And the Sun
Pursued
the
Moon

And the Sun
Pursued
the
Moon

Symbolic Knowledge and
Traditional Authority
among the Makassar

Thomas Gibson

University of Hawai'i Press
HONOLULU

Library of Congress Cataloging-in-Publication Data

Gibson, Thomas
  And the sun pursued the moon : symbolic knowledge and traditional authority among the Makassar / Thomas Gibson.
    p. cm.
  Includes bibliographical references and index.
  ISBN 0-8248-2865-8 (hardcover : alk. paper)
  1. Makasar (Indonesian people)—Science. 2. Makasar (Indonesian people)—Folklore.
3. Makasar (Indonesian people)—Kings and rulers. 4. Mythology, Indonesian—
Indonesia—Makassar. 5. Philosophy, Indonesian—Indonesia—Makassar.
6. Ethnoscience—Indonesia—Makassar. 7. Makassar (Indonesia)—Social life and
customs. I. Title.
  DS632.M25G53 2005
  959.8'4—dc22

                                        2004029026

University of Hawai'i Press books are printed on acid-free
paper and meet the guidelines for permanence and durability
of the Council on Library Resources.

Designed by University of Hawai'i Press production Staff
Printed by the Maple-Vail Book Manufacturing Staff

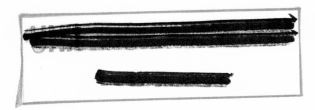

The Doctors added to all these Fooleries,
with which they amus'd the Vulgar People,
that the Heavens never had any Beginning;
that the Sun and Moon had always exercis'd a Sovereign Power there;
and had liv'd in peace with one another,
till a certain day that they quarrel'd together,
and that the Sun pursu'd the Moon
with a resolution to have abused her;
that being wounded in her flight before him,
she was deliver'd of the Earth,
that fell by chance in the same Situation as now we see it;
and that upon the opening of the Clumsie Lump in the middle,
two sorts of Giants issu'd forth;
that the one made themselves Masters of the Sea,
where they commanded the Fish,
rais'd Storms and Tempests when they were angry;
and that they never sneezed but that there happened some Shipwrack.
That the other Giants were thrust down to the Center of the Earth,
there to labour the Production of Metals
in concert with the Sun and Moon,
and when they bestirred themselves with too great Violence,
they caused Earthquakes, and sometimes overturned whole Cities.
Moreover, that the Moon was big with several other Worlds,
no less in extent than this,
that she would be delivered of them all successively, one after another,
to supply the Ruins of those that should be consumed
at the end of every hundred thousand years,
by the Excessive Heats of the Sun;
but that she should be delivered naturally, and not by Accident,
as she was the first time;
because the Sun and the Moon having found by mutual experience,
that the World cannot subsist without their reciprocal Influences,
were reconciled upon condition
that the Sun should reign one half the day,
and the Moon the other.

    —Nicolas Gervaise, *Historical Description of the Kingdom of Macasar*

Contents

Acknowledgments   ix

1. Introduction to South Sulawesi   1

2. Toward an Anthropology of Symbolic Knowledge   18

3. Androgynous Origins: Traces of Srivijaya in the Java Sea   39

4. Incestuous Twins and Magical Boats: Traces of Kediri in the Gulf of Bone   60

5. Noble Transgression and Shipwreck: Traces of Luwu' in Bira   91

6. The Sea Prince and the Bamboo Maiden: Traces of Majapahit in South Sulawesi   114

7. The Sea King and the Emperor: The Gunpowder State of Gowa-Tallo'   142

8. The Power of the Regalia: Royal Rebellion against the Dutch East India Company   169

9. The Return of the Kings: The Royal Ancestors under Colonial Rule   190

10. Knowledge, Power, and Traditional Authority   227

Notes   239

References   243

Index   253

Acknowledgments

The local scholar to whom I owe by far the greatest debt was my host and mentor, Abdul Hakim Daeng Paca. After serving in the Darul Islam militia in the 1950s, he served as village secretary, schoolteacher and school principal until the 1990s when he was appointed head of the Village Cooperative Unit (KUD). He was not only literate in Makassar, Bugis, Bahasa Indonesia, and Arabic, but was also an accomplished artist and musician. He had spent years compiling empirical materials on all aspects of local culture and history. Whenever he felt unsure of some specialized area of knowledge, he was eager to introduce me to the relevant local expert, whether the question concerned agricultural or artisanal techniques, the history and genealogies of noble families, Austronesian or Islamic ritual, or the history of the nationalist or Islamic modernist movements.

Among the many other experts who volunteered their time to instruct me in the finer points of the Makassar symbolic system were Haji Titi Daeng Toje, medium for the royal ancestors of Ara; Demma Daeng Puga, medium for the Bugis spirits of Ujung Lasoa; Hama Daeng La'ju and Palippui Daeng Puga, masters of the arcane sciences *(ilmu)*; Sirajang Daeng Munira, Alimuddin Daeng Mappi, and Muhammad Yakub Daeng Jagong, Imams of Ara; Muhamad Idris Daeng Buru'ne, Imam of Bira; Abdul Hamid Daeng Maming, former head of the Department of Education and Culture for Bonto Bahari; Daeng Pasau, Village Chief; Daeng Sibaji Daeng Puga and Muhammad Nasir, master reciters of Sinrili'; Bolong Daeng Puga, master boatbuilder; Haji Masa', master sailor; Banri Sau Daeng Baji, master goldsmith; Muhammad Idris Radatung Daeng Sarika, schoolteacher and master musician. Many other residents of Ara, Bira, Lemo Lemo, and Tanaberu provided practical, emotional, and spiritual support in ways too numerous to mention here. All were deeply proud of their culture and traditions and wished me to make them known to the wider world.

I also owe a deep debt of gratitude to Rusnani Babo and Drs. Aminuddin Bakry, my hosts and guides in Ujung Pandang, and to their extended families, who opened their homes to me and helped me navigate the capital city in many ways. Dr. Abu Hamid, professor of anthropology at Hasanuddin University, has provided generations of Indonesian and foreign researchers guidance in the field. I gratefully acknowledge his assistance in this respect and the access his seminar at the University provided me to the Indonesian academic community.

It is one of my deepest regrets that my parents, Dr. Count D. Gibson, Jr., and Katherine Vislocky Gibson, both passed away in 2001 before I could complete this manuscript. They provided steadfast support throughout my career and were always eager to read whatever I wrote. Their deep love of both the explicit knowledge contained in the writings of theologians and social scientists and of the implicit knowledge contained in ritual and symbolism provided the original inspiration for what has become my life's work. I can only hope that this installment would meet their high standards. My research on both the Philippines and Indonesia would not have been possible without my wife, Ruhi Maker, who opened up whole new areas of knowledge for me during her visits to the field and who has patiently listened to my endless reanalysis of the material for the last fifteen years. My sons, Taimur and Amir, have lived with this work in progress from the time of their birth. They, too, have patiently listened as I told and retold some of the many stories I heard in the field. I hope that they have helped me reproduce some of the narrative vigor that makes the original stories so entertaining to the Makassar themselves.

My initial comparative study of the cultures and societies of Island Southeast Asia in 1985 was supported by a grant from the Harry Frank Guggenheim Foundation for a project entitled "The Effects of Involvement in Regional Trading and Raiding on Attitudes toward Violence and Domination among Southeast Asian Shifting Cultivators." My first two visits to South Sulawesi in 1988 and 1989 were financed by a grant from the Harry Frank Guggenheim Foundation for a project entitled "Technology, Rank, and Ritual in South Sulawesi." Together with a return visit in 2000, my total time in the field came to eight months.

I wish to thank Professor James Fox for the opportunity to present my preliminary findings in 1989 when I spent some weeks in Canberra as a Visiting Fellow in the Comparative Austronesian Project of the Department of Anthropology, Research School of Pacific Studies, the Australian National University.

Historical research in the Netherlands was supported in 1994 by a Senior Scholar Award from the Fulbright Commission for lecturing and research in the Research Centre Religion and Society, University of Amsterdam, the Netherlands. I wish to thank my hosts at the Centre, Peter van der Veer, Patricia Spyer, Peter van Rooden, and Gerd Baumann, who provided me both exceptional hospitality and a new intellectual model for thinking about the relationship between global and local forms of knowledge.

James Siegel and Benedict Anderson provided me with many opportunities to present my evolving ideas to colloquia and graduate seminars organized by the Southeast Asia Program at Cornell University, especially during my year as a Visiting Associate Professor in 1997 and my year as a Visiting Fellow in 2000–2001. Without the lifeline to area specialists this program has so generously provided me, I would never have been able to stay abreast of the field while based at the University of Rochester.

I am particularly indebted to Anthony Day and Gene Ammarell, who read an earlier (and even longer) version of the current manuscript and encouraged me to see it through. I am also indebted to two anonymous reviewers of this manuscript who took the time to provide detailed comments on the entire work. They have enabled me to clarify and improve my argument in many particulars and, more generally, to stand back from the trees and see the forest again.

My understanding of Austronesian symbolic systems has benefited over the years from discussions with many fellow students of the area, including Greg Acciaioli, Leonard Andaya, Robert Barnes, Lanfranco Blanchetti-Revelli, Maurice Bloch, John Bowen, David Bulbeck, Fenella Cannell, Janet Carsten, Harold Conklin, Shelly Errington, James Fox, Ken George, Gilbert Hamonic, Robert Hefner, Webb Keane, Michael Lambek, Martin Manalansan, Robert McKinley, Jennifer Nourse, Michael Peletz, Christian Pelras, William Henry Scott, Heather Sutherland, John Wolf, and Mark Woodward.

I also wish to acknowledge the comments I have received from the participants at the conferences and seminars where I have presented portions of the argument. They include the Association for Asian Studies; the American Anthropological Association; the American Ethnological Association; the Fakultas Sosyal Politik, Universitas Hasanuddin, Ujung Pandang, Sulawesi Selatan; the Research School of Pacific Studies, the Australian National University; King's College, Cambridge University; the Department of Social Anthropology, London School of Economics; the University of Amsterdam; the University of Nijmegen; the Centre National de la Recherche Scientifique in Paris; the Department of Anthropology and the Southeast Asia Program, Cornell University; the Peabody Museum, the Department of Anthropology and the Southeast Asian Studies program, Harvard University; the Max Planck Institute for Social Anthropology, Halle, Germany; and the Institute of Social and Cultural Anthropology, Oxford University.

Finally, scientific work is by its nature a collaborative enterprise. This is particularly true of anthropological fieldwork. In the end, however, I must take full responsibility for the interpretations and arguments contained in this book. It is my hope that my audience will transcend the traditional boundaries of academic disciplines and appeal to a wide range of readers, including not just anthropologists and historians but those interested in emerging fields like oral literature, popular Islam, cultural studies, subaltern history, postcolonialism, globalization, and transnationalism. Such a diverse audience imposes an even heavier burden on the author to make his theoretical assumptions explicit. I have done my best to do so while avoiding the jargon of my own field of origin, anthropology.

Chapter 1

Introduction to South Sulawesi

T his book explores the relationship between local, regional, and global forms of symbolic knowledge and power in Ara, Indonesia. It is devoted to the process by which local communities were incoporated into regional political and economic systems over a period of about a thousand years, from 600 to 1600 C.E. I will argue that this process was facilitated in the whole area surrounding the Java Sea by the existence of a common Austronesian symbolic system. Although there is little discussion of Islam and European colonialism here, it is important to state at the outset that the kinds of symbolic knowledge I discuss here have coexisted with these global forms of knowledge for the past five hundred years.

Outline of the Present Volume

Two theoretical chapters frame the ethnographic portion of this work. In chapter 2, I outline my general theoretical approach to the anthropology of knowledge and power and situate the present volume within my larger project. In this volume, I am concerned with the relation between symbolic knowledge and what Weber called "traditional authority" in Makassar society. I argue for the importance of making a distinction between practical, symbolic, and ideological forms of knowledge. Ideological knowledge is dependent on symbolic knowledge, and symbolic knowledge is dependent on practical knowledge. None of them can be fully reduced to or explained in terms of the others.

The next seven chapters follow the introduction and transformation of symbolic and ideological practices through time and space. In chapter 3, I discuss the spread of the Austronesian people through Island Southeast Asia and the development of some of the basic features of Austronesian life, such as longdistance sailing, trading forest produce, and cultivating rice. Social intercourse intensified around the Java Sea when the Sumatran Empire of Srivijaya came to serve as an entrepôt between China and India in the seventh century. I analyze a group of myths that spread throughout the region during this period. In these myths, an initial antagonism between primordial male and female entities moderates into an acceptance of complementary opposition, upon which the two can come together in an orderly fashion and produce a pair of opposite-sex twins plus a third, androgynous entity. This scheme provides the key to much of the symbolic material discussed in subsequent chapters.

In chapter 4, I discuss the way little royal centers, modeling themselves on the Javanese kingdom of Kediri, sprang up along the coastlines of Sumatra, Borneo, and Sulawesi in the thirteenth century. These centers were loosely connected with one another and with the great civilizations of India and China by maritime trade. Traces of this period persist in myths recounting the adventures of a culture hero, often known as Panji. A version of this story is embedded in the enormous mythological cycle of the Bugis people known as the La Galigo. In the Bugis version, a pair of opposite-sex twins is separated at birth. The female twin remains fixed at her center of origin and becomes a *bissu* priestess with the power to move vertically between the Middleworld, the Upperworld, and the Underworld. The male twin is a great sailor, with the power to move horizontally across the sea. He uses a boat created by his sister to penetrate a new royal center where he marries a first cousin. In this maritime world, local royal houses reproduce themselves by sending noblemen across the sea to marry noblewomen from distant royal houses. Each local dynasty maintains its own links to the Upperworld and Underworld through local royal women.

In chapter 5, I analyze a set of myths in which the ordered exchange of sexual substances collapses through incest and adultery. The protagonists of these myths are worldly rulers unable to regulate their animal drives of lust and greed who are driven into exile or who are executed by their subjects. These sins interrupt the normal flow of life, resulting in epidemics that kill humans and animals, droughts that kill crops, and shipwrecks that send trade goods to the bottom of the sea. Androgynous shamans work to avert these calamities by performing exorcism rituals at the water's edge.

In chapter 6, I discuss the origin of wet rice agriculture in central South Sulawesi in the thirteenth century. A new ideology arose that legitimated royal powers in terms of an intrinsic difference between those with heavenly ancestors and the great mass of common farmers. In the foundation myths of inland Bugis kingdoms, kingship is based on a social contract in which rulers who descend from heaven provide their terrestrial subjects with social harmony and fertility in return for food, clothing, and shelter. In the foundation myths of coastal polities such as Luwu' and Bantaeng, royal houses traced their origin back to a wandering prince from the empire of Majapahit who encounters a heavenly maiden who has descended from heaven in a bamboo tube. They marry and produce monstrous offspring who become the first rulers. The female ancestor returns to heaven, only to descend to found different kingdoms elsewhere. The agricultural fertility of the land is associated in these myths with females of divine origin. It is contrasted with the long-distance trade that occurs on the sea and the temporal power of males from foreign empires. Like the myths discussed in chapter 4, these coastal foundation myths also serve as a template for a certain kind of royal wedding. In this case, it is a wedding in which a local kingdom allies with a more powerful foreign empire without losing its autonomy.

In chapter 7, I show how the symbolic system elaborated to legitimate kingship during the fifteenth century was linked to a new set of practical techniques in the sixteenth century to lay the basis for the centralized empire of Gowa and Tallo'. The legitimacy of local rulers was increasingly derived not from their own founding royal ancestors, but from their relationship to the royal houses of Gowa and Tallo'. This was the case in Ara and Bira, whose royal chronicles record their incorporation into the empire in the 1560s. The previously female symbolic function of agricultural fertility is now linked to bloodshed and warfare and absorbed by the agrarian kings of inland states. The complementary opposite of the ruler of the land now becomes the sea king of a coastal state, who continues to be associated with long-distance trade and diplomacy.

In chapter 8, I discuss the changing political functions of royal rituals during the colonial period. According to the traditional symbolic system, rulers were installed on the same stone on which the founding royal ancestor first descended from the Upperworld. Contact with the founding ancestors was maintained through sacred objects they left behind when they returned to the Otherworld. As the Dutch East India Company (VOC) established itself as a territorial power in South Sulawesi during the eighteenth century, control of these rituals and sacred objects became a matter of great practical concern to the Dutch as well as to local royal houses. The seizure of the royal regalia of Gowa by a rebellious slave in 1776 led to forty years of war in the area. After the VOC was abolished and replaced by the government of the Netherlands East Indies, the Dutch deliberately undermined the old royal rituals as they tried to remodel the local political system along the lines of a rational bureaucracy. In the face of rising nationalist sentiment in the 1920s, however, the colonial government tried to revive the old royal rituals, hoping to tap the residual traditional authority of the hereditary nobility for the colonial state.

In chapter 9, I describe the royal ancestor cults as they exist today in both Ara and Tanaberu. Although the political aspect of the ranking system was decapitated at the beginning of the twentieth century, the Dutch attempted to revive the ritual aspect in the 1930s, in an effort to forestall Islamic nationalism. This effort received support from a segment of the traditional nobility, because kingship anchored the social hierarchy. The royal ancestor cult in Ara is centered on a female spirit medium, a woman who is possessed only by male spirits and who is "married" to another woman. The cult is especially important to other noblewomen, who are excluded from most Islamic and bureaucratic offices. The cult in Tanaberu focuses on a pair of golden birds sent by the founding ancestor and his wife 150 years ago. Throughout the twentieth century, the central government has appointed men from other areas to rule this village, but they all found local wives descended from these founding ancestors. Here the cult remains important to both male and female nobles. These cults are paralleled by a cult of local Islamic saints, who always exist in male-female pairs as well.

Chapters 3 through 6 thus show how myth and ritual link practical forms of knowledge such as boatbuilding, navigation, agriculture, and warfare to basic social categories such as gender and hereditary rank and to basic cosmological categories such as the Upper-, Middle-, and Underworlds and the celestial and meteorological phenomena that tie them together. Chapters 7, 8, and 9 provide some historical and contemporary examples of how concrete agents put the symbolic infrastructure outlined in the earlier chapters to political and ideological use.

In the concluding chapter, I situate the material discussed in this volume in relation to Islam and life cycle rituals. I also return to the theoretical issues raised in chapter 2 concerning the relationship between practical, symbolic, and ideological knowledge, on the one hand, and between local, regional, and global forms of knowledge, on the other.

Methodology

The process by which I arrived at the view of knowledge outlined in chapter 2 was informed by the methods I used to gather empirical data for the present analysis, and the methods I used to gather the data were in turn informed by my growing understanding of the data. In other words, data and analysis were in a dialectical relationship. I take this relationship to be more central to the anthropological method than any one methodology such as participant observation. Indeed, in the course of this project I have grown to be somewhat suspicious of an overreliance on participant observation.

Participant Observation

My decision to study the Makassar was influenced by previous field research I had conducted among the Buid of the Philippines (Gibson 1985, 1986) and by a comparative study I had made on attitudes toward violence, domination, and aggression among Southeast Asian shifting cultivators (Gibson 1990a, 1990b). I came to the conclusion that the development of negative attitudes toward violence and aggression in societies like the Buid was strongly correlated with a history of victimization by predatory coastal states, whereas the development of positive attitudes in societies like the Iban of Sarawak was correlated with a history of successful predation. To fully understand the tribal societies of highland Southeast Asia, one thus had to study their interaction with predatory coastal societies. The Bugis and Makassar of South Sulawesi have long had a reputation as among the most aggressive maritime peoples of the region.

In many ways, Ara is an ideal site for research on the relation between the practical knowledge embedded in skilled labor and the symbolic knowledge embedded in ritual. On the one hand, three-quarters of the men are skilled carpenters who build large sailboats for a living and most women are skilled in weaving, embroidering, and marketing textiles. Many of these craft skills have been jealously guarded for centuries. On the other hand, even though almost

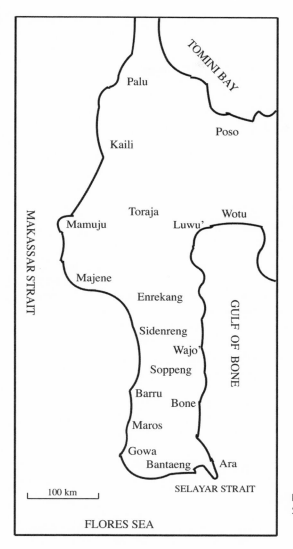

Map 1.1 South and Central Sulawesi

all boatbuilding is now done in settlements scattered across the whole of Indonesia, workers return with their accumulated wages to celebrate the most important ritual events in their lives. It is thus possible for a fieldworker to observe an almost unending round of rituals relating to birth, marriage, and death. Because my primary interest was in symbolic and not practical knowledge, I spent most of my time attending rituals and interviewing acknowledged experts in various forms of esoteric knowledge. Interviews were conducted in Bahasa Indonesia. Oral traditions and local texts were transcribed into the

Roman alphabet and translated from Makassar into Bahasa Indonesia by local scholars.

Regional, Textual, and Historical Analysis

In addition to the material I collected firsthand in the field, I have also used material drawn from the close reading of locally produced texts, from anthropologists and historians working on neighboring societies in the region, from Dutch missionaries and colonial officials, and from secondary sources on Islam and Asian history. This book is thus a hybrid of ethnography, geography, literary criticism, and history. This seems to me the only way to approach a highly literate society that made its living from trade with East Africa, Western Europe, the Middle East, South Asia, and East Asia for many centuries. The Makassar people were drawn into an expanding global culture in the twelfth century and have never withdrawn from it.

In my analysis of the mythology of Ara, I have drawn extensively on the writings of previous generations of Dutch, British, French, and American anthropologists and linguists working in Island Southeast Asia and beyond. As Claude Lévi-Strauss has shown, the meaning of a local myth or ritual is often revealed only when it is seen as a variant of a larger pattern. Only regional analysis can reveal whether a connection between two cultural practices is due to a common historical origin or to diffusion along chains of trade and communication (Gibson 1994a).

As soon as it became clear that Ara contained many highly literate individuals, I began to collaborate with them in compiling an archive of textual materials. Three scripts were in use in Ara: a local syllabic script known as *lontara,* Arabic, and Roman. A number of people could read and write all three scripts and I employed them to record, transcribe, and transliterate texts into Roman script and to translate them into Bahasa Indonesia. After leaving the field, I spent several years translating these Bahasa Indonesia texts into English and analyzing them. I draw on many of these textual materials in the present volume and will return to them again in future publications.

Internal analysis of the texts I gathered in the field was supplemented by historical research on the contexts in which they were originally created and the way they were introduced into local communities. I found the writings of Dutch missionaries and colonial administrators from the seventeenth century on to be especially helpful in this regard. Colonial administrators had a practical interest in power and legitimacy and paid close attention to political rivalries and rituals of legitimation. Missionaries paid attention to details of popular religious practices when they thought they could exploit them for the purposes of conversion.

Introduction to South Sulawesi and the Bira Peninsula

In this section I provide a general introduction to the province of South Sulawesi and a more detailed description of the hilly eastern part of the regency of Bulukumba inhabited by the speakers of a chain of Makassar dialects known as "coastal Konjo." A discussion of the symbolic meanings attached to various features of Ara's landscape will make it clear how deeply they remain rooted in this place, despite its apparent bleakness. A tour through the barren and rocky landscape of the Bira peninsula at the south end of the Konjo area will make it equally clear why its men have had to look toward the sea for their livelihood.

The villages of the Bira peninsula exhibit the apparently paradoxical features of a high degree of social and cultural autonomy, on the one hand, and of having been tightly integrated into a regional political economy for many centuries, on the other. Coastal villages throughout the Java Sea have engaged in an extensive exchange of trade goods, people, and ideas. The people of the Bira peninsula were more tightly integrated into this system than most because the poor quality of the soil forced them to specialize in boatbuilding and long-distance trade.

In 1990, the population of the province of South Sulawesi numbered about 7 million (Pelras 1996: 7). The last official census that enumerated the population by ethnolinguistic group was the colonial census of 1930, which found that roughly half the province was Bugis. Current estimates of the numbers of each ethnic group are usually extrapolated from the relative sizes of each group in 1930. Thus, the four largest ethnic groups in the province today are said to be: Bugis (3.5 million), Makassar (2 million), Toraja (600,000), and Mandar (400,000). The Mandar and Toraja occupy the mountainous areas in the north, the Bugis the fertile lowlands in the center, and the Makassar the hilly land at the southern end of the peninsula.

The 1930 census also found that 10 percent of all ethnic Bugis in the Netherlands East Indies were living outside their homeland, whereas only 2 percent of Makassar were doing so (Lineton 1975: 38). The Mandar and the Makassar tend to be assimilated to the Bugis when encountered outside their homeland in Sumatra, Java, Malaysia, or elsewhere in the archipelago, perhaps accounting for the disproportionate number of "Bugis" enumerated outside their homeland. Because of a scarcity of arable land, the Mandar and Makassar peoples have always relied on the sea for their livelihood at least as much as the Bugis.

The Coastal Konjo

Konjo refers to a string of Makassar dialects spoken in villages lying on the boundary between Makassar and Bugis areas. *Konjo* is the term for "over there" in this dialect and is used as a diacritic feature to distinguish it from other Makassar dialects that use the term *anjo*. Most Konjo live in mountainous terrain that is not well suited to wet rice cultivation, although some very impressive terraces have been built by the mountain Konjo in and around Malino in upper Gowa. Konjo Makassar shares about 75 percent of its basic vocabulary with standard Makassar. The Konjo dialects themselves are divided into two subgroups: "mountain Konjo," with about 100,000 speakers, spoken on and around Mount

Bawakaraeng, and "coastal Konjo," also with about 100,000 speakers, spoken along the coast of the Gulf of Bone. Coastal and Mountain Konjo are related to one another at the lexicostatistical level of 75 percent, making them no closer to one another at this level than each is to standard Makassar. At the morphophonemic, morphological, and syntactic levels, however, they are almost identical. The Mountain Konjo have been the subject of a number of publications by Rössler (1987, 1990, 2000) and Röttger-Rössler (1989, 2000).

In this book, I shall be concerned primarily with the coastal Konjo, who occupy the eastern *kecamatans* of the Kabupaten of Bulukumba. The *kecamatan* is the next smallest unit of administration beneath the *kabupaten,* or regency. Both terms are of Javanese origin. They replaced Dutch terms for division, regency, and district in the 1960s as a uniform administrative system was imposed throughout Indonesia. Some of these units correspond to ancient kingdoms, others represent an amalgamation or subdivision of such units. Of most significance for this book are the *kecamatan* of Kajang, Hero–Lange Lange (Herlang), Bonto Tiro, and Bonto Bahari.

The capital city of Bulukumba and its environs has had a large Bugis-speaking population since the late seventeenth century, when the area came under the control of the Dutch East India Company, which turned it over to the Kingdom of Bone. Konjo-speakers have a certain sense of ethnolinguistic identity, especially in the context of the local politics of the Regency, where they often form a faction opposed to the Bugis-speakers. In this context they refer to themselves in Bahasa Indonesia as *orang di atas,* "people up above." (This phrase also carries the connotation in Indonesian of "upper class.")

Historically, the northernmost coastal Konjo kingdom was Kajang. At the heart of Kajang is a village called Tana Toa, the "Ancient Land," famous throughout Makassar territory as a place of great mystical power. It is ruled over by the *Amma' Toa,* the Old Father. There is a tremendous mystique around this figure, who is believed to be the reincarnation of all previous *Amma' Toa.* Successful candidates to succeed a previous *Amma' Toa* are chosen by a long and complicated process. A series of omens (a buffalo, a cock, and incense smoke) must all indicate the same candidate, who must then be able to recite a series of myths and genealogies flawlessly without ever having studied them. To the south of Kajang, the ancient kingdoms of Hero and Lange Lange have been combined into the *kecamatan* of Herlang. They were in many respects within the sphere of influence of the much larger kingdom of Kajang, and participated in the cult led by the *Amma' Towa* (Usop 1985).

To the south of Hero and Lange Lange lay the ancient inland kingdoms of Tiro, Batang, and Bonto Tangnga. These were combined into the *kecamatan* of Bonto Tiro in the 1960s. They traditionally relied primarily on agriculture, particularly the cultivation of maize. The old kingdom of Tiro was considerably larger than any of its neighbors, and was itself composed of seven parts. Each part was ruled by an official with a different title, in the following rank order: the *lompo,* "Great One," of Ere Lebu; the *gallarrang,* "Titled One," of Kalumpang; the

Map 1.2 The Ten Realms of the Konjo Makassar

anrong tau "Mother of the People," of Caramming; the *kapala,* "Chief," of Hila Hila; the *macoa,* "Elder," of Basokeng; the *karadepa* of Salu Salu; and the *karabica* of Salumunte. Ara borders Kalumpang to the south, and Caramming to the southeast, so Ara's closest ties to Tiro are with these two settlements.

To the south of Bonto Tiro is the *kecamatan* of Bonto Bahari, "Land of the Sea." Because the soil in Bonto Bahari is too thin to support much agriculture, the villages of Bonto Tiro have traditionally provided much of the food eaten in Bonto Bahari in exchange for cash, fish, or trade goods. This agricultural specialization continues even among the migrant work force of Bonto Tiro, who are recruited to work on plantations in Sumatra rather than in boatyards.

Bonto Bahari is composed of the old kingdoms of Ara, Bira, Lemo Lemo, and Tanaberu. Close ties of kinship and economic exchange tied these four ancient realms together. All were largely dependent on the sea for their livelihood: Ara and Lemo Lemo relied almost exclusively on boatbuilding, Bira and Tanaberu on long-distance trade and fishing, with the women of Bira producing high-quality cotton textiles as well.

This division of labor among the four villages is so systematic that the men of Ara deny knowing how to sail, or even to rig, one of the boats they have built. The men of Bira can replace the rudders, masts, and rigging of a ship, but are incapable of building a hull. Because they are sailors, the men of Bira are best known to the outside world and Bira is often identified in the literature as the home of the boatbuilders. In fact, however, the men of Bira proper know nothing of boatbuilding.

Until the 1930s, the men of Ara relied almost exclusively on Bira for orders to build ships. They were paid in cash, to which the Birans had access because of their long-distance trading activities. Their monopoly position placed the Arans at their mercy, and the early part of this century is remembered as a time of hardship in Ara. Ara also engaged in some independent boatbuilding for the ruler of Bone far to the north. But even this did not bring in much cash, because Bone was off the major trade routes by the twentieth century.

The situation was rather different on the other side of the peninsula, in Lemo Lemo. In the nineteenth and early twentieth centuries, the boatbuilders of Lemo Lemo took their orders from the Makassar settlements along the south coast of South Sulawesi, as far away as Gowa. In the nineteenth century, this area had far more access to cash than did the Bugis areas around the Gulf of Bone, and as a result the boatbuilders of Lemo Lemo were much wealthier than those of Ara. The nineteenth and early twentieth centuries are remembered as a sort of Golden Age in Lemo Lemo.

Since the Second World War, the situation has reversed itself dramatically. The men of Ara, who had always held a monopoly of knowledge on building the large cargo-carrying sailing boats called *pinisi*, have acquired a national reputation and are sent for by entrepreneurs, many of them ethnically Chinese, to build boats of 250 tons and upward everywhere from Irian Jaya to Kalimantan and Sumatra. While the men are away, many for nine months out of every year, the women have learned to embroider with Singer sewing machines. They now earn ten times as much sewing as do the women of Bira weaving, while the men of Ara earn substantially more than the men of Lemo Lemo. The latter settlement is in fact almost deserted now, because it is far from any paved road and the only fresh water is at the bottom of a cave twenty meters deep. Most of the former inhabitants have moved up to Tanaberu, and recently the two *desas,* villages, have been combined into the Kelurahan of Tana Lemo.

Tanaberu is now the center of government for the entire *kecamatan,* and also for whatever boatbuilding still goes on locally. This is because it has the only broad, flat beach lying near the road, making it the only feasible place to bring timber in by truck. The boatbuilders of both Ara and Lemo Lemo who do not wish to go on temporary migration to another province now commute to Tanaberu or have moved there to work on boats. Very few have established the contacts or accumulated the capital required to serve as general contractors or entrepreneurs in their own right and tend to work for natives of Tanaberu as subcontractors, often for wages rather than a share of the profit. There is some considerable resentment about this in Ara, because Tanaberu has also received a good deal of attention in the national and even international media as the original home of the *pinisi* builders, which it has never been.

In 1988, the *desa* of Ara was divided into four *dusun,* wards. These were Bontona, Lambua, Pompantu, and Martin. Bontona, the upper settlement, was the area with the oldest and most noble houses. It was centered around Ere Lohe, the "Great Spring," next to which stood the oldest mosque. Lambua was formerly Lembanna, the lower settlement. It stretched down the slope to the sea and was the area where the commoners lived. Martin, at the southern end of the village, was recently created out of the scattered farming settlements of Maruangin and Tinadung whose populations had moved to the main road. Pompantu, at the northern end, was also a recent creation. The Great Mosque—Mesjid Raya—of the village was constructed in the 1960s on the boundary of Pompantu and Bontona.

The Symbolic Landscape of Ara

Just as the physical landscape is one of the most enduring features of Konjo society, so are the rituals that are attached to it. Physical singularities such as springs, boulders, and large trees tend to be associated with one or more invisible beings. Endicott, in his analysis of Malay magic, argued that the Malays view the universe as suffused with mystical power, called *semangat,* which tends to be concentrated in discontinuities in the landscape such as large trees, boulders, caves, and so on (Endicott 1970). Errington, in her analysis of a cognate Bugis term, *sumangé,* also speaks of an impersonal *mana*-like force that inheres in humans, houses, and other objects (Errington 1983). Though the people of Ara recognized the term, they did not make much use of it. Their view of the spirit world involved particularized spirits inhabiting particular points in the landscape, rather than a diffuse vitality that had to be caught and concentrated.

The chief foci of supernatural power in Ara are large rocks and trees, caves, and the summits of hills (for similar beliefs among the Malays, compare Endicott 1970). Each such feature tends to have a legend attached to it, and many have particular, recognized mediums who specialize in propitiating their spirit inhabitants. It is possible to draw a spiritual map of Ara that shows the location of many kinds of invisible being. Some belong to a category of *setan* and are propitiated by placing an offering on a *sangara,* a woven bamboo tray, in their tree or cave. Some are *jin*—an Arabic-derived term for invisible spirits—who may or may not be practicing Muslims. Some are the spirits of humans who died either in a state of great sin, such as incest, or great sanctity, such as Islamic saints, *wali.*

Certain places are associated with particular *setan,* more a kind of nature spirit than truly evil beings. The sort of ritual practices associated with *setan* are very similar to those I observed during my earlier fieldwork among the Buid of Mindoro and to those described among many other "tribal" Austronesian groups little affected by world religions or ideologies (Gibson 1986). They may be taken as transformations of a very ancient set of practices predating those discussed below. Although the legitimacy of making propitiatory offerings to *setan* is highly contested now, a century ago it would have constituted a normal method of dealing with certain illnesses.

Ara is composed of three plateaus that ascend from the beach to the central spine of the peninsula it shares with Tanaberu, Lemo Lemo, and Bira. The upper plateau occupies about two-thirds of Ara's area of approximately thirty square kilometers, but is only very sparsely inhabited. This is partly because there is no source of water on it. All drinking water must be laboriously hauled up from the middle plateau either by women who carry it on their heads or by men who lash great plastic containers to the backs of horses. The soil is also poorest on the highest plateau, and here fertile fields are separated from one another by barren rocky areas roughly ten times as large in area. A certain amount of cattle raising goes on here as well. Once or twice a day the cattle must be driven down to be watered on the middle plateau. From the ridge above Ara, the plateau slopes gently and continuously downward toward Tanaberu in the west. Beyond it lies the Gulf of Bulukumba and the broad plane of Ujung Lohe. Rising majestically over them all is Mount Bawakaraeng, "The King's Mouth," the volcanic cone that dominates the south coast of South Sulawesi.

At the north end of the village, the middle plateau rises to meet the upper plateau. At their intersection is a series of caves, boulders, and deep holes called Pilia. These caves were the focus of a cult of the founding royal ancestor, Karaeng Mamampang until the 1930s. Even now, it said that the skull of Karaeng Mamampang and his wife are hidden in these caves. Below the hills of Pilia lie the royal fields of Kaddaro, the produce of which traditionally belonged to the holder of the office of Gallarrang. *Kaddaro* means "to kick." According to a story in the *Chronicle* of Bira, it got this name in the aftermath of a battle between Tiro and Ara in which so many warriors died one could not cross the field without kicking the heads of the dead.

Below Kaddaro is Gua Passea, a cave that was used in pre-Islamic times as a burial place and in later times as a place of refuge from seafaring marauders. It is regarded by villagers as the premier tourist attraction of Ara, with good reason. It is in the middle of an overgrown area so that a new trail must be cut each time a visitor is taken to it. There is a central vault between ten and twenty meters high, with a hole in the roof through which light shines. The floor is covered with a thick layer of earth, in which many holes have been dug by treasure hunters. All that now remains are two wooden coffins two meters in length. The lids are shaped like peaked roofs. Villagers assert that these are the graves of their pre-Islamic ancestors who stood two meters in height.

Many villagers insist that their ancestors were forced to hide in the caves to escape capture by a race of black cannibals from the east, whom they variously call *To Seram,* a cover term for Moluccans, *To Belo,* a tribe from north Halmahera, or *To Pua-Pua,* "Papuans." Others argue that the purpose of these raids was not so much cannibalism as the taking of slaves. There is good historical evidence that these raids peaked between 1790 and 1810, when Sultan Nuku of Ternate took advantage of the disorganization of the colonial government that followed France's invasion of the Netherlands. At the back of the cave is a raised chamber known as the *tala tala,* dais of the kings. It played some role in the installation of the Gallarrang in the past. Local people are convinced that the Dutch also recognized the power, *karama,* of the place, because every controleur came to visit it with his wife soon after his appointment.

At the southern end of the village, the upper plateau falls to meet the middle plateau. At this point, a deep hollow was quarried in the 1930s to supply rocks for the new government road. It is called the hole of Buwi and is said by some to have a resident *setan* called *Topi Merah,* "Red Hat." The Hole of Buwi is just beyond the southern end of the settled part of Ara. To the south of Buwi is a broad, barren area known as Ela, where the most malicious of the *setan* live. A large *ara,* or banyan tree, called *Talise,* that grew in Ela before World War II was the focus of a cult led by a man named Taniasang and his wife Bungko Panasa. Bungko Panasa also served as intermediary for the spirit of Gua Pa'tungia, a cave surrounded by giant *pa'tung* bamboos. During the 1930s, the village chief, Gama Daeng Samana, singled out this tree and the cult surrounding it during his campaign to rid the village of what he regarded as un-Islamic practices. He personally cut it down to show the villagers that the evil spirits could do no harm to one who placed his trust in Allah. This act made a deep impression on the village, and I was told the story many times.

More generally, every tree is said to have a tutelary spirit referred to as its *kammi'na,* guardian. This spirit must be propitiated with an offering and invited to move elsewhere before its "house" is felled. There are various methods to determine whether the spirit has accepted the offering and left. One way is to lean your adz against the tree while addressing the spirit. If it falls over, the spirit is refusing to move. Today, trees are more commonly felled with chain saws. If the saw refuses to start, this is taken as another sign that the spirit is refusing to leave the tree. Another way is to observe the sky above it. If the clouds clear away, it means the spirit has left. Makka Daeng Koda told me a story about a spirit that once left the tree he was about to cut, but decided to move into a fieldhouse nearby. The spirit then had to be coaxed out of the fieldhouse. Otherwise, it would have become uninhabitable by humans.

Certain trees are inhabited by more formidable spirits that cause illness in humans. If such illnesses are diagnosed by a *sanro*, a traditional healer, an offering must be made at the place where the spirits live. These consist of a complete meal, which means, minimally, cooked rice, boiled eggs as a side dish, and the ingredients of a betel chew—betel leaves, areca nut, lime, tobacco, and gambir powder. These are all placed on a *sangara*. There is a high point near the coast in Ara, just south of the area called Ela, where the Dutch built a concrete benchmark in the 1930s. This spot was so frequently the site of offerings to *setan* that it is known as *Pasangarang*, "Place of the Bamboo Trays."

In the center of the village territory, the upper plateau drops abruptly to the middle one along a clifflike escarpment. This escarpment runs in a semicircle around the central settlement. There are only a few points at which it is feasible to build a trail down from the upper plateau. The most important of these is right in the center of the central settlement as it is now. A trail runs up from the Great Mosque to the upper plateau and then forks. The north fork takes one to Caramming, and the south fork due west to Tanaberu. The place where the trail climbs up to the plateau is called *Bataya*, "The Walls," because many stone walls were built across the trail in the old days to prevent quick entrances into and exits from the settlement by thieves.

At the base of the escarpment is a line of springs. Because of the need for ritual ablutions before entering a mosque, mosques tend to be built next to water sources. In the coastal Konjo area, this usually means that where there is a spring, there is a mosque. There are about five springs along the base of the upper escarpment. Ere Lohe is in the center of the current settlement, just on the border between Dusun Martin and Dusun Bontona. It forms a large pool that is deep enough for children to swim in during the rainy season when the waters rise. Next to it stands the Mosque of Dusun Bontona, the "Upper Settlement." To the north, in the center of Bontona is Ere Keke, the "Little Spring," and on the northern border of Bontona, Ere Balu, the "Widow's Well." In the nineteenth century, this well was still surrounded by forest. It was here that widows in mourning went to bathe secretly in the dead of night. Deeper in what was then the forest was an area of many small springs known as Ere Karaseya, the "Harsh Springs," because they were haunted by *setan*. This whole area is now heavily built up and the Great Mosque stands next to Ere Balu. Finally, a well has now been dug in the center of Dusun Pompantu, and a new mosque has been built next to it.

The old settlement of Ara was built around Ere Lohe. Just below it is the *possi' tana*, "navel of the earth." There is a navel of the earth in the center of every village in South Sulawesi, usually under a large rock. Indeed, the notion that the territory of each local community is centered on a navel of the earth is common throughout Indonesia (Schulte Nordholt 1980: 239; Traube 1980: 302). It is said that if one lifted the rock and looked down, one would see all the way to the seventh and lowest underworld. It thus links the Middleworld with the Lower- and Upperworlds and serves not only as the center of horizontal space, but also as a vertical *axis mundi.* The *possi' tana* is now in the charge of a woman ritual specialist, called Deda Daeng Kati. She was very old and almost deaf in 1988, but she read lips well and knew Indonesian. (I will discuss the rituals performed on the *possi' tana* in chapter 8.)

Most of the farmland in Ara runs along a narrow band in the center of the middle plateau. This band is about three kilometers long and half a kilometer wide. It thus constitutes only about 5 percent of the surface area of the village as a whole. At the southern end of it is a spring, Ere Tinadung. There used to be a separate settlement of farmers here with some sixty households. The people were intermarried with those of Kasuso, a village of fishermen that is the northernmost settlement of Bira. *Kasuso* means "the Corner," because it is built in a cove with almost square corners. Kasuso has belonged to Bira for a long time, although there is a legend that originally it belonged to Ara. Many of its customs are transitional between those of Bira and Ara. For example, half of its inhabitants follow the Ara inheritance rule by which the house passes to the eldest daughter. Conversely, many of the customs of Tinadung showed influences from Bira. For example, many men from Tinadung pursued a career as sailors for part of their lives and were the only ones in Ara to do so. The old settlement of Tinadung was abandoned to the monkeys in the 1960s, as the government forced people to resettle closer to the main roads. At the northern end of the fertile strip is the two-hectare field called Kaddaro.

The middle plateau runs right out to the sea at the northern and southern ends of the *desa,* ending in a series of cliffs falling straight into the sea. In the center, another escarpment falls abruptly down to the lower plateau that constitutes *Turunan Ara,* Ara's beach. It is this escarpment that prevents the craftsmen of Ara from pursuing their traditional occupation of boatbuilding in Ara anymore. In the old days, there was enough sandalwood growing in the extensive nonarable parts of Ara to supply all the need for raw materials, but this began to disappear in the 1930s. Now there is only low scrub that barely supplies the needs of the village for firewood. Timber for boats must now be brought in by truck, and so far there is only a footpath down to the beach. Almost all boatbuilding has now moved to the wide beach in Tanaberu that is easily accessible from the provincial highway.

What is a disadvantage today was an advantage up until about 1920. Before the Dutch built roads throughout the province, most travel in the area was by boat and settlements were built near sandy beaches. Maintaining law and order was also precarious until the 1930s. As late as the 1860s, pirates from Ternate and other Moluccan areas made frequent raids all along this coast. Ara's escarpments made it difficult for raiders to penetrate very far inland, and the population would withdraw to its fort, built near the edge of the middle plateau, or hide in one of the innumerable caves that honeycomb the local landscape.

At the base of the lower escarpment are at least two more springs that provided somewhat brackish drinking water for the old lower settlement of Lembanna. This lower plateau is only about 1.5 kilometers long from north to south, and 500 meters wide. The main spring is at the bottom of the Cave of Pasohara and is occupied by an Islamic *jin*. This cave ranks as the second tourist attraction of Ara after the cave at Passea.

To illustrate the dangers that derive from the fact that humans share the landscape with a host of invisible creatures, villagers told me about an event that had occurred just two months before my second trip to Ara: In March 1989, a group of boys was playing in the pool of Pasohara, when one of them urinated in the water. When the rest of the boys eventually decided to go home, they realized he wasn't with them. They went back to look, but could not find him. They hurried back to the village for help, and by the time a search party returned it was already dusk. They gathered dried coconut fronds to use as torches. Just as they were about to light them, they saw the boy hanging from the cliff face, as if his head were caught in a crevice. As they lit the torches, the boy suddenly appeared, sitting on a rock at the bottom of the cliff, unconscious. When he regained consciousness, he said that, just after he had urinated in the cave, a beautiful woman had appeared to him. She took him by the hand and asked him to come with her. He could not free himself until the torches were lit, at which point the spirit exclaimed, "They have come to burn my house down. You had better go away with them." And so he was released.

According to the villagers, this was not the first time this had happened at Pasohara. A few years before, a bus driver from Bulukumba had gone down to see the cave, defecated there, and been detained by the resident spirit for several hours. The explanation of these events lies in the fact that the cave is inhabited by a *Jin Islam*. These spirits are meticulously clean and will not let such offenses go unpunished. There is another spot inhabited by *Jin Islam* just south of Pasohara near the beach. This is *Batu Sibulan*, "One-Moon Rock." Although trees overhang it, one will never find dead leaves on it for it is swept clean by the spirits. This is true also of a boulder atop the caves at Pilia.

At the northern end of the beach is a cave called Kasorang Gama that is inhabited by the spirit of a giant crab (discussed in chapter 5). For about 500 meters north of Kasorang Gama, there is nothing but cliffs, and then *Sapo Hatu*, or "Stone House," the rock in which the first king of Tiro, Samparaja Daeng Malaja, was buried alive by disgruntled subjects (discussed in chapter 5). This rock marks the northern boundary of Ara. At the south end of the beach is a spring that comes up through the sand called Ere Labba, the "Neutralizing Waters." Here widows come to wash off the last vestiges of death pollution a year after the funeral of their husbands. Beyond Ere Labba is one kilometer of cliffs that hang over an area of shallow water. Here the Gallarrang used to organize large groups of villagers to construct bamboo fish traps. It was on one of these traps that Gallarrang Daeng Makkilo died in 1913 from cholera. Beyond these cliffs is another kilometer of cliffs that hang over deep water. At one point, the cove of Bili', it is possible to bring a large sailing vessel right up to the rocks without touching bottom. The southern border is marked by Soleng point. After that the coast turns inward due west for 800 meters before turning south at a right angle to form the beach of Kasuso, which lies in the *desa* of Bira.

The people of Ara thus occupy a landscape that is alive with both history and myth, where visible creatures coexist with invisible spirits. They think of this land as a place their ancestors have always lived and as the place where they and their descendents should be born, marry, and die, however much they wander in the intervening years. They take great pride in the preservation of those features of their own dialect, culture, and customary law that distinguish them from the neighboring villages of Tiro, Caramming, Tanaberu, and Bira. But as craftsmen and sailors who make their living from long-distance trade, they also feel quite at home everywhere in Island Southeast Asia. Life on the harsh peninsula of Bira would be almost impossible if the villages of Bonto Bahari were not part of a larger maritime region.

Chapter 2
Toward an Anthropology of Symbolic Knowledge

M y working hypothesis is that there is a hierarchy of kinds of knowledge, ranging from the implicit practical knowledge of everyday life to the explicit ideological knowledge used by conscious agents to achieve their individual goals. Between these two extremes is a vast body of what I call *symbolic* knowledge.

I end the chapter with a set of methodological reflections. I contend that a proper understanding of a complex culture like that of the Makassar requires a judicious balance between participant observation in the field, whereby one can gain access to implicit forms of knowledge, and textual analysis and thus gain access to explicit forms of knowledge generated independently of the researcher. Many attempts by anthropologists to overcome the limitations of classical ethnographic methods are vitiated by a failure to supplement field research with proper historical research. Conversely, many attempts by historians and cultural theorists to analyze colonial and postcolonial societies are vitiated by a failure to conduct any field research. Only participant observation can provide access to the implicit symbolic knowledge that underlies the explicit texts they study.

The Varieties of Knowledge

In both artisanship and ritual performance, it is easy to see that knowledge is not always an attribute of a conscious, speaking subject. It may be embedded in a whole network of social relationships, embodied practices, tools, raw materials, and implicit knowledge about the natural world. To put it another way, knowledge can be embedded in a variety of symbolic vehicles, only some of which are linguistic. Indeed, knowledge that can be expressed in language as a set of explicit propositions represents a relatively small proportion of knowledge as a whole. Speech often appears in ritual and handicrafts only as a supplement to embodied performance, in the form of the inaudible recitation of secret spells or sacred texts.

Practical Knowledge

As Bloch has recently argued, most of what people know is nonlinguistic in nature (Bloch 1991). Basic conceptual understandings of the natural world are learned in infancy through observation, imitation, and repeated practice well before language is acquired. Practical knowledge includes all the sensuous qualities of things in the world and of the culturally specific uses to which they can be put. Most practical knowledge is acquired in the first instance through bodily engagement with tools and raw materials. Children acquire the rudiments of many kinds of practical knowledge long before they learn to articulate them in language. It can be differentiated into the subjective skills required for interacting with both the natural and social worlds, the objective raw materials and tools through which these skills are enacted, and the linguistic statements people are capable of making about these skills and tools.

Among the types of practical knowledge discussed in this book are how to exploit the rain forest and the tropical seas (chapter 3); how to transform tropical hardwoods into boats suitable for long-distance trade (chapter 4); how to cope with illness and death resulting from epidemics and shipwreck (chapter 5); how to cultivate crops in irrigated terraces (chapter 6); and how to use firearms to coerce captives to produce agricultural surpluses (chapter 7).

Symbolic Knowledge

Lévi-Strauss argues, in *The Savage Mind,* that oral cultures store their accumulated practical knowledge of the world in a "science of the concrete." To do so, they employ a complex system of multidimensional metaphors that sets up correspondences and oppositions between elements drawn from many different domains of experience. Nature provides the human mind with a powerful model for thinking about and classifying the world in the form of plant and animal species. This is the true basis for the widespread distribution of so-called totemic systems, in which both social groups and natural phenomena are classified under the name of a species. Because individual members of a species are replicas of one another due to their common genetic inheritance, and because of the discrete boundaries between species due to their inability to breed with other species, they serve as a natural model for the essential identity of all the members of a class. Societies composed of identical segments thus often turn to species to symbolize what Durkheim called "mechanical solidarity of likeness." But each individual member of a species is also organized internally in a hierarchy of differentiated parts, thus serving as a natural model of societies composed of functionally differentiated groups. Societies with a complex division of social labor thus often turn to individual organisms to symbolize what Durkheim called "organic solidarity of difference" (Lévi-Strauss [1962] 1966).

Sperber clarifies this insight by showing that practical knowledge about the world is stored in a kind of mental encyclopedia, all of whose entries can serve as raw material for symbolic knowledge. "The symbolic value of 'fox' owes nothing to the sense of the word, and everything to what we know or believe about foxes: to their skill as predators, their look, their coat, etc. What matters, symbolically speaking, is neither how foxes are semantically defined nor what foxes actually are, but what is known of them, what is said of them, what is believed about them" (Sperber 1975: 108). To decode the symbolic meaning of a myth, one must often first acquire a thorough understanding of the ethnozoology, ethnobotany, and many other forms of a culture's practical knowledge.

Like practical knowledge, most symbolic knowledge also exists at an implicit, nonlinguistic level. Symbolic connections are made in the first instance on the basis of patterns encountered in everyday life. For the outside anthropologist who is not able to acquire these patterns of meaning over a lifetime of casual participation in everyday life, however, clues to the most salient symbolic connections are often accessible most quickly through participation in formal ritual settings. Ritual involves an encounter between the sensory and muscular systems of the body and symbolic objects with a rich density of potentially meaningful attributes, among them number, color, texture, smell, edibility, and durability. These objects are selected from the whole repertoire of possible objects because of the density of the symbolic connotations they carry. An enormous number of variables are processed simultaneously as the current object of contemplation is matched against a model learned over the course of many years.

Formal ritual may provide a shortcut into the heart of a symbolic system. But even ritual presents the anthropologist with a vast, complex, and obscure set of possibilities. The temptation is to ask informants to supply an explicit, linear interpretation of "the" meaning of a ritual sequence. This induces in informants an artificially reflective attitude. The need to formulate what one knows in explicit terms only occurs when a person needs to cope with a novel situation or guide someone else in the acquisition of knowledge. In fact, most anthropologists discover that only a very few informants are willing and able to supply the kind of interpretation they want. Many shrug their shoulders. A few provide a reference to a myth that is almost as obscure as the ritual (Bourdieu 1977).

As Leach pointed out long ago, "ritual" and "technical" activities are deeply embedded in one another and may only be distinguished for analytical purposes.

> In Kachin "customary procedure," the routines of clearing the ground, planting the seed, fencing the plot and weeding the growing crop are all patterned according to formal conventions and interspersed with all kinds of technically superfluous frills and decorations. It is these frills and decorations which make the performance a *Kachin* performance and not just a simple functional act. And so it is with every kind of technical action; there is always the element which is functionally essential, and another element which is simply the local custom, an aesthetic frill . . . it is precisely these customary frills which provide the social anthropologist with his primary data. (Leach 1954: 12)

Technical or practical and ritual activities both rely on an implicit understanding of the useful and meaningful properties of concrete objects like foodstuffs, raw materials, and tools. They are learned through lifelong participation in the activities themselves, and an explicit understanding of them may be acquired only by a few reflective individuals near the end of their lives. Ritual knowledge is difficult to communicate and is often deliberately kept secret. It thus tends to be localized in space, but, because it becomes so thoroughly embodied through repetitive practice, it tends to be quite persistent through time.

Ideological Knowledge

Symbolic knowledge of the sort just outlined must be distinguished from ideology, which I will define as the use of symbolic knowledge to acquire or maintain power. Social relations are part of the world that the systems of practical and symbolic knowledge must interpret. Social relations are based on both reciprocity and power. The kind of practical and symbolic knowledge a person develops and maintains will vary according to his or her position within the social structure. The most fundamental categories in Makassar society, as in many others, are those based on differences in gender, age, and hereditary rank. Senior men of the highest rank may well be able to impose their own interpretation of the symbolic system on the society as a whole, especially in formal public settings. It would be a mistake, however, either to assume that official statements of the system are the only ones or to reduce all symbolic systems to ideological deformations of practical knowledge.

Symbolic knowledge can never be reduced to or explained by the ideological uses to which it is sometimes put. Authors working in a Marxist or Nietzschean tradition are often tempted to reduce symbolism to ideology in just this way. In an early article, Bloch claims that ritual is but an extreme form of traditional authority. He argues that religious rituals typically place many constraints on the ability of participants to formulate new propositional statements about the world. Linguistic utterances produced during rituals often use an archaic vocabulary, follow a prescribed meter and are chanted or sung according to special rules. The same is true of the gestures used by participants, which are often so standardized as to resemble dance. For all of these reasons, Bloch argues that rituals seem to eliminate the creative freedom of individuals to contest the central authoritarian subtext of the rituals they are forced to attend (Bloch 1974).

Foucault, following Nietzsche, often writes as if ways of knowing the world are inextricably linked to ways of dominating it. "[T]he cause of the origin of a thing and its eventual utility, its actual employment and place in a system of purposes lie worlds apart; whatever exists, having somehow come into being is again and again reinterpreted to new ends, taken over, transformed, and redirected by some power superior to it; all events in the organic world are a subduing, a *becoming master,* and all subduing and becoming master involves a fresh interpretation, an adaptation through which any previous 'meaning' and 'purpose' are necessarily obscured or even obliterated" (Nietzsche 1966: 513).

Although Nietzsche was thus careful not to equate the origin of a thing to its current purpose, in the end the "origin" is lost in the past and becomes irrelevant to understanding the present significance of a thing. "Genealogies" of practices are of use only as polemical devices by which contemporary idols may be shown to have clay feet; thus, Christian morality was born out of the weakness and resentment of slaves.

I will argue, to the contrary, that the ability of an ideological system to persuade people of the legitimacy of traditional or charismatic rulers is based on the way it is inserted into a symbolic system that has a separate origin both in the past and in the present. Historically, symbolic systems preexist and outlast ideological systems. Psychologically, symbolic systems arise at an implicit and unconscious level. They preexist and are presupposed by any ideological attempt to acquire or maintain mastery over the world or other actors.

Thus, although later chapters increasingly stress the uses to which certain rituals are put, I view ideology as a tertiary phenomenon dependent on the symbolic knowledge that underlies it, just as the symbolic system is a secondary phenomenon dependent on practical knowledge. In sum, ideological, symbolic, and practical knowledge are inextricably intertwined yet irreducible to one another. People always know more about the world than they use for symbolic purposes, and their symbolic system is always richer than the ideological system that makes use of it.

The Varieties of Symbolic Knowledge

Having distinguished symbolic knowledge from practical and ideological knowledge, I now want to analyze symbolic knowledge itself in more detail. I will proceed from the most implicit, embodied forms of symbolic knowledge to the most explicit, objectified forms, from ritual and symbolism through oral myth, ending with a discussion of textual knowledge. As we will see, texts may themselves be classified according to the explicitness of the knowledge they contain. Thus, royal chronicles were meant only for the eyes of the nobles who wrote them. Sacred scriptures are meant for all humans of any era, although their inner meaning is restricted to those who have succeeded in transforming their inner selves in accordance with a fixed spiritual path. Official documents are addressed to interchangeable bureaucrats who have received a specific form of schooling.

Ethnographies aspire to be among the most explicit forms of symbolic knowledge there is, in that they are supposed to reveal the symbolic meanings of one culture to another. Some critics of the field believe that this aspiration marks the discipline as a tool of bureaucratic domination. This view is but another form of the reduction of symbolic knowledge to political function I noted above. Anthropological knowledge can no more be reduced to the political purposes to which it is sometimes put than can mythological knowledge can be reduced to the way it is sometimes used to shore up traditional authority.

Rituals

In his analysis of Australian aborigine rituals, Durkheim argued that the most fundamental material symbol is the human body itself: it is both the primary datum of subjective experience and the most important datum of objective observation. Collective sentiments and the notion of the sacred are generated by coordinated bodily sounds and gestures in obligatory, collective, and recurrent rituals. The sentiments generated in rituals then have to attach themselves to durable symbolic objects to form a continuing source of social solidarity (Durkheim [1915] 1995).

Twenty years later, Mauss pushed the argument somewhat further, when he outlined projects for the comparative study of the body ([1934] 1973) and the self ([1938] 1985). He directed our attention to the way the relation between the body and the soul evolved in the context of religious ritual in Asian history. "I believe precisely that at the bottom of all our mystical states there are body techniques which we have not studied, but which were studied fully in China and India, even in very remote periods. This socio-psycho-biological study should be made. I think there are necessarily biological means of entering into 'communion with God'" (Mauss 1973: 87). As Mauss indicates, in many mystical traditions, knowledge of the self may be reached only through a training of the body. The gnomic utterances of a Sufi master are, strictly speaking, incomprehensible to one who has not undergone the proper bodily training and are certain to be misunderstood by novices. Thus, the doctrines of the mystics are kept secret until the initiate has attained the proper level of experience. It is a commonplace in this tradition that statements that are true at one level of experience are false at another.

Ritual and Bodily Discipline

In the preindustrial age, it was incumbent on every person to learn a trade. In most premodern societies, children followed the trade of their parents. Bodies were seen as a sort of raw material for skill sets, with different bodies having different intrinsic properties suiting them for different trades. The goal of disciplinary forms under the apprenticeship system was to turn the dependent novice into an autonomous master. A master craftsman's most valuable capital inhered in his body. Mystical orders were based on the symbolic appropriation of these techniques of bodily training for profane purposes like handicrafts and warfare. Indeed, during the Middle Ages of Islam many mystical orders were based on craft guilds.

Taking his cue from a passage in Foucault, Asad has argued that in the European Middle Ages religious virtuosi entered monasteries and submitted themselves to a host of rituals that operated on the body to train the soul. "The novitiate is the road to beatitude: virtue leads to the latter, but it is discipline imposed on the body which forms virtue. Body and spirit are but one: disordered movements of the former betray outwardly *(foris)* the disarranged interior *(intus)* of the soul. But inversely, 'discipline' can act on the soul through the body—in ways of dressing *(in habitu)*, in posture and movement *(in gestu)*, in speech *(in lo-*

cutione), and in table manners *(in mensa)*" (Schmitt 1978: 9–10, cited in Asad 1993, 138). Thus, the monastic orders did develop a Christian version of the notion that access to divine knowledge required a training of the body.

The modern European approach to embodied knowledge culminated in what Foucault describes as the disciplinary foundations of the human sciences, disciplines such as the classroom and military drill.

> The classical age discovered the body as object and target of power. It is easy enough to find signs of attention then paid to the body—to the body that is manipulated, shaped, trained, which obeys, responds, becomes skilful and increases its forces. The great book of Man-the-Machine was written simultaneously on two registers: the anatomicophysical register, of which Descartes wrote the first pages and which the physicians and philosophers continued, and the technicopolitical register, which was constituted by a whole set of regulations and by empirical and calculated methods relating to the army, the school and the hospital, for controlling or correcting the operations of the body. (Foucault 1977: 136)

One may question how new any of this deliberate training of the body was. The great civilizations of Eurasia rested upon an extremely elaborate coordination of localized knowledge and skills by a political-military class. In particular, the controlled application of force rested on elaborate systems of bodily training, a process that began in early childhood. The Mongols were perhaps the ultimate masters of putting together military skill sets drawn from all of Eurasia into a whole that was more effective than the sum of its parts.

Symbolic Objects

In addition to the knowledge embodied in people's performances, rituals also involve reference to and the manipulation of symbolic objects. These may be subdivided into perishable materials that are consumed in the course of a ritual, durable artifacts that go on to help structure the perceptions and memories of people over an extended period of time, and permanent features of the landscape that serve as mnemonic foci for oral history.

PERISHABLE MATERIALS

All over the world, rituals commonly require the preparation of an elaborate display of perishable materials. In Indonesia, the most common are derived from wild and cultivated plants like rice, maize, bananas, coconuts, palm sugar, areca nuts, betel leaves, and tobacco; eggs and the meat of chickens, goats, and buffalo; and other perishable materials such as spring water, incense, and firewood. Foods offer the greatest possible number of sensory and conceptual axes of opposition. They may be used in a natural, raw, boiled, fried, or roasted form; they may contrast with one another in terms of taste, texture, number, color, gender, or manner of production and processing.

In Indonesia, as in India, the object of the manipulation of these materials is usually to construct a temporary vehicle for an otherwise invisible spirit. The world is filled with a whole host of spirits and spirit types that are attached to particular material vehicles. These spirits have their own identities, needs, and desires, some of which can be met only by humans. To interact with the material world, they must temporarily occupy a material vessel. The opening phase of many rituals then involves assembling the materials out of which an organic body can be constructed. Certain ritual procedures are then employed to invoke a spirit and to persuade it to descend into the vessel. Once they are embodied, one can communicate with them, propitiate them, ward them off, or banish them from the realm (for very similar notions in Nepal, compare Ortner 1978).

DURABLE OBJECTS

Rituals may also utilize or produce durable objects like elements of the natural landscape such as trees, caves, peaks, and springs; ancestral relics, regalia, shrines, or texts; scale model or actual boats or houses. A complex artifact like a house is both a utilitarian physical structure and a concrete symbolic structure. It embodies the knowledge of the carpenters who built it, but it structures the world of the children who grow up within it. Both ritual and everyday practices are conducted within the structure of the house. They gain part of their meaning from the way the house organizes time, space, and gender.

In terms of local understandings, these durable artifacts are the vehicles of spirits that are always present. A different kind of spirit is attached to each sort of vehicle. Just as human bodies have inner, invisible aspects that are closely tied to their external forms, things are also considered to have an invisible aspect. One must be sensitive to the subtle signs that reveal this inner dimension of the thing, in much the same way that one "reads" the inner character of a person from external bodily clues. This is the phenomenon often referred to in the literature as animism, the idea that natural objects contain souls or spirits. This includes the human body itself, which is seen as a complex physical whole, different aspects of which have different spiritual counterparts.

SYMBOLIC OBJECTS AND SOCIAL MEMORY

At around the same time that Mauss was speculating on the body and the self, another member of Durkheim's school, Maurice Halbwachs, was applying the same insight regarding the social relativity of thought and its embeddedness in socially constructed places and things to the topic of memory. For Halbwachs, memory, the body, and the self all provided more accessible means for investigating collective representations in contemporary "secular" societies than did the study of ritual.

Connerton argues more generally that social memory is structured by the material symbols that are used to evoke it, reproduce it, and transmit it. Like symbolic schemes in general, memories must be attached to a concrete material substrate. He makes a useful gross distinction between memories that rely on inscribing practices and those that rely on incorporating practices (Connerton 1989).

There are those in Ara who have access to Islamic forms of knowledge only in their incorporated form. That is, they encounter them only in the enactments of ritual and experience them as states of being. In Connerton's terms, they gain access to them in the form of habitual memory. Others have direct access to the original inscriptional forms of Islamic knowledge through literacy in the Arabic script. They thereby become more aware of the antiquity of these forms of knowledge. Thus, consciousness of the temporality of knowledge is unevenly distributed in society.

As we have seen, however, inscription is not the only way that memories or knowledge may be preserved in an objectified form. The ancient palace of a ruler holds within it a whole political history that may be read by anyone who has heard the stories that attach to its various features and to the regalia hidden within it, just as a medieval cathedral made the whole sacred history of the church available to those who knew how to decode its statues and stained glass.

I hesitate to call this externalized knowledge of the past "memory." The focus on memory seems inevitably to lead to a focus on childhood, because everyone's earliest memories are those of his or her own early childhood. A focus on knowledge is preferable because it assumes that knowledge is most perfect in adults. In the kind of knowledge acquired through long practice, memory would only be the recall of imperfect knowledge, whereas the best understanding of the knowledge would exist among the oldest members present.

In Ara, an individual's memories of the formative moments in his or her own development as an autonomous individual are less important than the knowledge he or she achieves as an adult. Access to the past is gained not by turning inward toward the earliest of one's own memories, but by turning outward toward the oldest members of the community. The elders in turn relate not their own earliest experiences, but what they learned from the oldest members of the community in their youth. The retention of childhood memories may thus be contrasted with the transmission of ancestral traditions as mediated by the acquisition of adult knowledge.

The recent fascination with memory among social theorists may reveal an obsession with childhood typical of rapidly changing "modern" societies. As Foucault notes:

> [The] child, the patient, the madman, the prisoner, were to become, with increasing ease from the eighteenth century and according to a curve which is that of the mechanisms of discipline, the object of individual descriptions and biographical accounts. The turning of real lives into writing is no longer a procedure of heroization; it functions as a procedure of objectification and subjection. The carefully collated life of mental patients or delinquents belongs, as did the chronicle of kings or the adventures of the great popular

bandits, to a certain political function of writing; but in a quite different technique of power. (Foucault 1977: 192)

In Ara, the chronicles of the kings and ballads of the bandits are still very much in use as techniques of power, legitimating both the system of social ranks as well as acts of resistance to colonial and neocolonial forms of power. The idea that earliest childhood is the site of the most important moments of spiritual development remains quite alien to a culture that sees one's whole life as a gradual movement toward ultimate knowledge through a disciplining of the self. In traditional societies, the oldest generation is the storehouse of wisdom not because it has the longest memory, but because it has had a lifetime to perfect its knowledge of the world.

Myths
Students of implicit knowledge are confronted by a paradox. On the one hand, they are likely to take much of the knowledge implicit in their own culture for granted and exclude it from their analysis. On the other, they usually only have a limited time to gain access to the implicit knowledge of a foreign culture, and they come to that culture as adults with an already formed implicit symbolic system that is likely to interfere with their understanding of the one they are studying.

One way to resolve this dilemma is to study a foreign culture, but to use explicit verbal knowledge as a guide into the implicit knowledge that underlies it. The most common way of doing this is to ask informants explicit questions about what a certain practice or object means. In many cases, however, informants cannot or will not provide an explicit interpretation. Even when an informant can articulate an answer, this approach runs the risk of imposing an irrelevant set of assumptions on the local situation. Imaginative informants who have made sufficient progress in understanding the anthropologist's own cultural categories may respond by generating an entirely novel interpretation that bridges the two cultures. In fact, most anthropologists rely heavily on such informants and would be lost without them. This has certainly always been my experience, and I am deeply indebted to a handful of people in both the Philippines and Indonesia who helped me in just this way.

But it is also imperative to not rely wholly on this form of local theory. Paradoxically, it risks leaving the anthropologist trapped in his or her own culture more than is necessary, because the questions one asks are, at least in the beginning, motivated by the preoccupations one brings to the field from home. Thus, explanations obtained in interviews should be checked where possible against types of symbolic knowledge that are generated independently of the anthropologist's research. Sometimes this happens spontaneously, as when a question about a ritual is answered by a reference to a local oral tradition like a myth. In literate cultures such as the Makassar, inferences drawn from interviews can also be checked against indigenous texts.

Myths and rituals often form complex commentaries on one another so that the meaning of one cannot be fathomed without the other. Indeed, the relation between oral myths and ritual performances is one of the main topics of this book. Just as Durkheim provided us with our introduction to the study of ritual and bodily performance, Lévi-Strauss will be our initial guide to the study of myth and verbal performance.

Like Durkheim, Lévi-Strauss began his investigations of collective representations by studying conceptual schemes governing group membership (i.e., with "kinship systems"). He argued that they were based on the exchange of women between groups ([1949] 1969). He went on to develop a unified theory of social life as systems of communication dealing in a number of different media. "This endeavor is possible on three levels, since the rules of kinship and marriage serve to insure the circulation of women between groups, just as economic rules serve to insure the circulation of goods and services, and linguistics the circulation of messages" (Lévi-Strauss [1958] 1963: 83). Having reached this conclusion, he turned away from the study of kinship. The material substrate of systems of kinship and marriage, human beings, was particularly resistant to use as a set of arbitrary signs. The order these structures tried to impose on the social world was always being thwarted by the vagaries of demographic chance. "Unlike other systems of classification, which are primarily *conceived* (like myths) or *acted* (like rites), totemism is always *lived*, that is to say, it attaches to concrete groups and concrete individuals because it is an *hereditary system of classification*. . . . In totemism, therefore, function inevitably triumphs over structure" ([1962] 1966: 232). Thus, the study of kinship systems provided only a very imperfect window on the functioning of the mental structures that underlie them.

To study mental structures in a purer form, Lévi-Strauss turned to the symbolic uses individuals made of other components of their natural and cultural environment in myth. "Mythology has no obvious practical function: unlike the phenomena previously studied, it has no direct link with a different kind of reality, which is endowed with a higher degree of objectivity that its own" (Lévi-Strauss [1964] 1970: 10). After analyzing a vast corpus of myths from North and South America, he concluded that the narrators of myths are always engaged in multiple dialogues: with their neighbors, with their own past, and with other parts of the contemporary social whole in which they are embedded. "Each version of a myth, then, shows the influence of a twofold determinism: one strand links it to a succession of previous versions or to a set of foreign versions, while the other operates transversally, through the constraints arising from the infrastructure which necessitate the modification of some particular element, with the result that the system undergoes reorganization in order to adapt these differences to necessities of an external kind" (Lévi-Strauss [1971] 1981: 629).

Mythical knowledge expresses much of the same symbolic logic found in ritual, but in a more explicit, verbal form. It is thus easier to communicate from one locality to another. As Lévi-Strauss points out, myths constantly pass from one community to another, undergoing systematic transformations as they engage with different local details of natural environment, productive techniques, and social organization. Mythical knowledge tends to be distributed across regions. But, because it is told and retold by individuals who relate it to their immediate experience, it is in a state of constant transformation through time.

Myths are the most ritual-like of linguistic forms. As Lévi-Strauss showed, they have much of the same internal symbolic redundancy as rituals. When recited, they appear to have a linear form, but when analyzed they turn out to be structured in several dimensions simultaneously. When placed into a group of other myths, the structure becomes even more complex. The words in a myth often refer to symbolic objects almost any of whose properties may become relevant depending on the other objects present in that myth. A set of myths does not explain a set of rituals; it only deepens and complicates their analysis.

Myths are, however, halfway toward the kind of explicit sequential knowledge required by academic monographs. As Lévi-Strauss showed, myths arise at the interface between local cultures. The rationale underlying a local symbolic system may be pushed further toward an explicit set of linguistic propositions when a carrier of the system is confronted by the questions of a visitor who does not share the same conceptual schemes. This is a common social situation, especially for maritime peoples who have been engaged in long-distance trade for millennia. Thus, cultures will always have some degree of explicit knowledge, and certain members of a society will always be better than others at putting what they know into words.

Myths represent the restatement of a culture's most significant symbolic knowledge in linguistic form. Because they do represent a simplification of the symbolic density found in ritual, they are more able to move across cultural boundaries. For the same reason, they may be offered by local people as a guide into the heart of their ritual symbolism. Lévi-Strauss also showed that, because of their internal symbolic redundancy, myths preserved much of their meaning when translated into neighboring languages or even into the languages of colonizing societies.

We must always remember, however, that, as we move from practical to symbolic to ritual to mythical knowledge, there is an impoverishment and simplification at each stage. Lévi-Strauss was apt to overlook this because he came to rely so heavily on the comparative analysis of myths across cultural boundaries, almost always working with versions translated into European languages. Because of the kinds of materials he used, he interpreted myths in terms of other myths, not in terms of the nonlinguistic ritual and symbolic practices in which they were originally embedded.

Although Lévi-Strauss recognized that there is a complex relationship between myth and ritual, he never got very far in analyzing it. This was due not only to what seems to be a real aversion to the sorts of emotions associated with many ritual experiences, but also to his interest in using myth as a way to get at cognitive universals. Rituals appear to be much more closely bound up with concrete experience in particular societies.

By not grounding his myth analysis in local fieldwork, Lévi-Strauss was able to pursue his interest in cognitive universals more easily. There is nothing wrong with this interest when handled correctly, but it does pose a temptation to view the most abstract and impoverished portion of a symbolic system as its basis. Lévi-Strauss's aesthetic sensibility—his openness to all the registers of human perception—save him from this error. He never makes the structural patterns he identifies in a set of myths the generative principle of a culture. Myths are always secondary and tertiary attempts to create an encompassing structure of meaning on the basis of all sorts of lower-level knowledges that have their own autonomous bases.

Whereas Lévi-Strauss tended to move from the analysis of particular symbolic systems to universal properties of the mind, I have followed authors like Hugh-Jones (1979) and Hammoudi (1993) in the opposite direction, focusing instead precisely on those symbolic practices most closely bound up with political and economic processes and thus most vulnerable to the vicissitudes of history.

That structural analysis can also be used to gain insight into the concrete experience of a particular society has been best shown by Hugh-Jones.

> Rather than reduce one to the other, I would see myth and ritual as drawing on a common set of cultural categories, classifications and ideas, expressed not only in the myths and rites themselves but also in the activities of daily life, and producing transformations of a common set of elements. But ritual is not the same as myth for it stands halfway between thought and action. It is through ritual that the categories of thought can be manipulated to produce effects. Myth may exhibit order in thought, but it is through ritual that this order is manipulated to produce order in action and in society at large. (Hugh-Jones 1979: 260)

Myths make explicit and play around with the cognitive elements implicit in ritual, but they do not exhaust their meanings. Conversely, rituals pick out certain aspects of myths for periodic reenactment, but they cannot exhaust their signifying potential.

> Without assuming either that myth is indissolubly linked with ritual or that myth, as a statement in words, necessarily "says" the same thing as ritual, as a statement in action, I have taken a complex involving both myth and rite as my unit of analysis. This complex involves, not simply one ritual overtly related to one myth in such a way that the myth is a recounted rite and the rite an enacted myth, but a number of different rites and myths, many of which bear no apparent or superficial relationship to each other. (Hugh-Jones 1979: 252)

Throughout this work, I will follow the lead of Hugh-Jones by integrating the analysis of myth with that of ritual.

In the next chapter, I will proceed by first establishing that the Java Sea was a coherent region whose peoples have interacted closely for millennia. Following Lévi-Strauss, I will then analyze several dozen myths from around its perimeter as a set of variants that respond both to the changing local "infrastructure" of natural environments, techniques, and rituals in each locality, and to the myths told by other societies in the region now and in the past. I collected these myths both directly from informants in the field and from the publications of English, French, and Dutch anthropologists, colonial administrators, and missionaries. As Lévi-Strauss also argues, the internal symbolic redundancy of myths means that much of their symbolic structure is preserved even through multiple translations. My reliance on these earlier publications does, however, raise more general questions about the relationship between written and unwritten forms of knowledge in Ara.

Texts

The knowledge contained in the myths and rituals discussed in this volume must be contextualized in relation to the written knowledge that has also been present in the village for many centuries. Goody and others have argued that writing has the potential to tear knowledge from a concrete time and place and to force knowledge to an even higher level of abstraction than myth and to enable the production and accumulation of entirely new forms of explicit knowledge (Goody 1977). Although this may be true of writing in certain times and places, the implication of the technology of writing for knowledge depends entirely on the social system within which it is embedded (Bloch 1968, 1998; Parry 1989; Robinson 2000).

Because of the existence in Ara of three scripts that are used for very different purposes, it is relatively easy to see that the significance of this technology varies according to the social practice within which it is embedded. The first script was introduced to South Sulawesi around 1400. It was derived from the syllabaries of India and inscribed on prepared leaves of the lontar palm, hence its name, the lontara script. It is used today primarily to record genealogies and deeds of the royal ancestors. I will refer to these texts as "Chronicles." The Arabic script was introduced along with Islam and is used today primarily to reproduce Islamic writings such as the Koran, Hadith, commentaries, and devotional tracts both in the original Arabic and in local translations. I will refer to all of these texts as "Scriptures." The Roman script was introduced by the Dutch East India Company (VOC) and was used primarily for official purposes, both in Dutch and in Malay. Today it is taught in schools along with the national language of Bahasa Indonesia. I will refer to these texts as "Documents."

ROYAL CHRONICLES

In his discussion of the role that literacy in the lontara script plays among the Bugis of South Sulawesi, Pelras comes to the following conclusion:

It seems to me necessary to distinguish three situations: that of societies where a grand literature dominates, generally printed, and where "oral literature" is a sort of negative of the grand literature from which it is markedly separated; that of the societies without writing, where only an oral literature exists; and finally that described in this article concerning the Bugis, but which is found more or less in other regions of Indonesia, in Sumatra, Java and Bali, in Malaysia, in certain countries of Asia and which was perhaps that of Europe before the Renaissance: in this situation, characterized by the existence of texts not printed but in manuscript, literature is one, of which the written and the oral are two separate expressions. It would be just as regrettable to study the written texts as if they were isolated works from the oral tradition, as it would be to interest oneself only in oral expression, ignoring all the richness of the written corpus. (Pelras 1979: 297)

I have come to the same conclusion: many of the oral narratives I was told while doing fieldwork showed every sign of having once been put into writing and then passed on again by word of mouth, whereas many writings showed every sign of being the recording of an oral tradition. One simply cannot study the "oral tradition" in South Sulawesi without paying attention to the written tradition. Many of the "myths" analyzed in this volume were in fact preserved in textual form as chronicles of this sort whose purpose was to preserve the words and deeds of the founding ancestors unchanged from one generation to the next. They constitute a sort of "frozen mythology," allowing us to peer back in time to the founding of the various Bugis and Makassar kingdoms in the fourteenth and fifteenth centuries.

The writing of local Chronicles began in earnest during the fifteenth century all over South Sulawesi (see Cummings 1999, 2000, 2001, 2002). They helped to solidify the power of local elites by providing them with an exclusive pedigree. In the sixteenth century, royal Chronicles became a tool of centralized empires like Gowa and Bone, whose power rested on a monopoly of gunpowder technology. Their Chronicles were taken as a model by the lesser states that became their vassals.

Today, local Chronicles are stored in attic shrines along with other relics of the most important local ancestors. They are taken down to be recited only during rituals designed to pay homage to these ancestors and to invoke their blessings. They allow the original words and deeds of the ancestors to be reproduced in much the same way that mediums who are possessed by the spirits of the ancestors can make the power of the past available in the present. I am fortunate to have at my disposal a collection of such documents relating to the villages of Ara and Bira obtained by a Dutch colonial official in 1936 (discussed in chapter 7).

ISLAMIC SCRIPTURES

Religious scriptures form the basis of whole civilizations spread over vast periods of time and areas of space. They may be used in rituals much like ancestral texts, as a means of invoking the blessings of a greater power. But because that power is universal and bestows its blessings on all humans who ask it properly, scriptures can also facilitate relatively abstract and individualized forms of thought and communication.

True conversion to a world religion requires that the explicit truths contained in a sacred text become integrated into the implicit symbolic system of a local congregation. In other words, relatively explicit texts must be translated into relatively implicit rituals. Over time, the Koran, the Hadith, and the canonical writings of mainstream Muslim authorities have come to structure a whole set of ritual practices and symbols that embed Islamic knowledge in people's bodies. These Islamic rituals supplement without displacing the rituals and symbols that are associated with local myths.

The relation between scripture and ritual is thus in some respects an inversion of the relation between myth and ritual. Myths arise as a commentary on implicit ritual knowledge, which itself is an abstraction from everyday practical knowledge. Scriptures form a fixed, universal template that must be adapted to local times and conditions. For the mystics who master Islamic symbolism at the deepest level of embodied experience, the practical understanding of the material world itself is transformed.

The descendents of a number of seventeenth-century Islamic saints live in Ara and Bira. Many serve in a variety of Islamic offices. They have at their disposal a number of Arabic, Malay, and Makassar manuscripts that they bring out for public recitations on appropriate ritual occasions. Among the most important of these texts are the Koran; the *barasanji,* or the *Life of the Prophet,* written by Jaffar al-Barzanji (d. 1766); and a text on death and the afterlife by Nur al-Din al-Raniri (d. 1658). While I was in the field, I had a number of these texts transliterated into Roman characters and translated from Makassar into Bahasa Indonesia. I soon discovered that they cast a whole new light on the ritual performances I had witnessed, especially the ones surrounding birth and death. Although I make some reference to these texts in the present volume, a systematic study of how thoroughly they were embedded in village ritual must be undertaken elsewhere.

OFFICIAL DOCUMENTS

The VOC was one of the most efficient bureaucracies in the world during the seventeenth century. Its officials were regularly rotated through the company's holdings throughout the Indian Ocean so that their loyalties would remain attached to the company and their power would continue to derive from it. As the VOC was transformed from a purely maritime enterprise into a territorial overlord in the seventeenth and eighteenth centuries, its officials were drawn into disputes over succession to high office within local polities and over rivalries between them. New administrators had to be provided with a concise, explicit set of instructions from their superiors and with a concise, explicit account of the local political situation. VOC documents thus functioned as instruments of state power, collating ever-changing data about a territory and its inhabitants so that they may be better exploited. The need for documents generated a vast archive that is a rich source of information for historians and anthropologists alike. Many of the myths discussed in this volume are taken from the publications of colonial officials who recorded them while trying to ascertain the "traditional" rules governing political authority and succession in local kingdoms.

At first, bureaucratic power and documentary knowledge were utterly unintelligible to the local population. They expected their political overlords to officiate at religious rituals and to form marriage alliances with their peers and subjects. Dutch Calvinists would and could do neither. The initial response by many Makassar was thus to declare a holy war against the company. (An example of the clash between these two forms of knowledge and power is contained in chapter 7.)

Ultimately, however, local people acquired the ability to manipulate documentary forms of knowledge and power for their own purposes. A crucial first step in this process was the introduction of European schools to the area by Protestant missionaries in the nineteenth century. When the colonial government decided it needed to staff the lower levels of the administration with native bureaucrats, it opened schools on a large scale. This soon had the effect of producing a whole generation of nationalists. Many of these nationalists went on to demand the declaration of an Islamic state after independence. In South Sulawesi, many joined the Darul Islam rebellion between 1950 and 1965. Several of my key informants in Ara had fought with this movement. Significantly, they were all schoolteachers. While I make frequent reference to these developments in the present volume, the account given here is by no means systematic. I have, however, discussed some aspects of these developments elsewhere (Gibson 1994b, 2000).

Writing of the use of the national language and print media in contemporary South Sulawesi, Pelras observes,

> It is interesting to note that a literature in the sense that we understand it in modern Europe has begun to develop in South Sulawesi with the support of printing, but its language is Indonesian, and its public, still not numerous on a provincial scale, is restricted to the urban intellectual milieu. However, if this development continues, it risks in the long run reducing the written expression of Bugis to a dead tradition, reserved for the study of scholars or savants, and of pushing oral expression into a folklore, still perhaps living, but relegated to a secondary place.
>
> A flourishing Bugis literature, productive and popular, would have a chance of maintaining itself and of developing parallel to the literature in the national language only on condition of taking maximum advantage of the modern means of diffusion which are most appropriate to it, to wit audiovisual means: cassettes, radio and television.

> Because, oral or written, Bugis speech is made for being heard. (Pelras 1979: 297)

My own experience of Makassar literature confirms Pelras's conclusions regarding Bugis. Little is written or published in Makassar, but tape recordings of traditional oral forms are eagerly sought and continue to circulate widely, at least among the older generation.

Ideology, Textuality, and Political Agency

Chronicles, scriptures, and documents are all profoundly implicated in what I earlier called "ideological knowledge," the use of symbolic knowledge to acquire or maintain power. Indeed, their fields of application correspond roughly to Weber's three types of political authority: traditional, charismatic, and rational-legal (Weber [1920] 1978: 212–255). I say "roughly," because Weber was at his best in delineating the rational-legal norms of the modern world, somewhat less convincing in his analysis of charismatic prophets, and, in light of his preoccupation with the development of the great literate civilizations, wholly unconvincing in his characterization of tribal societies.

Royal chronicles have as their main political function the legitimation of ruling houses by reference to their descent from the founding royal ancestors. Particular ruling families can mobilize warriors to fight for them only because the Chronicles draw on a dense network of rituals, symbols, and myths that make the existence of kingship, noble houses, and ancestral power part of the natural order. Particular kings may prove to be illegitimate, but the legitimacy of kingship itself can only be called into question by a competing symbolic system. It is this unconscious layer of symbolic meaning that Durkheim and Lévi-Strauss uncovered in their analysis of tribal ritual and myth and that escaped Weber entirely. The fact that these symbolic systems attribute extraordinary powers over both society and the world to political rulers in no way contradicts their traditional character.

Religious scriptures have as their main political function the subordination of particular traditional hierarchies to a universal hierarchy of the prophets and the saints, charismatic humans whose power derives from their knowledge of a God who transcends all local symbolic systems. I would argue that this sort of charisma must be sharply distinguished from the magical powers associated with traditional rulers, as I defined them above. The sultan who upholds the law and universal saint who upholds the existence of the creation in the mind of God are not tied to the same local traditions as are the kings. As with the institution of local kingship, the existence of a global hierarchy of sultans and saints is plausible only because Islamic rituals and scriptures make the mystical experience of an order of being that transcends local tradition available to the ordinary worshipper. Over the centuries, traditional kingship and charismatic sainthood have developed in tandem with one another, sometimes serving complementary functions, sometimes entering into open competition. Their interaction is also seen in the course of life cycle rituals that simultaneously define the individual as a person with particular rights and duties relative to their status in society and as an ethical individual with universal rights and duties whose conduct will be judged according to absolute criteria by God.

Official documents have as their main political function the collection of standardized factual information that can be utilized by interchangeable bureaucratic actors. Makassar has been exposed for three and a half centuries to domination by rational bureaucracies, beginning with the conquest of Gowa in 1667 by the VOC. As Weber defines it,

> Bureaucratic administration means fundamentally domination through knowledge. This is the feature of it which makes it specifically rational. This consists on the one hand in technical knowledge which, by itself, is sufficient to ensure it a position of extraordinary power. But in addition to this, bureaucratic organizations, or the holders of power who make use of them, have the tendency to increase their power still further by the knowledge growing out of experience in the service.
>
> Superior to bureaucracy in the knowledge of techniques and facts is only the capitalist entrepreneur, within his own sphere of interest. He is the only type who has been able to maintain at least relative immunity from subjection to the control of rational bureaucratic knowledge. (Weber [1920] 1978: 225)

As both a bureaucratic administration and a capitalist enterprise driven by the need to accumulate profits, the VOC comes very close to the ideal type of rational domination.

Weber also stresses the central role in rational-legal domination played by the accumulation of impersonal knowledge in the form of official documents. "Administrative acts, decisions, and rules are formulated and recorded in writing, even in cases where oral discussion is the rule or is even mandatory. This applies at least to preliminary discussions and proposals, to final decisions, and to all sorts of orders and rules. The combination of written documents and a continuous operation by officials constitutes the "office" *(Bureau)* which is the central focus of all types of modern organized action" (Weber [1920] 1978: 219). And, indeed, the archives of the VOC are famous for their scope and thoroughness.

Rational bureaucracy did not become a form of legitimate authority in Makassar, however, until the introduction of graded classrooms in the twentieth century gave rise to the demand for national independence and the control of the state by members of the nation. The modern developmental state now obtains the consent of the citizenry because they have internalized the modalities of documentary knowledge in school. At present, the legitimacy of any particular government rests on its ability to develop the nation, but the goal of development is never itself in doubt. Rational developmentalism interacts in complex ways with Islam and with local tradition: none may be said to have achieved complete hegemony within the social whole.

At different points during the twentieth century, the symbolic knowledge embedded in chronicles, scriptures, and documents have been used to further political ends. To understand the ability of traditional, charismatic, and rational authority to mobilize people politically, one must first understand the symbolic infrastructures on which they are built. The deepest of these are the mythological and ritual structures discussed in chapters 3–6, for they arise from the practical knowledges produced by everyday life as it has evolved over millennia. Islam and modernity are relatively recent forms of knowledge cultivated in relatively restricted domains of experience. Each of these domains of experience produce a different sense of both the self and the world.

Because of the functional specialization of scripts in Makassar, it is unusually easy to see in this case how all three forms of authority may coexist in a single society. As a result of these political functions, we may say that textual knowledge has clear ideological functions in Makassar, but we still cannot reduce it to these functions. As Bloch has argued, the best way of disentangling meaning from function in ritual is to examine how rituals behave in time. As he showed in the case of the circumcision ritual of the Merina, the symbolic structure of the ritual has changed very little since it was first described by missionaries in 1800, while it has been used to legitimate many different political orders during the past two hundred years (Bloch 1986). I will return to the relation between ritual and history in the concluding chapter.

Objectified and Embodied Knowledge

It may be useful to contrast my conception of practical, symbolic, and ideological knowledge with another recent approach to the anthropology of knowledge proposed by Lambek. He began his investigation of Islamic knowledge, cosmology, and spirit possession in Mayotte by classifying Islam and cosmology as forms of knowledge that were "objectified" in texts and in explicit verbal exegesis, and spirit possession as a form of knowledge that was "embodied" in spirit mediums. He came to realize, however, that each form of knowledge was "characterized by a particular dialectic of objectification and embodiment" (Lambek 1993: 307). Islamic knowledge is encoded in texts, but it is also memorized and performed. He concludes, "Embodiment and objectification are interdependent, each partial and unrealized without the other. Embodiment provides the ultimate ground of legitimating objective knowledge, rendering it experientially real and confirming its presence in and for the bearer or recipient. Objectification makes embodied knowledge graspable by others, loosening its attachment to the immediate crucible of its production and reinscribing it in the public domain. An understanding of this dialectic is critical for relating knowledge to questions of authority, legitimation, accountability and power" (Lambek 1993: 307).

What Lambek here calls "objectified knowledge" corresponds most closely to what I call "explicit symbolic knowledge." Many other things besides sacred scriptures would fall under the heading of "objectified knowledge" in Makassar society, including formalized oral genres like myths and epic ballads that circulate relatively independently of any particular social agent or situation and implicit forms of objectified knowledge such as architectural, artisanal, and agricultural practices that leave a material residue that both structures ongoing sensuous experience of the world and evokes memories of past experience.

These are all forms of objectified knowledge, but their meanings are implicit and do not circulate in the same way as written texts. Each bears a different relationship to embodied knowledge. As Lambek argues, many forms of objectified knowledge are internalized in ritual performances as a set of bodily experiences and capacities. But other forms of objectified knowledge are internalized in nonritual situations like everyday social and economic activity. Thus, the "technical" process of building a house and the "everyday" practice of living in it both create a sense of how one aspect of the world really is. Lambek's main point, however, remains valid. There is a dialectic between practical, symbolic, and ideological knowledge and between implicit and explicit forms of each.

Methodological Implications

The study of complex societies requires a judicious blend of participant observation and textual analysis. An overreliance on participant observation exposes the anthropologist to the constant temptation to commit the sins of localism and its temporal equivalent, presentism. That is, anthropologists are apt to ignore the textual knowledge that reveals the extent to which people are engaged in global circuits of knowledge exchange and the extent to which contemporary rituals, symbols, and myths are rooted in ancient texts.

By contrast, an overreliance on the study of texts exposes historians to the constant temptation to reduce knowledge to the explicit propositions endorsed by ruling elites. Chronicles produced in royal courts are useful sources for the explicit, official ideology of the state, but they must be contextualized in terms of the implicit practices of violence and popular ritual. An overreliance on local chronicles produced for and by royal elites is evident in many anthropological writings on the Southeast Asian state (e.g., Geertz 1980).

Historians are trained to take advantage of the full range of archival material in a way that anthropologists making brief forays into history often are not. These earlier writings must be read critically with an eye to what they reveal about the cultural presuppositions and personal agendas of the authors. Colonial administrators often give a more complete account of the role of violence and warfare in local society than is available in the royal chronicles. But many were good observers and were, moreover, present at events such as warfare and succession disputes that anthropologists can seldom observe directly after full colonial pacification.

Even trained historians, however, are likely to miss the extent to which textual knowledge gains its significance and efficacy only from the implicit systems of knowledge in which it is embedded (i.e. the kinds of knowledge found in ritual, symbolism, and myth). For all of these reasons, it is important to try to strike a balance between a range of methodologies (see Schulte Nordholt 1996).

Chapter 3
Androgynous Origins
Traces of Srivijaya in the
Java Sea

I n this chapter, I argue that the Austronesian peoples of Island Southeast Asia developed a distinctive civilization over the past five thousand years based on their exploitation of the tropical forests and seas. The shared symbolic underpinning of this civilization is expressed in a widespread myth of origin in which the male and female principles learn how to generate new life by separating and recombining in an orderly fashion.

The Origins of Maritime Trade

By the middle of the third millennium B.C.E., the Austronesian adaptation to the natural environment included the cultivation of a mixture of grain, root, and tree crops adapted to the humid tropics. Coastal settlements separated by hundreds of miles of sea could still maintain regular economic and social contacts with one another by sailing large canoes across the shallow tropical seas.

Austronesian Origins (5000–1 B.C.E.)

Peoples who spoke a language ancestral to Austronesian appear to have originated in a part of southern China where agriculture first developed between 5000 and 4000 B.C.E. Part of this population moved to Taiwan between 4000 and 3000 B.C.E., where the initial Austronesian languages first developed. By 2500 B.C.E. agricultural people were moving southward through the Philippines, where Proto-Malayo-Polynesian (PMP) separated from the Formosan family of languages. A reconstruction of the vocabulary of PMP "indicates an economy well suited to marginal tropical latitudes with the cultivation of rice, millet, sugarcane, the domestication of dogs and pigs and the use of some kind of watercraft" (Bellwood 1995: 99). PMP speakers continued to move south through the Philippines, apparently domesticating such tropical crops as taro, breadfruit, banana, yam, sago, and coconut along the way. "The PMP vocabulary also has terms for

pottery, sailing canoes and several components of substantial timber houses"
(Bellwood 1995: 99, citing Zorc 1994).

Bellwood puts forward the hypothesis that, as the PMP speakers moved
south through the Philippines, they developed a particular complex of institutions that stimulated further geographic expansion. These included the development of sophisticated sailing canoes and methods of navigation leading to
rapid movement along coasts in search of inshore fishing grounds adjacent to
virgin land for swidden agriculture; a stratified social system based on the
deification of ancestors who founded new settlements; and networks of long-
distance exchange that stimulated demand for prestigious trade goods. The
hinterlands of the larger islands were often occupied only centuries after the
coastal areas (Bellwood 1995: 103).

After reaching the Java Sea, PMP speakers split into an eastern group that
went on to colonize the Pacific and a western group that colonized the islands
bordering the Java Sea. When they moved eastward into New Guinea, however,
they encountered relatively high population densities, because of the independent development of agriculture by speakers of Papuan languages. The same was
true when they reached the western shores of the Java Sea, where Austronesian
peoples encountered the agricultural civilizations of Mainland Southeast Asia.
Austronesian expansion stopped at the Malay peninsula, but extensive trade
soon developed between the cultures of Island and Mainland Southeast Asia. By
500 B.C.E. to 0 C.E., evidence from bronzes and megaliths show that "a very
strong Mainland Southeast Asia-Indonesian linkage of trade and influence existed" (Bellwood 1978: 225). Bronze and iron metallurgy techniques spread
throughout Island Southeast Asia at this time (Bellwood 1995:107).

Austronesian speakers probably first arrived in South Sulawesi between
2000 and 1000 B.C.E. Pelras follows the linguist Mills in ascribing an origin to the
South Sulawesi peoples in northeast Borneo, with the Saddan River delta as the
original point of colonization. He points out that the Saddan River gave access to
the gold and iron of the Toraja Mountains and would have been a logical base for
peoples already engaged in extensive sea trade (Pelras 1996: 42–43). According to
Bulbeck, however, the simplest explanation for current population densities and
linguistic relationships on the peninsula is that the Makassar-speaking peoples in
the south have been in place the longest and that the Bugis represent groups that
split off and gradually colonized the lands to the north (Bulbeck 1992: 512–513).

If Bellwood is correct, by the time PMP speakers entered Borneo and Sulawesi four thousand years ago, they had already developed many of the distinctive institutions we will be encountering in this volume. Seagoing sailing vessels,
timber frame houses, ranked kinship groups, and long-distance trade are all characteristic features of coastal populations throughout Island Southeast Asia.

> [There] seems to have been a phase of very rapid and continuous colonizing
> activity between 2000 and 1000 B.C., when we find the first archeological
> traces of Neolithic colonists all the way from the Philippines through eastern

Indonesia and into Melanesia, western Polynesia, and western Micronesia. This is an impressive colonization, perhaps the most rapid, successful and widespread in the history of humanity prior to the recent dispersals from Europe. . . . [By] the time Austronesians moved beyond the Philippines they were undoubtedly getting into high gear, colonizing purposefully and extremely skillfully, searching in the case of the remote Pacific Islands for colonizing opportunities in order to establish new founder-focused lineages of high status. (Bellwood 1997: 311)

The speed of this process was aided by the absence of preexisting agricultural populations in the Philippines and Indonesia. The very low density of hunting and gathering communities presented no obstacle to settlement.

The geographic and climatological features of Island Southeast Asia opened up certain possibilities and set certain constraints for the Austronesian peoples. On the one hand, seas and rivers made a large proportion of the land area accessible to long-distance trade and to the transport of bulk materials such as rice. This meant that from very early times there was a trade in staples as well as luxury goods (Scott 1982) and that the population was highly mobile. Boats are used as metaphors for social organization itself in many societies (Manguin 1986). On the other hand, much of the land was highly mountainous and covered with tropical rain forest, so the land tended to obstruct social intercourse while the sea facilitated it.

The low fertility of mountainous tropical soils limited the population densities achievable with shifting cultivation and required enormous amounts of labor investment in terracing whenever the population passed those limits. In general terms, returns to labor from wet rice cultivation are far lower than from dry rice, and irrigation is only adopted out of necessity. In the fertile lowlands, until a century ago, it was usually a necessity engineered by a despotic state more interested in its absolute revenue than in returns to labor invested (Dove 1985). It was in the few fertile river basins of Java and Mainland Southeast Asia that great agrarian kingdoms first developed between 300 and 800 C.E. (van Leur 1955). They did not do so in South Sulawesi until after 1300 C.E.

Until well into the colonial era, basic productive activities in Southeast Asia were carried out with very simple tools and, aside from irrigation works, did not require a great deal of capital investment. Even the largest artifacts such as buildings and boats were constructed for the most part from readily available vegetation with simple hand tools. A great deal of knowledge and skill went into their production, however, so that skilled boatbuilders, ironsmiths, carpenters, and other artisans constituted the main forces of production. It is virtually impossible to differentiate purely technical from purely ritual activities within such craft traditions. The mnemonic role ritual and symbolism play in the transmission of such implicit knowledge is great. Technical skills like boatbuilding were thus embedded in cultural traditions, handed down through a process of emulation from one generation to another, and often jealously guarded from outsiders.

Specialized skills were likely to be the monopoly of certain ethnic groups and not easily transferable to new groups. One result of this was that the acquisition of new technologies and the construction of more complex social systems often involved the integration of new cultural groups, through either persuasion or capture. This was all the truer in Southeast Asia, where the population density were very low and labor power hard to find and keep. Power, wealth, and prestige derived as much from the political techniques used to control people as it did from the control of land and capital (Reid 1983: 8).

Differential access to high-value trade goods allowed certain groups within a society to acquire prestige at the expense of other groups and some societies to acquire regional hegemony over other groups. Prestige goods were used for such social payments as bridewealth and dowry, compensation for injury and death, tribute to political superiors, and fines for violating religious and legal norms. Failure to pay could lead to the pawning or enslavement of the debtor or one of his or her dependents. The peculiar disproportion between movable and immovable wealth thus also helps explain the centrality of debt bondage in Southeast Asia. As Reid has argued, debt bondage and enslavement for nonpayment of fines are characteristic features of Southeast Asian slavery not encountered to the same degree in the rest of Asia, in Europe, or in Africa (Reid 1983).

Societies with flexible ranking systems tended to flourish in this environment. A minimal division of society into three hereditary classes of noble, commoner, and slave was pervasive in the region, even among the shifting cultivators of Borneo, where the Kayan, Kenyah, Melanau, Ngaju, and others kept slaves. These slaves played a key role in ritual and were often associated with the earth in contrast to the nobles who were associated with the sky (compare Schärer [1946] 1963; Rousseau 1979; Morris 1980; Metcalf 1982; King 1985).

In the kingdoms of South Sulawesi, power rested on a fragile pyramid of dyadic ties of super- and subordination and on competition between equals at all levels of the pyramid. Only those rulers who could prove themselves effective could command respect. Conversely, only those rulers who could command respect could be effective. Within these groups, a notionally ascribed hierarchy was combined with intense competition to legitimate one's presumed place within it, and claims to high status had to be backed by effective control over subordinates to be taken seriously.

This principle applied all the way down the chain of ranks: claims to status had to be validated continually. The higher up the hierarchy one went, the greater the symbolic role of the political leader in unifying the polity. In the absence of a stable bureaucracy, fixed capital investments, or even permanent buildings, the political leader and his loyal entourage were, in a very real sense, the state. Entire cities built of bamboo could spring up in a matter of weeks, and the wealth of a kingdom could be easily loaded into boats and carried away. In such a situation, there was every reason to identify the state of a ruler's health with the health of the ruler's state.

Just as important as methods of economic production, then, were the political methods of controlling the laborers who embodied these techniques. The technology of power involved both coercive military techniques and hierarchical ideologies that legitimated submission to social superiors. The same principal applied to political as to productive techniques. They were acquired through apprenticeship within a cultural tradition. There was an intimate relationship between purely military technique and hierarchical ideology, for the qualities of loyalty to military leaders, courage, and pride are often decisive in hand-to-hand combat. And it is in relation to these psychic qualities of the efficient warrior that ritual techniques to instill confidence and to legitimate leaders are essential. Thus, those groups within a region that best combined military skill with legitimate ranking are likely to have an edge over their neighbors and be able to put together larger and more complex polities over time.

Early Trade with India and China

Because of its geographic position between the great civilizations of China and India and its maritime technology, a great deal of highly concentrated wealth was continually circulating in Southeast Asia in the form of spices, precious metals and gems, fine silk cloths, and goods gathered from the forest, such as aromatic resins, and from the sea, such as pearls and tripang. Maritime linkages between South Sulawesi and the Indian Ocean go back more than two thousand years. At the beginning of the first millennium C.E., there is already evidence of Southeast Asian trade with South India. "Many of the beads were probably made in Southeast Asia itself, and in addition it appears that scrap glass for the industry may have been imported from the Middle East and the Mediterranean area. Roman trade with South India is well documented and a small number of polychrome beads from Southeast Asia may actually be of Roman origin" (Bellwood 1978: 230). Indian glass beads dating to the second or third centuries B.C.E. have been found in Ara itself (Pelras 1996: 26).

By the time of the appearance of the first Indianized states in Mainland Southeast Asia around 300 C.E., the Bay of Bengal and the southern Indian Ocean were already being widely navigated by western Austronesians. "It is possible that a great deal of linguistic assimilation of prior diversity occurred from this time onwards, for instance by the Malayic languages (especially Old Malay itself), Javanese and perhaps other languages or subgroups (cf. Blust 1991, for the possibility of some kind of linguistic leveling in the Philippines). By A.D. 500 the Western Austronesian area was perhaps a zone of continuously-flourishing inter-island travel and trade" (Bellwood 1995: 107). Sollheim has gone so far as to suggest that Southeast Asians had a virtual monopoly on the sea in the period up to 300 B.C.E. and that early Indian influences must have been brought back to Southeast Asia on Southeast Asian ships. By the same token, they must have had an influence on the cultures of South India and Sri Lanka so that "it would not be unreasonable to think that they had something to do with the Cholas becoming a sea power" later on (Spencer 1983: 72, quoting an unpublished paper by Sollheim).

According to Horridge, in time the maritime influences flowed in both directions. The basic boatbuilding techniques used in Ara and much of western Indonesia today originated in South Asia.

> The basis of all Austronesian boats, beyond the simple dug-out and the raft, is the lashed-lug construction technique, in which projecting perforated lugs are left in the dug-out base of the hull and on additional planks which are sewn onto its sides. . . .
>
> Annual trade between China and India through the Malacca Straits had opened by about 200 B.C.E. Perhaps by that time Austronesian sailors were regularly carrying cloves and cinnamon to India and Sri Lanka, and perhaps even as far as the coast of Africa in boats with outriggers.
>
> The fixed mast, doweling techniques, the quarter rudder and the trapezoid sail appear to have spread eastward into Indonesia from the Indian Ocean during the past 2000 years, since the initiation of trade through the Straits of Malacca. Before the arrival of western explorers these details spread no further than the early trade routes to the Philippines and New Guinea. . . . Sanskrit words and possibly some rigging techniques could have started to spread east of Peninsular Malaysia by 200 B.C.E. (Horridge 1995: 137, 138)

Adelaar argues that Madagascar was colonized some time after the seventh century C.E. by Malays and Javanese who brought large numbers of subject peoples from the southeast coast of Borneo. The languages of these subjects became the basis of the Malagasy dialects, which contain a number of borrowings from Malay and Sanskrit as filtered through Malay. There is also evidence in Malagasy of borrowings from Arabic filtered through Malay, which indicates that contact between Madagascar and Indonesia must have continued after conversion to Islam, at least up through the fourteenth and perhaps into the fifteenth centuries (Adelaar 1995). The trans-Indian Ocean colonization of Madagascar was, then, a collective project of peoples from all around the Java Sea that lasted for several centuries.

In addition to technological methods, western Indonesians also began to borrow many political and religious ideas from India early in the first millennium C.E., often in the form of Hindu and Buddhist myths. On the basis of the presence of Sanskrit loanwords in early Bugis myths, Pelras is of the opinion that Buddhist traders of Sumatran origin may have been present in Sulawesi as early as the fifth century C.E. Stylistic analyses of Buddhist bronzes unearthed in Bantaeng indicate Southeast Indian influences dating to the seventh or eighth centuries C.E. (Pelras 1996: 25, 54). As Indic mythology filtered into the region, equivalents were found for the original celestial characters of Austronesian mythology so that Vishnu or Shiva might be substituted for the Sun and their consorts for the Moon. This process was facilitated by the gender dualism at the heart of both symbolic systems.

Austronesian civilization also came into contact with Chinese civilization in the first half of the first millennium. In classical times the "center of gravity" of the Chinese population was in the northern interior, and the bulk of long-distance trade went overland along the great silk road to Rome. During the disintegration of the Later Han dynasty in the third century C.E. this route was disrupted by "barbarians." Only then was China drawn into the ancient maritime network created by the peoples of the South Seas. The shift of trade from the northern land route to the southern sea route accelerated as the population of China shifted toward the southern coast from the sixth century onward.

Intermittently denied access across the steppes in later centuries, Chinese interest in trade through the southern seas continued to fluctuate. It regarded the goods sent from Southeast Asia itself as "tribute" from the "barbarian" nations of the south (Abu-Lughod 1989: 305). The first trade-based state recognized by the Chinese in Southeast Asia was Funan in the Mekong Delta. It flourished from about 200 C.E. until 400 C.E. Trade then shifted toward Sumatra, and toward coastal polities that could draw on locally produced goods. A large proportion of these trade goods were gathered by nomadic tribes in the forested interior of the islands, such as the Sumatran pine resins that were adopted as substitutes for Southwest Asian aromatics like frankincense. Other perfumes and drugs such as camphor and benzoin were gradually added to the list of goods traded (Spencer 1983: 103–104). Other goods were collected by wandering boat people like the Bajau, such as edible bird's nests collected from remote caves and *tripang,* "sea cucumbers," collected from the sea floor. Goods such as these were then bulked for long-distance export by stratified coastal chiefdoms and small states situated at the mouths of navigable rivers.

Beginning in 618 C.E., direct trade expanded across the Indian Ocean as Persians began sailing all the way to China. Not entirely happy with this influx of foreigners, the T'ang dynasty again tried to move most trade with western Asia offshore to Southeast Asia. In 670 C.E., it recognized the Sumatran state of Srivijaya as the successor to the tributary trading state of Funan. Antiforeign sentiment hardened even further in the following century. Between 758 and 792, the T'ang dynasty closed the southern ports of China to Middle Easterners entirely. "When, in the eighth century, Arab seamen joined their Persian precursors in making direct calls on Chinese ports, the T'ang were relatively unprepared for these different and perhaps less ceremonially sensitive entrepreneurs. . . . China's response to them was simple: she again interdicted her ports to these nonsubservient trading partners. They could go as far as the Straits area, but no farther. The representatives of Srivijaya, who ostensibly remained docile 'vassals' of China, were not barred from Chinese ports, a fact that may explain their 'mysterious,' if only temporary, power" (Abu-Lughod 1989: 305).

Between 792 and 878, large numbers of foreigners were again permitted to settle in southern China. But in 878 a rebel army under Huang Ch'ao captured the port of Kwang-chou and slaughtered 120,000 Muslims, Christians, Jews, and Parsis. Middle Eastern traders then pioneered a new eastern route to Japan and Korea that avoided the China coast. This route passed through the waters of

Borneo and the Philippines, drawing a new set of peoples into the global trading system. The earliest reference to the Philippines in Chinese texts concerns the arrival in 982 in Canton of an Arab ship with a load of goods from Ma-i. "Ma-i" may refer to the island of Mindoro, or to the northern Philippines in general (Hourani 1951). In eastern Indonesia, the Arabs discovered the source of many of the exotic spices that had long been traded to the Middle East. Because of the fragmented and hierarchical nature of the polities they found there, they dubbed the area *Maluku,* from the Arabic *al-Muluk,* "Land of Many Kings."

Southern China became safe for Middle Eastern traders again after the Sung dynasty reunified China in 979, and most of them returned to the shorter route along the coast of Vietnam. Their place in the eastern part of the archipelago was taken by Chinese ships from the southern ports of Hangchow and Zaytun, which sailed through the Philippines to reach the spices of Maluku. Centralized chiefdoms arose in the northern Philippines to handle the annual fleets of Chinese vessels. A Chinese account of trade to "Ma-i" written in 1225 gives some idea of what it was like to trade with the tribal chiefdoms in the southern seas in the Southern Sung era.

> When trading ships enter the harbor, they stop in front of the official plaza, for the official plaza is that country's place for barter and trade, and once the ship is registered, they mix together freely. Since the local chieftains make a habit of using white umbrellas, the merchants must present them as gifts.
>
> The method for transacting business is for the savage traders to come all in a crowd, and immediately transfer the merchandise into baskets and go off with it. If at first they can't tell who they are, gradually they come to know those who remove the foods so in the end nothing is actually lost. The savage traders then take the goods around to the other islands for barter, and generally don't start coming back till September or October to repay the ship's merchants with what they have got. Indeed, there are some who do not come back even then, so ships trading with Ma-I are the last to reach home. (Chau Ju-Kua [1225] 1984: 68)

This system remained in place until the southern Sung dynasty was defeated by the Mongols in 1280.

Macknight suggests that among the places these Filipino traders went was South Sulawesi. Some 10 percent of the 14,000 ceramics catalogued between 1973 and 1977 by the History and Antiquities Service pertain to the Sung dynasty (960–1279), yet there is no mention of South Sulawesi in the Chinese records of this time, which indicates that these ceramics were acquired through middlemen. The earliest Chinese reference to Sulawesi that Pelras has been able to find is in a passage concerning Donggala in Central Celebes, referring to a trip made after 1430 (Pelras 1981: 154, citing Mills 1975). Macknight notes that the similarity of the Philippine and Sulawesi writing systems, both based on Indic syllabaries, indicates an ancient link between the areas (Macknight 1983: 96).

Thus, both Indic and Sinic influences on South Sulawesi continued to be mediated by other Austronesians in this era.

At the same time the Sung were removing privileged access to Chinese
ports from the Malays in the tenth and eleventh centuries, the Chola state of
South India began to take a more active interest in seafaring. In the ninth to
eleventh centuries, the Chola state backed up the activities of organized guilds
of traders in Southeast Asia, going so far as to launch a military expedition
against Srivijaya in 1025. With their trade routes being squeezed by the Cholas
in the west and the Sung from the east, the power and influence of Srivijaya
shrank during the eleventh century (Abu-Lughod 1989: 305–306).

The argument about the antiquity and centrality of long-distance trade
in the region that I have developed in this section should lead us to pay particular attention to certain aspects of the ethnographic and historical record if we
wish to understand why certain groups succeeded in expanding their power
and influence within the regional system at the expense of others. These aspects include the political techniques they employed both in warfare and in legitimating a flexible ranking system; the operation of the marriage system both
in uniting and in dividing groups at different levels in the system of ranking;
and the success of the rulers in putting together multiethnic coalitions. Finally
the centrality of trade-raiding organized along hierarchical chains of command
in the political economy should lead us to expect a fetishism of violence, instant wealth, and the person of the ruler.

The Cosmology of the Java Sea

By the end of the first millennium c.e., a region of loosely integrated societies
had developed around the Java Sea. Participants shared a material culture, including timber-framed houses, sailing canoes, and swidden agriculture based on
the cultivation of grain, root, and tree crops. But the societies of the Java Sea also
shared a symbolic culture inherited from their Austronesian ancestors. Austronesian classification systems privileged siblingship and gender complementarity as models for social solidarity over filiation and unilineal descent. Their
mythological system put these models into play in a natural environment made
up of forested islands, shallow seas, and heavens dominated by the seasonal re-
versal of the monsoon winds.

Austronesian origin myths center on the conflict between a male principle
associated with the sun/sky/Upperworld and a female principle associated with
the moon/water/Underworld. The female principle is an aspect of the male principle from which it is yet repelled. The male principle must forcibly overcome the
antagonism of the female principle to produce new life, at which point the principles are able to live in harmony as a couple. The resolution of the conflict between the two principles leads to pregnancy and to the birth of new life, which
is also a form of unity-in-duality, in this case that of opposite-sex twins.

My first example of the Austronesian symbolic system of western Indone-

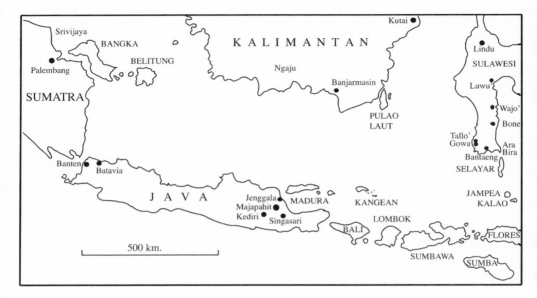

Map 3.1 The Java Sea

sia will be taken from the Ngaju of Central Kalimantan. We have exceptionally rich data on both the mythology and ritual of this people, which was collected by Mallinkrodt and Schärer early in the twentieth century. During mortuary rituals, Ngaju priests, the female *balian* and the male *basir,* had to be able to chant a creation myth to prove that they have the right to enter the Upperworld and to invite the spirits to guide the deceased into the afterlife. These priests were drawn from the ranks of hereditary slaves. Male priests dressed as women and were said to be hermaphrodites or impotent. Both male and female priests were expected to engage in ritual intercourse with men from the middle and upper ranks. They were trained from youth as singers and dancers.

A version of the origin myth chanted by the priests was first published by Mallinckrodt and Mallinckrodt-Djata in Ngaju (1928). It was translated into German by Schärer (1946) and then into English by Needham (Schärer 1963). My own summary of Needham's translation runs as follows:

M 3.1 The Hornbills Quarrel over the Tree of Life (Ngaju: Borneo)
The male hornbill Mahatala dwells atop the gold mountain of the Underworld. His sister-wife, the female hawk Raja Tempon Hawon, dwells atop the jewel mountain of the Upperworld. The mountains clash together seven times, creating clouds; the sky; mountains and cliffs; the sun and the moon; the Hawk and the Fish; an animal with golden saliva and an animal with jewel eyes; and finally a magical object, a gold-and-jewel headdress.

Mahatala has another sister-wife, Putir Selong Langit, who may be the same as the hawk Raja Tempon Hawon. Mahatala creates a daughter-wife, Jata, by dropping rainwater from his hands into the sea. Jata uses the jewels of her earrings to create earth and hills. Mahatala uses thunder and lightening from his fingers to create mountains and streams. As *sanger* (coparents-in-law), Mahatala and Jata together create the human and divine families.

Mahatala raises the gold and jewel headdress and it becomes the Tree of Life. Putir Selong Langit creates rice from the buds of the Tree. A male hornbill emerges from Mahatala's dagger [phallus]. A female hornbill emerges from Putir Selong Langit's golden cage [pudenda]. The hornbills fight over the Tree and destroy it. The blossoms become a golden boat in which a maiden created from ivory tree knots sails away. The male bird kills the female. From her blood emerges a youth, who sails away in a jewel boat created from the Tree's stump.

The gold and jewel boats collide, and the youth asks the maiden to marry him. She demands first dry land and then a house before she agrees. Mahatala provides them. They marry and give birth to three sons. [According to a different myth, she first gives birth to a pig, a dog, and a hen.] The man and woman mate again, and from the woman's flow of blood a magical elephant covered in gold and jewels is born. When the sons are grown, they fight over this elephant on a forbidden mountain. The elder brothers fail to kill it by using iron, which emerges from the depths. The youngest, white-colored, brother kills it in the end with iron that descends from heaven. The youngest son settles in the Middleworld and becomes ancestor to humans. (Condensed from Schärer [1946] 1963: 28–38)

The first striking feature of this myth is the symbolic importance accorded to gold, ivory, and jewels, portrayed as the cosmic source of all creation. This would be surprising in an acephalous tribal society unless it was closely integrated into networks of long-distance trade in which such rare and high-value commodities flowed from peripheral areas to political and economic centers.

In the first generation, a conflict between a male and female bird associated with a pair of mountains representing the Upperworld and the Underworld create a series of entities with ambivalent qualities. These entities can be grouped into three sets. The first set consists of natural phenomena that combine complementary qualities within themselves: clouds, which are half water/Underworld and half air/Upperworld; the sky itself, which links the Middleworld to the Upperworld; and mountains and cliffs, which reach from the earth/Underworld through the Middleworld up to the sky/Upperworld. The second set consists of pairs of complementary entities: the sun/fire/Upperworld and the moon/water/Underworld; animals inhabiting opposed worlds (hawk/Upperworld and fish/Underworld); and animals with opposed characteristics (golden saliva/Underworld and jewel eyes/Upperworld). The third set consists in a single magical object that contains the essence of the two mountains within itself, the gold and jewel headdress.

In the second "generation," a male figure of the Upperworld, Mahatala, is ambiguously paired with two female figures. One is associated with the moon, which, Ras argues, symbolizes the Underworld in its nocturnal aspect, when the Underworld is ascendant in the sky. Mahatala creates moon-shaped ornaments for this sister/wife. The other female figure is associated with the diurnal Underworld, when the Underworld lies beneath the Middleworld. Mahatala creates this female figure by dropping rain (celestial water) onto the sea (abyssal water). His diurnal daughter/wife thus represents another phase of his nocturnal sister/wife.

The magical object from the first round of creation gives rise to a tree that also unites the two worlds. Ras describes the function of this tree as follows: "This tree of life symbolizes the unity of the two supreme deities: the total ambivalent godhead. It stands between the Upperworld and the Underworld. . . . *The trunk of the tree is formed by the sacred spear, emblem of Mahatala and, again, a phallic symbol. It rests on the primeval hill, suggestive of the female pudenda.* . . . In its simplest form we find the tree represented as a combination of spear and cloth: as a *banner*" (Ras 1973: 447; emphasis in original). Cloth is to women as spears are to men. The banner is thus an androgynous magical object. Male and female birds emerging from the symbolic genitalia of the male and female divinities tear this unity to pieces in their struggle with one another.

From this creative destruction, a third generation appears that can unite as a couple only after the second generation creates dry land between the sky and the waters. The man and woman of the third generation produce three sons. Schärer notes that, in other myths, they also engender the three main domestic animals found throughout Austronesia, the pig, the chicken, and the dog. The pig mediates between the Middleworld and the Underworld and the hen between the Middleworld and the Upperworld, whereas the dog belongs purely to the Middleworld (compare Gibson 1986). The youngest son receives a gift from the heavens that allows him to kill the entity that unites the two worlds in his generation: the elephant. Not only is the elephant covered in both gold and jewels, but elephants are themselves an amalgam of Underworld water snakes (*naga*) and land animals. From this act of creative destruction, all the riches of the world derive.

As Schärer never tires of stating, mystical power among the Ngaju always derives from an ambivalent unity of two elements, a unity-in-duality. In every generation of this myth, the same pattern is repeated: pairing, separation, violent collision, and the production and dispersion of new life in triadic form: male, female, and a supplementary, androgynous entity.

On the basis of our preliminary analysis of this myth, we can construct a schematic diagram showing the basic structure of the Austronesian cosmos. It will serve as a sort of cognitive map for much of the analysis in this book.

My next example of an origin myth comes from a seventeenth-century account by Nicolas Gervaise, a Jesuit priest who learned to speak Thai during his time in Siam. Pelras has recently shown that Gervaise probably obtained his in-

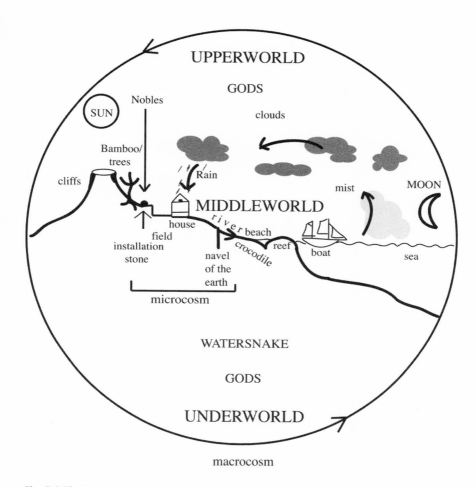

Fig. 3.1 The Austronesian Cosmos.

formation from two young princes who were born to a Makassar noble living in exile in Siam. They probably served as pages in the royal court in Gowa between 1680 and 1685 when the eldest was between eleven and sixteen and the youngest between five and ten. Their knowledge is thus somewhat imperfect, but still quite detailed. After their father led a rebellion against the Thai king, they were taken prisoner and sent to France in 1686, where they came under the care of Gervaise, with whom they could converse in Thai (Pelras 1997, 1998).

In a book published in France in 1688, Gervaise described a former Makassar cult of the Sun and Moon, who were represented by gilded idols kept in every house. According to Gervaise's informants, before conversion to Islam, the Makassar sacrificed oxen, cows, and goats to the Sun and Moon on the first and fifth days of each month. These animals were held to be reincarnations of humans. When the divinities were believed to be particularly angry and there were no more cattle available for sacrifice, people would offer their own children. Pigs and chickens, on the other hand, were not treated as inherently sacred, because human souls were never reincarnated in such lowly vessels.

Gervaise goes on to record the following myth concerning the role of the Sun and Moon in creating the cosmos:

M 3.2 The Sun quarrels with the Moon (Makassar: Gowa)
The Doctors added to all these Fooleries, with which they amus'd the Vulgar People, that the Heavens never had any Beginning; that the Sun and Moon had always exercis'd a Sovereign Power there; and liv'd in peace with one an-other, till a certain day that they quarrel'd together, and that the Sun pursu'd the Moon with a resolution to have abused her; that being wounded in her flight before him, she was deliver'd of the Earth, that fell by chance as now we see it; and that upon the opening of the Clumsie Lump in the middle, two sorts of Giants issue'd forth; that the one made themselves Masters of the Sea, where they commanded the Fish, rais'd Storms and Tempests when they were angry; and that they never sneezed but that there happened some Shipwrack: That the other Giants were thrust down to the Center of the Earth, there to labor the Production of Metals in concert with the Sun and Moon, and when they bestirred themselves with too great Violence, they caused Earthquakes and sometimes overturned whole Cities. Moreover, that the Moon was big with several other Worlds, no less in extent than this; that she would be deliv-ered of them all successively, one after another, to supply the Ruins of those that should be consumed at the end of every hundred thousand years, by the Excessive heats of the Sun; but that she should be delivered naturally, and not by Accident, as she was the first time; because the Sun and the Moon having found by mutual experience, that the World cannot subsist without their re-ciprocal influences, were reconciled upon condition that the Sun should reign one half of the day, and the Moon the other. (Gervaise [1688] 1701: 120)

In the first generation, an angry male figure wounds a female figure, caus-ing her to miscarry and give birth to two races of giants, associated with the sea and with subterranean fire, respectively. They reconcile, and after this first birth the Moon begins to give birth to new worlds in a regular fashion. The Sun's ex-cessive heat eventually destroys each world, but new ones are continually created by the Moon, now working in harmony with the Sun. The male principle is as-sociated with heat, death, and destruction, the female with coolness, life, and creation. The two principles work together to generate a continuous flow of life.

Some years ago, Hamonic published a five-page manuscript he acquired from the widow of the former Opu Pa'bicara of Luwu' in 1978 (for an account of his life, see Errington 1989: 20–23). It is the only other text I know of from South Sulawesi that refers to the offspring of the Sun and the Moon. Hamonic notes that he had great difficulty in persuading the royal family to allow him to see and copy this manuscript, which was held as part of the sacred regalia of the king-dom. This was also true of the other texts to which he compares it. All were re-garded as containing secret, esoteric knowledge not available to ordinary people. Their function was thus not to serve as public charters legitimating divine king-ship, but as sources of mystical power for those who held them in private.

M 3.3 The Sun and Moon Explode, Begetting Twins (Bugis: Luwu')

The One God creates the light called Zatulbukhti/Ruhul Kudus (the Angel Jibril), then the seven levels of the heavens and of the earth. Then within the Light of Muhammad, God's Majesty and Magnificence combine to produce the first god, Datu Dewata (the Prince of Gods).

The male Sun is produced from his right thigh and the female Moon from his left. The stars are also produced and disperse in constellations. The Sun becomes pregnant with light from Datu Dewata's right thigh, and the Moon from his left. The two then marry. They tour the universe and separate. The Moon descends and the Sun ascends, but then turns, catches the Moon and they fuse momentarily into one. They blow apart with a clap of thunder, leaving behind a man and a woman.

The woman is carried to the edge of the sky, the man to the highest throne. After twelve years they meet in the center of the sky and are married. They en-gender three sets of twins; one of iron, one of silver and one of gold [i.e. earth, moon and sun] and one single child who is without bones, but who is twin to both silver and gold. He gives rise to the first rice. The first son marries the sec-ond daughter, the second son marries the third daughter and the third son marries the first daughter. Each couple has, in turn, nine children. The first man and the first woman then withdraw from the earth and return to the Sun and Moon, respectively. (Condensed from Hamonic 1983: 50–54)

This myth presents evidence of the process by which Islamic cosmology was first harmonized with indigenous Austronesian themes. Pelras argues that the initial conversion of all South Sulawesi began in Luwu' when a Sumatran Sufi linked indigenous notions of an androgynous creator deity to the Islamic no-tion of an asexual Allah.

> According to local traditions, Dato' Pattimang, who was to spend, from then on, most of his life in Luwu', centered his teaching on *tauhid* (Arabic for Unic-ity), not in the usual Muslim way, but by using Bugis beliefs about the One God (Dewata Seuwae) and about Sawerigading. No text, to my knowledge, permits us to know what his teachings were exactly, but I suspect that many stories found in *lontara'* (manuscripts) concerning the Creation, giving Adam and Eve as the parents of the former Bugis gods or showing Sawerigading as a kind of prophet *avant la lettre* who, before his descent to the Underworld, an-nounced the coming of Islam, and so forth, may at least represent some of their offshoots. (Pelras 1985: 120)

In this version of the creation myth, the original Unicity of God engenders the divine light and the Seven Grades of Being. Within the Light of Muhammad there emerges the first duality of Majesty and Beauty, two attributes of God that often have male and female associations in Sufi literature. These attributes combine to produce another kind of unity-in-duality, Datu Dewata, who is clearly androgynous in character.

This androgynous whole generates the Sun and the Moon from his right and left thigh. Each becomes pregnant asexually by light from the same thigh that originally produced them. Only then do they come forcibly together, creating a second androgynous whole. This results in a violent explosion and produces a second set of opposite-sex twins, the first man and woman. They must be separated for twelve years (the time required for sexual differences to mature) before coming together in marriage. Their union engenders three more sets of twins. Each set is associated with a different element (iron/earth, silver/water/moon, gold/sky/sun), plus a supplementary individual who is twin to both gold (solar male) and silver (lunar female) metals. This androgynous individual is the ancestor of rice. The three sets of twins then combine with one another in marriage in an orderly fashion. Each couple then engenders four more sets of twins, plus a supplementary ninth child. Their work in filling the earth completed, the first man and woman withdraw to the heavens.

As with the creation of the magical headdress, the Tree of Life, and the elephant in the Ngaju myth, the creation of each new generation in this myth is accompanied by the production of a third, ambiguous element alongside the male and female pair: the constellations, the boneless child, the ninth child.

Hamonic shows that the cosmological conceptions found in the texts of Gervaise and of Luwu' also exist in two other Bugis texts that have, however, undergone a further revision in Islamic terms. Adam and Eve (Hawa) substitute in these texts for the Sun and the Moon, but many of the same symbolic oppositions are preserved. Matthes published the first of these texts in 1864. As with Hamonic's text of Luwu', Matthes acquired it with great difficulty. The knowledge it contained was regarded as a powerful secret, and various rituals had to be performed before he was allowed to copy it.

M 3.4 Adam and Eve Quarrel over Cain (Bugis: Matthes)

When Kabele had killed his brother Habele, Adam wanted to put him to death, but Sitti Hawa opposed it. In the course of their dispute, Adam let escape his semen, and from it was born a beautiful young girl with white blood, Sitti Anise'. The latter married La Saidulilla, son of a serpent and a peacock. From that union was born seven sets of twins, each time a boy and a girl. The eldest son, Sangkuru Wira la Patigana Aji Patoro, married the twin sister of Guru ri Selleng, that is Mutia Unru' Datu Palinge', while Guru ri Selleng married the twin sister of Aji Patoto. (Hamonic 1983: 39, citing Matthes 1872 vol. 3: 252)

We have here three generations of marriages. Adam and Eve produce a pair of same-sex brothers, one of whom kills the other. Adam is so angered by this that he wishes to kill the remaining brother, but he is prevented by Eve. His anger boils over, as it were, and his white semen escapes and engenders a white-blooded daughter. At some level, both Adam and his daughter are androgynous, because Adam was capable of producing a female on his own and his daughter has nothing but the white blood of Adam in her veins. In the second generation, this female-born-of-a-male marries a male figure, who is also androgynous at some level, because he is the offspring of creatures from the Underworld and the Upperworld, the serpent and the bird. Only in the third generation do these androgynous entities begin to differentiate into stable opposite-sex pairs as the second generation gives birth to seven sets of opposite-sex twins, who begin to marry the members of other sets of twins in an orderly fashion.

Hamonic recorded the next myth in 1975 from the mouth of an old *bissu* priest in Wajo'.

M 3.5 Adam and Eve Quarrel over Sex (Bugis: Wajo')

God created Hawa from the left side of Adam. But he could not marry her, they could not have children; and Hawa was constantly arrogant, wanting always to be in the right, wanting to be superior, wanting the same power as Adam, and the matter could not be settled because there were still no relations between male and female. . . .

Time passed and the woman found herself pregnant, without being approached by the man. And Adam, who could not understand it, called Hawa and said to her, "What you have in your belly, it is necessary for there to be two for it to succeed, let us thus be together!" But Hawa didn't want to understand anything and said she would give birth alone; and the quarrel continued without their being able to resolve it. Adam thus turned to Dewata Seuwa To Papunna and asked him to resolve it. He sent them two great jars, one to contain the female semen, the other, their mixed semen, so that one would discover which was sterile. And so it came to pass: the man and the woman filled the jars one by one with their semen during seven seasons, seven days and seven nights, which they then closed. The set time having elapsed, they opened them again at the same instant. They saw then that their mixed semen had remained intact, while the semen that came solely from Hawa had "rotted." From that day man and woman have married. . . .

From their mixed semen contained in one of the jars was born, in one day and one night, nine pairs of twins, but two of them, imperfect, did not thrive. Datu Patoto' was thus the twin brother of Guru Ri Selleng, while Datu Palinge' was the twin sister of Sinau Toja. From the rotten semen of Hawa contained in the other jar, were born forty divinities, also twins, who married among themselves. They dispersed on the land, in the sea and in the sky. Among them were the stars, the thunder and lightening which fill the skies, the veins of iron in the earth, and the kin of the crocodile in the waters. (Hamonic 1983: 40)

In this myth, the quarrel between the first man and the first woman leads the *woman* to conceive without help from the man. She gives birth on her own to twenty sets of twins who intermarry and go forth to fill the three worlds with natural objects and animals. But God also makes them mix their fluids and from this mixture is born nine sets of human twins, two of whom die, leaving sixteen children.

Hamonic summarizes the parallels between the four myths he discusses as follows:

When we compare the schemes of our different narratives, we have in every case:

1. A masculine-feminine couple who take the form either of Adam and Eve (Matthes, "narrative of Wajo'"), the sun and the moon (cf. Gervaise), or both under different avatars, as in the "text of Luwu'" (male-sun creature — La Tepulangi' — La Patigana/female-moon creature — We sengngeng lingnge' — We lette' sompa).

2. A quarrel arises between them (cf. Matthes, Gervaise, "narrative of Wajo'") followed by a chase or a race which, according to the texts, results in the birth either of a single male creature (Matthes)—but this birth will give birth, by the intermediary of Sitti Anise', to the generation of Datu Patoto and the other divinities of the La Galigo; or to the birth of a single female figure (cf. Gervaise, "narrative of Wajo'") giving birth to the earth and to giant monsters, who number in total forty divinities. The "text of Luwu'," for its part, makes no allusion to the consequences of the first coupling between La Tepulangi' and We sengngeng lingnge', but one knows that on that occasion "the sun and the moon swallowed each other" and that the coupling resulted in a sort of exile of We lette sompa to the limits of the sky (cf. III, 3–4; III, 13–14).

3. Finally, this dispute is soon followed by a reconciliation (cf. Gervaise and the "narrative of Wajo'") or a conciliation which can take the form of life as a couple ("text of Luwu'") from which are born the sovereign divinities at the origin of the genealogies of the La Galigo. (Hamonic 1983: 45)

References to the birth of several sets of twins occur in the three Bugis texts discussed by Hamonic: seven sets in Matthes, nine sets in the Wajo' text, and three in the Luwu' text. Hamonic notes that while incest among groups of twins constitutes a second focus of interest in the Bugis myths he examines, it is absent in Gervaise's Makassar myth.

Where the Bugis myths recorded by Matthes and Hamonic ostensibly set out to explain the origin of the Bugis pantheon, Acciaioli recorded a myth among lower-status Bugis migrants in Central Sulawesi that uses similar elements to explain the origin of social stratification:

M 3.6 Adam and Eve Quarrel over Cain (Bugis: Lake Lindu)

Adam and Hawa were having a fight with each other, they were quarreling. A child named Kabel had been born to them. Adam declared it was his child because he placed it [in the womb]. Hawa declared it was her child, because she had stored it [in her womb]. So they each hoarded their genital fluids. From these each gave birth to a child. Adam's child eventually became hard, but Hawa's child was soft. It could not even stand. It had to be lifted up, since it was as if paralyzed. It was just carried around. Its elder sibling was always ordered to carry it. So they considered how it could be arranged that this child of Hawa would still [always] be cared for by its elder sibling so that it could live. Thus the descendents of Hawa were raised to the status of nobility because they were not able to work, to hoe the fields. Each child married and had children. Eventually, the child of Hawa's son Kail came to regard his father as rajah. He was always being carried around. Even if his father wanted to go out to defecate, he was carried. And so it has been passed down for those who become rajah. Though when you think of it, there is really only one humankind. (Acciaioli 1989: 294–295)

In this myth, the first man and the first woman again quarrel over their first child. As a result of this quarrel, each gives birth to another child without benefit of intercourse. Both children are incomplete: the child of the male is hard, the child of the female so soft it cannot walk. Rather than this child becoming the ancestor of rice as in the Text of Luwu', however, he becomes the ancestor of the ruling class.

Acciaioli's Bugis myth is reminiscent of one I recorded in Ara. I learned of it from Imam Muhammad Yakub of Dusun Martin, who is originally from Selayar. He told it to me during a funeral as a means of explaining Islamic funeral customs, but it clearly belongs to the same group of origin myths as the others in this chapter.

M 3.7 Cain and Abel Quarrel over Iklimah (Konjo: Ara)

Adam and Hawa had two sets of twins, each made up of a boy and a girl. The elder pair were called Kabil (Cain) and Iklimah, the younger Habil (Abel) and Labuda. Now, because there was no one else for Kabil and Habil to marry except their sisters, they were commanded at least not to marry their own twin. Thus, Kabil was destined for Labuda and Habil for Iklimah. But Iklimah was by far the most beautiful, and Kabil began to plot a way to keep her for himself. So he said to Habil, let us prepare sacrifices to the Lord, and the one whose sacrifice is most acceptable will get Iklimah. But it was Habil's sacrifice that was accepted, because his intentions were sincere.

Then Kabil formed another plan. There were but six people on the earth, but the animals had all been created, including Serigala, the jackal. Kabil asked Adam for permission to take Habil to the edge of the woods to play, but Adam forbade it, saying, "No, you mustn't take him there; he might be eaten by Serigala." Because his desire for his twin was so great, Kabil kept coaxing and deceiving Adam, until finally he gave in, because he loved Kabil. Off they went to the edge of the woods, where Kabil attacked and killed Habil. He removed his clothing to take back to show Adam as evidence that the jackal had killed and eaten Habil. But he couldn't figure out what to do with the body, because no one had died before and burial was still unknown.

While mulling this over, he noticed two crows fighting in a tree. Finally, one killed the other and it fell down on the ground next to Habil's body. The other crow flew down and dug a hole in the ground with its talons, dragged the body into it, and covered it. And so Kabil got the idea to bury Habil. This practice was later confirmed as the ritually correct procedure by God's revelation to the prophets.

Hawa was now left with just three children, but she went on to give birth to eighteen more sets of twins, and to one last single son. Each boy married a sister from the next younger set of twins, except for this last, youngest son, who had to marry the eldest sibling, Iklimah. In the next generation, everyone was able to marry a cousin. (Muhammad Yakub Daeng Jagong, Imam Dusun Martin, February 8, 1989)

In this myth, the quarrel occurs not between the first man and the first woman, but between the male members of the first two sets of twins, and it results in the first death rather than the first birth. The eldest brother does not want to give up the eldest sister to his brother. Kabil's greed leads to deceit and then to murder, which results in a lack in the sibling sets rather than a supplement as was typical in the other myths. Hawa then gives birth to eighteen more sets of twins, each of whom marries a younger sister when their own twin is taken by an elder brother. It is Kabil who finally marries Labuda. A supplementary individual child is required to take Habil's place.

In all of the myths discussed in this chapter, the creation of new life requires the splitting of an original androgynous unity into two complementary halves, which must then learn how to come back together in an orderly way to generate new life. The androgynous unity that pervades the myths exists at several levels, from the abstract cosmological level of two worlds to the increasingly concrete levels of heavenly bodies, paired animals, and opposite-sex twins. The next generation generally consists of two separate halves of the original whole, plus a third thing that itself perpetuates the original androgynous whole. Androgynous unity is best expressed by magical objects such as the headdress and elephant made of gold and jewels of the Ngaju. Such objects played a key role in the rituals of many of these societies and were often manipulated by priests who were themselves of androgynous gender. This was certainly the case in South Sulawesi, where transvestite priests called *bissu* were guardians of the sacred regalia right through the nineteenth century, and survived in places well into the twentieth century (Hamonic 1987). We will encounter many other such objects in the chapters to come.

Conclusion: Ara and Regional Analysis

This chapter presented the archeological and linguistic evidence for the origins of the Austronesian people in southern China and their spread through Island Southeast Asia and beyond. This evidence indicates that basic features of Austronesian life—including the shifting cultivation of grain, root, and tree crops, the collection and export of forest produce, and maritime trade—date back several thousand years. These activities provided a common framework of practical knowledge within which shared symbolic knowledge contained in myths and rituals could circulate widely. This circulation accelerated during the first millennium C.E., when the Sumatran empire of Srivijaya came to serve as an entrepôt between China and India.

It is against this historical background that I have analyzed a set of myths found throughout western Indonesia that must have been circulating around the Java Sea at least since the time of Srivijaya in the seventh century. These myths provide a sort of symbolic baseline for Austronesian systems of gender and marriage. They concern the origin of sexual complementarity between primordial male and female beings, often identified with the Sun and the Moon. The male figure is simultaneously attracted to and repelled by the female figure. They either attempt to reproduce asexually, giving birth to incomplete beings, or the male realizes his need for the female and chases her until they come violently together. Their union produces a pair of opposite-sex twins, plus an androgynous supplement that often takes the form of a magical object. By the end of the myth, the initial antagonism between male and female has moderated into an acceptance of complementary opposition. Orderly procedures are adopted for the pairing of male and female figures and for their exchange of sexual fluids.

Chapter 4
Incestuous Twins and Magical Boats
Traces of Kediri in the Gulf of Bone

I n this chapter, I discuss a widely distributed set of myths in which the world is portrayed as a series of royal centers distributed along the coasts of the islands surrounding the Java Sea. These centers are linked together by marriages contracted between seafaring male heroes and local female princesses, who serve as mediators between humans and the gods of the Upperworld and of Underworld. Following Ras, I argue that these myths originally served as charters for a set of royal rituals that legitimated the power of local dynasties in terms of their privileged access to distant royal centers. The key figures in the myths are a male hero who sails around the archipelago on a quest for wealth, power, and a bride of sufficient rank and beauty; a female demigod who meets these criteria; and a magical boat capable of carrying a whole army of followers. The boatbuilders and sailors of the Bira Peninsula have long played a pivotal role in this narrative. Because I was based in Ara, my material relates primarily to boatbuilding.[1]

Royal Alliance in the Java Sea

After the decline of the Sumatran Empire of Srivijaya in the eleventh century, the center of cultural influence in Island Southeast Asia shifted to the Javanese Empire of Kediri. A new kind of civilization had developed in the interior of Java that relied as much on tribute extracted from wet rice cultivators as it did on the control of long-distance trade. The rise of agrarian states throughout Southeast Asia created a new demand for labor power, because irrigation was capable of absorbing an almost unlimited amount of seasonal labor. One source of new labor was slaves captured in war (Tambiah 1976: 120; Reid 1980: 243).

The rulers of agrarian states in Southeast Asia frequently borrowed Hindu and Buddhist ideas from South Asia to legitimate the exalted position of the king. In the eleventh-century Javanese Empire of Kediri, the King was represented as an incarnation of Vishnu. By the twelfth century, Kediri had come to serve as a model for innumerable little polities scattered around the Java Sea, including Luwu' at the north end of the Gulf of Bone. Over the next few centuries, Luwu' came to control the major coastal estuaries of the Gulf of Bone, dominating the export of metals and forest produce from the highlands of central Sulawesi and the import of silk and Chinese porcelain transshipped from the Philippines and Java. Sanskrit words and Indic symbols entered into the local languages and cultures of the area at this time.

Local ruling dynasties throughout the Java Sea attributed their origins to semidivine ancestors who descended from the Upperworld or who ascended from the Underworld. The high-ranking nobility of each local realm sought the recognition of the high-ranking nobility of other realms to maintain its local prestige. The sign of this recognition was the acquisition of exotic goods through long-distance trade and the exchange of noble children in marriage. Long-distance trade was a source of both great power and great danger.

Royal origin myths thus combine a concern with travel along a vertical axis between the Upper-, Middle-, and Underworlds with a concern for horizontal movements across the sea between distant realms. One way they do this is by linking the vertical dimension to a princess who remains in one place but is able to communicate with the gods and the horizontal dimension to a seafaring prince who travels from one kingdom to another.

Hamonic has argued that the cosmological myths analyzed in the previous chapter reflect the position of South Sulawesi as a cultural "crossroads" between western and eastern Indonesia (Hamonic 1983: 46). On the one hand, he sees the concern with sexual antagonism displayed in the quarrel between the Sun and the Moon as typical of western Indonesia. On the other hand, he sees the theme of marriage among the gods and incest among their offspring as typical of eastern Indonesia. The theme of royal incest is also present throughout western Indonesia, however, in the tales recounting the adventures of a hero named Panji. In these tales, the seafaring prince and the immobile princess are opposite-sex twins who are separated in childhood. Only after many difficulties are they able to reunite with one another or a close substitute.

Rassers on Panji and Archaic Social Organization

In 1922, Rassers published a study of the tales of Panji that was instrumental in inaugurating the Leiden school of structural analysis. He began his analysis with a 110-page summary of an 800-page Malay text called the *Hikayat Cekel Wanengpati*. Ras condensed this to two pages, which I will condense further as follows:

> M 4.1 *Hikayat Cekel Wanengpati* (Malay)
> In heaven the god Naya-kusuma has two children, one of each sex, by the nymph Nila Utama. The boy is named Indra Kamajaya and the girl receives the name Dewi Nila Kencana. The children are like the sun and moon. They grow up separately, but when they meet they fall so deeply in love with each

other as to become inseparable. Because a marriage is, of course, out of the question, the father decides that they must incarnate themselves on earth. . . . The young prince is born on earth as the crown prince of Koripan and is named Raden Inu Kertapati. . . . His sister is born on earth as a princess of Daha and receives the name Candra Kirana (Princess Moonbeam). . . . When he grows up, Raden Inu vows he will touch no other woman before he is united with the princess of Daha. [After several hundred pages of adventures that prevent their union], Raden Inu reaches Daha (in disguise). [Raden Inu and Candra Kirana are finally married]. Inu defeats all his rivals and in doing so captures most of Java. (Ras 1973: 417–418)

In Javanese stories of this type, the Raden Inu character is generally known as Panji. "Panji is often represented as an incarnation of Vishnu, creator and lord of the Upperworld. His twin/wife Candra Kirana is represented as an incarnation of Dewi Sri, who represents 'the primeval waters and the Underworld, which is auspicious for the fertility of the earth and the good fortune of the human community'" (Ras 1973: 439).

Following the 1903 essay by Durkheim and Mauss, *Primitive Classification,* in which all cognitive classifications are held to derive from social groupings, Rassers argued that Panji and his twin sister must have represented the exogamous moieties of the original Javanese social structure. The adventures they underwent in the course of the story before they were united in marriage at the end represented tribal rites of passage (Durkheim and Mauss [1903] 1963; Rassers 1922, 1959).

Explaining a later set of symbolic structures in terms of long-vanished social structures fell out of fashion in the 1940s, in part because of the influence of Lévi-Strauss's reformulation of structuralism. Nevertheless, Rassers was on the right track in trying to link the myth in question to wedding rituals. There is, however, no need to project these rituals into the distant past.

Ras on Panji and Medieval Royal Weddings

In 1973, Ras published a reevaluation of Rassers in which the tales of Panji were more plausibly interpreted as a charter for marriages between distant royal families during the Kediri period in Java.

Interpreted in this way the drama of Panji and Candra Kirana was an appropriate stage-play to be performed on the occasion of every pre-Islamic *royal wedding* in Indonesia. . . . In my opinion it is this *social function* of the Panji drama as the conventional stage-play for royal weddings in the twelfth through thirteenth centuries rather than its deeper religious meanings which explains the large number of existing Panji stories both in Java and outside. In this period a large number of Javanese princes and princesses must have been sent abroad to be married off to members of befriended royal houses. Available historical data testify to this. The retinue of such a prince or princess most probably in-cluded a *dalang* with a *wayang gedog* outfit, or even a whole group of *topeng* dancers, or both. As part of the festivities the Panji drama was put on the stage in the desired form, translated into Malay, Balinese, Cham or Thai for the benefit of the audience. (Ras 1973: 439–440)

According to Ras, the "Kediri period" of Javanese history (1037–1222 C.E.) "was a period in which Wisnuism, 'the religion of the Mahabharata and Ramayana epics,' was the most prominent religion in Java. Characteristic of the Panji story is the identification of Panji and Candra Kirana, respectively, with Wisnu and Sri. In the *wayang purwa lakons,* we find a similar identification of Kresna and Rukmini or of Rama and Dewi Sinta with Wisnu and Sri" (Ras 1973: 442). Such marriages became more frequent in the twelfth century as long-distance mari-time trade between coastal kingdoms became more important to royal power.

Ras goes on to compare several Panji stories from Java and Bali with the Ngaju Dayak creation myth discussed in chapter 3. He reaches four main con-clusions. First, the Ngaju Tree of Life plays the same role as the *kayon* in the Jav-anese shadow theater: both are ambivalent male-female symbols that link the three worlds. Indonesians readily adopted the symbolism of the Shiva's *lingga* (phallus) growing up out of the *yoni* (pudenda) as it could be made to represent the same complex of ideas. Second, the male protagonists in both stories have two wives: a regular partner at the beginning of the story and a quasi-incestuous relationship with a second woman later on. One is associated with the water snake in the diurnal underworld, and the other with the Moon in the nocturnal sky. Third, the goddess associated with the Moon is responsible for the origin of rice, whereas the Sun, identified by the Ngaju as the Hornbill, is transformed in Javanese myth into the grandson of a great ruler like Erlangga of Kediri, and with various incarnations of Vishnu. Fourth, the whole complex of myths functions as a charter for life cycle rituals in general and royal weddings in particular. These were conducted between agricultural cycles that required the construc-tion of a Tree of Life at their beginning and its destruction at their end (Ras 1973: 448–454).

The Bugis I La Galigo Epic

The period of Kediri's efflorescence is precisely the same as the period Pelras and others have suggested for the origins of the La Galigo epic of the Bugis people, named for the character who is said to have composed it. In the nineteenth cen-tury, Dutch scholars collected 113 manuscripts containing more than 31,000 pages of La Galigo tales (Kern 1939, 1950; Pelras 1996: 34). Most of these texts consisted of but one or two episodes. In the 1850s, the missionary Matthes com-missioned a compilation of the entire work from Arung Pancana, the Queen of Tanete. She managed to put together a single work containing 2,800 folio pages, each with fifty lines of ten to fifteen syllables. But this still only covered one-third of the entire cycle; a "complete" text would contain some 300,000 lines, half again as long as the "critical edition" of the Mahabharata produced in India between 1925 and 1944, itself compiled from some seventy manuscripts that had been winnowed down from a collection of 235 (Koolhof 1995: 1; van der Veer 2001: 118).

Pelras argues that the I La Galigo contains a great deal of information about Bugis society in the twelfth and thirteenth centuries. He reconstructs the local political situation at that time as follows:

> During the epoch in question, the southern part of Celebes was divided into three zones of influence: that of Luwu', that of Tompo'tikka and that of Wéwang Riwu'. Luwu', centered at the time in Ware' (near the present-day Palopo) and in Wotu-Malili, dominated the east, north and northwest coasts of the Gulf of Boné. The country of Cina, in the present-day territory of Wajo', as well as, it seems, the island of Selayar and the peninsula of Bira which faces it, were more or less tied to it. . . . These three coastal powers owed their existence without doubt to the control of certain products: for Luwu', nickeliferous iron from the region of Matano, accessible by Malili—which furnished the best *pamors* [damascened blades] even in the nineteenth century, much sought in Java—and the gold of the Toraja country, to which Ware' commanded access. (Pelras 1981:177)

Pelras analyzes the La Galigo mostly to reconstruct the internal organization of medieval Bugis society. If one reads it as a variant of the Panji tales, however, one can also use it as evidence of extensive external contact with Java during the Kediri period. Like the Panji tales, a central theme of the I La Galigo is the birth of opposite-sex twins, their necessary separation, their desire to reunite, and the resolution of this conflict when a princess in a distant kingdom is found to be an acceptable substitute in marriage.

The Panji character in the I La Galigo is Sawerigading, father of La Galigo. In the Sulawesi myths, Sawerigading spends years sailing the seas seeking to unite with his pseudo-twin sister, who lives in a distant kingdom. Their marriage provides a charter for politically useful marriages between widely separated royal houses and for the process of household reproduction in general. Stories concerning Sawerigading are now found all along the coasts of Sulawesi (e.g., Nourse 1998).

It is worth quoting Pelras's summary of Sawerigading's adventures at length, because I will later show that they share many of the same themes as the rituals surrounding houses and the life cycle.

M 4.2 Sawerigading and We Cudai' (Bugis: La Galigo)

Sawerigading's mother We Opu Seng'eng had an "adopted" sister called We Tenriabeng, who had been carried in We Opu Seng'eng's mother's womb as a foetus and was later taken away to Cina in the heart of the Bugis country to marry its *to-manurung* (he or she who descended) ruler La Sattumpogi'. Each of the "sisters" had promised the other that should one of them have a daughter and the other a son, they would marry the offspring to each other; We Opu Seng'eng gave birth to Sawerigading, and We Tenriabeng to a girl, called We Cudai'.

Sawerigading is himself born as the twin brother of a girl called We Tenriabeng, who is brought up in a separate part of their parents' palace without his knowledge, for fear of a prophecy saying that should he meet his sister he will fall in love with her. Once grown to adulthood, he sails away on a journey to Taranati (Ternate) to represent Luwu' at a gathering of princes held on the occasion of the ceremonial tattooing of Taranati's ruler. In fact, he has been sent away from Luwu' because his twin sister is to be ordained as a *bissu* in a public ceremony which he must not attend lest the prophecy be fulfilled. During his journey, however, he is told about his twin sister, and once back home he manages to see her through a hole in the loft of the palace: he falls in love with her and decides to marry her. No one can persuade him to give up his intention, even when he is told of the cataclysms which will surely result if he realizes his wish. Finally, We Tenriabeng tells Sawerigading of the existence in Cina of their cousin We Cudai': she is, says We Tenriabeng, her own exact likeness, and as proof she gives her twin brother one of her hairs, one of her bracelets and one of her rings so that he can verify her assertion. Should We Cudai's hair not be as long as her own, and should the bracelet and ring not fit her wrist and finger, she, We Tenriabeng, will accept marriage with her brother. [Sawerigading sails to Cina in a magical boat made from the Welenreng tree. See M 4.3.]

During the journey to find his cousin, Sawerigading meets several of We Cudai's suitors at sea and defeats them. Arriving in Cina, he goes to the palace in the disguise of an Oro peddler [Negrito]; having discreetly ascertained that We Cudai' really does resemble his sister, he asks for her hand in marriage. The match does not, however, proceed smoothly. The Cina rulers have accepted Sawerigading's proposal, but We Cudai' herself, having heard that her suitor is a savage Oro, refuses him and the bride price is returned. Sawerigading takes this as a *causus belli* and conquers Cina by force of arms. All sorts of incidents follow before We Cudai' eventually accepts Sawerigading as her husband and a son is born to them, named La Galigo.

Many episodes then occur in which Sawerigading, while remaining the most honoured figure, stays in the background. He reemerges as the major protagonist at the end of the cycle, after La Galigo's son has been installed as the new ruler of Luwu'. On this occasion all the main figures of the cycle convene in Luwu'—including Sawerigading, despite his vow never to set foot there again. Setting sail after the feast to return to Cina with We Cudai', his ship is engulfed by the sea near Ussu'; but, far from being drowned, the couple become the new rulers of the Underworld, while Sawerigading's twin sister We Tenriabeng and her heavenly spouse become the new rulers of heaven. They beget more children, Sawerigading a daughter, We Tenriabeng a son, who are married and themselves produce a child for whom a great feast is given in Luwu', again in the presence of all the main participants in the cycle. On this occasion the gods inform them that they are all to leave this world for either heaven or the underworld. Only the new ruling couple of Luwu' and their offspring will remain; and the rainbow will no longer permit passage between the divine and human worlds. (Pelras 1996: 88–89)

In the first generation, two sisters are linked not because of their parentage, but because they shared the same womb. Sharing a womb at the same moment in time, as happens in the case of twins, creates such an intense tie that the identity of the twins fuses. The two female twins are fated to be separated by marriages to distant royal spouses, but pledge their children in marriage as a means of reuniting with one another. Thus, this sort of close-cousin marriage is conceived as an act of reunification.

In the second generation, it is opposite-sex twins that share a womb. This sort of twinship is more dangerous than same-sex twinship, since the desire to reunite with the twin through marriage may lead to incest. Sawerigading must thus be separated at birth from his twin sister. At the moment that his sister is to be initiated as a *bissu* priestess, serving as a vertical intermediary with the Upperworld and Underworld, Sawerigading is sent out across the seas as a horizontal ambassador from the earthly realm of Luwu' to the realm of Ternate. When he hears of his twin, he returns home only to be sent out again by his sister to fulfill the promise of his mother to her sister. Sawerigading crosses the sea to the distant realm of Cina in a magical boat. This part of the myth will be dealt with in more detail below, where it provides a template for the building of actual boats.

Sawerigading finds in his mother's sister's daughter an acceptable substitute for his sister in his own generation. Not only is she as beautiful as his sister, but, as several texts stress, she is higher in rank than his sister. This means that she is higher in rank than Sawerigading himself and that, by successfully marrying her, he is raising his prestige. He marries uxorilocally in Cina and sends his son back to Luwu' to rule in his place. Because of his irresistible desire for his sister, his exile must be permanent. The final reunion of the twins can only take place when Sawerigading's daughter marries We Tenriabeng's son. With the birth of a son to this final couple, the original split is healed, an earthly dynasty is established, and the gods return to the Otherworld forever.

Like the Panji tales, the story of Sawerigading is able to represent even the marriage of a prince and princess from distant kingdoms as the reunification of an original set of twins and as the fulfillment of individual desire. In the Panji tales, the prince and princess are earthly incarnations of celestial siblings. In the La Galigo tales, the prince and princess are very closely related cousins, the children of parallel female twins. In both cases, the royal wedding is represented as predestined; a marriage with a distant partner that was negotiated for the purposes of political and commercial alliance is represented as the product of a promise between two sisters or a brother and a sister.

As I have argued elsewhere, all marriages are symbolically treated in ritual as the transformation of siblingship into affinity and back into siblingship again (Gibson 1995). In light of the practice of cousin marriage, the full developmental cycle of a household takes four generations, just like in the myth.

As for Rassers's argument concerning the historical influence of the Javanese court of Kediri on other kingdoms, there is indeed much evidence for trade between Kediri and Luwu' in the thirteenth century. It is quite easy to imagine a prince and his retinue coming from Kediri in East Java in the thirteenth century, marrying a local princess, and establishing a Javanese colony in Luwu'. They would have introduced a number of Sanskrit terms to the local elite. For example, Sawerigading's grandfather is called *"Batara Guru,"* a common term for Shiva in Java. Sawerigading is himself more like Vishnu in his incarnations as Krishna in the Mahabharata, as Rama in the Ramayana, or as Panji in the tales of that name. But such Sanskrit terms and concepts were laid on top of preexisting Austronesian notions of kinship and marriage, in which the sharing of a womb with your siblings is the key symbol.

The Mythological Origins of Boats

The I La Galigo cycle of myths is confined to the Bugis areas of the peninsula with the significant exception of the Makassar people of Bira and Selayar living at the mouth of the Gulf of Bone. The La Galigo texts refer to the inhabitants of the Bira Peninsula as *waniaga,* from the Sanskrit *vaniyaga,* trader, indicating the presence of a maritime community there at a very early date (Pelras 1996: 74).

Sawerigading has great significance for the people of the Bira Peninsula, and his maritime travels make him the patron saint of seafaring. A central episode of the La Galigo concerns the magical construction of his boat from the trunk of a single Welenreng tree. The following version of the story is based on an 1887 Bugis manuscript summarized in Dutch by Kern (1939: A XIV) with interpolations from several other manuscripts (A XV, A XVI, A XX, A XXI, A XXII). Each manuscript develops a different aspect of the episode. The oppositions at work become clearest when all the versions are considered together.[2]

M 4.3 Sawerigading's Welenreng Boat (Bugis: La Galigo)

[XVI: 209 We Tenriabeng remained firm in her refusal to marry Sawerigading. But she told him of a princess in Cina who was her exact image, I We Cudai. If he did not believe her, she would give him an armband, a ring and a hair from her head. When he arrived in Cina, he must remove the skin of an Oro, put it on and thus disguised as a merchant go ashore and offer his goods for sale in the palace of La Tanette where We Cudai lived. When he saw her he would be able to tell whether she was We Tenriabeng's double, whether or not the armband and ring fit exactly and whether her hair was identical to the one he brought with him. If all this was not the case, then he could return to Luwu' and she would marry him.]

We Tenriabeng showed him We Cudai's image by placing special leaves on her fingernail. He admitted she seemed beautiful but wanted more proof. We Tenriabeng put him to sleep by rubbing him with heavenly oil and he dreamed he was coupling with We Cudai. He awoke convinced he should go, but first he would need a new fleet, as the old one was worn out.

We Tenriabeng told him which tree he should use to build a new boat, where he would find it, and what day work should begin. Sawerigading told his father, Bataralattu', to order his workers to make axes. The princesses brought provisions. We Tenriabeng had gifts brought from the treasury for the two priests (Puang) of Luwu' and Ware' who would make offerings to the tree before it was felled. Bataralattu' and Sawerigading dressed in royal costumes and were carried on palanquins with their regalia in a procession to their boat.

They sailed to Mangkuttu', an island made of benzoin incense. When they arrived, the priests placed an offering of chicken eggs, betel leaf and rice in the sea before going ashore dressed in full bissu costume with burning candles. They put the blood of sacrificed chickens on the Welenreng tree and performed certain ceremonies. Only then did the others disembark, followed by Bataralattu' and his kin. Bataralattu' explained to the tree that he had to cut it down to obtain food and shelter for his family. The animals who lived in it lamented: a pair of deer of the forest, snakes and centipedes of the earth, birds of the air and so on.

[XV 193: Bataralattu' had huts built for the workers who came from Toraja, Mengkoka (Mekongaka), Metang, Merokoli, Silaja (Selayar) and Waniaga (Bira). . . . But when they began cutting, a storm arose. The priests tried to exorcise it, but it only became worse. Bataralattu' sacrificed great numbers of albinos, pygmies and Oro tribesmen from the forest, all to no avail.]

Emissaries were sent back to Luwu' to ask We Tenriabeng for advice. [XV, XVI: Because it was a heavenly tree, commoners could not cut it, but only nobles dressed in full regalia.] She told them to fetch two axes that had descended from heaven with Batara Guru. The axes were to be honored like nobles on ceremonial occasions. The two priests and their *bissu* helpers were to use the axes to sacrifice an Oro tribesman. [XVI 211: Two times seven *oro kelling* must be sacrificed with these blades, and just as many albinos, as well as costly buffaloes and a great number of chickens of specified color and markings. When their blood was placed on the Welenreng tree, the heavenly beings living in its crown would fly away.]

The sacrifices were performed. Then the ax was given to Bataralattu' and further rites were performed that caused the demons *(raksasas)* of the deep forest to fall out of the tree. [XV 194–196: The birds, the monkeys, the deer, the horse, the buffalo, the king of the wild boars and their entourages all lamented the loss of their home. In response to the lamentations of the heavenly beings, the Creator lowered a seven-colored rainbow so they could escape to the Skyworld. They were then finally able to cut down the tree, which killed the commoner wood cutters and caused widespread devastation. Sawerigading stroked the trunk of the Welenreng tree and made a vow. Just as he had ended the life of the Welenreng in its place of origin, so would he never return to Luwu'. Only his son and heir would one day return. A branch of the tree covered with sevenfold leaves flew through the air to Cina. It landed on the palace, its leaves glowing like coals. The priest of Cina told the queen that these leaves signified a new offer of marriage for We Cudai, and that therefore she would not be wed to her current fiancée. The new suitor would best the old one at sea, devastate the kingdom and marry We Cudai. Together they would have one son and two daughters.]

Suddenly, the Welenreng descended into the Underworld, to the great distress of all. Sawerigading returned to his boat. The next day, Bataralattu' mounted the palanquin in which his mother We Nyli'timo had originally emerged from the foam. Enveloped in the smoke of burning leaves, and burning a candle, raw rice was scattered and betel leaves were offered to the sea. In the midst of a thunderstorm, the palanquin descended to the Underworld. A great number of boatbuilders was gathered there at the royal hall under the tamarind trees. They had just completed three hundred boats, one of great size. The guards wanted to detain him, but Bataralattu' told them he was the son of We Nyili'timo and showed them the rings he had received from Sang Pencipta and his wife. They brought him to Guru ri Selleng and his wife Sinautoja in the palace.

Sinautoja explained that she had made the tree descend so it could be transformed more quickly into a boat that would carry Sawerigading to Cina. She would fill it and the accompanying fleet with gifts for her beloved nephew and his sister. Bataralattu' returned to earth, and while telling Sawerigading what had happened the whole fleet suddenly emerged. A buffalo was sacrificed to the boat, raw rice was scattered and verses were sung. Sawerigading boarded Welenreng and then named the other boats, bestowing each on one of his followers. They raced them for three months before returning to Luwu'.

[A XX, XXI, XXII: Later, when he is in Cina and wishes to spy on We Cudai without being recognized, he flays an Oro alive, dries his skin and pulls it over his body. The father, mother and sister of this Oro had been sacrificed earlier during the building of the Welenreng boat. He dresses as a merchant and tricks We Cudai into coming to see his wares.] (Kern 1939: 153–213, 258–284).

Sawerigading must forever exile himself from Luwu' because the temptation to commit incest with his sister is too great for him to remain there. Only his son may return to Luwu', and he is promised to We Tenriabeng's daughter before either is even conceived. At one level then, this myth is a charter for patrilateral cross-cousin marriage, or delayed direct exchange. Only because of a rule of uxorilocality, it is men, not women who are exchanged between royal centers.

At another level, this episode of the myth is about the crossing of the dangerous zones of forest and sea that separate centers of civilization. Two sorts of vessels appear in this myth. One consists of the magical palanquins that are used by the demigods to pass back and forth on a vertical axis: between their houses on land and their boats at sea and between the Middleworld and the Upperworld and Underworld. These are templates for the bamboo palanquins that are still used in rituals to carry nobles undergoing a major change in status.

The other sort of vessels are the boats that carry people horizontally from one kingdom to another. These boats are built from ironwood trees that grow deep in the tropical rain forest. These trees are so large they provide a habitat for hundreds of species of insects, animals, and birds. A whole society of creatures or, as we now like to say, a whole ecosystem, must be destroyed in order to obtain the wood for one boat. In the myth, the very largest of these trees, one which reaches from the earth to the sky, must be felled to provide Sawerigading with a magical vehicle. This Welenreng tree is reminiscent of the Ngaju Tree of Life discussed in chapter 3, which must also be cut down so that a man and a woman can marry.

Thus, a vertical tree that connects the Upperworld and the Middleworld must be transformed into a horizontal boat that can connect one earthly kingdom with another. The transformation of a tree into a boat can be accomplished only by a *bissu* priestess who is an expert in magic that connects the Middleworld to the Upperworld and Underworld.

The powerful spirits that inhabit hardwood trees must be appeased through an escalating series of blood sacrifices. First, chickens and buffaloes must be sacrificed. Chickens mediate between the earth and the sky, water buffalo mediate between the earth and the Underworld. Their meat is offered to the spirits of the Underworld by being placed in the sea and to the Upperworld by rubbing their blood on the trunk of a heavenly tree. Next, white-skinned albinos who mediate between the world of humans and the world of the sky spirits and black-skinned Negritos *(Oro Kelling)* who mediate between the world of civilized men and the deep forest must be sacrificed. Finally, the civilized but common woodcutters are killed by the tree itself when it is finally falls down from the sky to the Middleworld. Among them are men from Selayar and from Waniaga, the ancient name for both the Bira Peninsula and its inhabitants.

All life in the Middleworld thus seems fair game to those of noble blood. Since it is a heavenly tree and has a heavenly child living in its crown, only nobles who have a heavenly origin can cut it, using heavenly blades. The iron tools that descend from the heavens are reminiscent of those used by the youngest brother in the Ngaju myth (M 3.1), who could only slay the magical elephant with "iron that descended." The concept of heavenly iron is also possibly a reference to the famous nickeliferous iron of Lake Matano near Wotu that was traded to Java in the Middle Ages. Because this iron comes from the remnants of a meteor, it is indeed "iron that descended."

Finally, the tree must descend from the Middleworld to the Underworld to be turned into a boat by carpenters who live under the sea. Transforming a tree into a boat thus requires a mastery both of the forest in order to cut it down without offending the spirits who live in it and of the sea so that the wood can be turned into a vessel that will not sink.

The transformation of a tree into a boat involves vertical knowledge of the

Upperworld and the Underworld that belongs only to *bissu* priestesses, in this case, to We Tenriabeng. The use of a boat to travel from one royal center to another requires knowledge of both the sea and the forest. This is what Sawerigading has in abundance. We Tenriabeng tells Sawerigading that he will later have to transform himself into a Negrito merchant when he arrives in Cina. Although they are portrayed as wild men of the forest, Negritos are not seen as completely independent of centers of civilization. Rather, they traverse the forest from one center to another, entering agricultural settlements to exchange goods. The transformation is accomplished when Sawerigading skins a Negrito alive, whose whole family had been sacrificed previously to the Welenreng tree.

We Tenriabeng is thus the paradigmatic woman, in that she controls vertical movements between the three worlds and the transformation of trees into boats. Sawerigading is the paradigmatic man, in that he has the ability to traverse the wild forest and the sea. The skills required to build a boat and to sail are complementary and distinct.

I will now turn from the Bugis texts to oral myths told in and around Ara about Sawerigading, his magical boat, and his son, La Galigo. This version of Sawerigading's adventures in the land of Cina comes from an old boatbuilder in Ara, Daeng Tontong.

M 4.4 Sawerigading in Wotu (Konjo: Daeng Tontong, Ara)

Sawerigading rejected all the girls his mother found for him to marry, as they were not beautiful enough. Then, one day, he saw a girl who was so beautiful, he proposed to her on the spot. When he told his mother about the girl, she said marriage was out of the question since the girl was his twin sister. He could not believe it, since she had grown up in a different house. He persisted in his desire to marry the girl. Finally, his twin told him that a girl exactly like her lived in Cina. She was called Coda Jung ri Sompa. She gave him a ring with a strand of her hair bound up inside it.

To reach Cina, his twin told him he must build a boat out of a great eel tree in Wotu [*kuaya lenrengngia konjo ri Otu*, north of Luwu' at the head of the Gulf of Bone]. It was so hard to cut, they had to bring together the men of Ara and Lemo Lemo to help, using their *pangkulu manurung*, "axes that descended." It finally fell when the Wotu (worms) were cut. All the eggs (*bayao*) that had been laid in it tumbled out and smashed, giving rise to the Bajo (Bayo) people who went on to serve the twin sister. The men of Ara and Lemo Lemo finally finished the boat, and have been famous for their skills in doing so ever since.

The boat was loaded with trade goods and set sail for Cina. When it arrived, Sawerigading fired its cannon. The Datu' of Cina came down to find out their intentions. They told him they had only come to trade peacefully. When the types of goods they had brought were called out, a messenger came to say that Coda Jung wanted them brought into the palace so that she too could buy. All the women tried on Sawerigading's ring, but it only fit Coda Jung. Then she took out the hair and saw that it was exactly the same length as her own.

Coda Jung accepted Sawerigading as her mate, but when he said he wanted to eat with her, her father got angry. Sawerigading also got angry and burned incense that placed everyone in a trance except Coda Jung. She told him to release the others. He promised to return the next day and challenged the Datu' to a cockfight. The Datu' accepted, wagering his palace and its contents against the boat of Sawerigading. Sawerigading's cock was actually a magical white cat in disguise. It easily defeated the Datu's cock.

The villagers were enraged, and Sawerigading retreated to his boat. For ten days the villagers fired on it without damaging it. Meanwhile, Sawerigading secretly rode his cat to the palace every day and impregnated Coda Jung. Seven sanro failed to discover who had done it. Finally, Coda Jung told them it was Sawerigading, and the Datu' finally acquiesced in their marriage. Sawerigading succeeded him as ruler of Cina. (Condensed from Daeng Tontong's oral version, recorded 1988)

In this version, the Welenreng tree of the La Galigo story is interpreted as a *lenreng,* or eel, tree and the place where it grows, Wotu, is interpreted as meaning *otu,* or worm. The village of Wotu still exists. Its inhabitants "stress their own special relationship with Selayar and Buton, two islands located respectively at the southwest and southeast of the entry to the Gulf of Bone. Recent preliminary linguistic research has indeed found a relatively high percentage of correlations between their language and the Wolio dialect of Buton and the Layolo of Selayar" (Pelras 1996: 13).

This version does not mention the use of Oro in human sacrifices, either for the building of the boat or for tricking We Cudai/Coda Jung. But the tree does contain eggs that give rise to the Bajo sea people. As nomadic hunter-gatherers, the Bajo may be seen as the maritime equivalent of the Oro Negritos of the forest. Both live so close to untamed nature that they can mediate between other humans and the spirits that inhabit the wild places.

In this version, the sea people become the servants of the sister, We Tenriabeng and Sawerigading is portrayed as a master mariner and merchant. Both sister and brother are thus linked to the sea.

It is the same magical creature, a white cat, who allows Sawerigading to win Coda Jung's hand in marriage through a cockfight and to enter her chambers undetected at night. Success in cockfighting is thus linked to success in seduction. As we will see, his success in cockfighting is also stressed in other versions of the story.

A nephew of Daeng Makkilo, the Gallarrang of Ara, who died in 1913, told me another version of the Sawerigading story to explain the origin of boatbuilding in the area.

M 4.5 Sawerigading Creates Islands (Konjo: Daeng Majannang, Ara)
Once Sawerigading and his son La Galigo both built boats and decided to race them. They agreed to sail from Selayar around Gantaran to Kabaena. They met up at dinner time and ate together. They washed the rice from their

hands in a finger bowl and poured the contents in the sea. From the rice grains arose the islands of Tarupa, Great Rajuni and Little Rajuni, Great Latondu and Little Latondu [coral islands southeast of Selayar].

Sawerigading filled his boat, called Raja Somba Manakku, with lontar fruit, intending to plant lontar palms everywhere he went. He sailed first to Maumere, where a storm blew up and caused the boat to heel over. A stone from the hearth fell into the sea and became the island of Palu. He planted his lontar in Maumere and sailed on to Bima. Again a storm came up and caused a hearth stone to fall into the sea. The wind was called Kolonnya Sanggara, and that is still the name of the first cape one sees on the right side of Bima. The hearth stone became the island of Sangiang, situated to the left of the Bima river. He planted his lontar in Bima, then sailed on to Sumbawa, Lombok and Mataram in Java, planting lontar everywhere.

Sawerigading continued on to Sumatra, ending his journey in Aceh. There he abandoned his boat, and it was swept away by the sea. Its boards eventually washed ashore in Ara, its bow and stern in Lemo Lemo, and its keel, bowsprit and sails in Bira. The men of the three villages pooled all the pieces and reassembled the boat. Although they each tried to master the part of the boat that had washed up in the other villages, to this day the men of Ara specialize in the hull, the men of Lemo Lemo in carving the bow and stern, and the men of Bira in sailing.

In this myth, we can see that the creation of the seascape itself is closely linked to the creation of boats. Coral islands and beaches are the result of specialized magical knowledge and power no less than boats themselves. They too are amphibious entities, halfway between the world of the sea and the world of the mainland.

Both this myth and the one recounted by Tonton link the origin of the specialized skills of Ara, Lemo Lemo, and Bira to the great trade route between Luwu' at the head of the Gulf of Bone and southern shore of the Java Sea, from Sumbawa in the east to Sumatra in the west. Mention of the Bajo people in these myths may provide a clue as to the origin of boatbuilding expertise in the Gulf of Bone. These "sea nomads" are found from the southern Philippines to the Straits of Malacca to eastern Indonesia and have long been present in the Gulf of Bone and the small islands south of Selayar. They may have brought the new techniques from the west long ago.

Horst Liebner collected a rather similar story in Ara from Johari, the son of a Bajo from Pulao Sembilan, a group of islands off the coast of Sinjai. They claimed to have once owned a *lontara* manuscript recording the origins of the Bajo people. This version thus pays less attention to boatbuilding and more to the fortunes of the Bajo people.

M 4.6 Sawerigading in Cina (Konjo: Johari, Ara)

Sawerigading has a sister called Abeng. It is she who finally fells the tree with her weaving knife and who then supplies him with a fleet of seven boats when the tree sinks into the sea. Eggs that were in the tree smash and the resulting flood washes a girl out to sea in a boat who might somehow be Sawerigading's first child (the informant was unclear). Her crew were Bajo, and she became the first Bajo noble. They sailed to Makassar, where she married the King. Meanwhile, Sawerigading wins the princess of Cina in a cockfight. She is called We Cudai. Sawerigading's cat is left in Sumatra, where it becomes the ancestor of the tigers. Upon their return, We Cudai gives birth to La Galigo in Selayar. Sawerigading urinates on a leaf there. The urine is licked up by a pig, who becomes pregnant and gives birth to the first Selayarese noble. (Condensed from Liebner 1998: 119–121, 130)

Here Sawerigading's sister is identified with the founding ancestress of Gowa. In other versions of the Gowa foundation myth, a female Tomanurung is discovered there by a male ruler of the Bajo, or Karaeng Bayo, from Bantaeng (see chapter 7). Johari's myth reverses the gender of the ruler of the sea nomads and the ruler of Gowa.

According to Liebner, the detail about the pig was intended to denigrate the Selayarese. This detail is also present, however, in another version of the story I collected, in which Sawerigading's son, La Galigo, is himself born from a pig.

M 4.7 Sawerigading Impregnates a Pig (Konjo: Daeng Majannang, Ara)
[Sawerigading] is a boatbuilder from Ara. He goes to Pamatata in Selayar to build a boat. So great are his powers that he always places a mark on the spot where he urinates, because any animal that drinks it will become pregnant. One day, while carrying a board back from the forest, he urinates on the leaf of a breadfruit growing in the middle of the path. A pig comes along, drinks it, and becomes pregnant. She gives birth to a boy.

When this child grows up, his mother brings him back to where she had drunk the urine. The child walks around the boat for two or three days, singing that he will be the Captain of the ship. Finally, the boatbuilder catches him and asks him why he has been singing there for several days. The pig comes and says, "I am going to bite you." So the boatbuilder throws his adze at the pig. The boy tells him not to, since the pig is his mother. When the boatbuilder proves skeptical, the boy and the pig show him the exact spot where he had left a mark that he had urinated. The man acknowledges the boy as his son, and promises to care for his mother.

Then the boy insists that the man exchange the bow and stern boards of the boat before he assumes command of the boat under the name of La Galigo Daeng Mangeppe. He collects a crew and they launch the boat.

Meanwhile, the father, Sawerigading, sets sail in his boat. This boat was made from the trunk of an eel tree in Luwu' *[battu ri lenrengngia ri Tana Luhu']*. The two boats sail between Selayar and Kabaena when they are struck by a storm. Sawerigading puts his hands together and says a spell, causing the waves and the winds to die down. The two boats come together and Sawerigading and La Galigo share a meal. When it is over, they wash the rice off their hands in a finger bowl, and pour the water into the sea. The rice grains turn into the coral islands of Terupa, Great Rajuni and Little Rajuni, Great Latonda and Little Latonda.

Then Sawerigading sails off to Manggarai to plant lontar palms, while La Galigo returns home to Pamatata to find passengers and embark on a trading expedition. They sail around visiting coral reefs. La Galigo tells his men to fetch rocks from the bottom, but rejects those containing first copper, then silver and finally gold as being insufficiently valuable to take on as cargo. Finally, they arrive at a place where the boat sticks fast and will not move. They lower a dipper into the sea and it is filled with fish. They fill the whole boat with fish and return to Pamatata. La Galigo decides to take the cargo to the great city, where its value proves so great they not only obtained all the money in the city, they leave all the merchants and residents in debt to them.

On their way back to Selayar, the crew conspires to throw La Galigo overboard and keep all the profits for themselves. La Galigo is saved by a rayfish and an octopus, which hold him up by the foot and hand. A perch defends him from attack from below. A mackerel defends him from attack on the right, and a *kaso* [?] fish defends him from attack on the left. They carry him to Pamatata, arriving there before his mutinous crew. In return for their help, La Galigo promises that he will never eat any of the fish who saved him again. The fish lay a curse on his descendents: if he breaks his promise, the skin of his descendents will become spotted like those of the fish who saved him.

La Galigo goes into his house and hides in a trunk. When the boat lands, his relatives tell the crew to bring all the goods they have collected up to the house to be divided. When they ask where La Galigo is, they pretend to cry and say that he fell overboard. The crew places all the coarse goods of little value in a pile for La Galigo's heirs, and keep all the refined valuable goods for themselves. La Galigo then jumps out of the last trunk and declares them hereditary slaves of the sort who can never redeem themselves. They are forbidden to erect certain emblems or hold certain festivals in their village unless they are freed by their master.

And to this day, the descendents of La Galigo are forbidden to eat the spotted *ila* fish. (*Pomacentrus Lividus,* according to Cense 1979:249)

In this myth, Sawerigading has multiple powers over water, especially through fluids exuded from his own body. His urine is capable of bringing forth life in whatever it touches, and the saliva washed from his hands in the finger bowl is capable of bringing forth coral islands from the sea. Coral islands and beaches are not really considered part of the land: they are transitional spaces that arise out of the sea and can resubmerge under the tides. This power over water and the Underworld is further associated with maritime trade.

In light of Sawerigading's son's later affinity with fish, we might interpret the wild pig in this story as another representative of the underworld, associated with the wild forest rather than the sea. Just as pigs are relatively smooth and hairless, mackerel, rayfish, and octopuses lack scales. Pigs are thus the terrestrial equivalents of octopuses and rays. Indeed, it is because the scaleless fish recognize La Galigo as the son of a hairless pig that the fish decide to help him in the first place. La Galigo's ability to pass as a denizen of the sea, because of the similarity of his skin with certain fish, is thus parallel to Sawerigading's ability to assimilate the skin of a Negrito and pass as a denizen of the forest whom we encountered in M 4.3.

Despite the strong aversion to pigs inculcated by Islamic dietary rules, it would seem that a more ancient association of pigs with subterranean powers was never wholly lost. Pigs are used in other forms of magic in this area. For example, one of the most powerful forms of invulnerability magic is derived from an iron chain found under a pig's skin. This argument is reinforced by the existence of an almost identical myth among the non-Muslim Toraja people.

M 4.8 Bonggakaradeng the Ironsmith Impregnates a Pig (Toraja)

Bonggakaradeng came from a village called Batu Tandung, near the Masuppu River. He was another person who found his wife inside a bamboo; her name was Datu Baringan, and she had a sister who was a python. Once while out in the forest on a hunting trip, Bonggakaradeng stopped to rest beneath an *uru* tree at a place called Pokka Uru on Buttu Karua (a mountain in Simbuang). He urinated on a fallen tree, unaware that in doing so, he had impregnated a spirit pig inside the tree. The pig gave birth to twin boys, Buttu Karua and Buttu Layuk. When they were about six years old, the mother sent them to look for their father, and they came to where Bonggakaradeng was working in his forge. They offered to help him in the forge, but he refused, not seeing how they could be of any use to him. But while he was eating his lunch in the house, they finished all his work for him, and to a standard exceeding his own. According to another version, they made a sword of gold *(labo' penai bulawan)* called Tonapa. This sword became a famous heirloom whose sheath is still kept in Sawitto, while the blade is in Simbuang. Eventually they persuaded the astonished Bonggakaradeng that he was indeed their father, and lived with him for a time, but, offended by his persistence in eating pork, they set off again by boat down the Masuppu River, taking their mother with them, until they reached Sawitto, where the pig-mother eventually turned into stone. They made magic there, causing the sky to go dark except around their own house, until the local people begged for an explanation. The brothers told them that they would bring back the sunlight if the people would agree henceforth always to show them various marks of respect, and to abstain from eating pork or the meat of any animal that died without being slaughtered. Thus the Bonenese became Muslim, while the two bothers married the daughters of a great aristocratic family, and had several children who became important ancestors in their turn. (Waterson 1997: 68–69)

In this and in several other myths, the Torajans interpret the Muslim aversion to pork as a sign of respect for a porcine ancestress. Again, this may be a secondary elaboration of an older association between pigs and the powers of the Underworld and the interpretation of food taboos as a sign of respect for the thing avoided, rather than as a sign of aversion to unclean things as in the Abrahamic tradition.

Mastery of the powers of the Underworld is signified in the case of the landlocked Toraja by the mastery of metalwork. In the case of Ara, it is signified by knowledge of boatbuilding and sailing. In fact, the two skills were connected historically, in that the gold and meteoric iron of the mountains above Luwu' drew maritime traders past Ara up through the Gulf of Bone for a thousand years. One might say that metalwork is the terrestrial equivalent of boatbuilding and navigation. Indeed, the two were linked explicitly in the La Galigo episode recounted above as M4.3, where Bataralattu's workers manufacture axes with which to cut down the Welenreng tree, even though in the end axes made in heaven must be used.

The Boat as Symbolic Vessel

As we have just seen, boats may be thought of as hollow, horizontal tree trunks, operating as mediators between terrestrial realms, just as bamboo internodes serve as hollow vertical trunks operating as mediators between the Upperworld, Middleworld, and Underworld. I will now turn from myth to the ritual symbolism embedded in the process of building the type of boat whose origins are attributed to Sawerigading.

Boatbuilding rituals are modeled on the biological processes of conception, gestation, and birth. One significant difference exists. Whereas the biological reproduction of humans and agricultural crops is almost completely in the hands of women, the production of boats and houses is almost completely in the hands of men. In both cases, however, both male and female principles must be combined to create new life.

Apprenticeship and Mastery

In Ara, master boatbuilders are called *punggawa,* a term that exists also in Malay. It has the general sense of boss, commander, or captain in an economic, military, or naval enterprise. Abdul Hakim was of the view that five sorts of skill were necessary to become a *punggawa.* They were the ability to lead a crew; the ability to obtain commissions through connections with shipowners; the ability to conceive the model of a ship and carry it through in practice; knowledge of the properties of wood; and the possession of the appropriate spells, *mantera.* The fifth sort of knowledge was often the most difficult to obtain. *Mantera* had to be purchased with traditional valuables such as white cloths and gold coins. You might get them from your father, but only after you had demonstrated to him mastery of the other four skills.

The process of apprenticeship begins as soon as a boy is able to fetch water and to cook for the adult crew. In general in Southeast Asia, the hull of the boat is built first and the ribs added later. Boards are carved to the correct curvature from a block of wood with a simple adz and then fitted edge to edge with dowels inserted into holes carved with a hand drill. When they are big enough to handle a drill, boys are set to work fitting together the boards that have been carved by the others. These boys receive one quarter of an adult share at the final division of the payment. Your share increases by degrees to a one-third share and a one-half share before you are eligible for a full adult share.

The *punggawa* receives an equal share along with all the other adult men, plus a 10 percent commission deducted from the share owed to labor out of the total price of the boat. This is usually 30 percent of the total cost. A crew usually consists of eight or nine workers, so the *punggawa* earns about twice what each member of the crew earns. Disputes within a crew over payment are submitted for binding arbitration to the *liden,* a body of four master boatbuilders with the village head serving ex officio as a fifth member. The village head chooses four new *punggawa* every four years from a list of nominees. Disputes over boats are never taken to authorities outside the village.

Until the middle of the twentieth century, the boatbuilders of Ara relied entirely on the merchant captains of Bira for access to cash in exchange for large *pinisi* boats. The soil was so poor in the village that staple foods were acquired mostly by bartering small fishing vessels for rice with agricultural peoples living around the Gulf of Bone. Fishing boats were traded for wet rice with Bugis from Bone on the western shore of the Gulf. Fishing boats, rings made out of copper coins and sarongs were traded for hill rice with tribal peoples from the eastern shore of the Gulf. Abdul Hakim told me that tribesmen speaking the Lahui (Laa'iwoi) and Bengkoka dialects of Tolaki and Marnene (Moronene, related to Kobaena) used to sail across the Gulf to Ara after the rice harvest each year and barter away all their rice, subsisting on cassava for the rest of the year (Noorduyn 1991: 111–119). The rice was packaged in flexible baskets called *balase* that held about thirty liters of rice each. Three *balase* of rice would trade for one cotton sarong. The same amount of rice purchased on the market would have cost about one ringgit or two and a half rupiah in the 1930s. A buffalo cost thirty rupiah at that time.

Traditionally, the men of Ara never sailed the boats they made. I commissioned a retired boatbuilder, Bolong, to build me a scale replica of a *pinisi*. The making of model boats is an old tradition because such boats were required in many rituals to carry away spirits, both good and evil (see the description of the *lope lope* ritual in chapter 9; compare Nourse 1999: 129–174). After a month of work, everyone approved of the finished product until an actual sailor from Bira, Haji Masa, saw the rigging. He immediately took it all off: Bolong had used the wrong kind of wood for the masts (he should have used, *jati,* teak), he had made the rudders half the right size, and so on. Bolong explained that, because boatbuilders never sail the boats and sailors have to be able to replace the rigging at any time, it was not a skill the men of Ara needed to know.

It was the men of Bira who specialized in sailing. Dessiboja Daeng Kala of Bira told me that in times past a boat's crew was also paid in shares of the profits from each voyage. Profits made from trading merchandise were divided in two, half to the owner of the boat and half to the crew. Food costs were deducted from the crew's share, and the remainder was divided equally among the sailors, including the captain. The captain also received 15 percent of the boat owner's share. In the case of fees charged for freight consigned by third parties, one-third went to the boat owner and two-thirds to the crew. Again, the captain received an equal part of the crew's share and 15 percent of the owner's.

It was thus only the sea captains of Bira who could accumulate the capital required to commission the building of a boat. The wealthiest owned as many as twenty or thirty boats. Until the 1950s, the boatbuilders of Ara were dependent on the wealthy merchants of Bira for almost all their employment. The situation of the boatbuilders in Lemo-Lemo was quite different. At least since the beginning of the nineteenth century, they had established colonies in other areas, including the Dutch colonial capital of Ujung Pandang (Liedermoij 1854). They grew wealthy while Ara remained poor.

Men from Ara did go to work at boatyards at Pelengu in Jeneponto and at Lempongan in Bone in the 1930s. Then the whole province was thrown into turmoil by the Darul Islam rebellion, in the 1950s. The boatyards in Bira and Bone closed down. Many families fled from Ara and settled on neighboring islands such as Selayar, Jampea, and Flores. Punggawas began making contacts with new sources of commissions, especially ethnic Chinese merchants located throughout Indonesia. They returned to Ara to recruit boatbuilding crews and take them away for nine months out of the year to build boats on site. As their fame spread, boat owners began to come directly to Ara to recruit crews. As an example, Abdul Hakim told me about Mappisau Toton, a Punggawa who was working with a crew in Kota Baru on Pulau Laut in South Kalimantan. Pulau Laut is where the largest boats of all are built, up to 600 tons in size. A Chinese merchant was so impressed by their industry and skill that he invited them to come to Balikpapan in East Kalimantan. A permanent colony was established there. The men of Ara build boats so much faster and their product is so much sturdier than those built by Bugis or Mandar that they are able to command a premium: a boat that cost five million rupiah in 1988 when built by Mandar would cost eight million when built by men from Ara.

In places like Balikpapan, where work was steady, men began to bring their families across from Ara. In 1988, colonies of people from Ara existed in Jampea, in Selayar; in Merauke and Sorong, in Irian Jaya; in Kupang, in West Timor; in Ambon and Ternate, in Maluku; in Tarakan and Balikpapan, in East Kalimantan; in Batu Licin, Kota Baru, and Banjarmasin, in South Kalimantan; in Sampit, Kuala Pembuang, and Kumai, in Central Kalimantan; in Pontianak, in West Kalimantan; in Jakarta and Surabaya, in Java; in Belitung, in Lampung; in Palembang, in South Sumatra; in Jambi; and in temporary camps in many other places. During the 1990s, Abdul Hakim became head of Ara's KUD, the government-sponsored development agency. He spent a few years visiting many of these colonies to find out whether they were in need of government loans. He found 800 people in Batu Licin alone. So far, however, it seems that most of the migrants returned to Ara for all major life-cycle rituals, including marriage.

Engines are now added to most boats, which cost as much as the boat itself. A 500-ton *pinisi* that cost 80 million rupiah in 1989 would carry an engine that cost another 78 million rupiah, then equivalent to about U.S. $100,000. Few merchants from Bira can afford these prices, and boat ownership is increasingly concentrated in the hands of ethnic Chinese merchants. Bira has generally fallen on hard times since the 1940s, while Ara has prospered. Workers are no longer paid in strictly equal shares. The Punggawa is now free to pay workers according to their industry. On motorized boats, the crew is now paid a fixed sum per trip.

Mastery of the Forest: Selecting and Felling Trees

The following account of boatbuilding ritual relies heavily on the work of Usman Pelly, who spent five months in Ara in 1975 and produced a detailed report for the Universitas Hasanuddin (Pelly 1975, 1977). I have paraphrased and condensed his rich ethnography, and interpolated my own commentary. I have tried to note where his interpretation differs from my own.

The first task in building a boat is selecting, collecting, and storing wood in the forest. The master boatbuilder must persuade the anonymous spirits inhabiting the trees to leave before he can use the wood for his own purposes. When the intended forest is in sight, the master waves his arms several times, pointing to the forest, while whispering to himself, "Hai, inhabitants of the forest, get ready to move, I am coming to cut the trees of your forest."

The master immediately goes to visit the tree that will be cut first. All adzes, saws, and bush knives are propped around the tree as a sign to the spirit of what is in store. Then the master, together with the workers, backs away several steps, and sits down to concentrate on the tree. At this point a sort of conversation takes place between the master and the tree spirits. If they do not want to move to another place they give a sign. For example, one of the adzes leaning against the tree falls, or the tree moves. The master must then be ready with an offering. A worker sets out a "complete" set of dishes *(kanre sangka)* and a newly hatched chick. The master lights a fire and burns incense, inducing the tree spirit to enter the chick. The chick is then freed and allowed to go wherever it likes. After this, the master looks up and makes a sign for the inhabitant of the tree to move immediately. This ritual follows the same pattern laid out in the Welenreng myth, where the various inhabitants of the archetypal tree must be induced to leave through sacrifices and invocations.

The other workers stand in a semicircle. With an adz in his hand, the master circles the tree counterclockwise and then recites a prayer as follows:

Kutabbangi kayunna Nu'manulhakim   I cut the tree Nukmanulhakim
Nukuhayuang i lopina 'i-anu   To make a boat for X

Barang nasabaki nanaidallena'i-anu	Hoping it will bring wealth to X
Sada'nu ri Karaennu	Confess yourself to your Lord
Manyila' matanna allo	Who caused the sun to exist
Rate intu Karaennu.	Above all is your Lord.

The master controls his breathing until he feels sure that his breath is leaving his right nostril more quickly than his left. Men contain both a male and a female aspect, whereas women are wholly female. The male aspect is associated with the right, the female with the left. At the moment the male principle is uppermost in his body, he strikes. The first blow of the adz should be upward, with the intention that the fortunes of the ship will continually go upward. He wields his adz in this way three times before a worker advances to help him, striking alternately with him until the tree falls.

Laying the Keel

The point of this ritual is to animate the nascent boat with life force and a spirit. The owner and his wife sit facing the master on the left side of the keel, with the captain and a group of novices sitting behind them. It is necessary to have one or two pregnant women among them. Pelly says that this is intended to symbolize the contents of a loaded boat, but I think it also symbolizes the intention to bring a new life into being. They take the place of the human sacrifices mentioned in the Welenreng myth.

The master sits on the right side of the keel with all his workers behind him. The master waits for calm, focusing his attention on the face of the owner until he feels sure the ritual can begin respectfully. A member of the owner's family then covers the master with a white cloth, to indicate that he is in a ritually pure and liminal state. The owner next burns some incense to establish contact with the spirit world, and the master sacralizes a chisel in it. The chisel is placed on the line marking the front of the keel. Before hitting it with the hammer, the master recites the following *mantera:*

Dalle membua' ilaa	The sun rise in the east
Si'buntulangko sicini	You meet the view
Namaramu pa'mainnu	Let your feelings be joyous
Nammakang nahang-nahangmu	Your thoughts calm
Arrungan jinni kuarung	The path I once endured
Lu'lu' jinni kupinahang	I follow the edge of a good path
Kuerang baji	I bring you peacefully
Kuerang ri mate'nea	I bring a thing to please you
Ikambe lalang massurangan.	We are friends of the owner.

Then to himself, without moving tongue or teeth, the master pronounces the sound of the three letters: A – I – U. After reciting U, the hammer is brought down on the chisel. The resultant chip of wood is divided in two. One half is given to the owner, who puts it in a bottle filled with coconut oil, and the master puts the other away.[3]

The owner will later hang this bottle containing the oil and wood chip from the front mast of the boat. Whenever the boat is in danger, a little of the oil from the bottle may be brushed on the *naga* beam of the boat, which lies just above the keel, to make it safe from danger. The first chip from the keel and the dust from the navel is thus equivalent to the umbilicus of a child, which is also preserved to treat misfortunes later in life. The master preserves his half of the chip to ensure he is paid for his work later. He can use it to magically prevent the ship from moving when it is being launched.

After making the first cut, the master can continue his work without being covered by the white cloth. He gouges out holes in both ends of the keel as points of connection for the keel extenders. The master wraps a collection of objects in a cotton cloth and places the bundle in each of the two holes. The collection includes a grain of gold to symbolize magnificence, iron to symbolize strength, a grain of unhusked rice to symbolize prosperity, and other objects such as copper, a piece of a leaf, a crust of cooked rice, and a bit of coconut.

The master then cuts the comb of a white rooster and sprinkles its blood on both joints. White is the color of rain and purity and is associated with the divinities who descended from the Upperworld, whose blood was white. Then a black hen is taken and treated the same way. Black is the color of the earth and biological fertility, which is in turn associated with the female principle. The red of the blood is the color of fire and is associated with the life force that animates both male and female, sky and earth. The elements of earth (black), fire (red), rain (white), and male and female genders are thus combined to animate the keel with the beginnings of a new life. Only after the blood is applied can the two joints be pushed right together. Their union, and the spilling of the blood of a male rooster and female hen, symbolize the consummation of a marriage. To end the ritual, the master separates himself from his liminal state by washing his face with water. The owner gives him a ring and some raw husked rice and unhusked rice as a gift. Rice cakes are placed on the keel and eaten in a festive manner.

Building the Hull

After the keel is laid, the building of the boat can continue without further ritual intervention until it is ready to be launched. The size of a *pinisi* is determined by the length of the keel. According to Pelly, a fifteen-foot keel will produce a 100-ton boat, a seventeen-foot keel a 150-ton boat, and a nineteen foot-keel a 200-ton boat. After the keel is cut to approximately the right length, the master determines the destiny of the boat. Taking the width of the keel as his measure, he counts from front to back in a cycle of five possible outcomes: enjoyment, profit-seeking, sinking, being pirated, and dying on land (that is, not sinking at sea). When he reaches the end, the outcome on which he finishes reveals the destiny of the boat. Most owners prefer the fifth outcome, and so the length of the keel will be adjusted so the count will end on this one.

The board immediately above the keel is called the "pincer." It helps to hold the front and back keel extenders to the keel. Above the pincer are several layers of *papan terasa*, "basic boards." The length of the keel determines the length of every basic board in the boat. The keel is divided into six equal units, called *tarip-taripang*. Each of these units is divided into a *tambuku* and a *ruang*. Boards in the hull are measured according to whether they should be three, four, five, or six *tarip-taripang* long. The number of layers of boards, *urat*, is determined by the tonnage of the boat. A 100-ton boat will have eleven *urat*, a 200-ton boat thirteen *urat*. The number must always be odd.

The arrangement of these boards is strictly determined by tradition. Running up the center of the boat are a series of *papan* boards. At either end of the *papan* are *panapu*, linking boards that connect the ends of the *papan* to the boards that meet the prow and stern. The latter are referred to with terms like *bengo* ("twisted"), *sangahili* ("lopsided"), and *rakkasala* ("messed up") because of their complex curvatures as they bend around from the side of the ship to meet the prow and stern. The connections between these boards and the *panapu* are the weakest part of the boat.

A number of rules of thumb govern the placement of the boards. For example, a five board must have a four board on top of it. Connections must never be made over knotholes in the next lower level as this would cause the boat misfortune or epidemics among the crew. Each layer of boards must be a little wider than the one beneath it, or the owner's life will be shortened. All knots must be chiseled out or the boat will have a tendency to run into coral reefs. The *bengo* is the target of black magic, and so the builder must take extra care to make it smooth and neat. Women must not climb on the boat while the *papan terasa* are being fitted, because they symbolize things easily broken. The *rakkasala* boards on the right must be slightly wider that those on the left, because the right is the captain's side. Wood must not be taken from trees that have fallen down or been washed away.

Once the hull is complete, alternating ribs and floors are installed at intervals of fifteen to seventeen centimeters and fixed to the hull with treenails. Fourteen or so of them are allowed to extend up above the deck to form posts for fixing the rigging. When the ribs are complete, a beam is installed over them the length of the keel. This is called the *naga*, "watersnake" beam. The invisible realm beneath the sea is the abode of the *naga* whose movements determine the auspicious times for different ventures. The *naga* beam is extended at either end by *buaya*, "crocodile" beams which run up the stem and stern posts. Crocodiles are the mediators between the depths and the surface of the water. As master of sea trade, the rulers of Luwu' were symbolically identified with crocodiles. Finally, further longitudinal beams are fixed to the ribs up the inner sides of the hull. Thwarts are installed across the top of the hold and the deck is covered over except for two hatches giving access to the interior.

In 1988, I hired a retired master boatbuilder, Bolong, to make me a scale model of a modern *pinisi*. The diagrams shown in figure 4.1 are based on his model of a small *pinisi* with seven layers of basic boards.

Launching a Boat

Once the deck is complete, the boat is physically ready to be launched, but it must undergo a number of rituals before it is spiritually ready. Before 9:00 A.M. on the day before the boat is to be launched, a buffalo is sacrificed near it. Its blood is caught and poured on the *naga* beam exactly in the center of the keel,

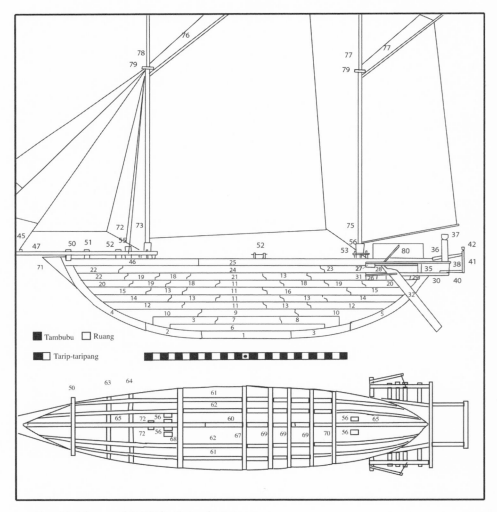

Fig. 4.1 *(above and right)* The Parts of a Boat.

where the boat's navel will later be carved, transferring its life force to the boat. Buffalo contain the largest amount of life force aside from humans.

That evening, at about 8 P.M., a reading is begun of the *barasanji* (Jaffar al-Barzanji's "Life of the Prophet"; see Kaptein 1992). While it is being recited, a ritual specialist called a *panrita* stirs a pot filled with well water and several types of leaf, including *tinappasa* and betel, and a stalk of areca palm blossom. This

1. Kalebiseang:
   "center of boat"
2. Panyambung
   kalebiseang riolo
   "front keel extender"
3. Panyambung
   kalebiseang riboko:
   "rear keel extender"
4. Sotting riolo:
   "front sotting"
   [pamuru in Bira]
5. Sotting riboko:
   "rear sotting"
6. Pangepe: "pincer"
7. Uru Sangkara:
   "first sangkara"
8. Uru sangahili/kanjai:
   "First lopsided/hooked"
9. Papanganam:
   "six board"
10. Sangahili bakka:
    "great lopsided"
11. Papanglima:
    "five board"
12. Bengo: "twisted"
13. Panapu tallu:
    "three connector"
14. Padolang: "out to sea"
15. Mula rakkasala
    "First easily messed up"
16. Panapu gulung-gulung
    "wobbly connector"
17. Sambung tallu:
    "three connector"
18. Panapu tallu lalang:
    "inner three connector"
19. Panapu tallu pantara:
    "outer three connector"
20. Rakkasala
    "easily messed up"
21. Sambung tallu:
    "three connector"
22. Tungku-tungku jangolang
    "direct penetrator"
23. Rembasanng:
    "thrown outside"
24. Papang lammah:
    "flexible board"
25. Balo-balo
26. Sangkilang:
    rudder support
27. Baratang
28. Padongki
29. Ambing
30. Sareang guling:
    "rudder rest"
31. Pangepe guling:
    rudder pincer
32. Guling: rudder
33. Pansara guling
34. Lete ambalahona
35. Pa'riring
    jamba-jambanga
36. Lemba-lembarana
37. Laba-labana
38. Rembasana
39. Pa'todo jamba-jambanga
40. Dasere jamba-jambanga
41. Benteng kajang-kajang
42. Tempat tiang bandera (I)
    "place of the flag pole"
43. Parenreng kajang-kajang
44. Taju ayana
45. Tonko duni
46. Balo-balo tampaka
47. Pasipi' anjong:
    "prow pincer"
48. Anjong: prow
49. Patanrana (ujung anjong):
    "supporter (of the prow)"
50. Tampakong
51. Tajo' anjong: "prow post"
52. Tajo' patambera jalan:
    "adjustable shroud post"
    (two front, two rear)
53. Tajo' patambera puli:
    "fixed shroud post"
54. Pangepe tajo':
    "post pincer"
55. Panumbu
    bangkeng salara:
    "mast foot support"
56. Bangkeng salara:
    "mast foot"
57. Patokopeta ri tangnga:
    "middle hatch"
58. Patokopeta ri boko:
    "rear hatch"
59. Palu-paluna: "striker"
60. Naga-naga: "watersnake"
61. Lepe lalang:
    "inner lateral beam"
62. Lepe: "lateral beam"
63. Soloro: half rib
    (45 in a 100-ton boat)
64. Kelo: full rib
    (45 in a 100-ton boat)
65. Bua-buaya: "crocodile"
66. Dek: "deck"
67. Kalang ri rangnga:
    "middle transverse beam"
68. Kalang timong: crossbeam
69. Kalang: crossbeam
70. Kalang pangepe:
    pincer beam
71. Ditamping sotting
72. Panumpu':
    front tripod base
73. Palayain bakka (two)
74. Pa'joli
75. Palayain ri boko
76. Bau ri tangnga:
    center top mast
77. Bau ri boko: rear top mast
78. Bau ri olo: front top mast
79. Pampang: top mast brace
80. Kamar: cabin

water will later be sprinkled around the boat as a form of *songkabala*, "warding off of danger." When the *barasanji* reading is over the owner comes and exchanges greetings with the reciters and gives them gifts. After this he sets out food and invites the reciters and other guests to eat.

Carving the Navel

Later that night, the ritual carving of the boat's navel *(possi)* takes place. First, the master locates the midpoint of the keel with a torch and marks it. The owner sits facing the master on the left side of the keel while the captain sits on the master's side. The master takes a chisel and smokes it in incense. Traditionally, the master conducted this ritual naked. At this point the owner covered the master with a white cloth. According to Pelly, the owner's wife usually attends this ritual at present, and the master no longer strips himself. Before the hammer is brought down on the chisel, the master recites the following *mantera:*

Bismillahirrahmanirrahim	In the name of Allah the Merciful the Forgiving
Nabbi Summa tettong	The Prophet Summa stands
Riolonna loppi	In front of the boat
Nabbi Hilir ajjaga	The Prophet Hilir guards it
Ri laleng ri saliweng	Inside and outside
Patimbonakko buttaya	You are the highlands
Kayu annako Nukmanulhakim	You are the Nukmanulhakim wood
Laku sareangi Nabbi Hilir.	You are guarded by the Prophet Hilir.

The master regulates his breathing until it feels as if the breath from the right nostril flows more quickly than from the left, as he did before felling the first tree for the boat. Only then is the chisel struck with the hammer. The wood chips are taken by the master and put in his mouth, along with a ring given him by the owner. Then the master takes a drill and smokes it in the incense. Still covered by the cloth, the master begins to drill the keel on the spot where he chiseled. A worker waits below the keel with a frying pan to catch the sawdust. This sawdust is put in the bottle of coconut oil along with the chips from the keel-laying ritual.

When he finishes drilling the hole, the master removes the ring and wood chip from his mouth. He gargles with some water and spews it on the hole, using his own mouth to sacralize the "protective water" *(songkabala)* instead of a basin. Then the owner hands over a cock. The cock's comb is cut with an adz and the blood is spattered on the hole. The same is done with a hen. The master ends the ritual by rinsing his face and eating a rice cake.

It should be noted that the carving of the boat's navel has exactly the same structure as the ritual conducted when the boat's keel was laid. The master is put into an appropriately liminal state by stripping and being covered with a white cloth. Incense is burned to establish communication with the spirit world while a *mantera* is recited. Wood shavings are taken from the keel and preserved in oil. The blood of a rooster and a hen is placed in holes. Finally, the master separates himself from his liminal state by rinsing his face. This second ritual marks the completion of the process of gestation. A fully formed spirit now animates the vessel and can receive its first regular feeding.

Feeding the Boat Spirit

The next rite is called *a'pakanre balapati*, "feeding the boat spirit." It is usually led by a ritual specialist (*panrita*) from the owner's family, because the *balapati* is connected more with sailing than with boatbuilding. In the middle of the *naga* beam near the boat's navel a clear surface is made. The *panrita* begins the rite by lighting incense and then reading from a book written in Arabic script. The owner and his wife, as well as the captain, sit to the *panrita*'s left. When he has finished reading, the owner's wife gives him a newly hatched chick. The specialist takes a bush knife and chops the twittering chick into fine pieces, starting from the head. This violent sacrifice of an immature creature transfers a life force that is still more potential than actual to the navel of the boat. The *panrita* then takes a red banana blossom, chops it finely, and mixes it with the remains of the chick. The mixture is divided into several portions, wrapped in banana leaves, and placed around the periphery of the boat. Packages are given to the captain to place at the joints between the central keel and the front and rear extenders. Two more packages are placed on the front and rear "crocodile" beams, which extend from the central dragon beam. Additional packages are placed at the joints above each bollard and scattered on the right and left sides of the boat. The wife of the owner then empties a basket containing red and black glutinous rice, egg, and curried chicken in front of the *panrita*. The *panrita* places these materials on a banana leaf and divides them into two equal parts with a knife. One package is placed near the boat's navel on the right side, and one package is placed on the left. This ends the *a'pakanre balapati* rite. The owner gives the *panrita* a gift of money on a betel leaf. This rite will be repeated later, when the boat is at sea.

Burnt Offering of a Goat

A final sacrifice, the most violent of the cycle, is then held for the spirits of the earth. A one-meter hole is dug exactly beneath the navel of the boat. A black goat is put in the hole and buried in wood chips left over from the building of the boat. The chips are set alight and the goat is burned until it is completely incinerated. Pelly says that this is a rite of tribute to the inhabitants of the earth in the place where the boat was built, a way of expressing thanks to them. But it would also seem to be a means of transferring the life force of the goat to the navel of the boat from below by means of smoke, thus supplementing the transfer of the life force of the chick from above by means of liquid blood. Fur-

ther, the black goat is a creature of the earth, while the yellow chick is a creature of the wind and sky.

The boat is launched the following morning. As the men push and pull it
toward the sea, the wife of the owner and several other women scatter yellow tur-
meric rice on it. When the keel of the boat touches the water the master recites a
mantera to introduce the boat to the sea. The rite closes with a feast on the beach.

The keel-laying, navel-carving, and boat-launching rituals involve the creation of a singular spirit called a *balapati* and its infusion into an artifact. Similar
procedures are performed when building a house. The boatbuilding rituals also
involve the extraction, concentration, transfer, and binding of an impersonal
spiritual energy or life force called *sumanga'* within the artifact. Similar procedures are performed on newly born infants, on agricultural fields, and on
houses. The life force of an animal may be extracted by burning it alive and allowing the life force to be carried upward in the smoke and downward into the
ashes; by cooking and eating the meat; by collecting and applying the blood to
another object; or by some combination of these methods. The life force is
bound inside an entity by circling them with magical substances seven times in
a counterclockwise direction and by setting up magical barriers at the perimeter
of the entity.

These procedures often focus on young and immature beings. Immature
beings both absorb and lose additional life force more easily than mature beings,
because their boundaries are softer and more permeable. One objective of the rituals surrounding pregnancy and childbirth is to infuse additional life force in the
fetus and to bind the life force that is already there more firmly in place. Conversely, the sacrifice of a fetus or newborn creature is more effective if the objective is to transfer its life force to another material or spiritual being. Beings at an
early stage of their growth contain the life force as potential energy, so to speak.

A vivid expression of this principle is contained in the following anecdote
from Collins:

> Later in the evening I told them of launching Viking ships, saying:
> "Long ago some of my people used to launch their prahus over living men
> instead of wooden rollers. I'm not sure how many they used—probably
> twenty or thirty or even more for big prahus."
> And in a few minutes they were admitting that before cock's blood took
> their place two human heads were impaled on stem and sternpost. . . .
> The mention of the Viking ships moved the Karaeng to tell me of a parallel
> among Celebes prahu builders.
> "When a palari was to be launched," he said, "seven young women in their
> first pregnancy were taken and bound and used as rollers." (Collins 1936: 221)

Without further evidence, one may doubt that this was ever a real practice, especially because Collins had just primed his informant with the example of the
Vikings. Nevertheless, his informant's choice of victim was highly significant:

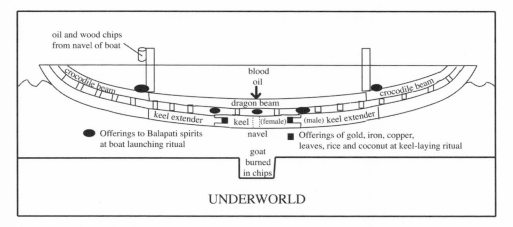

Fig. 4.2 The Symbolic Aspects of a Boat.

seven women in their first pregnancy. As I have discussed elsewhere, the first pregnancy is more highly elaborated than the rest and is the occasion for a ritual particularly concerned with the life force of the fetus (Gibson 1994a, 1995).

Throughout Island Southeast Asia, the sacrifice of human fetuses and infants is a subject of fascination, although it occurs more in the realm of myth and rumor than of actual practice. People in the Philippines, Borneo, and Sulawesi all fear that, when the foundations of a bridge are being laid, a child will be kidnapped and buried alive to give the structure life. Despite the imaginary quality of many of these reports, one should not neglect the presence of ritual headhunting and human sacrifice throughout this culture area until only a few generations ago. In practice, when potential vitality is at issue, the most likely immature victim today is a chick. When a large amount of actual vitality is required, a mature buffalo is the ideal victim.

The rigging of the boat is added later by the crew who will sail it. *Pinisi* have two masts. The forward mast is a tripod, with a topmast and diagonal spar running from the top. The rear mast is a single post with a topmast and a diagonal spar running from the top and a boom at the bottom. Each mast carries two sails. Three more jib sails are attached to the long bowsprit in front, giving the *pinisi* its characteristic seven-sail sloop rigging.

Conclusion: Transoceanic Alliance and Royal Potency

In this chapter, I discussed the historical and literary evidence for intensified maritime interaction around the Java Sea in the thirteenth century. This is when the Javanese kingdom of Kediri promoted the worship of the King as an avatar of Vishnu. Little royal centers modeling themselves on Kediri sprang up along the coastlines of Sumatra, Borneo, and Sulawesi. Traces of this period persist in the form of myths found all over coastal Southeast Asia recounting the adventures of a hero called Panji. In these myths, the hero has a twin sister in heaven from whom he is separated when they are incarnated in widely separated kingdoms. After many adventures, he manages to reunite with her. Ras argues that the Panji myth served as a template during the Kediri period of Javanese history for royal weddings between distant kingdoms linked only by maritime trade. This set of myths takes place in a world composed of multiple royal centers. Alliances between them are maintained through the balanced exchange of royal men, while each maintains its own links to the Upperworld and Underworld through local royal women.

A version of this story is embedded in the enormous mythological cycle of the Bugis people known as the La Galigo. In the Bugis version, a pair of opposite-sex twins are separated at birth. The female twin remains fixed at her center of origin. She becomes a *bissu* priestess with the power to move vertically between the Middleworld, the Upperworld, and the Underworld. Only she is able to fell the great tree that connects the three worlds and turn it into a boat. The male twin is a great sailor, with the power to move horizontally across the sea. He uses the boat created by his sister to penetrate a new royal center where he marries a first cousin who is identical to his own twin sister. He settles uxorilocally, but his son returns to rule the original royal center.

Oral versions of these myths remain current in Ara, Bira, and Selayar because the peoples of this area continue to play a central role in the maritime trade of Island Southeast Asia. They provide a mythical charter for the practical and ritual activities that accompany the building of boats to this day.

Chapter 5
Noble Transgression and Shipwreck
Traces of Luwu' in Bira

I n this chapter I discuss a set of myths and rituals that deal with the negation of this world of seafaring, long-distance trade, and royal marriage, a world in which royal incest and adultery result in discord, epidemic disease, and shipwreck. These forces of disorder are ritually combated by hermaphroditic mediums with the help of the spirits of foreign princesses. The seafarers of Bira traditionally claimed knowledge not only of boatbuilding and navigation, but also of the power to control the dangerous forces of wind, current, and tide. Like the origins of boatbuilding discussed in the previous chapter, these forces were also linked to the royal families of Luwu' and Cina. A beach in Bira is known as Panrang Luhu', Luwu's graveyard, because of the many wrecked ships that once washed ashore there. The narrow passage between Bira and Selayar is filled with reefs and complex crosscurrents that turn into whirlpools under certain conditions. Bugis ships sailing down the Gulf of Bone, intending to head west toward the Java Sea, used to stop off in Bira and take on a local pilot before rounding Ujung Lasoa.

In the first part of this chapter, I analyze a group of myths that link shipwreck and drowning to royal incest. The male protagonists of these myths overturn both generational and gender hierarchies by marrying their own mothers. They are thus the opposite of Panji and Sawerigading, who marry distant cousins to avoid incest with their sisters. In the local version of the incest myth, a prince from Luwu' accidentally marries his mother in Cina. The two flee down the coast of the Gulf of Bone. They finally drown themselves off the coast of Bira, calling down a curse on the sailors of Luwu' so that they cannot round Ujung Lasoa without risking shipwreck.

In the second part of the chapter, I turn to a group of myths about an opposite form of royal sexual transgression. In these myths, a ruler linked to Luwu' commits adultery with the wives of his subjects while their husbands are away at sea. Like those guilty of incest, this ruler may not be buried in the earth. Rather than being drowned at sea, however, when his subjects rebel they bury him alive in a stone tomb located on the boundary between land and sea.

In the final part of the chapter, I relate these myths of transgressive sexuality to four types of ritual. The first is a rite of exorcism meant to expel ill fortune. The example I discuss was a ritual performed in 1935 to expel a malaria epidemic. The second is a rite, also performed in 1935, to protect the local fleet as it set out on its annual voyage to Maluku. The third was a rite performed in 1989 to fulfill a vow made to the local spirits by a farmer who had made a good return on his cash crop of peanuts. Finally, I describe a ritual performed on the seashore to propitiate the spirit of a giant crab that causes skin disease.

This group of myths and rituals indicates the profoundly ambivalent character of Ujung Lasoa in particular and of the boundary between land and sea more generally. The extreme southeastern tip of South Sulawesi is associated both with shipwreck and other calamities and with windfall profits like bumper harvests of cash crops and lottery winnings. To help explain this ambivalence, I note that, although shipwreck is a dire threat for long-distance traders, it is a source of regular income for local pilots and of sudden wealth for local scavengers. Such income is morally ambiguous and can leave as rapidly as it comes. Long-distance sea trade itself has ambiguous implications. It can lead to great wealth for adventurous men, but it also puts the contents of their houses at the mercy of unscrupulous rulers.

Myths of Incest

As Boon has pointed out, if the most auspicious form of marriage in central Indonesia is that between first cousins, who are seen as the closest acceptable substitutes for opposite-sex twins, the most inauspicious form of incest is that between a mother and a son, whose union confounds not only generational but gender hierarchies. "Balinese ancestor-group endogamy appears to be a series of flirtations with sibling incest. 'Mother'-son and at least real father-daughter unions are excluded from consideration by the principle of distinct, ranked generations; 'brother-sister' or same generation incest is the ambivalent problem area, highlighted by the concern with twins" (Boon 1977: 139). But the possibility of the most transgressive sort of incest is not completely excluded from at least mythological consideration, as shown by the following story in the *Babad Tanah Jawi*:

M 5.1 Watu Gunung and Dewi Sinta (Java: Babad Tanah Jawi)

King Watu Gunung was unwittingly married to his own mother, Dewi Sinta [Javanese for Sita, the spouse of Rama]. She had struck him on the head with a ladle because he had bothered her while she was cooking rice. One day while Dewi Sinta was delousing her husband's hair she noticed the scar on his head from the wound she had formerly inflicted on him, and then realized what position she was in. She persuaded the king to wage war on Sura-laja (heaven) in order to obtain a heavenly nymph as a wife. She hoped that Watu Gunung would be killed in battle against the gods and that in this way her incestuous marriage would automatically be dissolved. (Ras 1968: 146)

A similar story appears in the Hikayat Banjar, where the role of Watu Gunung is played by the founder of the second *kraton,* Raden Sakar Sungsang. The latter is said to have left the Banjar *kraton* after being struck on the head by his mother while she was cooking. He went to Java, where he married a nymph. Later, he returned to Banjar and married the widowed queen, who later turned out to be his mother. Ras argues that the parallel between the founder of the second *kraton* and Watu Gunung was probably made by a later ruler in order to delegitimate the preceding dynasty. But it is also the case that this sort of incest, horrific as it might appear, may be a source of great supernatural power, which can be tapped by those who know how.

An almost identical story links the kingdom of Luwu' to one of the most sacred sites in Bira, the southeastern-most cape of South Sulawesi, known as Ujung Lasoa. The waters off Ujung Lasoa are full of reefs and crosscurrents, making them extremely dangerous to navigate. The origin of the danger surrounding Ujung Lasoa is recounted in a myth about royal incest. I heard a few versions of this story in 1988–1989, but the one recorded by Collins in the 1930s is more detailed. I reproduce it here, with some condensation:

M 5.2 Maroangin and Aru Cina (Konjo: Bira)

Aru Cina was a beautiful Queen of Luwu whose husband had died. She had a ten-year-old son named Maroangin who was always getting into mischief. He harassed the slaves and the Queen's ministers, and was always greedy for food. One day while his mother was weaving he came and demanded food although he had just eaten a big meal. She refused him and in a temper he grabbed the loom and broke many threads. Enraged Aru Cina hit him across the head with the "sword" of the loom, a long flat wooden bar used to tamp the cross threads tight. He turned and ran away deep into the woods until he was lost. He wandered for days living off roots and berries, moving all the time away from Luwu'. Finally he came to some hamlets built near the shore and a man took him in and fed him. One of the hamlet chiefs said to another that the boy must have come down from the sky, he had appeared so far away from any other human habitation.

Meanwhile, Aru Cina sank into a deep depression when months passed and her son failed to return. After many years she finally ran away into the woods, planning to kill herself. She walked and walked until she too reached the same hamlet her son had. A hunter found her and brought her to the Chief. They all thought that she too must have come down from the sky. The Chief decided that it would be best if they married and bore children so that the hamlets would always have sky people to rule over them. Maroangin was fed even more food than usual by the men of the mountains and urged to marry Aru Cina. Although much older than him, she was much fairer than the coarse mountain women, and still very beautiful.

They married and had a daughter, Sampanena. One day Maroangin got lice in his hair and asked Aru Cina to hunt for them. She did and discovered the scar that her loom sword had left on him. She asked how he had got it, and when he explained she realized he was her son and that they had committed incest. The consequences of incest are that no rain falls, and crops fail. Animals miscarry and the fish swim far from shore. Death and disease spread through the land. The only way to avert this is to drown the guilty ones.

Maroangin decided they would have to run away in case their sin was discovered. One night, they took their child Sampanena and fled, moving through the forest only at night and avoiding human habitation. They ran south, away from Luwu'. At last they came to Ujung Lasoa in Bira, the southern-most point of land. At that time there was no settlement near the point, and they settled there in seclusion.

Aru Cina was still afraid they would be discovered by men from Luwu'. She would often gaze out at the Gulf of Bone. She began to fear that every boat was from Luwu' come to look for her, so she cast spells that made a whirlpool rise up and swallow every boat as it tried to round the Cape. This went on for years, and soon it became an insatiable appetite with her. The sight of the drowning men made her belly feel full. Sampanena meanwhile was growing up. At first she did not realize what was happening, that when a boat sank, men were dying. But one day her mother sank a ship right beneath the cliff they were standing on, and she heard the cries of the sailors. She felt pity for them, and afterward whenever she saw a boat she would run back to the house and distract her mother by searching for lice in her hair until the boat had safely rounded the cape. (Condensed from Collins 1936: 176–183)

There is indeed a whirlpool that often springs up in the strong currents that run between Cape Lasoa in Bira and Selayar Island. According to Collins's informant, the *karaeng* of Bira Andi Mulia (r. 1901–1914, 1920–1941), sailors from Luwu' were particularly afraid of this passage, even in his youth. Before 1900, they would anchor in the Gulf of Bone at the beach of Marumasa or at Panrang Luhu' and let a Biran crew take their boats round the point while they crossed the peninsula on foot and reembarked in Tanaberu. *Panrang Luhu'* means "Luwu's graveyard," because it was here that bodies from wrecks off the point would wash up. In the 1930s, Bugis sailors were still either avoiding the straits completely or taking on local Biran pilots. They called Cape Lasoa *Sombah i Opu*, "Lord and Emperor," and cast an offering of rice, eggs, and betel on the waters as they passed. Sampanena, the daughter, is thought of as the protector of sailors generally, and Bugis whose men were late coming home from a sea journey would come to the point where Aru Cina lived to make offerings to her (Collins 1936:174–176).

Abdul Hakim added that there were four capes at which the cursed couple stopped along the way, causing dangerous currents to arise at each. They include Ujung Palate, in Bone, Ujung La'bu, in Kajang, and Ujung Tiro, in Tiro. The most powerful, and the most dangerous, is Ujung Lasoa, in Bira. According to Hakim, the guilty couple drowned themselves when they reached Ujung Lasoa, calling

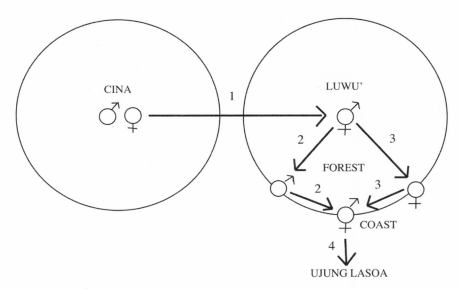

Fig. 5.1 Maroangin's Incest with Aru Cina.

down a curse on all people from Luwu' that tried to pass that point. He made no mention of the child, Sampanena. Hakim confirmed that people from Luwu' still avoid the cape. If they order a boat built in Tana Beru, they have local people sail it around to Ara or Tiro before they take possession of it.

In this myth, a princess from one royal center marries virilocally in another. Her son cannot control his impulses and is driven away from the royal center into the wild periphery. He becomes the chief of an uncivilized tribe living along the seashore. His mother regrets her attack and sets off to search for him. She does not recognize him when she finds him and they marry. They discover their sin after they consummate their marriage, and flee ever outward along the boundary of land and sea until they reach the uttermost point of South Sulawesi in Bira.

This marriage reverses the normal hierarchies of age, since husbands should be older than wives; gender, since men should pursue women; and space, since women should move from periphery to center or from center to center, and not from center to periphery. These reversals interrupt the normal flow of life, resulting in epidemics that kill humans and animals, droughts that kill crops, and shipwrecks that send trade goods to the bottom of the sea.

If one compares the myths that deal with the "good" incest of opposite-sex twins and those that deal with the "bad" incest of mothers and sons, one finds many of the same themes, among them: ignorance of a relationship to a female relative, passage through the wild forest, adoption by tribesmen, incest, and the production of a powerful child (compare Nourse on a myth of father-daughter incest among the Laujé 1999: 110–111).

But the myth of Maroangin is also a systematic inversion of the myth of Sawerigading on a number of levels:

1. Sawerigading is initially ignorant of the existence of his sister; Maroangin becomes ignorant of the identity of his mother.
2. When Sawerigading learns of his sister, he desires her. When Aru Cina learns the identity of her son, she is horrified.
3. Maroanging's incest with his mother is the result of an earlier quarrel and separation. Sawerigading's marriage to his cousin is the result of an earlier agreement with his sister.
4. Maroangin and Aru Cina flee into the wilderness in fits of mad rage and despair; Sawerigading enters it deliberately as a ruse to inform himself about We Cudai.
5. Sawerigading's incestuous love for his sister is transformed into legitimate marriage to his cousin. Maroangin's hatred for his mother is transformed into illegitimate desire for her.
6. Sawerigading's virtuous sublimation of his desires transforms him into the benevolent ruler of the watery Underworld. Maroangin's evil indulgence of his desires transforms him into the malevolent ruler of whirlpools.
7. Sawerigading is the consummate lover, sailor, and merchant. His mastery of the circuits of long-distance exchange enable him to marry a princess of the highest status, one who outranks his twin sister, and therefore himself. Maroangin's inability to master his impulses drives him into permanent exile in the wilderness. Instead of sailing, he travels along the shore on foot, causing whirlpools to spring up that are an impediment to navigation.
8. These whirlpools cause shipwrecks, leading to an interruption in the flow of trade goods and, therefore, of long-distance marriage alliances. The myth contains the following syllogism: If prestige trade goods facilitate proper weddings, and shipwrecks inhibit trade, then improper weddings can cause shipwrecks.

The difference in outcome between the two sorts of incest—one between opposite-sex twins sublimated by a series of mediations into a marriage between cousins of the same genealogical level and one between a younger male and an older female belonging to adjacent genealogical levels—reflects a fundamental feature of kinship in the area. Incest between an "elder brother" and a "younger sister" is, as it were, entirely grammatical at the level of social classifications. Incest between a mother and a son confuses the hierarchical structure of the universe at so many levels only madness can result (compare Errington 1989: 244–247).

Mother-son incest is the most extreme instance of a short circuit of the proper channels through which the forces of fertility should flow. The earth itself is offended by this sort of transgression. The miscreants cannot be buried in the earth, for they would cause it to become dangerously hot and dry. The rain and the crops would fail, and the land would be invaded by the forces of anti-fertility. The only thing to do with these offenders is to throw them into the sea.

Myths of Adultery

The myth of Maroangin and Aru Cina is not the only one that attributes transgressive sexuality to the nobility of Luwu'. Another set of myths describes the excessive lust of a ruler from Luwu' who takes advantage of the wives of his subjects while their husbands are away at sea.

M 5.3 The *Karaeng* of Tiro Is Buried Alive (Konjo: Ara)

The first ruler of Tiro was a prince from Luwu' called Karaeng Samparaja Daeng Malaja. According to the Department of Culture in Tiro, he ruled from 1468 to 1516. Local informants told me that he used to send his men away on long expeditions, if they were not planning long sailing trips anyway. While they were gone, he would systematically seduce their wives. When they returned each year, the *karaeng* would give them a big feast, serving the men in bowls made from coconut shells. Now some of these bowls had been polished smooth, and others left quite hairy. After a few years, the men began to notice that the same men were always given the same bowls. They compared notes and discovered that the amount of coarse fibers left on the bowls corresponded exactly to the amount of pubic hair on their respective wives and that he had been mocking them in this way all along. The men then conspired to kill him. They told the *karaeng* that they wanted to build him a tomb worthy of his greatness. They hollowed it out for him in a huge boulder that lies on the beach between Ara and Tiro. The *karaeng* was pleased and agreed to climb inside to see if it was the right size. They told him to stay inside while they tested the fit of the covering stone, and again he agreed. Twenty-five men then lifted a massive stone over the top and sealed him in. After his death, he was known as *Sapo Hatu,* meaning "Stone House" in the dialect of Selayar.

In contrast to the myth of Maroangin, where incest led to insufficient trade, in this myth the ruler orders his subjects to undertake excessively long sea voyages. This leaves their wives open to his advances on land, leading to excessive sexual intercourse that transgresses social rules. Adding insult to injury, the ruler feeds them in split coconuts that resemble their wives' genitalia, making them eat symbolically from the containers he has defiled.

The ruler's transgression of sexual boundaries leads to the most extreme inversion of proper hierarchical relations, regicide. Normally, this act would result in the state of *busung,* a condition in which the belly of those who offend the powerful swells up and bursts. So great is the ruler's sin, however, that he in effect abdicates his status as king. Because his sin is of a sexual nature, he, too, cannot be buried in the earth. Because he is not guilty of incest, he is not drowned at sea either. In the end, the subjects come up with the solution of burying him in a boulder that stands on the boundary of the land and sea. Despite its dubious contents, this rock is regarded as a site of great power. Supplicants seeking favors often come to pay homage to Samparaja and to leave offerings for his spirit.

On a visit to Ere Lebu, the home village of the *karaeng*s of Tiro, I asked one of Samparaja's descendents, Andi Bangun Daeng Ma'gau, about this story. He vigorously denied that Samparaja had been an unjust ruler. He reasoned that no one would have gone to the trouble of hollowing a tomb out of a solid boulder for a hated king. Further, there were many graves of his *gallarrang* close by, which also would not happen had he been disliked.

He went on to give me an alternative explanation for the fact that Samparaja could not be buried normally in the earth, but had to be placed in a stone tomb.

M 5.4 The *Karaeng* Squeezes Oil from the Earth (Konjo: Tiro)

One day a child was walking home with a jar of oil it had been sent to buy. The child spilled the oil outside Samparaja's house and burst into tears. Samparaja came out to see what was wrong. The child said he was afraid his mother would be angry. Samparaja told it not to worry and picked up the earth and squeezed the oil back into the bottle. The earth complained that it was being hurt by the squeezing and that it would retaliate later when Samparaja was buried in the earth. But Samparaja was able to defy the earth, because he knew that he would later be buried in stone.

This myth attributes Samaparaja's offense against the earth to excessive compassion for a small child, leading Samparaja to defy the earth itself. In this version, it is Samaparaja who outwits the superior party, escaping the wrath of the earth by having himself buried in a stone.

In 1935, the *karaeng* of Bira told Collins an almost identical story to the first myth about Samparaja in Bira. He, however, attributed these actions to an early ruler of Bira called Malanra. According to some genealogies, Malanra was the great-grandson of Samparaja and ruled at the beginning of the seventeenth century.

M 5.5 The *Karaeng* Is Crushed by a Boat (Konjo: Bira)

Malanra used to take advantage of his men's wives when they set sail every year and to feast the men every year on their return. He served them in coconut shells with different amounts of fiber adhering to the shells. Eventually the men realized that the hairiness of the shells corresponded to that of their respective wives' pubic hair, and they resolved to kill him. They waited until a boat was stuck on the beach and asked Malanra to come down to help push her free. They waited until he was alongside pushing, and on a predetermined command all the men on his side leapt clear and the men on the other pushed the boat over on top of him. (Condensed from Collins 1937: 217–219)

In both stories, the excessive absence of men at sea leads the ruler to take advantage of their wives and then to insult them. In this version, they also retaliate by killing him at the water's edge, but do not bury him in a stone tomb.

In both versions, women and their sexuality are identified with the land and with plant life. The duty of the territorial ruler is to protect them while their husbands are away at sea in his service. A breach of this duty justifies a breach of the normally sacred authority of the ruler. As we shall see in the next chapter, the justice of the ruler is a necessary condition for the health and fertility of the land and its people. Conversely, a land that has lost its fertility and become subject to drought and disease must be under the rule of an unjust king. An unjust ruler brings a curse on his land and may not be buried in it.

Rituals of Transgression

The myth of Maroangin and Aru Cina ended with the intervention on behalf of sailors of their child, Sampanena. The act of her parents that led to her conception may have been an abomination, but Sampanena herself is good and has pity for other humans. Because of her role in deflecting the dangerous curses of her mother, she may be supplicated to avert other ill fortune such as epidemics. Because of the association of the Ujung Lasoa with plunder from shipwrecks, it is also an appropriate place to seek other forms of good fortune such as bumper harvests.

In this part of the chapter, I will discuss two sets of rituals conducted at Ujung Lasoa. The first set was conducted by a pair of male and female spirit mediums in 1935 to exorcise evil spirits that were causing a malaria epidemic. The second was conducted by a hermaphroditic spirit medium in 1989 on behalf of a farmer's peanut crop and to determine the winning lottery number.

The Malaria Epidemic of 1935

During Collins's time in Bira, there was a severe malaria epidemic. In addition to the quinine he dispensed, the people resorted to a number of different ritual measures to expel the spirits causing the disease. The simplest of these involved building a little bamboo house out in the fields and placing offerings within it. The hope was that the spirits would mistake it for the real house and enter it instead. If people had already fallen ill in a household, an offering of cooked food would be carried to the nearest road. The spirits would follow the smell out to the road, and in the morning they might forget which house they came from.

A more elaborate exorcism involved an attempt to send the evil spirits out to sea. Collins describes the preparation of a small dugout canoe with two outriggers, complete with a full set of sails and a crew made out of figurines woven from palm leaves. The canoe was carried down to the shore on a palanquin, together with a complete food offering of colored rice, eggs and roast chicken, green and yellow bananas, and coconuts. Informants explained to me that this sort of preparation provides the invisible and intangible spirits with temporary bodies into which they can materialize. The rice is colored red, black, white, and yellow to represent the four elements of fire, earth, water, and air that compose all material bodies. Eggs and chickens represent the life force that animates them. Hands of bananas resemble rib cages and coconuts resemble heads. Thus, the spirits are attracted to the offerings by their smell and can then adopt them as their bodies.

A newly hatched chick was placed in the middle of the canoe. A cock and a hen were placed forward and another pair aft. The canoe was placed in a boat along with a black goat and rowed far out to sea. The canoe was put in the water along with the live goat and the whole assemblage was abandoned. Rituals like this that are designed to appease and expel hostile spirits require the absolute sacrifice of whole animals. They are either abandoned to the sea to drown or burnt to ashes (Collins 1937: 46–48).

Even more elaborate rituals to expel the spirits of disease were held at the shrine of Sampanena at Ujung Lasoa. The *karaeng* of Bira, Andi Mulia, did his best to dissuade Collins from attending any of these rituals. First he claimed they would be of no interest; then he tried to stage other attractions. But Collins persisted. He writes that in a single day he saw three parties from different villages arrive to use the pavilion, each with its own *sanro,* and they had to wait their turn to use it. He gives a detailed description of one séance he observed that was designed to cure a group of children of malaria. Bira was in the midst of a serious epidemic during Collins's stay, and he spent much of his time distributing quinine.

Collins described the shrine to Sampanena as follows:

The cliffs at this point are about a hundred feet high, and among the bushes by their edge is a small pavilion about eighteen feet long by twelve in width. It has a red tiled roof, and is built of old ships planks and timbers. On the right, just inside the doorway, stands an upright stone about eighteen inches high, resting on a low platform and protected by a wooden barrier. It is smooth and fat and black with oil, in the form of a huge elongated egg.

The inner half of the floor is raised about two feet, and in the centre of this dais are two heavy blocks cut from ships' planks. Set upright in holes in the wood are four more stones; a pair in each block, each stone about the shape and size of that by the doorway. And between the two in front is a smaller stone. Like the others, it is smooth and black with oil; but it is only nine inches high and three in width, swelling at the top to four.

This stone has three names, according to the nature of the rites that are performed before or on it. When its help is invoked to keep danger from ships it has a girl's name, Sampanena; when women who want children sit on it and wriggle, it takes a male name, Pangorisang; and when it helps to drive away the demons of disease it is called The Body. The big stones round it are named, for disease rites, Earth, Water, Fire and Air. . . . A photograph I took of the stones at this time shows the central stone not in its usual position but with the narrow pointed end on top. It had been reversed not long before by a woman who hoped that by becoming truly linked with it she would become pregnant. (Collins 1937: 50–51)

The area is still much as Collins described it, except that the pavilion has been torn down and replaced by a three-foot-high fence. The dais at the back is now covered by a tin roof, but no walls. Informants told me that this dais was the grave of a woman from Luwu', and the smaller stone dais was that of her child, although my informants did not give me their names. It was clear that these graves were felt to be repositories of power in and of themselves.

The four outer stones representing the four elements surrounding a central oval stone representing the whole, reflects a common arrangement in ritual and myth first described by van Ossenbruggen in his article on "Java's moncapat" system. "The cardinal points shall divide the earth into four equal parts," says a Hindu-Javanese creation myth (van Hien 1906: 1: 7). "The first part shall be white, the second yellow, the third red and the fourth black" (van Ossenbruggen [1918] 1977: 55). In many rituals in South Sulawesi, the four elements are represented by mounds of red, yellow, black, and white rice and the whole by an egg. Van Ossenbruggen cites examples of a similar symbolic system in many other parts of Indonesia, showing how it is integrated in different places with either Hindu or Muslim ideas.

The central stone can apparently change gender depending on the purpose of the ritual, acting either as a sort of male *lingam* for the transmission of potency into the wombs of women or as a female protector to shield sailors from the wrath of Aru Cina. Thus, in addition to the Vaishnavite resonances of the story of Sawerigading discussed in Chapter 4, there would seem to be some evidence of a Shaivite cult as well. I will elaborate on this point in chapter 6. For the moment it is important to note that the shrine has an ambivalent male-female, or hermaphroditic, character.

When Collins arrived for the séance soon after dawn, women were dressing the peripheral stones in white cloths and gold chains, while the central Body stone was left bare. A basket containing coconuts, bananas, and a number of small figurines woven out of palm leaves was brought up from a canoe that had been brought to the base of the cliffs. It was placed in front of the pavilion door, next to an eight-foot-high bamboo pole, "its top so split and bent outward as to form an inverted cone" (Collins 1937: 52). A young husked coconut called "The Head" was placed inside it. Collins is clearly describing a *tompong,* a bamboo tube used in many rituals to connect the Middleworld to the Upperworld (see, for example, the To Kambang rituals in chapter 9). Its juxtaposition to the basket of little men brought up from the sea suggests that the latter were meant to connect the Middleworld to the Underworld.

The ritual assistants then laid out the usual array of colored rice, eggs, and bananas. When the decorations were complete, drums and gongs were beaten while a female medium sat in front of a coconut shell filled with burning incense.

The pavilion was crowded with women. The medium's body began to tremble, and the spectators said a "god" was entering it. After a while, the female medium began to abuse the bystanders, throwing eggs and stones into the crowd and hitting Collins with a bunch of green bananas.

The female medium began to pick up articles of men's clothing from a pile and to sniff them one by one. When she found a sarong, jacket, scarf, and cap her possessing spirit liked, she was helped into them by an assistant. This is how possessing spirits identify themselves to this day, by choosing a costume appropriate to their ethnicity, rank, and gender. In all of the séances I attended, the medium was always possessed by a spirit of the opposite gender.

When the female medium was fully entranced, a sheathed *keris* was thrust into a scarf tied around her waist. It appears from Collins's photograph that this *keris* had seven waves in it. As this is the largest number of waves found in local *keris,* and, because the number of waves indicates the power of a *keris,* it must have been a particularly potent instrument.

The medium drew the *keris* and waved it about in the air, before resting it against the Body stone. She smeared oil over the head, face, and back of a goat that had been tethered next to her. She passed an incense burner around the head of the goat three times. She then snatched up the *keris* and began slashing at the goat with it. The goat was led out of the pavilion, followed by the possessed medium and several other *sanro.* They walked in procession around the pavilion three times and around the bamboo Head post three times. All this time, the medium was screaming wildly and trying to stab the goat. The circling of the goat, pavilion, and Head post with the incense linked the sacrificial animals to the spirits of the place, binding them to help exorcise the evil spirits in exchange for the offering.

Finally, the medium was led back into the pavilion and seated on the dais. A nine-month-old baby was placed on her knees. The medium rattled the *keris* against the Body stone and then placed its tip first in her own, then in the baby's mouth. She then slashed the air with it and drove it straight at the baby's throat, causing the women round her to scream and cover their eyes. But she caught the tip with the fingers of her other hand, so the baby was unharmed. The *keris* was rattled against the Body again, jabbed at the baby's throat, navel, and fontanel, and finally laid flat along its back. These are the points on the body that are most vulnerable to the entry of evil spirits or to the loss of the life force. Six or seven more children between the ages of one and eight years old were treated in this manner.

The *keris* was thus charged with power from the Body stone before being used to drive out the spirits of disease. Spirits cannot be destroyed; they can only be transferred from one container to another. In this case, they were transferred to the basket of figurines that had been brought up from the sea and to the coconut Head on the bamboo pole. When the medium was led out of the pavilion again and over to the basket, she began to slash at it with the *keris.* She was then carried back into the pavilion. A male medium seized the *keris* she had dropped. In a frenzy, he attacked first the basket of figurines, then the coconut on the pole, then the basket again. He, too, was in a trance, not even noticing when he knocked the coconut to the ground. After the attacks on the basket and the coconut were completed, the *keris* was returned to the female medium, and she continued to slash about with it for another hour inside the pavilion.

At about noon, a second phase began, culminating in the sacrifice of a goat. The medium and goat were again led out and taken to two trees, one dead, called the Black Tree, and one living. A five-foot-high bonfire was built, and the medium and goat were led around it and the living tree three times. The medium then rubbed more oil on the goat's horns, head, face, and back. Then she embraced it and had to be dragged away by two male *sanro*. She then tried to kill it with the *keris* but was too weak. Finally, the chief male *sanro* took it from her, did a short leaping dance, and stabbed it several times in the throat, continuing even after it was dead. The carcass was placed on top of the bonfire and left to burn.

Collins tried to question the medium after the ritual was over, with the following results:

> "What do you think about when you're stabbing the children?" I asked.
>
> "I can't remember. The god's inside me, and makes me stab them."
>
> I have been told that formerly, if children did not lose their sickness as soon as the point of the kris was put in their mouths, they were killed.
>
> "And what do you think about the coco-nut called The Head and the stone called The Body?"
>
> "It's a man," she replied. "His body's with the big stones and his head's on the bamboo."
>
> "Try to remember what you thought about when you stabbed the dead men in the basket."
>
> "I forget, Tuan."
>
> She was silent for a while. Then she began to mutter a few of her spells, and I let her go on. Soon she trembled slightly, still muttering, and I told her cousin to ask her again about the dead men, and how they came to die.
>
> "Did they die of malaria?" I asked. "Or in a fight?"
>
> "Not in a fight," she answered. "They were not killed by sickness or accident. They are real men, and they died as they used to die by the stones."
>
> She went on muttering her spells for a while, then added:
>
> "They sail away in the boat. They eat the food we give them. They carry away the sickness, far from the land."
>
> Her body shook, and she cried:
>
> "The men are burning! I see the dead men burning, burning!" (Collins 1937: 58–59)

As with many of the references to the previous practice of human sacrifice in Collins, the claim that children who failed to recover immediately were killed must not be taken too literally. From this passage, it would seem safe to say only that the spirits of disease were thought to require the life of some creature before they would depart.

Once one has driven the spirits of the disease out of the bodies of the children, one must provide them with other bodies to move into. One must give them the whole body of the sacrificial offering by burning it, or, as we saw earlier, abandoning it to drown in the sea. The human figurines are another set of substitute bodies. In the imagination of the medium, the figurines represent human sacrifices that are burnt to death in the same manner as the goat.

The ritual ended when the basket of figurines was carried back down the cliff to the dugout canoe. A sail was set, and the basket was carried far out to sea. In chapter 9, I discuss another ritual in which good spirits that have been deliberately induced to enter the body of a spirit medium are also transferred to another body and sent out to sea in a boat. In that ritual as well, a live chick was placed on the boat before it was launched. But only token amounts of cooked food were abandoned. The rest of the offerings were consumed by the participants because the point of that ritual was to maintain a close connection with benevolent ancestor spirits.

On another occasion, Collins was invited to observe a ritual at Ujung Lasoa designed to invoke the spirit of Sampanena to protect the Bira fleet during a trip to Maluku. A female medium sat before the central stone in the pavilion burning incense while a group of women sang a slow song. The medium brought the smoke to her forehead and mouth. The incense was carried around the stones three times. A goat was brought into the pavilion. Rice was thrown on the goat, on the stones, then on the medium. The medium went out and circled the pavilion three times before walking to the very edge of the cliff, to the place where Sampanena used to watch for passing boats. There she fed a hen, threw food over the cliff for Sampanena, and requested her to guard the ships until they returned home.

The party returned to the pavilion, where a male medium worked himself up into a dissociated state and attacked the goat violently with a *keris*. When it was wounded but still alive it was thrown on a pyre, but came to and ran off into the bush. This caused some alarm among the participants, but the female medium reassured them that the spirits of the stones had received the offering as soon as it was placed in the fire, and that it was they who had allowed the goat to escape (Collins 1937: 213–215).

Demma Daeng Puga

We will now jump forward more than half a century to a séance I observed at Ujung Lasoa conducted by Demma Daeng Puga, an individual who claimed to be a hermaphrodite. Hermaphrodism is a well-recognized condition in South Sulawesi, by both the local culture and Western medicine. It involves the shrinkage of the male genitalia some time after puberty and the development of secondary female characteristics like breasts. A hermaphrodite is like a male and female twin contained in one body, potentially the most powerful of all intermediaries with the spirit world.

Demma was born in about 1940 and died in the mid-1990s after my second visit to the field. His father, Tanggo, was a farmer in Tinadong who had a certain power to cure wounds with bespelled water but was not a spirit medium. In the 1930s, Tanggo moved his house up above the main road, and three of his children have since built their houses on the land around it. Tanggo's mother, Bungko Engka, specialized in making offerings to *setan*.

Demma is of the same generation as my host Abdul Hakim, who said that Demma was *luar biasa*, "out of the ordinary," even as a schoolboy. Demma told me that he had been a normal boy but that at some point in his adolescence the spirit of a fifteen-year-old Bugis princess from Bone had possessed him. After that he grew increasingly androgynous. His genitals started to shrink and his breasts to grow, and he became a physiological hermaphrodite. Although he did marry a woman, they had no children and were soon separated. He then began to travel quite widely, visiting Sumatra and Singapore before coming back to settle in Ara. Since then he has had a series of *suami angkat* (I), "adoptive husbands," mostly Bugis from other *kabupaten* such as Bone, Soppeng, and Selayar. Demma sometimes still adopted male roles, as when I saw him help wash the corpse of Baso Marepa, his brother-in-law's male cousin. Usually, however, he adopted a female role, sitting in the back room of a house and gossiping with other women in a way a man never would.

Demma deliberately played up these ambiguities. His house was a tiny affair that had probably once been a field hut, but since he lived alone most of the time, it was sufficient for his needs. He turned the area between the two front tiers of posts into a sort of reception parlor and consulting room for his clients. All of the walls and ceiling were painted a bright blue, and all the walls hung with photographs. There were two large black-and-white photographs of himself. He had colored them by hand to emphasize his ambiguous character: in the photos, he was wearing men's spectacles, and he had drawn in a moustache as well as red lipstick and a beauty spot. There were several other photographs of him standing next to newlyweds. Like many other *calabai*, "false women" or transvestites, in South Sulawesi, he specialized in dressing and making up the faces and hair of brides. Pictures of women fashion models were glued to the walls (this is not in itself unusual in Indonesian houses), alongside frilly decorations constructed from empty cigarette boxes. The coffee tables were littered with seashells painted blue and beige, and with chunks of pink coral. At the west end of the room, opposite the door, was his bed. It was covered in lace curtains and frilly cushions. Next to it was a small doll's bed, similarly decorated, and on it sat a blonde doll made up with mascara. The total effect could only be described as campy.

Demma greeted his visitors in this room and offered them coffee and cakes in the normal way. But he also liked to prey on the unease of visitors in these slightly bizarre surroundings, especially that of men. Hakim, for example, had never been in the house until I asked to be taken to it and could not bear to stay for more than a few minutes. He left me alone, and Demma immediately proposed that I spend the night. He was much more relaxed with women. They found him quite amusing, and he spent most of his time dressed in a woman's sarong and gossiping with his female relatives.

The spirit that first possessed him, and that most affected his personality, was that of Andi Muliati, a pretty young girl from Bone. It is for this reason that he often affected the mannerisms of a young girl, primping and making himself up like a maiden. But he was also possessed by a host of other spirits, all of them "foreign" to Ara, that is, none of them were ancestral spirits. They could come from Luwu', Bone, Gowa, or even Java and Malaysia. While possessed, he spoke in the native language of the spirit concerned: Bugis, Makassar, Javanese, or Malay. Like the medium observed by Collins, Demma never knew in advance which spirit would possess him. He had to bring a whole wardrobe of clothes with him whenever he conducted a séance away from his house, for the possessing spirit would demand he dress in a costume appropriate to her ethnic origin.

Demma conducted most of his séances at Ujung Lasoa, on the very spot described by Collins above. He explained that it was the best place for séances because of the *karama'* (imbued with power) stones there, which he described as boat shaped. The spirits were more likely to enter him there, and, once they did, anyone could approach and ask them questions. He listed as necessary ingredients for an offering to the spirits a goat sacrificed on the spot, or at least some chickens, green and yellow bananas, and four kinds of rice: red, black, and white sticky rice and ordinary rice.

Demma had a reputation as a bit of a charlatan in Ara and had even been arrested and jailed for fraud in the village. His activities seemed to be barely tolerated by government officials. He seemed to have quite a loyal following in other areas, however, especially among the Bugis of Bone and Sinjai. In contrast to most other *sanro*, Demma boasted quite openly about his powers and described miraculous feats that could quite clearly be performed through sleight of hand. For example, he claimed that he could crumple a piece of blank paper in his hand and, after waiting for half an hour, open it to find the paper covered with magical writings in the lontara script of Luwu'. Or he might instruct someone to open a coconut and have them find objects inside.

I heard stories from other people, however, about how he had been caught out in his tricks. Many of these stories I heard from the friends and relatives of one of his main rivals as a medium, Titi Daeng Toja, who is discussed in chapter 9. One girl in her house told me of a time when he was treating a woman called Lebu. After chanting for a while in a trance, he told the people that if they dug a hole in the ground they would find fresh leaves at the bottom. But he got so carried away with his chanting, the leaves he had concealed in his armpit fell out and gave him away.

Another time, Demma gave a man a big jar and said that, after a certain time had elapsed, money would appear inside it. The man opened it before the stated time and found only dry corn husks. Demma explained that he had ruined the magic by opening it too early. Another time, he was paid 40,000 rupiah to

cure someone, but they died the next day. Once, a man from Liukang Lohe became so enraged by his tricks that he beat Demma unconscious, and it was some
time before he could walk again.

Although there seemed to be an inexhaustible supply of such stories about
Demma, Titi's group did not categorically deny he had any power. Their position was that he mixed in tricks with his real powers because he was greedy.
They said that a proper *sanro* should help others out of kindness. If grateful clients then want to give a gift later, that was fine, but Demma asked for cash up
front, and played on the baser motives of his clients. Many went to him not to
seek cures for illness, but to get rich.

Demma's attitude toward Titi was that his spirits were stronger, because
they were from more varied origins and thus had more knowledge of the world.
Although Titi's spirits would only diagnose a disease and refer the patient to
other specialists for treatment, Demma's spirits provided the cure as well. There
was thus a constant rivalry between the two main mediums in Ara. Demma was
well aware of the criticisms about his greed and touting for business. He coun-
tered them by saying people came to seek him out, he did not seek them out. He
denied using black magic, *sihir*, pointing out that he never used yellow rice in
his offerings, which he claimed was given only to *setan* in Ara. Finally, he attributed whatever good came from his rituals to God.

Demma at Ujung Lassoa

After several false starts, I was finally able to attend a séance held by Demma
at Ujung Lasoa. My experience was almost the same as that of Collins fifty years
earlier in that my main informant, Abdul Hakim, was quite anxious that I not attend this ritual and tried various stratagems to dissuade me from going. After he
failed to do so, he showed up himself later in the day, when the ceremony was in
full swing. Because he had made his disapproval evident to all concerned, he had
to be persuaded to leave before Demma would carry on with it.

The séance was sponsored by a farmer from Caramming named Subu.
Subu had made a vow when he planted his cash crop of peanuts earlier in the
year. If his eighty liters of seed yielded more than 4,000 liters of produce, a fifty-
fold increase, he vowed to go to Ujung Lasoa and to the Peak of Pua' Janggo in
Bira to make offerings. He was successful, and sold his crop for 175 rupiah per
liter, earning about 700,000 rupiah. By contrast, Abdul Hakim's peanut crop
only yielded 1,000 liters on fifty liters of seed that year, a twenty-fold increase.
Demma estimated the total cost of Subu's ritual at 250,000 rupiah, including the
cost of a goat, several chickens, fifty liters of rice, and the rental of one of Haji
Baso's jeeps for the day. He thus paid more than a third of the value of his crop
to the spirits.

On the day of the ritual, a dozen people came down from Caramming, including Subu and his first wife. (He has a second wife in Ara and is divorced from
a third.) Accompanying them were six young women, including his daughters
and nieces, and four young men. Several more people joined the group in Ara,

including Demma's sisters Densa and Dengi and three young men who were his acolytes. They stayed close to him throughout the day, supporting him when in trance, and helping him dress.

The jeep set off for Bira at 8:30 A.M. and went first to the peak of Pua' Janggo'. Pua'Janggo' means "Lord Beard," indicative of the Islamic piety of the saint who used to meditate there. This saint's given name was Abdul Haris (born ca. 1675–1700). He practiced a mystical variant of Islam that dispenses with many elements of *syariah (shari'a)* law and withdrew to meditate on a mountain peak overlooking Bira. This spot is the object of many Islamically oriented pilgrimages *(ziarah)*, but also attracts mediums like Demma.

A simple offering was laid out in the enclosure at the top of the peak. It included five plates of cooked white rice, with boiled or fried eggs on top. Two of these also had two hands of bananas on them. There were two plates with assorted side dishes (boiled eggs, beans, and fish) and a plate of fragrant *pinang* leaves. While some incense was burning, first Demma then Subu smeared oil on the wall of the enclosure.

The group then set off for Kabongkolang, a white sandy beach in Bira that enjoyed a limited popularity until the mid-1990s with German tourists of the "traveler" sort when a big investment was made in beach houses to attract wealthier tourists. The economic crisis of 1997 soon put an end to that hope. There is a level stone platform nearby know simply as *Karamaya*, "the Place of Mystical Power." A cylindrical stone has been placed upright on it, as they have on so many old places of power to make them resemble the tombs of Islamic saints. No one knew whose grave this was, but it did not seem to matter. Here the ritual was even more perfunctory. Demma scattered betel leaves, cigarettes, and fragrant *pinang* leaves on it and rubbed some oil on the upright stone. Subu followed suit, and we all went back to the jeep.

Demma went into the enclosure and sat on the dais at the south end with his acolytes behind him. Subu sat at the north end, and the older women sat on the ground to the east. The other young people paid less attention to the ritual and wandered in and out. The enclosure was then decorated. Bright new sarongs were hung from the roof of the shack, and a white cloth was suspended horizontally above Demma. Young fronds were hung over the entrance of the sort used to decorate doorways at a wedding. Demma began to make himself up. He changed out of the tee shirt and jeans he had worn while riding pillion on a motorcycle and walking to the point. He changed his earrings, pinned on a hair piece, and changed into a woman's sarong and a *baju bodo*, a traditional formal blouse. He first tried on a white blouse, but rejected it for a green one. He later explained that the green blouse meant that he had been possessed by a spirit from Luwu'.

At noon Demma was ready to begin the séance. He started chanting, frequently mentioning the name of his favorite familiar, Andi Muliati. Then he came out of the enclosure and approached the sacrificial goat. It, too, had been made up. Although it was a billy goat, it was combed and powdered as if it were female. A white cloth was laid across its back. Demma smashed a raw egg on its head, in the same way that a bride's mother shows her approval of the groom's sacrificial buffalo. He then combed its hair and powdered its face, showing the goat its image in a mirror. Then a tray containing several shapes and sizes of sweetened rice cakes steamed in containers woven from coconut fronds was held over its back. Demma waved the incense over the goat's face and then over the tray of cakes. All of this is reminiscent of the way that a goat is prepared for sacrifice on the seventh day after a funeral when it is sent to carry gifts to the spirits that have received the dead soul in the afterlife.

Demma and the women filed back into the enclosure, while the men took the goat away to be butchered. This was done under what may have been the same tree Collins saw used for the burnt offering fifty years before. The slaughter was done according to *syariah* law by Abdul Hakim's son-in-law, Mustari, who is an orthodox modernist. He also killed a black and a white chicken. Some of the blood was collected in a little blue cup and placed inside the enclosure. Blood is offered to honor spirits on many other occasions, particularly when homage is being paid to the regalia of the royal ancestors.

Demma, meanwhile, had sat down on the dais again. He began to speak in rapid Indonesian/Malay. He invited anyone who had a serious request to approach but warned those who just wanted to fool around to stay away. He continued to alternate chanting with ordinary speech for the next hour, while the women got on with cooking the meat.

By this time it was 3 P.M. Abdul Hakim and a fellow schoolteacher showed up unexpectedly in a state of exhaustion. They explained that they had never been to the shrine before and had spent the last hour hunting all over the bush for it. Because the food was cooked, everyone except the older women, Subu, and Demma ate. Demma refused to go on with the ritual until Hakim and his friend left, which they did after half an hour.

Demma then changed into a white blouse, took off his gold jewelry, and replaced it with "diamonds." He later told me that this meant a new spirit possessed him. This one was from Gowa. She was called Andi Karaeng and was the daughter of Karaeng Opu and his wife Andi Opu. All three names are in fact just combinations of royal titles. Opu is used mostly in Selayar, Andi is Bugis, and *karaeng* is Makassar. Andi Karaeng engaged Subu and his wife in an intense conversation while Subu kept some incense burning.

Meanwhile, Demma's elder sister Densa and the guide from Tanettang began preparing three small offerings on banana leaves. The offerings each included two mounds each of white, red, and black rice, a boiled egg, five betel leaves folded *deppo*, "squatting," corn husk cigarettes, raw yellow rice, and puffed rice. One was placed under the tree where the goat had been killed. One was put on the small dais in the enclosure, and one was carried out to the very tip of the point. Demma later told me that the one in the enclosure was for the child (Sampanena) of the chief spirit (Aru Cina), and the other two for its *anak angkat*, "adoptive children," although he would not name them.

At 4 P.M. Demma started laying out a quite elaborate offering on the dais. It included the usual two trays containing coconuts and bananas and plates of red, black, and white glutinous rice and of plain rice, each topped by a boiled egg. In addition, there were side dishes of chicken, goat, beans, fish, and eggs, a plate of sweets, including *songkolo* (a pudding made of rice flour, coconut milk, and palm sugar), and assorted fried cakes, a plate of cigarettes and betel ingredients, two glasses of coffee, and two glasses of water. It would seem that two spirits were expected to come partake of the offering. The offering was left for a moment, and then everyone closed in on it and started eating.

At 5 P.M. we all filed out to the place at the edge of the cliff where the female medium had invoked Sampanena's protection for the fleet in 1935. Subu carried a magnificent large cock. Demma had changed his clothes again and was now wearing a local sarong colored with somber natural dyes. He chanted as he walked unsteadily out to the point and had to be guided by his acolytes. There he danced a little, took hold of the cock, and squatted down. He stroked it and chanted to it until it went into trance. Its body became completely pliable and stayed in whatever position it was put. Then Demma began reciting a string of numbers to it. Subu held a piece of paper with what he thought would be the winning lottery number on it in his right hand. Finally, the cock was set down on the ground. If, when it came out of trance, it preened itself on the right, the number would win. If it moved its head to the left first, it would lose. We watched tensely for a few moments, and then it woke up and moved to the right. Everyone breathed out at once, *Ya, itu mau jadi* (I), "Yes, it will work."

We then went back to the enclosure. Demma put betel and *pinang* leaves into each of three deep depressions carved into a block of wood. This may well have been the block in which some of the egg-shaped stones observed by Collins had once been set. That was the end of the ritual. People packed up and made their way back to Tanettang, where the jeep picked them up and took them back to Ara.

Kasorang Gama

Rituals conducted at the water's edge are concerned with repairing a breach in the boundaries between natural or moral categories. As a concluding example of such rituals, I will describe a cult designed to cure diseases of the skin by appeasing the spirit of a giant crab that lives inside the cave of Kasorang Gama. According to some informants, this crab is responsible for causing—and, according to others, for curing—all manner of skin diseases: fungus infections, suppurating wounds that will not heal, and so on. If a person is afflicted with a skin disease, he or she makes a vow to give an offering to the giant crab if it heals the disease. With its hard and impenetrable shell, crabs are able to cross the barrier between land and sea with impunity. This makes them particularly appropriate symbols for rituals designed to repair damage to the skin, the boundary of the human body.

Abdul Hamid told me that, in the old days, the spirit of Kasorang Gama really did materialize as a crab three feet across, but that the grandfather of a man named Bolong had killed it just to prove that it did not really have supernatural powers. Now one can see only small crabs in the cave. Because Bolong is now a grandfather, the story must date to the 1920s or 1930s, to the time of a general campaign by Muslim purists against the spirit cults.

A *sanro* named Dia is one of the specialists in offerings at the Crab's cave. Her clientele comes mainly from the Dusun of Lambua and Pompantu, while the Kasorang Gama specialist for Maroangin and Bontona is called Deda Dongi. One morning, Dia led a procession of women down from the village to the beach and up into the cave. Deep inside the cave there is a small tree that grows from the sunlight let in through a small hole in the roof. Dia watched the tree carefully until she saw its branches move, indicating the presence of the spirit. She then took a leaf and placed it inside a coconut that had been split in half. She held the halves together and threw the coconut in the area, observing how it fell. On the first three throws the halves each fell "open," that is, with their concave surface upward. Finally, on the fourth throw, one half fell "closed" and the other open. This indicated that the spirit had been successfully induced to remain present to accept the offering, and she was able to begin.

The first step was to create a ritual simulacrum of a body into which the evil spirits causing the illness could be transferred from the body of the patient. The ritual body was constructed out of an egg, a coconut, and some bananas. These three articles are present in almost every ritual designed to influence spirits. Eggs are considered natural receptacles for spirits and are used to materialize them either to establish communications or, as in this case, break them off. The combination of coconuts and bananas is also used to create the simulacrum of a body, with the coconut as head and the bananas as rib cage.

The body was then placed in a small boat. A little boy was told to cast it away into the sea, carrying the sickness with it. As soon as the boat was handed over to the boy, however, it became irrelevant to the participants, and the boy was free to eat the offerings inside it before launching it. This procedure is often resorted to all along the coast of Sulawesi if people desire to expel spirits from a village (Nourse 1999). The model boats can be quite elaborate and may sail for long distances before washing up on a beach somewhere else. Whoever finds such a boat considers themselves lucky and will eat the offering without fearing that they are thereby absorbing the evil. An elaborate instance of such a ritual is described in chapter 9, where the intent is not to expel evil spirits but to bring a séance to a conclusion by providing an ancestor spirit and his entourage with a means of returning to the other world.

The next step was the preparation of an elaborate offering to the spirit of the giant crab. It consisted of the following materials:

1. Two boiled eggs on top of sticky white rice.
2. A dish of chicken curry.

3. A dish of chicken liver.
4. Four hands of bananas and a coconut.
5. A complete set of miniature home furnishings, skillfully woven out of palm leaves, which included a pillow, a blanket, a sleeping mat, a storage basket, and seven *pussa pussa*, figurines meant to represent humans.

The simulated home furnishings are similar to those given by a groom's family to the bride when a marriage is finally about to be consummated. They have a similar purpose—to provide the recipient with the means to lead a separate existence.

When the offerings had all been laid out on the floor of the cave, Dia began to mutter a spell while throwing handfuls of uncooked rice into the cave, toward the tree. She addressed the spirit as *bohe,* ancestor. She then had the patient and another man and woman throw some rice as well. The woven items were hung from a hook in the ceiling of the cave, next to some which were left over from a previous offering. The intent here was to invoke the spirit to descend into the cave so it could receive the offerings, but to then ensure that contact with it was broken off at the end of the ritual. The food offering was then packed up and taken home to be eaten by the participants.

In this ritual, the boundary of a supplicant's body has been undermined by spirits who have attacked its skin. Its integrity can be restored by appealing to the crab spirit, whose bodily boundaries are exceptionally strong and firm. In the rite of exorcism, the boundary of the body, the skin, is mapped onto the boundary of the land, the shore. The invasive spirits are induced to cross over both boundaries and into a newly constructed body, which is then sent away out to sea.

Conclusion: Boundaries, Transgression, and Sterility

I began this chapter with a set of myths in which the ordered exchange of sexual substances collapses. In these myths, normal hierarchies of age, rank, and gender are transgressed or collapsed. Sons marry mothers, subjects kill kings, and male bodies are occupied by female spirits and vice versa. These inversions short-circuit the normal flow of trade goods and marriage partners. This short circuit normally brings about disaster, but, handled correctly, it may be turned to the advantage of whoever can divert the flow to themselves.

Spirit mediums may avert these calamities by performing certain rituals on the water's edge. Surrounded by reefs and dangerous currents, the narrow peninsula that forms Ujung Lasoa acts as a portal to the Underworld for the whole east coast of South Sulawesi. Its reputation draws people from far and wide who seek cures, protection, or favors from its tutelary spirit. This spirit, Sampanena, is herself the product of a breach in the rules regarding gender, age, and marriage. Her conception opened up a dangerous but powerful hole in the boundaries between this world and the spirit world.

The first ritual discussed in this chapter was a ritual of exorcism, designed to expel the forces of death and infertility by pushing them across the boundary between the land/Middleworld and the sea/Underworld. The second ritual was intended to prevent the annual fleet from crossing this boundary by sinking into the sea. The third ritual was meant to open up a channel across the boundary between this world and the spirit world to thank the spirits for having bestowed good fortune on a petitioner in the past, and to request help in obtaining good fortune in the future. The good fortune in question was of the purely amoral, monetary sort that accrues to those who salvage a shipwreck. One does not go to the portal of Ujung Lasoa to seek fertility. The fourth ritual, like the first, was meant to send hostile spirits across the boundary and to close off communications between the two worlds.

Thus far, I have focused on the importance of seafaring and long-distance trade to the peoples of the Java Sea. These activities are marked in many ways as exclusively male activities. Only men go deep into the forest to fell trees for building boats. Woodcutters and sailors are likened in myth to the wild hunter-gatherers of the forest, the dark-skinned Oros, and to the wild hunter-gatherers of the sea, the Bajo sea nomads. The life of a wandering man is full of danger but also of opportunity for reaping the rewards of luck, skill, cunning, bravery, and strength. It is a life devoted to achieving wealth, fame, and the higher social rank that comes from marrying a well-born wife. Although the myths and rituals portray these activities on a heroic scale, in fact many men do set out to sea in their youth hoping to return with significantly increased social standing. The world of men, however, is only one half of the picture. We must now turn to the world of women.

Chapter 6
The Sea Prince and the Bamboo Maiden
Traces of Majapahit in South Sulawesi

I n the La Galigo myths discussed in chapter 4, the power of male rulers was based on their control of navigation and on trade goods extracted from the forests, seas, and mines. Women were present in these myths as the complementary opposites of the sea kings. They remained fixed in royal centers and communicated with the gods in the heavens. At the end of the La Galigo, the whole class of rulers returns to the Upperworld and Underworld, leaving humanity in a state of savage anarchy. Social conflict leads to disease and infertility in crops, domesticated animals, and women. In this chapter, I explore the historical and symbolic connections between women, agriculture, and kingship. Agriculture is symbolically female in contrast to the male activities of boatbuilding and sailing. Social rank and, hence, eligibility for political office was symbolically transmitted through women, although the occupants of most offices were men.

The royal foundation myths found throughout the province tell of a second coming of divine beings who bestowed social harmony and natural fertility on the people in exchange for feudal service. These myths vary depending on the location of the original pair of rulers. I explain these variations according to how closely an area was integrated into the regional system of maritime trade. In the inland Bugis kingdoms that developed around Lake Tempe around 1300, the origin myths attribute the foundation of the first kingdoms to entirely endogenous otherworldly beings that ascend or descend on a vertical axis from the Upperworld or the Underworld. In the coastal Makassar kingdoms and in the coastal Bugis kingdom of Luwu', the foundation of the kingdoms is attributed to an endogenous otherworldly female being who descends from the Upperworld and to a wandering prince who represents the chief worldly power of the time. The female being is associated with agriculture and the domestic arts, and the male being with long-distance trade and warfare. The terrestrial arts enjoy a higher ascriptive status, as indicated by the divine origin of the female founder, whereas the maritime arts allow for a greater degree of achieved status as indicated by the ability of a worldly male figure to marry a divine female, to settle in her domain, and to become a royal ancestor. I argue that these coastal myths indicate the growing hegemony of the Javanese empire of Majapahit in the region during the fourteenth century, exerting a cultural influence even stronger than that of its predecessor, Kediri.

In the first part of this chapter, I discuss the evidence for the origins of irrigated rice agriculture among the Bugis who lived along the shores of Lake Tempe in the thirteenth and fourteenth centuries. Fixed field agriculture enabled local rulers to extract larger amounts of tribute in the form of surplus rice. In Polanyi's terms, the local political economy was transformed from one of reciprocity to one of centralized redistribution (Polanyi 1957). A form of agrarian kingship appears to have arisen spontaneously in this area with little evidence of direct borrowing from Indic models in the royal foundation myths of these kingdoms. The political elites of these kingdoms did, however, depend on their ability to acquire for prestige goods from foreign sources by way of coastal intermediaries and some cultural influences must have penetrated along with them.

The Makassar kingdoms of the coast were more heavily engaged in long-distance trade. In the second part of the chapter, I discuss the evidence for the influence of the Javanese Empire of Majapahit on the kingdoms of the Makassar coast of South Sulawesi in the fourteenth century. Archeological and ethnographic evidence indicates the presence of a form of Shivaism in the area. I then discuss a number of Makassar foundation myths that have much in common with what Ras calls the "Malay Myth of Origin." In the Panji tales discussed in chapter 4, equal royal centers were tied together by the reciprocal exchange of men in marriage. In the Malay myth of origin, a peripheral kingdom allies itself with an imperial center by inviting a prince from the center to marry a local princess and to settle uxorilocally. Similarly, in the myths discussed in this chapter, a prince is born in a central kingdom and marries a divine princess in a peripheral kingdom. The relation between the two kingdoms is hierarchical. The myth restores a rough equality between center and periphery by balancing the political power of the husband against the divine status of the wife.

The Descent of the Kings: The First Inland States, 1300–1400

Caldwell and Macknight date the earliest origins of centralized agrarian states in South Sulawesi to the area around Lake Tempe in the thirteenth century (Macknight 1983: 99–100; Caldwell 1988: 180). At the time, the lake was much larger than it is today, forming a kind of shallow, freshwater sea. It gradually silted up over the centuries and has been reduced to three discontinuous bodies of water and a series of swamps (Pelras 1977: 139–142, 1996: 64; Bulbeck 1992: 9). It is precisely along the shores of such a lake that one would expect a transition from the cultivation of dry rice to wet rice to occur. Dry rice cultivation exhausts the fertility of the soil in a few years and requires a population to make new clearings in old growth forest on a regular basis. The fertility of the original clearings can only be restored after abandoning them to the forest for a decade or more. The seasonal inundation of the land bordering the lake by the monsoons would create the perfect conditions for sowing wet rice simply by broadcasting the seeds into the mud. The lake would shrink back to its original dimensions during the following dry season, allowing the rice stalks to ripen for harvest. The seasonal inundation of the land would have maintained soil fertility from one year to the next, allowing a dense population to occupy permanent settlements. Once the transition to wet rice agriculture is made in this way, it is relatively easy to take the next step of deliberately inundating fields by terracing the land, damming rivers, and digging canals.

During the fourteenth and fifteenth centuries, a shift took place in the balance of power from coastal chiefdoms to the inland kingdoms surrounding this lake. These kingdoms had access to much larger populations and agricultural surpluses than did the old coastal realms and began to exert a growing influence on their neighbors (Macknight 1983: 99–100). On the basis of his analysis of a number of early Bugis texts from kingdoms bordering the lake—such as Soppeng, Sidenreng, Cina, and Luwu'—Caldwell comes to the following conclusion: "With the possible exception of Luwuq, the emergence of the kingdoms of South Sulawesi appears to be largely unconnected to foreign technology or ideas. Unlike all other literate, pre-European-contact Indonesian societies, those of early South Sulawesi developed largely uninfluenced by Indic ideas, and the small number of Indic elements one does find are superficial and poorly assimilated" (Caldwell 1995: 403). This assessment appears to be particularly true of inland Bugis kingdoms like Soppeng, one of the earliest agrarian kingdoms in South Sulawesi.

Backdating from the first historically verifiable ruler of Soppeng, Bulbeck places the origin of the kingdom around 1280 (Bulbeck 1992: 475). The chronicle of Soppeng recounts the foundation of the kingdom as follows:

M 6.1 The Foundation of Soppeng

For seven generations, the people of Soppeng were without lords. Those whose ancestry could be traced to the age of Galigo were no more, and the sixty headmen alone ruled the land. Then our lord descended at Sekkanili. His appearance was made known by Matoa Tinco. The headmen gathered and went to beseech the one who had descended [*tomanurung*], saying,

"We take you as lord. You protect our fields from birds so that we do not lack food. You cover us so that we are not cold. You bind our rice sheaves so that we are not empty and you lead us near and far. Should you reject even our wives and children, we too will reject them."

They agreed to build him a palace, provide him with servants, open fields to grow crops for him, and not depose him wrongfully. After the agreement was made, the lord was carried in a procession to Soppeng, led by a great number of *bissu*.

When the people assembled to climb a hill and cut down trees for the palace, the *tomanurung* told them not to. A great storm came in the night and knocked down all the trees, and a flood washed them into the river. The people built a palace from the wood.

The *tomanurung* told them that his cousin had descended at Libureng and that they should submit to him as well. They found that he had descended in a great jar, from which he hatched. They made the same agreement with him: the Lord would protect the fields from birds and bind the rice sheaves, and the people would serve the Lord. (Condensed from Caldwell 1988: 109–112)

The notion that seven generations of anarchy intervened between the ordered society described by the La Galigo myths and the founding of kingship is a common one in South Sulawesi. It will be noted that kingship is conceived as a contract between the ruler and his subjects, whereby he provides them with agricultural fertility and they provide him with labor. The subjects must pledge to put loyalty to king over loyalty to kin.

The king's power and status are symbolized by the building of a palace out of trees that are cut down by a storm from the heavens. This process is reminiscent of the felling of the Welenreng tree in the La Galigo story. The king's symbolic power is thus based on his continued access to the power of the Upperworld, as mediated by an entourage of androgynous priests, the *bissu*. The first *tomanurung* is paired with a second, who appears to have an Underworld association in that he hatches from an earthenware jar. The latter reference may also allude to an association between kingship and imported porcelain goods.

A text recording the origins of kingship in Sidenreng contains four versions of this event. The first three accounts connect Sidenreng to a series of neighboring kingdoms, Tana Toraja, Rappang, and Luwu', while the fourth accounts for the conversion of the kingdom to Islam. No attempt has been made to make the different accounts consistent with one another. The first and third stories are of most interest for our purposes.

M 6.2 The Foundation of Sidenreng

1. There were nine brothers in Tanatoraja. La Ma'daremmeng, the eldest, abused the others so they decided to leave and live down in the plains in Sidenreng. They wandered until they came to the lake. They settled at the western end and agreed that the seven younger brothers would defer to the eldest. Later, a daughter of La Ma'daremmeng arrived with her husband. She was accepted as the first noble ruler, *a'daoang*. She had three children. At first, the eldest refused to be made *a'daoang*, saying, "I am poor and foolish." But he finally agreed. The people pledged to obey him, to cultivate the land and to build him a palace.

2. La Malibureng had eight children. The second youngest became the *adatuang* of Sidenreng. He had seven children. The second oldest became *a'daoang* of Sidenreng and married the daughter of the *pajung* of Luwu'. It was he who formalized the laws of Sidenreng, making an agreement with his

seven brothers, who were called the Ploughmen. They agree to fill his palace with servants; to give him a monopoly on the sale of salt, betel, and tobacco; to give him all uncanny people such as transvestites, dwarves, and albinos; and to pay a tax of five reals on all confiscated goods.

The seven headmen said, "It is our decision that only you are the great *a'daoang*. As for the contents of your palace, once they have gone up to the palace we shall have no further claim to them." [The *a'daoang* said,] "I alone send [goods] down [from the palace], it is also I who ensure that you maintain traditional law." (Condensed from Caldwell 1988: 144–148)

Here we encounter a number of common themes. In both stories, the original federation is composed of seven or eight siblings plus one who is placed above the others. In the first story, the second ruler is portrayed as inherently poor and foolish and so dependent on his subjects: the relationship between lord and subject rests on reciprocal rights and duties (compare M 3.6 and M 7.5). As in the chronicle of Soppeng, the primary service owed to the king is defined in terms of cultivating the land and building a palace. In the third story, the seven headmen are defined by their agricultural function, while the king is granted a monopoly on the sale of luxury goods. His extraordinary status is symbolized by his entourage of uncanny beings. The story concludes with a succinct state-ment of the principle of centralized redistribution: surplus from the entire kingdom is accumulated in the palace, and the king alone controls how it will be distributed.

In the neighboring Bugis realms of Suppa' and Bone, the rulers traced themselves back to male and female figures both of whom descended from the heavens (Caldwell 1988, cited in Bulbeck 1992: 474–475). Bone originated at the center of the broad plain that runs along the east coast of South Sulawesi around 1350. In 1400 it was still a tiny realm, no bigger than Bira. Under the long reign of its third ruler, the Arumpone Kerrempelua (1410–1482), it gradually absorbed its neighbors until it was about thirty-five kilometers from north to south and twnty-five kilometers from west to east. The fourth *arumpone*, We Banri Gau (1482–1512) purchased "the hill of Cina" from Katumpi'. This places the north-ern limits of Bugis territory at the Cenrana river by the beginning of the sixteenth century (Macknight and Mukhlis, n.d.), bringing Bone into contact with the ris-ing powers of Wajo' to the north, and of Soppeng to the northeast.

In summary, the ideology of agrarian kingship that arose in the fourteenth century is embedded in a set of Bugis foundation myths. In these myths, ordi-nary people are divided into quarreling factions, threatening the fertility of the earth, domesticated animals, and humans. The people encounter both male and female supernatural beings from the Upperworld called "those who have de-scended," or *tomanurung*. The common people beseech the *tomanurung* to be-come their rulers, reasoning that their divine origin will allow them to resolve disputes impartially, thus maintaining social harmony and biological fertility. The people arrange for their own *tomanurung* to marry a *tomanurung* who descended in a neighboring realm. In these foundation myths, kingship is based on a social contract in which rulers provide subjects with social harmony and fertility and subjects provide rulers with food, clothing, and shelter. The social world is composed of multiple agrarian kingdoms that are tied together through the intermarriage of their rulers.

Traces of Shiva on the Coast of South Sulawesi

As we have seen, Caldwell argues that there is little evidence that kingship in South Sulawesi was originally inspired by Indic and Javanese models. His skepticism about this influence is corroborated by the Bugis foundation myths just discussed, in which the royal ancestors have purely autochthonous origins. In the chronicles of the Bugis realms of Soppeng, Suppa, and Bone, both male and female founders descend from the sky. In the realms of Luwu', Cina, Wajo', and Ajatta-Parreng, the rulers trace themselves back to a male founder who descends from the sky and a female founder who ascends from the Underworld. In all these cases, the founders of Bugis kingdoms arrive on earth by traveling along a vertical axis.

But Caldwell also notes that even these inland kingdoms were heavily dependent on long-distance trade in the fourteenth century.

> What is certain is that at least by the fourteenth century the agricultural kingdoms of South Sulawesi were linked, probably via the north coast ports of Java, to places as distant as Thailand, Vietnam and China, and perhaps directly with the Southern Philippines (Macknight 1983: 95–96). The rise of the "southern" kingdoms of Ajatappareng, Wajoq, Boné, Soppéng and Makasar was closely linked to the centrally directed expansion and intensification of agriculture, although the remains of large numbers of high-quality celadon and blue and white ceramics at sites within Soppéng show that trade continued to form an important part of the economic basis of political life. (Caldwell 1995: 413–414)

Although it may be true that the kingdoms that arose in the interior of the peninsula were able to import foreign goods without importing foreign ideas, it was not true in the coastal kingdoms. To understand what was happening on the coast of South Sulawesi while the Bugis kingdoms were forming in the interior, we must return to developments in the Java Sea as a whole in the fourteenth century.

The rise of the first agrarian kingdoms in South Sulawesi coincided with the brief period of Mongol world hegemony. The Mongols defeated the last remnants of the Southern Sung dynasty in China in 1280, establishing the Yuan dynasty. In 1292, they launched an abortive naval expedition against Java to put a stop to Javanese interference in the straits of Melaka. During the same period, maritime trade in Southeast Asia was dominated by the Chinese, whose ships began visiting Maluku to trade for small quantities of cloves in the 1340s (Ptak

1992; Reid 1993: 4). They still probably did not themselves reach South Sulawesi, but their trade goods did in growing numbers, perhaps after passing through the hands of middlemen in the Philippines.

Then Chinese power suddenly collapsed in the fourteenth century, because of the bubonic plague. In 1331, 90 percent of the population of Hopei province died, and plagues followed in Fukien (Zaytun), in 1345–1346, and throughout southern China, between 1351 and 1360. The Mongols were so decimated that they were forced to withdraw to Mongolia in 1368. A native dynasty, the Ming, succeeded them. The Ming spent their first thirty-five years in power consolidating their hold on the north of China. Thus, between 1350 and 1402, Chinese imperial forces disappeared from the southern seas.

The vacuum in maritime trade created by the collapse of China was filled in the west by Gujarati merchants, who now began to sail directly to China. In the east, the new Javanese Empire of Majapahit now became a maritime power, expanding along the trade routes passing between Borneo and Sulawesi up through the Sulu Sea to Mindoro, Luzon, and Taiwan. Indic syllabaries and a certain amount of Sanskrit vocabulary probably diffused northward at this time all the way to the Philippines, perhaps carried by the Bugis and Makassar, who developed very similar syllabaries at this time.

Majapahit was founded in 1293 by Jayavadhana. Stability did not come to the new realm until Gaja Mada became its chief administrator in 1330. Over the next thirty-eight years, this capable man built up a remarkably centralized and powerful inland state. In 1365, the Emperor Hayam Wuruk ordered the chief of the Buddhist clergy, Prapanca, to compose a poem extolling his rule. In the resulting *Nagarakertagama*—royal chronicle of Majapahit—Prapanca claims as tributaries of Majapahit more than 100 overseas realms scattered around the archipelago on the islands of Sumatra, Malaya, Borneo, Sulawesi, Bali, Sumbawa, and numerous smaller islands; he recognizes as neighboring kingdoms such mainland states as Siam, Ayuthia, Campa, Cambodia, and Annam.

After the death of the chief minister, Gaja Mada, in 1368, Hayam Wuruk increasingly turned his attention to religious matters. The royal court of Majapahit portrayed itself as the product of a dynamic cosmic tension between the older Javanese kingdoms of Kediri/Wengker-Daha in the west and Singasari-Janggala in the east. Kediri was associated with Vishnu and the Underworld; Singasari with Shiva and the Upperworld; while Majapahit mediated between the two and controlled the Middleworld. Court ritual centered on the worship of dead kings as Shaivite or Buddhist gods; on the worship of Vishnu's consort Sri, who was the patron of agriculture; and on the worship of another avatar of Vishnu connected to rice. The Emperor also worked to integrate the cults of indigenous local spirits with the cult of the Indic world gods of the court. Shaivite, Buddhist and local priests known as *resi* each had a complementary role to play in rituals conducted outside the court centers at shrines located on the estates of local nobles (Hall 1996: 102–103). The *Nagarakertagama* describes in great detail the emperor's participation in local rites that invoked the ancestral spirits of provincial elites, thus integrating local priests into the imperial religious hierarchy. The standardization of ritual performance achieved during his reign is evident everywhere in east Java in the ubiquity of ritual water beakers dated between 1321 and 1430, but mostly dating to around 1350 (Hall 1996: 112).

Hall thus argues that the kings of Majapahit tried to co-opt village religion in the period 1350–1400 without suppressing regional differences. Village priests were recognized as masters of local chthonic forces, while the court asserted control of celestial ritual. The court acknowledged these chthonic forces both in court rituals and during annual royal progresses around ritual sites located throughout the realm. These annual circuits created a sense of shared historical experience that was the basis for Majapahit's central place in Javanese historical memory. Even so, villagers continued to maintain a degree of local ritual autonomy. Rural shamans, *jangga*, officiated over worship of the rice goddess at the village level but were deliberately excluded from the system of royal ritual. Thus, in the Empire of Majapahit, royal legitimacy was based on periodic rituals in which the king and local priests mediated between the Middleworld and the Upper- and Lowerworlds.

There are several sorts of evidence that Majapahit exerted some degree of economic, political, and religious influence on coastal South Sulawesi, including the integration of local spirit cults into the central royal cult. First, the *Nagarakertagama* lists the Sulawesi dependencies of Majapahit as follows: "[Of] the countries of Bantayan [that is, Sulawesi], the principal is Bantayan, on the other hand Luwuk, then the countries of Uda, making a trio; these are the most important of those that are one island, altogether. Those that are (enumerated) island by island (are): Makasar, Butun, Banggawi, Kunir, Galiyao and Salaya" (Pigeaud 1960: 17). The identities of most of these places are not in dispute: On the Sulawesi mainland, Bantayan is Bantaeng and Luwuk is Luwu'. Of the smaller islands, Butun is Buton, Banggawi is Banggai, and Salaya is Selayar. The referent of Uda is less clear, although Pelras suggests Southwest Sulawesi.[1] Makasar may be any of a number of small islands where "Makasar" people lived. It has now been established that Galiyao refers to the Galiyaoi Watang Lema alliance of the islands of Alor and Pantar (Barnes 1982; Dietrich 1984; Rodemeier 1995). As far as I am aware, the identity of Kunir remains uncertain.

Second, the earliest historical chronicles and genealogies in South Sulawesi begin some time in the fourteenth century as writing was adopted. Because writing was introduced at the very time Majapahit was extending its reach to Sulawesi, however, Majapahit seems the most likely source for it.[2] The royal chronicles of all the major kingdoms of Luwu', Gowa, and Bone trace the origins of the ruling dynasties back to the early fourteenth century, when Majapahit's influence was at its height. The chronicle of Bira asserts that the concept of "*karaeng*ship" was introduced by a shipwrecked prince of Majapahit, I Ma'rakki Kalapaya (reigned circa 1350; see chapter 7).

Third, there are signs that new techniques of terracing and irrigation spread from Majapahit that made wet rice agriculture possible in the relatively hilly lands of the Makassar coast. The rise in population densities that this made possible would have allowed the kingdom of Bantaeng, centered at Lembang Cina, in a rice plain near the coast, to dominate its older rivals, centered on hills immediately to the west and to the east (Bougas 1998: 90).

Finally, the cult of Shiva promoted by the emperor of Majapahit seems to have made a deep impression all along the Makassar coast. As the centralized agrarian kingdom of Bantaeng came to dominate the older mercantile chiefdoms in the area, new forms of court ceremonial borrowed from Majapahit were probably introduced. Archeological evidence of this influence appears in the form of graves oriented on an east-west axis all along the Makassar coast, a burial form found nowhere else on the peninsula but common in Java (David Bulbeck, personal communication). Terra-cotta figures have recently been unearthed at some of the older sites in eastern Bantaeng. They were found buried with their heads pointing to the east in the same way as humans were in the same period, although they were not found in the human graves themselves. They have many features similar to those found in terra-cotta figurines produced in Majapahit (Bougas 1998: 98). Thus, they may represent another instance of a synthesis of local spirit cults and the imperial religion of Majapahit.

In light of this recent archeological and historical work, it is worth reassessing some of the claims made by nineteenth-century Dutch authors for Javanese influences on Makassar myth and ritual. Bantaeng remained the center of a cult of a spirit called Karaeng Lowé well into the nineteenth century. toe Water was the first Dutch author to remark on this cult. He claimed that, when the annual ceremony in honor of Karaeng Lowé was celebrated during the month of August, "no native of this district will undertake, except by force, a sea voyage" (toe Water 1840: 587). The missionary Donselaar later gave a more detailed account of this key feature of the cult. He wrote that an annual feast was held at the shrine of Karaeng Lowé in Gantarang Keke, a settlement high on the slopes of Mount Bawakaraeng. The feast lasted for eight days, during which time no boat was allowed to leave the coast of Bantaeng and Bulukumba, because the spirits of neighboring islands sailed to Gantarang Keke to attend the feast and one risked colliding with them. Offerings of gold were placed in the attic of the shrine, where they mysteriously disappeared. Donselaar concludes, "Further offerings of foods are also made, meals are held and outings organized, which not rarely, according to the national character, end with a bloody riot *(amok)*" (Donselaar 1855: 180).

Another Dutch missionary, Goudswaard, devoted a great deal of effort to the study of this cult during his ten years in Bantaeng ministering to the colony of mixed race Indo-Europeans that had grown up around the Dutch garrison since the 1730s. Because the members of this cult were neither Muslim nor Christian, Goudswaard claimed that these descendents of Dutch soldiers were among the most devoted adherents of Karaeng Lowé's cult. Goudswaard noted that the feast in honor of Karaeng Lowé was held not in August as such, but in the month following Ramadan. By his time, there was no longer any special taboo on sea voyages during the festival.

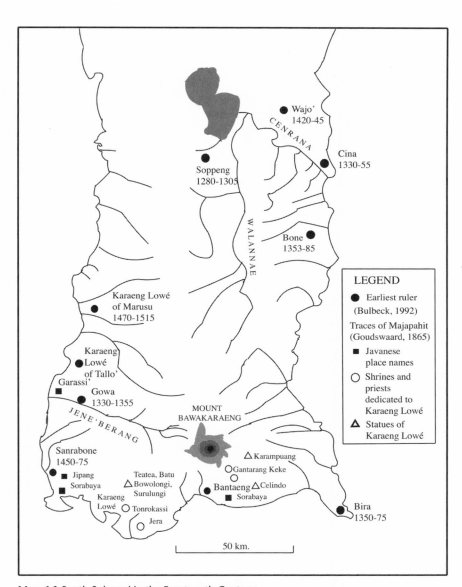

Map 6.1 South Sulawesi in the Fourteenth Century

After many attempts, Goudswaard was finally able to visit the central shrine of the cult in Gantarang-keke. He described it as follows:

> In the middle of the chamber stood a little miniature house, a copy of a royal dwelling, provided with a royal stairway. Around the little house a klamboe was stretched, which had once been white, and various *pabongka setan* [repel-

lers of demons] attached to it. With tense expectation I sat down before the palace. The curtain was opened and I saw there nothing but an oblong box, in the form of an ordinary rather large music box. Now the pinati went in front of the stairway, made a sumba, and then dared to open the box and show me its contents for the day to witness. What was in it? Nothing but four objects, two of which were Japanese porcelain jugs decorated in blue, one of which was half filled with water and the other a quarter full of oil; and two black stones which I must describe further. The first stone was oval, about two palms long, thicker at one end than the other, exactly in the shape of a carrot from which the tip has been cut. The other stone was a flat, round oval, the greatest length of which was about 1 1/2 palms and the greatest breadth 1 palm. In the middle of this was an indentation and was provided with a groove which had apparently been made with a sharp instrument. (Goudswaard 1865: 88–89)

Goudswaard argues throughout his article that the *lingga-yoni* stones found all along the coast of South Sulawesi are evidence of a cult of Shiva and his consort and that Karaeng Lowé, the Great Lord, is the local name of Shiva, and he traces the origin of the cult back to Majapahit (Goudswaard 1865: 93–94).

In 1883, a Dutch colonial officer called Kooreman noted that the *gaukang* (royal regalia) of Bantaeng was a golden Hindu statuette (Kooreman 1883). The following year, another Dutch official, Englehard, agreed with Goudswaard's argument linking Karaeng Lowé to Shiva and Majapahit. He went on to note that

[One] finds the worship of Karaeng-Lowé along the whole south coast of South Celebes, from Bira to the Turatea lands. Further, local histories make mention of Karaeng-Lowé ri Bajeng and Karaeng-Lowé ri Galimporo, who reigned respectively in the present districts of Polombanking and Bangkala, and who lived around 1400 or earlier. Further, among the divisions of the Gowan realm, Karaeng-Lowé ri Sero is named as the first ruler of Tallo', while his brother Batara-Gowa remained lord over the realm proper. . . . Finally mention is made of Karaeng-Lowé-ri-Marusu (= Maros) whose daughter married Tu-nipasulu-ri-Tallo', son of Tu-nilabu and great grandfather of the celebrated Gowan chancellor Karaeng Patingaloang. (Englehard 1884a: 394)

Englehardt continues:

If one now takes a look at the areas where Karaeng-Lowés have been or are still found . . . one sees that without exception they are all situated along the coast, never in the mountains such as the subdivision of the Mountain regencies and Bikeru, and that all, without exception, are situated in a more or less fertile terrain, that of a valley or river mouth, separated from each other by a mountain ridge or inhospitable or stony part. (Englehard 1884a: 395)

We may safely conclude, then, that the title of Karaeng Lowé, found all along the coast of South Sulawesi, represents a trace of Majapahit's influence in the area in the fourteenth century.

The fourteenth-century Javanese expansion sparked a qualitative shift in the organization of many states in South Sulawesi, particularly those lying along the sea lanes. The process by which new centers of power were established in response to changes in the mode of agricultural production and in the flow of long-distance trade is reflected in the origin myths of the ruling families in these areas.

Traces of Majapahit in Royal Foundation Myths

The foundation myths that link the origin of kingship in South Sulawesi to the Javanese empire of Majapahit show marked similarities to dynastic foundation myths found in the opening passages of royal chronicles all around the Java Sea. Unlike the inland Bugis foundation myths discussed earlier in the chapter, however, in these coastal myths the divine being who descends from the sky in a bamboo tube is always a woman, and she is discovered not by a local man but by a prince associated with a powerful overseas kingdom. The factionalized local people approach and implore these two exotic beings to rule over them. They agree to do so in exchange for food, housing, and servants. After engendering a race of white-blooded nobles, the founding ancestress withdraws again into the sky, often to descend again elsewhere and establish another royal center.

This narrative is a transformation of the one Ras identified as the "Malay Myth of Origin."

M 6.3 The Malay Myth of Origin

[The] purport of this Malay myth of origin was to symbolize, by the marriage of the princess from the foam to a prince who descended from heaven, the creation of a union between two opposite cosmic elements: the waters (the nether world) and the sun (heaven). This first marriage is followed by a second one in which the son of the first couple is married to a princess who has emerged from bamboo. Since the latter princess may be considered as a daughter of the earth, the entire myth must be assumed to have symbolized a threefold union involving the cosmic elements of sun, water and earth, and which was effected in two successive stages. This mythical union was represented as the origin of the local royal dynasty and, by extension, that of the entire community. (Ras 1968: 98–99)

He concludes his extensive analysis of the transformations the Hikayat Banjar underwent as follows:

The stories contained in the Salasilah Kutai, the Rama tale and the Pandji tale all centre around two successive marriages and may all be interpreted as symbolizing the union of the earthly community with that of the ancestors in heaven and the union, on a lower level, of the two moieties which together constitute the earthly community. They are therefore intrinsically equal to each other. This explains how the Bandjarese story could so easily be changed from a pseudo Rama-tale into a pseudo Pandji-tale. Since, however, the societies in which these stories circulated were strongly conservative, it is likely that two other conditions would have to be fulfilled for adaptations such as those seen in the case of the Hikajat Bandjar, namely recognition of the cultural superiority of the foreign society from which that parallel tradition originated and the presence of a sufficiently strong motive. (Ras 1968: 155)

The superior foreign society in question was that of the royal courts of Java, and the motive in question was a political one. At a certain point in history, the court of Banjarmasin found it politically expedient to portray itself as linked to the regional power of Kediri and Majapahit.

Ras suggests that the stories found at the beginning of the chronicles of the western Malay kingdoms of Sumatra and the Malay peninsula represent remnants of an original "Malay myth of origin" that lost its function as a charter for ritual at an early point in history. "Once the connection between a myth and a corresponding ritual is severed the myth becomes a story, a legend like any other, and it becomes much more prone to changes and corruptions in the course of time than would otherwise have been the case" (Ras 1968: 97).

Variations of this myth are found all along the trade routes that stretch from Aceh in the far west of the archipelago to Maluku in the far east (compare Traube 1980, 1986; Hefner 1985; Nourse 1999). In most cases, the local version of the myth makes some attempt to link the local dynasty to both the Upperworld and Underworld and to the fourteenth-century Javanese Empire of Majapahit, which is taken to represent the most powerful center of the Middleworld. In the following discussion, I will begin with Ras's discussion of the foundation myth of Kutai in eastern Borneo, followed by a discussion of three myths from the Gulf of Bone and another two myths from the south coast of South Sulawesi.

Majapahit and Coastal Borneo

Ras found what he regarded as the most complete versions of the Malay myth of origin among the Ngaju of South Kalimantan and in a text from Kutai in East Kalimantan. In both cases, it had preserved its integrity by serving as a charter for a set of rituals that continued to be celebrated into the twentieth century. I have already discussed the Ngaju at some length in chapter 3. I will use Ras's summary and analysis of the Kutai myth as the starting point for my analysis because it contains in a single narrative most of the elements that appear in a fragmentary form in the foundation myths of the coastal kingdoms in South Sulawesi.

M 6.4 The Foam Princess and the Bamboo Maiden (Kutai)
Aji Batara Agung Dewa Sakti is born from a golden bowl that is lowered by seven gods from heaven. It is received by the chief of Jaitan Layar and his wife

who must hold the bowl on their laps for forty days and nights before a boy emerges holding an egg in one hand and a keris in the other. Meanwhile, the chief of Hulu Dusun splits a rafter of his house for firewood and finds a snake inside. He rears it with his wife until it is very big, when it descends into the river and churns it into foam. The princess Karang Melenu is born from the foam, lying on a flat gong, which lies on a naga, or mythical serpent, which lies on an ox with tusks, which in turn stands on a stone. After five years, a series of initiation rituals is performed for them: the first walking on the ground *(tijak-tanah)*; the first bathing in the river; headhunting to obtain human sacrifices. At the end of the rituals, Karang Melenu is carried on the head of her ox to the palace. Aji Batara stages a series of cockfights, first with a Chinese king who arrives at Jaitan Layar, then in Brunei, Sambas, Sukadana and Matan.

When he is grown, Aji Batara Agung has a dream about whom he is to marry. His fighting cock escapes and after a long chase arrives at the house of Karang Melenu. Aji Batara marries Karang Melenu. They have a son, Paduka Nira. Karang Melenu forbids Aji Batara to engage in any more cockfights, but he cannot resist and rides the ox to Majapahit. Shortly thereafter, Karang Melenu drowns herself in the river. Aji Batara Agung follows her to his death in the river.

When Paduka Nira reaches adulthood, he has a dream that he is to marry a princess who emerges from an exploding bamboo. He soon receives reports that the princess Paduka Suri was indeed found in an exploding bamboo by the hunting dogs of the chief of Bengalon, who is also childless. She was swaddled in silk and held an egg containing a female chick in her left hand and a hollow golden tube in her right. Paduka Suri agrees to marry Paduka Nira after he proves he is equal to her by being able to wear her jacket and ring. They have seven children, including five sons (Maharaja Sakti, Maharaja Surawangsa, Maharaja Indrawangsa, Maharaja Dermawangsa, and Maharaja Sultan) and two daughters (Raja Puteri and Dewa Puteri).

After the death of Paduka Nira, the youngest son, Maharaja Sultan, is proclaimed king; the other brothers become ministers. A ship arrives from Muara Kaman with the king Maharaja Indra Mulia. Maharaja Sakti, Maharaja Sultan, and Maharaja Indra Mulia are chosen to go together to Majapahit to study the *adat*. They travel by air through the heavens and the seven spheres. Upon their return, Maharaja Sultan undergoes a proper royal installation (condensed from Mees 1935 and Ras 1968: 81–83)

Ras notes that the chronicle of Kutai is unusual in that it preserves two generations of marriages, in the first of which a woman arises from the sea foam and in the second from the earth within a bamboo. Most chronicles from the western part of the archipelago collapse these two marriages into a single marriage between an earthly prince and a princess who emerges either from the foam or from a bamboo (Ras 1968: 88).

The first generation narrates the marriage between an ambivalent male figure holding an egg and a keris (female and male symbols) who is contained in a round golden object from the sky (the sun) and an ambivalent female figure who arises from the river resting on a water snake and an ox. Thus, although both have androgynous aspects, they are also from opposite worlds. The prince wins the princess and riches through the magical powers of his fighting cock. After completing his mission of giving birth to an earthly son and founding a local royal house, the male figure finds himself irresistibly drawn to the center of cosmopolitan civilization, Majapahit. The emperor of Majapahit was seen as an avatar of the Hindu Sun Gods Vishnu and Shiva. The local female figure despairs at this and returns to the watery Underworld from whence she came, drawing the male figure down after her.

In the second generation, their son combines the Upperworld and the Underworld. He marries a maiden found in the middle of the forest by a hunter. The maiden is contained in a bamboo tube rooted in the soil. She is also androgynous in that she holds in her hands both a round egg, pregnant with new life, and a phallic tube, much like her father-in-law.

In the third generation, the youngest son becomes ruler and his four brothers become ministers or advisers. This introduces the distinction between territorial lord and master of speech, which we will also find among the Makassar in chapter 7. It also introduces the widespread symbolism of a central element surrounded by four others that was first noted by van Ossenbruggen ([1918] 1977). Once this structure is in place, the local king sets out to acquire cosmopolitan knowledge from Majapahit, returning to create a replica of the center on the periphery. The ruler's claim to legitimacy thus rests on both his connection to the sky, the water, and the earth and his ties to the imperial center of Majapahit.

Ras rejects the notion that parallels between the origin myths of kingdoms located throughout Indonesia are to be explained solely in terms of borrowings from literary sources. He argues instead that as each dynasty came to write down a history of its origins, it drew on a protomyth common to the whole area. But the existence of a common cosmological framework throughout western Indonesia did facilitate the communication of certain modifications and elaborations to the basic theme. Thus, the modifications identified by Ras in Borneo that link refined kingship to Majapahit are also found in South Sulawesi, but only in areas that were directly exposed to maritime trade in the fourteenth century. There appear to have been two separate centers in South Sulawesi from which the new ideas about kingship diffused: the Bugis kingdom of Luwu' at the north end of the Gulf of Bone and the Makassar kingdom of Bantaeng on the south coast.

Majapahit and the Gulf of Bone

Unlike the purely endogenous origins of the founding royal ancestors of the inland Bugis states discussed in the first part of the chapter, the founding myth of Luwu' shows clear signs of having followed models derived from Majapahit.

As we saw in chapter 4, Luwu' long served as a link between the maritime world of Panji and Sawerigading, on the one hand, and the inland peoples of central Sulawesi, on the other. The version of Luwu's founding myth that I will discuss is taken from Caldwell. Caldwell notes that this text is probably just a small fragment intended to help in the recall of a much more elaborate oral tradition in which the various rituals would have been discussed in greater detail.

M 6.5 Simpurusia and We Patia'jala (Luwu')

1. Simpurusia descends from the celestial kingdom of Botillangi' in a bamboo tube and marries We Patia'jala, "She who was caught in a fish net," who arises from the sea foam. They have one daughter. Her mother promises her in marriage to two different first cousins. Upset, Simpurusia uses incense to travel to the Upperworld and ask the Creator's advice. He is told to make a duplicate daughter by taking the placenta that accompanied his daughter from a jar and placing it in a Garuda basket, of the sort used by *bissu* to seek contact with spirits.

2. Simpurusia also has a son, Anakaji, who becomes ruler of Luwu'. He marries We Tappa'cinna, the daughter's daughter of the *tomanurung* of Majapahit. We Tappa'cinna's mother gives her three gifts: incense, sacred oil, and a yellow silk thread. When she is insulted by her mother-in-law, We Patia'jala, she uses the gifts to magically cross the ocean back to Majapahit. Her husband follows and promises to place her interests before those of his parents. There she is given some heavenly soil that descended from heaven with her grandfather and brings it with her to Luwu', where she remains.

3. Anakaji has a son, To Panangi, who becomes ruler of Luwu' [reigned circa 1475–1500]. They also have a daughter, We Mattengngaempong, "Middle of the Sea," who becomes Queen of the Crocodiles. She marries La Tuppusolo Acang Kuling, who is from Uriliung, "the Bottom of the Ocean." They have a daughter, Da La Ia, who goes to live with her father in his underwater realm.

4. We Mattengngempoang has a son, La Malalae, who is inconsolable at the departure of his sister. He is finally allowed to visit the Underworld for nine nights. He is given three magical objects: a headdress worn by *bissu*, a clay incense holder, and a musical instrument played at birth rituals. The censer is carried up by a female *bissu*, We Demmikoro, who remains on earth. (Condensed from Caldwell 1988: 42–47; see also Kern 1929)

In the Simpurusia myth, a constant commerce is maintained between the Middleworld, the Upperworld, and the Underworld and between distant centers in the Middleworld. Like the La Galigo stories, the Simpurusia myth clearly functioned as much as a charter for a number of rituals surrounding the births and marriages of royal children as it did as a charter to legitimate the local dynasty.

In the first generation, a man from the Upperworld and a woman from the Underworld marry and live on earth, one might say neolocally. A mistake on the part of the wife causes the husband to return to the Upperworld by means of in-

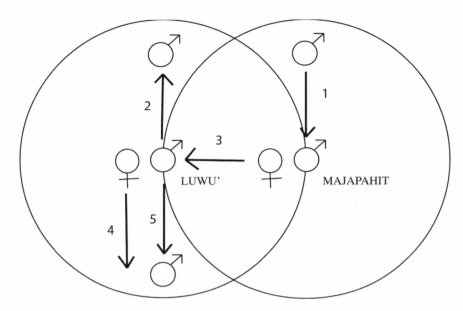

Fig. 6.1 Simpurusia's Marriage to We Patia'jala.

cense. He is taught how to channel the power of the Creator downward through a bird basket into a placenta, thus bringing to life a twin daughter, who is associated with the sky.

In the second generation, a man brings a wife from across the sea from Majapahit to Luwu'. A mistake on the part of his mother causes his wife to return home by means of three magical objects: incense, oil, and a yellow thread. The husband persuades her to come back, but, before she will agree to live permanently in her husband's house, she must become its undisputed mistress. He swears to disown his parents if they insult her again, and she brings some soil back with her from Majapahit, symbolically transforming a virilocal marriage into an uxorilocal one. She is thus associated with the earth.

In the third generation, a woman from the Middleworld marries a husband from the Underworld. She is known as the Queen of the Crocodiles, creatures who live on the boundary of the land and water. They have a daughter and a son but fail to settle on a permanent residence and separate, each returning to their natal home.

In the fourth generation, a woman follows her father to the Underworld while her brother remains on land with his mother. After much begging, he is allowed to visit his sister in the Underworld. Like his mother, the Queen of the Crocodiles, he can cross the boundaries between land and water. In the Underworld, he is given three magical objects for use in ritual—a costume for dancing, an earthenware holder to burn incense, and an instrument to play music. His sister is associated with the sea.

To summarize, a man descends from the Upperworld in a bamboo tube and marries a woman who arises from the foam. He later visits the sky world for advice. Their son remains in Luwu' and marries a woman from across the sea. She later visits there for advice. Their daughter marries a male figure from under the sea. Their son remains in Luwu' but later visits the Underworld, where he is given ritual instruments to maintain contact.

The narrative connects the founding rulers of Luwu' to the Upperworld, the Underworld, and the most powerful center of the Middleworld, Majapahit. In this myth, it is men who act as *bissu*, traveling between the three worlds on a vertical axis. It is women who act like sailors, crossing and recrossing the sea on a horizontal axis. In these respects, the myth is an inversion of the story of Sawerigading the sailor and his sister We Tenriabeng the *bissu*.

Caldwell notes that the names of the characters in the Simpurusia myth differentiate it from the names found in the royal genealogies of inland Bugis kingdoms like Cina and Soppeng. In the latter texts, one only finds personal names that

> contain elements reflecting the concerns of a settled agricultural community: genealogical names are, furthermore, closely linked to inland settlements, many of which can be identified on modern maps. We do not find more than the barest hint of a world outside the agrarian kingdoms of South Sulawesi.
>
> The names of the Simpurusia legend are, however, more like those of the I La Galigo. These may be characterized as referring to natural phenomena, such as thunder, lightning and storm, or features of the natural landscape. Reference to water is frequent. . . . The names of the [Simpurusia myth], coupled with the crocodile queen, underwater kingdom and aquatic elements of the proto-Malay myth of origin (cf. Ras 1968), produce a vivid impression of a coastal and riverine world very different from that provided by the names found in the genealogies, with their emphasis on agricultural activities and the minutiae of everyday life in an inland, farming community. (Caldwell 1988: 36-37)

As a coastal state dependent on maritime trade, Luwu' had more in common with the Makassar coast of South Sulawesi than with the Bugis interior. Both areas were more heavily influenced by Javanese models than the inland kingdoms were.

Luwu' and Toraja

Luwu's hinterland was the mountainous region of Toraja. Although the Toraja never formed a centralized kingdom on the same scale as the Bugis, they did link their ruling families to those of the lowlands.

M 6.6 Laki Padada and the Princess of Gowa (Toraja)
Laki Padada is represented in several genealogies as a grandson of Timboro Langi', one of Toraja's most famous *to manurun*. His father, Puang Sanda Boro,

married a woman whom he discovered inside a bamboo; she was called To Bu'tu ri Pattung (One Who Appeared from a Bamboo), or Puang Ao' Gading (Lady of the Bamboo). She gave birth to two children—a son, Laki Padada, and a daughter, Puang Mate Mangura or Puang Mate Malolo (both names mean Lady Who Died Young). Distraught at his sister's death, Laki Padada vowed to travel the world in search of the secret of eternal life. His journeys eventually brought him to the Makasarese kingdom of Gowa. There, after many adventures, he married the ruler's daughter. Of their three sons, one, Pattala Merang, became the ruler of Gowa. The second, Patala Bunga, became the ruler of Luwu', and the third, Patala Bantan, returned to Toraja and married Petimba Bulaan (Golden Dipper), variously depicted as the daughter or granddaughter of Manaek, founder of *tongkonan* Nonogan in Sanggalangi' district. Pattala Bantan went to Sangalla' and ruled over that part of Toraja known as the Tallu Lembangna, or Three Districts of Ma'kale, Sangalla', and Mengkendek. These southern districts formed a federation, the closest Toraja ever came to emulating the centralized kingdoms of the lowlands. Later descendents of Laki Padada are said to have married into the royal family of Bone. (Waterson 1997: 67–68)

This myth is a transformation of the Simpurusia story in which Laki Padada plays the role of the *tomanurung*'s son Anakaji and Gowa plays the role of the distant empire of Majapahit that supplies him with a wife. In this case, however, it is a woman who descends in a bamboo. It is also a transformation of the Sawerigading myth in which the hero spends his life in the quest to be reunited with his sister. In this respect, Gowa plays the role of Cina, supplying the hero with an acceptable substitute as a wife. As we will see in the next chapter, Laki Padada also appears in Gowa's own foundation myth, but there it is his brother Karaeng Bayo who marries the princess of Gowa.

The Foundation of Kajang

The foundation myth of Kajang appears to refer to the time when this part of the Gulf of Bone was under the control of Luwu'. The following version was told to me by Abdul Hamid, a noble from Kajang who married into Ara.

M 6.7 Lady River and Lord Sea (Kajang)

Once a man, Pu' Temparang (Lord Sea), was fishing in the sea with a cast net. He cast it out, but all he pulled in was a bamboo internode. He threw it away, and again caught only the bamboo. Again and again he threw it away, but it kept coming back. Finally, he gave up and took the bamboo home. There he put it next to the clay water jar. That night and for several nights thereafter he would wake up to hear someone shivering from the cold, but he could not figure out where the sound was coming from. Then one day he happened to move the bamboo on to a rack above the fireplace. After that, every night he heard someone complaining about the heat. Finally, he realized that it was the bamboo that had been first cold near the water then hot near the fire. So he placed it next to the loom.

Every morning Pu' Temparang and his wife went off to work in the fields. When they returned in the evening, they found that the cloth on the loom was much longer and that all the drinking water had been used up. After three days, the piece of cloth was almost finished. The husband decided to pretend to leave, but to then creep back to spy on the mysterious weaver. He looked through a chink in the wall and saw a beautiful woman sitting in the room. Her name was Pu' Binaga (Lady River). He leaped inside and grabbed her, telling her he was going to marry her. She agreed, but warned him not to be surprised if their children turned out to be peculiar. They had four children:

1. *Tu Kale Bojo*, The One with a Melon's Body. This child had no limbs and was perfectly round. He became the ruler of Lembang Lohe in Kajang.
2. *Tu Tentaya Matana*, The Cross-Eyed One. He became the ruler of Na'nasaya, Place of the Sandalwood, in Kajang.
3. *Tu Sapaya Lilana*, The One with a Cleft Tongue. He became the ruler of Kajang proper.
4. *Tu Kaditili Simbulena*, The One with a Small Hairknot. This was the only daughter, whose hair was so kinky that her hairknot was only the size of a candle nut. She became the ruler of Tana Toa.

After the children were born, Lady River vanished and reappeared in Bone. There she married and had seven children, who became the rulers of the seven realms that provided the electors *(hadat)* of the *arumpone*, Lord of all Bone. She then went to Luwu', where she had six children, who became the first electors of Luwu'. Finally, she went to Gowa where she had nine children, who became the first electors of Gowa.

The Bamboo Princess in this story is a universal mediator between the three worlds: Abdul Hamid called her a *tomanurung*. Before the myth begins, she has thus descended from the heavens to a bamboo growing on the land, from the land to the sea by way of a river, much like rainwater.

After she is caught by Lord Sea, Lady River reverses her original journey through the three worlds. She ascends from the sea to the land and is placed in the middle level of the house. She then completes the whole cycle again on a microcosmic scale. She ascends from a low, cold position near the clay water jar to a high, hot position above the hearth until she comes to rest in the middle next to the loom. At the end of the myth, she ascends again to the heavens, completing the macrocosmic circuit.

At the beginning of the myth, Lord Sea is already married. His first wife goes out each day to work in the fields producing subsistence crops, a low-status occupation. His second wife, Lady River, remains indoors to weave cloth, a high-status female activity. Cloth is one of the paramount items in long-distance sea trade. The export of trade cloth from the house complements the import of fish and foreign princesses into the house. At this level, the myth is a meditation on the need to balance two forms of marriage. Marriage to a local woman of low status provides for domestic subsistence, whereas marriage to a foreign woman of high status provides access to trade goods.

Before Lord Sea can actually unite with her, the exotic Lady River must be domesticated by a process of cooling, heating, and weaving. She is already well established in the center of the house when Lord Sea discovers her identity and declares his intention to marry her. Even so, she remains quite alien in nature, pointing out to Lord Sea that, if they marry, their offspring will be peculiar. As in the foundation myth of Gowa, the offspring of the union between a goddess and an earthly lord are uncanny (see M 7.1). Their four children are all deformed, although in declining degrees. The first has no limbs, the second defective eyes, the third a defective tongue, and the fourth defective hair. Despite their physical defects, the uncanny children of Lady River are so potent that they are chosen to rule ordinary humans all over the peninsula. As noted in chapter 3, myths that account for the origin of a class of idle nobles in terms of their descent from a child who is born without the ability to care for himself and becomes dependent on a sibling are found widely in South Sulawesi (compare M 3.6).

A transformation occurs between the foundation myth of Kajang and that of Toraja. The Kajang myth traces the origin of all of the great kingdoms back to a single woman and multiple husbands. After the *tomanurung* of Kajang returns to the Upperworld, she descends again three more times, founding the kingdoms Gowa, Luwu', and Bone. This is an inversion of the foundation myth of Toraja, in which a single man, Laki Padada, marries multiple local wives and fathers the first rulers of Gowa and Luwu' as well as of Toraja.

Both Toraja and Kajang have always cut rather minor figures on the political stage of South Sulawesi. But they have always enjoyed a reputation throughout as places of great, and potentially dangerous, mystical power. Kajang's reputation carried forward into the Islamic period. Of the three Sumatran saints who converted South Sulawesi, the eldest settled in Luwu', where he converted the first king; the middle settled in Gowa, where he induced the ruler to enforce the shariah law by the sword if necessary; and the youngest settled just south of Kajang in Tiro, where he taught the inner, mystical aspect of Islam, the *tarekat*.

Majapahit and the Makassar Coast

We saw above that, by the 1350s, the Majapahit cult of Shiva had been adopted all along the Makassar coast under the name of Karaeng Lowé. By 1400, Majapahit's overseas networks had collapsed and its role as exemplary center had been taken over by its former peripheral vassals. For the Makassar people, the paramount royal center in the fifteenth century was Bantaeng. The foundation myth of Bantaeng will thus serve as the starting point for my discussion of Makassar royal foundation myths.

In 1865, Goudswaard published the following version of a local legend "which concerns the origin of the seven offering places of Karaeng Lowé" in Bantaeng.

M 6.8 Bungko and the Prince of Java (Bantaeng)

Seven orphaned sisters live under the care of the eldest. The youngest, Bungko, has the job of collecting firewood in the forest each morning. One day she catches a *julung-julung* [*Zenarchopterus dispar.,* an edible sea fish with a long sharp snout] while bathing in the river. She decides to keep it as a pet in a basin in the cave of Celindo-lindo. She feeds it half her rice every day and it soon grows to a great size. She sings it a little song each time she visits it: "*Julung-julung* come up; eat rice from a stone plate that is washed in milk."

Bungko grows very thin. Concerned, her sisters follow her. The next day, they send her to another forest while they go to the cave, sing the song, catch, cook and eat the fish. Bungko goes to the cave later and finds the fish missing. She returns home grief-stricken and covers herself with a sarong. A cock crows to her: "The bones of your *julung-julung* fish are hidden under the hearth." She digs them up and reburies them in the cave, saying: "You must grow up to be a tree, and your leaves must fall on Java, which the king of Java shall pick." The bones do grow into a tree, the trunk of which is made of ivory, the blades of silk, the thorns of iron needles, the blossoms of gold and the fruits of diamonds.

When the tree is big, one of its leaves falls on Java. The leaf is brought to the king. When he sees it, he decides to go in search of the tree from which it came. He sails to Bantaeng, and while hunting in the forest accidentally comes upon the tree. He calls all the inhabitants together to find out who owns it, but no one knows. Last of all, the king has Bungko brought to him. As soon as she appears the branches lower themselves down so low that little children can pick them. Now the king knows whom the tree's real owner is. Bungko offers him some leaves and fruit. He is so touched by this gesture that he takes her as his wife. He takes her and her sisters to Java, but they all return shortly afterwards to Bantaeng.

The eldest sister settles in Gantarang-keke; the second at the shrine which houses a golden statue of the *karaeng* at Bantaeng; the third at Bisampole; the fourth at Bontorappo in Binamu; the fifth at Karang-batu; the sixth at Karam-puang; and the seventh at Celindo-lindo.

Upon separating, they agreed the eldest will give a feast once a year which all the people of Bantaeng must attend, and that the six other sisters would permit their people to come to her whenever they wished. (Condensed from Goudswaard 1865: 96–99)

The founding ancestress is here associated with the Underworld, via her attachment to a sea fish that is kept in a basin of water in a cave. She gradually transfers half her bodily substance to the fish by feeding it half her rice. The fish is further transformed by being cooked on the hearth. When its remains are buried in the earth, it grows into a magical tree that produces all manner of prestige trade goods such as gold, ivory, diamonds, and silk, very much like the Ngaju Tree of Life. The tree is thus in a sense a transformation of the young girl herself, who sacrifices her own bodily substance to bring forth a magical plant. In this she resembles the Bugis goddess of rice, Sangiang Serri. Sangiang Serri was the daughter of Batara Guru, the first god to descend to earth. She died only three days after birth and was the first divinity to be buried on earth. A few days later, Batara Guru visited her grave only to discover that it had been overgrown by different kinds of rice (Kern 1939: 37–38; Pelras 1996: 90).

The beauty of the tree draws a prince outward from the royal center of Majapahit toward the peripheral realm of Bantaeng. But the branches of the tree define Bantaeng as the sacred center of the world and reposition Majapahit on the periphery. Because the rulers of Majapahit were identified in court ritual with the sun gods of the Hindu pantheon and the maiden from Bantaeng is identified with the sea and the Underworld, their union can also be seen as a union of the Underworld and the Upperworld.

When the maiden offers him the fruits of her tree, he accepts and takes her back to Java as his wife. This attempt at virilocality fails, and the couple settles uxorilocally in Bantaeng with her six sisters. This is an inversion of the foundation myth of Luwu' in which the royal couple is able to settle virilocally. After an initial failure, the princess converts her husband's house into an outpost of Majapahit by bringing some of its soil, and after she displaces her mother-in-law within the household. In both cases the question of who is to preside over the household is resolved in favor of the woman.

Bantaeng and Bangkala

The realm of Bangkala lies just west of Bantaeng along the Makassar coast. The Dutch controleur Goedhart published the following version of its foundation myth:

M 6.9 Banri Manurung and Karaeng Lowé (Bangkala)
Bangkala was once divided into many small realms each governed by a Kare. One day, a strange man and woman appeared in Kalimporo, the realm furthest to the east. They said they were beings who had descended from the sky *(tomanurung)* and were accepted by the local people as kings. Their title of Karaeng Lowé made them the equals of the Karaeng Lowé of Bantaeng, Katingang, Bajing, Maruso, Bone, and Luwu. The people of all the little realms came to pay them tribute.

Their daughter married Karaeng Paurang, son of the Karaeng Lowé of Bantaeng. One day Karaeng Paurang went hunting in the forest of Ujung Moncong. One of his followers told him he had seen a beautiful young woman while following his dog. Karaeng Paurang looked for her, but found only a fingernail and some human hair. Then he saw a *patung* bamboo, from which human hair of the same color protruded. He called out: "If someone is in this bamboo, come out and show yourself. Otherwise I'll cut the tube in two." A beautiful young woman emerged called Banri Manurung [The Gold that Descends]. She declared that she had descended from heaven. Karaeng Paurang immediately asked her to marry him, and she agreed.

When the Karaeng of Kalimporo heard that Karaeng Paurang was going to marry again, he offered to sponsor a great marriage feast. Banri Manurung advised Karaeng Paurang to accept the invitation. When he admitted to her that he had no followers to accompany her to Kalimporo, she wet her hair and sprinkled a large number of *patung* bamboos with the water. Men soon emerged from them. Then she sprinkled blades of grass with the same water, and women came into being. They went to Kalimporo with these men and women in their train, and were festively received by the *karaeng*.

Right away Banri Manurung observed that her husband's father-in-law had fallen in love with her. She told her husband to flee with her back to where she had been found at Ujung Moncong in Bangkala. The local chiefs of Ujung Moncong and Patiro asked them to become their kings and settled near them with their dependents. When the *karaeng* of Kalimporo came to attack them, he was defeated.

Bangkala became a great power, while Kalimporo's prestige declined. The settlements of Garasikang and Palengu withdrew themselves from the authority of the Karaeng Lowé of Kalimporo and later became autonomous *karaeng*ships. The name Kalimporo was altered to Tanatowa, and the title Karaeng Lowé ri Kalimporo became Karaeng Tanatowa. Thus were constituted in ancient times the *karaeng*ships of Bangkala, Tanatowa, Garasikang and Palingu. (condensed from Goedhart [1920] 1929: 312–313)

In the first generation of this myth, a male and a female figure descend and are accepted as Karaeng Lowé by the people of Kalimporo. Their high status is confirmed by the marriage of their daughter to Karaeng Paurang, the son of the Karaeng Lowé of Bantaeng. In this regard, Bantaeng plays the same role Majapahit played in the foundation myth of Bantaeng, that of a powerful realm that provides a suitor for a local princess. Karaeng Paurang marries uxorilocally in Kalimporo.

After Karaeng Paurang marries the daughter of the *tomanurung* of Kalimporo, he discovers another supernatural being in a bamboo tube growing out of the earth. The Karaeng of Kalimporo also desires the bamboo maiden for himself, but the maiden favors Karaeng Paurang, despite his poverty. The maiden's power over biological reproduction is so great that she can produce a whole crop of people by sprinkling water from her hair onto different sorts of grass. Hard *patung* bamboos produce men, and soft blades of grass produce women. They escape back to Bangkala where the maiden first emerged. Thus, Karaeng Paurang marries uxorilocally a second time, moving steadily west from his origin in Bantaeng.

The union of Karaeng Paurang and Banri Manurung represents a union between the sky and the earth. Together they are more powerful than the pair of *tomanurung* who descended in Kalimporo, both of whom are linked only to the sky.

Conclusion: The Sea Prince, the Heavenly Maiden, and the Bamboo Tube

Generally speaking, the coastal kingdoms of South Sulawesi traced themselves back to a union between two figures: a prince from a powerful kingdom who sails from across the sea and enters the local forest and a woman who is discovered in the forest inside a bamboo or under a tree and holding a magical object. The tree is an axis mundi that links the three worlds and defines the center of a realm. The local people, often represented as followers of a set of seven same-sex siblings, recognize the prince and the princess as overlords and settle around the central palace/tree. In exchange for feeding, sheltering, and protecting the king and his successors, the kings guarantee the fertility of all the crops, animals, and people within the realm.

The Sea Prince: The Precedence of Majapahit

In his analysis of the historical transformations the Malay Myth of Origin underwent in Banjarmasin, Ras convincingly demonstrates that when borrowings from Hindu mythology occurred, they were mapped onto a preexisting western Austronesian cosmological scheme. Thus, the figure of Shiva/Rama or even Iskandar could take the role of the sun god without fundamentally altering the structure of the myth.

A similar process occurred in South Sulawesi. The already established myth of a male *tomanurung,* perhaps associated with the sun, seems to have been fused with aspects of the Javanese cult of Shiva in the fourteenth century. Rulers all along the south coast linked themselves to Shiva under the name of Maheswara, Sanskrit for "the Great Lord," or, in Makassar, Karaeng Lowé. Because of the association between Shiva the Sun God and Majapahit at the peak of its maritime power, the figure of Karaeng Lowé at the trading colony of Bantaeng was able to condense in himself the powers of both the Upperworld and the Overseas Empire. Thus, it is sufficient for Karaeng Lowé or his son to find and marry the figure representing the Underworld for all the main oppositions contained in the protomyth to be preserved.

The western Makassar realms recognized the precedence of Bantaeng as the center of long-distance trade, whereas Bantaeng linked itself to Majapahit. There are indications that the early dominance of Bantaeng was based on a special relationship with the Bajo sea nomads. In myth 4.4, Johari of Ara traced the origin of Gowa to a marriage between a queen of the Bajo and a local king of Gowa: the Bajo hatched from eggs that tumbled out of the Welenreng tree and became the servants of Sawerigading's daughter. They sailed with her as far as Gowa, where she married a local lord. This inverts the story found in Gowa's foundation myth (M 7.1), which traces Gowa's origin to a *queen* of the Bajo who arrives from the east and marries a local king. But in both cases, the foundation of the kingdom required the collaboration of a local agrarian realm and a people adapted to the sea.

The Bamboo Maiden: The Precedence of Local Women

The foundation myth of Luwu' is similar to the Makassar myths in many ways. Like many of the Makassar myths, the Luwu' myth traces its foundation back to one ancestor who descended from the sky in a bamboo tube and to another ancestor who was from Majapahit. But in the case of Luwu', the ancestor from Majapahit was female and the local ancestor who descended in a bamboo tube was male, the opposite of the Makassar myths.

The precedence of local women over foreign men in the foundation of kingdoms is clear in all the Makassar myths. Although the princess who plants a magical tree or who is found inside a bamboo is immobile and appears to play a passive role, in fact it is she who chooses her husband and pulls him inward toward a new center of power. Bungko of Bantaeng deliberately plants her tree to attract the prince of Majapahit. Banri Manurung of Bangkala leaves a trail of fingernails and hair for the prince of Bantaeng to find and chooses him over his more powerful father-in-law. Lord Sea of Kajang repeatedly tries to discard the bamboo tube he finds, but Lady River keeps returning to his net. The message is clear: men may be the masters of the forest and the sea, but women are the mistresses of the household and by implication of terrestrial kingdoms.

The same is not true for the Bugis. In addition to the cases of Luwu' and Toraja just discussed, we saw at the beginning of the chapter that the Bugis kingdoms of Soppeng, Suppa', and Bone were all founded by a pair of male and female figures who descended together from the Upperworld. Bulbeck notes that the Bugis kingdoms of Cina, Wajo', and Ajatta-Parrang were all founded by male figures who descended from the Upperworld and female figures who ascended from the Underworld (Bulbeck 1988: 474). In all these cases, the power of the founding king derives from his local descent, not from his ties to powerful foreign kingdoms. The male and female principles are either not contrasted at all or are contrasted on a purely vertical axis.

This difference between the inland and the coastal kingdoms may be explained in terms of the relative importance of trade and agriculture in the two cases. Bugis kingship originated largely for endogenous reasons through the gradual intensification of agriculture in the swamps of the interior. Makassar kingship evolved out of maritime chiefdoms as intensified trade with Majapahit introduced Hindu Javanese ideas of kingship and perhaps wet rice agriculture as well, first to Bantaeng and then to Jene'berang delta, where Gowa later developed.

Androgynous Ritual Objects

Bamboo tubes often serve in the myths as a means of communication between the Upperworld and the Middleworld. They also appear as symbolic me-

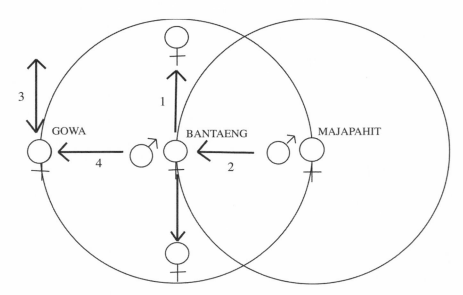

Fig. 6.2 The Sea King's Marriage to the Bamboo Maiden.

diators in many rituals. Thus, bamboo is used to make palanquins that convey a groom to the house of his bride and a corpse from the house to the grave; it is planted in the earth to receive blessings from the sky at rituals held at the navel of the earth to honor the royal regalia or to install new kings; and it is filled with clay pellets to make sacred rattles. This recalls the general symbolic point made in chapter 3, that male-female pairs always appear in myths as part of a triad in which the third element is an androgynous ritual object with both male and female characteristics.

In chapter 3 I discussed a myth in which a white-blooded princess engendered solely by Adam marries the son of a serpent and a peacock (M 3.4). Commenting on this myth, Hamonic remarks, "In Bugis country itself, the union of a serpent and a bird evoked here cannot fail to bring to mind those two ceremonial objects used by the *bissu* priests, the *arumpigi* and the *alosu* (instruments made of long tubes of bamboo filled with little fragments of porcelain or pottery). The *bissu* priests shake them during their ritual dances in a fashion which imitates a bird who pecks. The body of these bamboo objects represent in effect a serpent, while the head and tail represent those of a cock or calao" (Hamonic 1983: 39). A similar symbolic object is central to the ritual of the royal regalia performed in Tanaberu (chapter 9). This magical object has the body of a stiffened snake, symbol of the Underworld, and the head of a bird, symbol of the Upperworld. The *bissu* are themselves androgynous: men who dress and live as women.

More generally, we might note, as have many cultures from New Guinea to the Amazon, that a hollow tube is capable of representing both phallus and

CHAPTER	MALE	ANDROGYNOUS	FEMALE
3. Cosmos	Sun	Earth	Moon
4. Sea	Sawerigading	Boat	We Tenriabeng/ We Cudai
5. Shore	Maroangin	Sampanena/ Shaman	Aru Cina
6. Land	Lord Sea	Bamboo tube	First wife/ Lady River

Fig. 6.3 The Three Genders of Austronesia.

vagina, both *lingga* and *yoni,* at the same time. In the form of an upright bamboo stem, the hollow tube also unites the three levels of the cosmos. It serves as a universal mediator, bringing together the powers of the three worlds and authorizing the origin of divine kingship. Bamboo thus condenses in itself all three worlds and both genders. Like the *bissu* priests, bamboo embodies an androgynous, mediating power, both active and passive.

Androgynous Totality in Austronesia

To summarize the argument so far, a fundamental aspect of Makassar symbolism is the conceptual scheme that life and power are generated through the interaction of three genders—an active male principle, an attractive female principle, and an encompassing androgynous principle. This scheme is found throughout the myths analyzed in the first half of the book.

In chapter 3 we saw that the Austronesian cosmos begins when a male being from the Upperworld and a female being from the Underworld come violently together to produce an androgynous Middleworld. In chapter 4 we saw that a male twin, Sawerigading, accepts the need to separate from his female twin when she provides him with a boat that will enable him to substitute his cousin for her as a wife, thereby reproducing an alliance between separate royal houses. In chapter 5 we saw the consequences of asymmetric incest, even when it is inadvertent: drought, disease, shipwreck, and infertility. The union of the son and the mother still produces a benevolent third being, however, their daughter Sampanena. She is female, but when she takes possession of a male spirit medium they form a hermaphroditic whole that can reverse evil effects of the original union, bringing health and good fortune to her devotees. In chapter 6 we saw the way the institution of kingship transformed the equal exchange of cousins between noble houses into a an asymmetrical relationship between a royal center and a noble periphery when a prince from Majapahit is united with a local maiden found inside an androgynous bamboo tube.

Chapter 7

The Sea King and the Emperor
The Gunpowder State of Gowa-Tallo'

I n this chapter, I describe the process by which the dual kingdom of Gowa and Tallo' rose from being just one among a number of competing principalities along the Makassar coast to hegemony over all South Sulawesi. It did so by adopting a number of new military, agricultural, maritime, informational, and administrative techniques and by astutely manipulating the existing symbolic system. The royal houses of Gowa and Tallo' incorporated rival royal houses through a process of military conquest; political and marital alliances; and the formation of a variety of tributary relationships.

The Expansion of Gowa, 1300–1605

The domination achieved by Majapahit over the Java Sea proved short-lived, and this may account for the relative superficiality of Hindu influences on the Makassar coast as compared with Java and Bali. Majapahit's center was weakened when a factional war broke out between its western and eastern halves at the beginning of the fifteenth century. Majapahit's control of its maritime periphery was then undermined by an initiative undertaken by the third ruler of the Ming dynasty, Yongle, who came to the throne of China in 1402. His control of the Chinese mainland was secure enough to allow the Chinese state to direct its attention to foreign trade for the first time since the plagues of the early fourteenth century. It was at just this time, however, that Timur was completing his conquests in central Asia (1370–1405). The disruptions of the central Asian trade routes caused by these conquests prompted Yongle to outfit a series of six expeditions into the South Seas between 1405 and 1432. They were commanded by a Muslim eunuch named Zheng He (Cheng Ho).

Each Chinese expedition consisted of hundreds of ships and thousands of men. They spent long periods refitting in the ports of east Java. Many Muslim Chinese stayed behind and married Javanese women, leading to a "creative melding of Javanese and Chinese maritime technology" along the coasts (Reid 1993:

39). On his first voyage, Zheng He recognized Melaka on the Malay Peninsula as the legitimate heir to Srivijaya, China's ancient trading partner in the area. Melaka soon replaced Majapahit as the chief naval power in the Java Sea. During the fifteenth century, Malay merchants began to build and sail cargo ships as large as 1,000 tons, chiefly to China, Maluku, and the Coromandel coast of India, but also as far west as the Maldives, Calicut, Oman, Aden, and the Red Sea. In the early sixteenth century, the Portuguese transcribed still vivid memories in Melaka of earlier voyages to lands as distant as Madagascar (Manguin 1993: 199).

Influenced by Muslim merchants from north India, the ruler of Melaka converted to Islam some time between 1411 and 1436. This conversion marked the culmination of a long-term shift in cultural influence in Island Southeast Asia from the Hindu-Buddhist cultures of South India to the Islamic cultures of North India and the Middle East. The power of the Hindu Chola state in South India had been in decline since the twelfth century, whereas the power of the Muslim Delhi sultanate in North India had grown in the same period. Delhi was in direct control of the maritime region of Gujarat from 1303 to 1398 and left behind a Muslim sultanate after it withdrew. In the fifteenth century, growing numbers of Muslim Gujaratis began to trade in Southeast Asia, displacing the Hindu Tamils. As the Indian Ocean basin as a whole became a Muslim lake, many Hindu rulers along the north coast of Java followed Melaka's lead and converted to Islam.

Then, in 1453, the Ming dynasty suddenly withdrew from direct involvement in maritime trade. The sultanate of Melaka was able to call on its prestige as the heir to Srivijaya, the recognized partner of China, and one of the first kingdoms to convert to Islam to assert its preeminence in regional trade and diplomacy. But by the end of fifteenth century, it appeared that the more populous Islamic states of coastal Java were about to reassert the hegemony Majapahit had enjoyed in the fourteenth century. The ruler of Japara outfitted a huge war fleet to attack Melaka. The fleet included sixty ships averaging 350 to 500 tons each, but some reached 1,000 tons and carried a thousand men.

Java's conquest of Melaka never occurred, however, because of the sudden appearance of a new power in the Indian Ocean, the Portuguese. From the time of Cabral's expedition in 1500, the Portuguese declared their particular hostility to Muslims in the Indian Ocean and their willingness to ally with Hindu rulers against them. The royal council in Lisbon commissioned Almeida in 1505 to establish fortifications around the Indian Ocean to cut off the Muslim spice trade to the Red Sea. In 1509, he succeeded in destroying the combined Mameluk and Gujarati fleets off Diu. In 1510, D'Albuquerque took the island of Goa from the sultan of Bijapur in the Deccan and the Malay port of Melaka in 1511. The Portuguese reached Ternate, in the Spice Islands, in 1512 (Chaudhuri 1985: 68–69). In 1513, the Japara fleet that had been built for the conquest of Muslim Melaka was used against Portuguese Melaka instead, but it was entirely destroyed by the superior firepower of the Portuguese (Manguin 1993).

The Portuguese thought that they could monopolize the spice trade by simply taking and holding Melaka. When they occupied it in 1511, however, many Muslim merchants simply shifted to the nascent sultanates of Aceh in north Sumatra and Banten in west Java. Despite numerous attempts, the Portuguese failed to conquer Aceh. They then attempted to blockade the entrance to the Red Sea to prevent spices reaching the markets of the Middle East and, through them, of rival Italian merchants. Although still outgunned by the Portuguese, Muslim vessels soon learned to outrun the Portuguese patrols. By the time Ala al-Din Ri'ayat Shah al-Qahhar (reigned 1539–1571) began his reign as sultan of Aceh, the pepper trade had not only recovered, but had reached new heights. "From the 1550s European dealers began to note that pepper was once again available in substantial quantities in Alexandria and Italy" (Chaudhuri 1985: 75). Acehnese pepper shipments reached a peak during the 1560s, when at least five large ships from Aceh were reportedly arriving in the Red Sea each year (Reid 1975: 46). The Portuguese became just another player on the local scene, albeit one with certain technological advantages.

Bantaeng and the Origins of Gowa, circa 1300

The decline of Majapahit's influence in the eastern part of Indonesia was accompanied by the decline of Luwu' and Bantaeng as local powers in South Sulawesi. The rise of Melaka in the western part of Indonesia was accompanied by the rise of a new kind of kingdom on the west coast of South Sulawesi, the twin kingdom of Gowa and Tallo'. Like its Bugis counterparts, Gowa first developed as an inland agrarian kingdom around 1300. We have two sources for the early history of Gowa, a Chronicle written for its own rulers, and a Chronicle written for the rulers of the neighboring kingdom of Tallo'.

One version of the Gowa foundation myth was first published in 1855 and reprinted by van Eerde in 1930:

> **M 7.1 The Tomanurung and Karaeng Bayo (Gowa)**
> A heavenly maiden descends from the Upperworld to the forest in Gowa. A man from Bantaeng called Karaeng Bayo [King of the Sea Nomads] enters the forest with his men in search of wood to build a boat. After cutting the trees they need, they climb the hill of Tingi-mae to begin work. Then they are seized with a great thirst. They can find no water on the hill until a dog returns, wet and covered in mud. Karaeng Bayo follows it to a spring in a garden at the center of which is a palace. Inside he sees a woman sitting on an ivory throne, under a multicolored roof inlaid with jewels. Karaeng Bayo casts down his eyes but the woman says she had chosen him of all mortals to be her husband. The Tomanurung gives birth to a son called Massalanga-bairayang and disappears back into the clouds. Her son becomes the first king of Gowa. (Condensed from van Eerde 1930: 820–821)

As in the foundation myth of Bangkala (M 6.9), a dog leads a wandering prince from Bantaeng to a bamboo maiden in a forest. In this case, he is a sailor in search of wood, not a hunter in search of game. As in the Bangkala myth, the maiden is associated with water. As in the Bantaeng myth, she is associated with fabulous treasures. This version of the story ends with the birth of her son, Massalanga Barayang. This name means "he with the crooked shoulders," or "hunchback."

The version of the chronicle of Gowa published by Matthes tells the story of the *tomanurung* as follows:[1]

> Tumanurunga took as a husband Karaeng Bayo, the father of Tumassalangga Baraya[ng]. The reason she was called Tumanurung by the people of ancient times was because it was not known [whence] her origin was and the manner of her passing on; it was said only that she disappeared.
>
> She was married by Karaeng Bayo. We also do not know Karaeng Bayo's country [of origin], we know that he was brother to Lakipadada; who was the owner of [the sacred sword] Sudanga.
>
> Karaeng Bayo married the Tumanurung, and I Massalangga Baraya[ng] was born. Three years he was in the womb. When he was born he could walk and talked right away.
>
> But his father and the people all sorrowed and shouted, "He is deformed!"
>
> The reason he was called Tumassalangga Baraya[ng] was because his shoulder was high on one side and low on the other, and his ear on one side was knoblike and broad on the other, the soles of his feet to the length of his heels were twisted to the front, his navel was as big as a *baku'-karaeng,* a king-size basket, and that is why he was called the Deformed One. (Wolhoff and Abdurrahim [1960]: 9)
>
> But his mother said: "Why do you say that my son is a misshapen man? For his shoulders are *barayang* shoulders, his ears are flanking mountains; a hair snapping in Java he hears; a dead white buffalo in Selayar he smells; the white spot of a leech in Bantaeng he discerns; his feet are like scales; his navel is a great well; his hands are hollowed-out extremities; when they scoop they have taels of gold; when they scoop they fold *karoa'* cloth, when they scoop they let his men walk in multitudes. (translated by Noorduyn 1991: 464–465)
>
> When her child had grown, her necklace was cut into two parts. One part was set for the child, then she entered into a room and disappeared [with the other].
>
> The chain that remained was called I Tanisamanga.
>
> Nothing is known concerning the wife Tumassalangga Barayang and the manner of his passing on. The old people say only that he disappeared. He said to the people "Stay here." Then he went toward the northern mountains of Jongowa. A thunderbolt crashed and rain fell on a hot day, and he disappeared from sight. (Wolhoff and Abdurrahim [1960]: 9)

One purpose of this version is to account for the origin of the most important regalia of Gowa: the Sudanga sword and the Tanisanga chain. As we saw in chapter 6, the Toraja people claim the original owner of the Sudanga as their ancestor. In chapter 8, I discuss a protracted civil war that resulted in Gowa when the Sudanga and the Tanisanga fell into the hands of rival claimants to the throne. Another purpose is to position Gowa as the successor to the maritime kingdom of Bantaeng. As in the myth of Bangkala, a prince from Bantaeng marries uxorilocally in the west. His son retains an association with the older maritime realms of Majapahit, Selayar, and Bantaeng through his deformed body. According to his mother, Tumassalanga Barayang's head is designed for hearing, smelling, and seeing what goes on in those distant realms. His body is designed for dealing in prestige trade goods: gold bullion, cloth, and servants.

Division and Unification: Gowa and Tallo', 1450–1535

The "historical" part of these chronicles of Gowa and Tallo' begins with the generation born between 1425 and 1450. According to the chronicle of Gowa, the sixth ruler of Gowa, Tunatangka Lopi, divided the kingdom between Batara Gowa and his brother, Karaeng Lowé ri Sero (Wolhoff and Abdurrahim [1960]: paragraph 16). According to the chronicle of Tallo', however, Karaeng Lowé ri Sero was the rightful ruler of the entire realm. This is the version contained in that chronicle:

> ### M 7.2 The Foundation of Tallo'
> This is the story of the ancestors of the people of Talloq. Tunatangkalopi had a child, Karaeng Loe of Sero. After Tunatangkalopi died, his part [of the kingdom] was taken [by Karaeng Loe, who] then lived in Sero. The two brothers quarreled. [Karaeng Loe of Sero] went over to Java. A portion of the *gallarrang* went to his older brother, to Batara Gowa. For example, Tomboloq-keke, Saumata, Borongloe, Pacciqnongang, Pao-Pao. Those [*gallarrang*] who did not go were not summoned [by Batara Gowa]. They lived waiting for their *karaeng* [Karaeng Loe of Sero]. Arriving back from Jawa, Karaeng Loe of Sero learned that not all the people had been taken by his older brother. He went to dwell on the north side of Bangkalaq [at a place] called Passanggalleang. After some time there, one of his *gallarrang* built a ship. After the outrigger was finished he rowed out to the river mouth. . . . [He later told Karaeng Loe] "I went out, my Lord, to the river mouth to look around, and it would be good for us to build a settlement there, because here is a bad location, neither on the coast nor in the mountains." Then the *karaeng* agreed. . . . We do not know how long [Karaeng Loe lived or ruled] and we also do not know of his wives. These are the words of I Daeng of Buloa, named I Kanrebajiq. (Translated by Cummings, 2002: 81; compare Manyambeang and Mone 1979: 7–8)

As Cummings points out, the chronicler here is aware that his information about the founder of Tallo' is insufficient to follow what has become a standard account of a king's reign, such as the marital alliances he formed.

As we saw above, Karaeng Lowé's very name, meaning Great Lord or Shiva, associated him with the older Javanese civilization of Majapahit, the one that gave rise to an entire belt of Shaivite cults along the south coast of South Sulawesi. The coastal region of Java into which Karaeng Lowé ri Sero ventured was one that was fast converting to Islam. Karaeng Lowé was succeeded by his son, Tunilabu ri Suriwa, who confirmed the kingdom's maritime orientation by marrying princesses from the coastal states of Garassi' and Siang, and from Surabaya in Java. He died while sailing to Manggarai in about 1500 (Cummings 2002: 82). He was succeeded as ruler of Tallo' by his son Tunipasu'ru'. The latter was also a great sailor who visited Johore and Melaka before the Portuguese conquest in 1511. The chronicle of Tallo' thus emphasizes the maritime orientation of the kingdom from its very inception.

While Karaeng Lowé was shifting his palace to the coast, his brother, Batara Gowa, was consolidating his hold on the inland kingdom of Gowa. He then made a move toward the sea by marrying a daughter of the *somba* of Garassi', the realm at the mouth of the river on which Gowa was located. As an indication of Gowa's rising power and prestige, the throne of Garassi' passed through the *somba*'s daughter to one of her sons by Batara Gowa. Because rank and office pass bilaterally to the highest-ranking offspring of a marriage, it was possible for a very high-ranking lineage like that of the royal house of Gowa in the sixteenth century to absorb titles from its lower-ranking affines. Garassi' disappeared as a distinct political force, and the capital of Gowa was later moved to Somba Opu, in Garassi'. The title of the ruler of Garassi' was downgraded from *somba* to *karaeng,* and the title of *somba* was henceforth reserved for the ruler of Gowa.

Batara Gowa was succeeded by a son, Tunijallo' ri Passuki', who died without heirs about the same time the Portuguese captured Melaka in 1511. He was succeeded by his half brother, Tumapa'risi Kallona. According to the chronicle, Tuma'parisi Kallona's mother was a slave given in tribute by a camphor merchant. His ability to take and retain the throne is thus a testament to his great personal charisma. Soon after he was installed as ruler, Tumapa'risi Kallona exchanged sisters in marriage with his cousin, Karaeng Tunipasu'ru' of Tallo'. Their sons and grandsons reaffirmed the alliance in subsequent generations by also exchanging their sisters in marriage. Such an exchange also expressed the exact social and political equality of the two houses, because women were never allowed to marry men of lower rank.

Meanwhile, a third Makassar power was developing to the north, in Siang, where many Malays had settled after the Portuguese capture of Melaka. Between 1520 and 1535, a struggle developed between Gowa, Tallo', and Siang over control of the mouth of the great Jene'berang River at Garassi. About 1520, Tallo' seized Garassi' from Gowa. Around 1530, Siang seized it from Tallo', and in about 1533, Gowa seized it back again from Siang.

From this point on, it became clear that Gowa was threatening to become the hegemonic power in the area. Around 1535, Tallo' formed an alliance with the coastal states of Marusu' to the north and Bajeng to the south to attack Gowa. Tumpa'risi' Kallona defeated this alliance in a great battle with the help of his

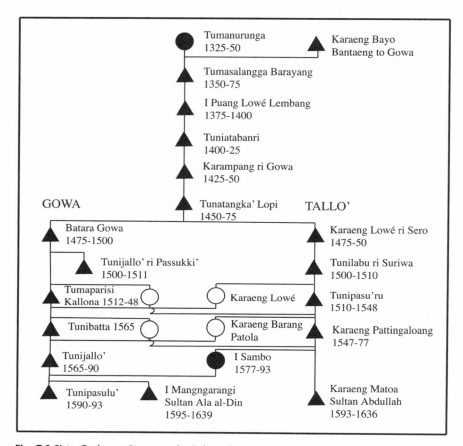

Fig. 7.1 Sister Exchange between the Rulers of Gowa and Tallo'.

sons Karaeng Lakiung and Karaeng Data, who commanded the flanks of his army. Both later became rulers of Gowa in their own right. Tallo' sued for peace and signed a treaty of perpetual friendship with Gowa. For the next two centuries, this alliance never wavered.

Each kingdom contributed unique resources to the alliance. Gowa was an inland realm with a dense population subsisting on irrigated rice cultivation. Tumapa'risi' Kallona used his superior manpower and earth-moving skills to drain the swamps of Maros and Takalar for large-scale rice cultivation, allowing him to maintain a large standing army. He also used them to build a fort with earthen walls at the mouth of the Jene'berang River at Somba Opu capable of withstanding artillery barrages.

For its part, Tallo' retained a distinct identity as a maritime power with a unique access to advanced technology. The chronicle of Tallo' records that new sorts of firearms and warships began to be manufactured during Tunipasu'ru's reign, and that the system of writing was also improved. His trading activities were so extensive that he had extended many loans to people as far away as Johore, on the Malay Peninsula (Manyambeang and Mone 1979: 10–11).

Tumapa'risi' Kallona appointed the first nonterritorial functionary of the kingdom, a *sabarana* (from the Malay *shahbandar*), or harbormaster named Daeng Pamatte. The chronicle of Gowa attributes the invention of the Makassar script to this man. Although the script had probably already been in existence for over a hundred years, it was now put to use by the state. Among the most important innovations of Tumapa'risi' Kallona's reign was the standardization of the royal chronicles in the Makassar area. These chronicles provide us a key to what local actors understood as the most important events in each reign. They usually begin with some version of the royal foundations myths discussed in the last chapter, but then quickly move on to a more practical account of the politically relevant marital, military, and administrative achievements of individual rulers. Many of these chronicles have been published over the past forty years in the original and in Indonesian, Dutch, or English translation, including those of Wajo' (Noorduyn 1955), Gowa (Wolhoff and Abdurrahim [1960]), Tallo' (Manyambeang and Mone 1979), and Bone (Macknight and Mukhlis, n.d.; see also Macknight 1983).

The Bugis and Makassarese peoples of South Sulawesi have long been noted for an approach to recording their own history that is unusual in Southeast Asia: their chronicles are "written in simple prose; they are terse, objective, matter-of-fact, and relatively short" (Brown 1988: 101, summing up the following historians: Noorduyn 1961, 1965; Soedjatmoko 1965; Andaya 1979; see also Cense 1951, 1966). The chronicles of Malay and Javanese kings are by contrast full of mythological elements, backdated prophecies, and hagiography. Brown ascribes this concern for accuracy to the openness of Bugis-Makassar social structure, in which the achievements of individual rulers count for more than their ascribed social status. Be that as it may, it is clear that these documents contain a great wealth of "factual" information that can be cross-checked against other sources.

This view has recently been challenged by Cummings, who notes that the principle function of *lontara* writings in South Sulawesi were to record the genealogies of the elite and the achievements of the rulers (Cummings 2000). They were stored along with the regalia of the kingdom and were considered to be possessed of great intrinsic power. Writing provided Bugis and Makassar with the means for preserving not just material relics of the founding rulers, but also their very words. Reciting the words and deeds of a powerful royal ancestor was a way of making the past present. Lontara recording the "things of those who came before," *patorioloang,* were carefully preserved and recopied so as to maintain a continuing ancestral presence. Possession of these manuscripts brought power and prestige in the same way as possession of the *gaukang* and *kalompoang*.

Cummings links the origin of writing to the origin of social stratification in South Sulawesi. Indeed, he sees writing as a primary causal force in this process. I would prefer to say that writing was only one of a number of technological innovations that led to a transformation in temporal consciousness, innovations such as the expansion of wet rice agriculture in the thirteenth century, exposure to Indo-Javanese models of kingship in the fourteenth century, and the introduction of firearms in the sixteenth century, as I argued in earlier chapters. Nevertheless, Cummings is right to note that the recording of oral traditions concerning the origin of local polities enabled a new way of thinking about the past, a new sense of the implications of technological innovation for political change.

The Fall of Luwu', 1500–1530

By the end of the fifteenth century, the preeminence of Luwu' over the east coast of the peninsula was threatened by the rise of these new agrarian kingdoms. Around 1500, the ruler Luwu' died. The Bugis kingdom of Wajo' took this opportunity to challenge Luwu's hegemony over Sidenreng and Soppeng with which it shared the shores of the Lake Tempe. Soon after Luwu's last great warrior king, Dewaraja, came to power around 1505, he recognized Wajo' as an equal power and ceded it a number of former vassals. Wajo' and Luwu' then allied to defeat Sidenreng.

In 1512, Luwu' attacked Bone. The queen of Bone had just ceded power to her eleven-year-old son, La Tenrisukki (1512–1543). La Tenrisukki proved to be as skilled a warrior as was Tuma'parisi Kallona of Gowa. He defeated Luwu' decisively, seizing Dewaraja's red umbrella in battle. From this battle, La Tenrisukki acquired the title Mappajungngé, "He of the Umbrella." Dewaraja was able to escape by ship with only twenty of his men. (Andaya 1981: 22; Bulbeck 1992: 476; Macknight and Mukhlis, n.d.).

This defeat by Bone was the beginning of the end for Luwu' as a regional political power. Dewaraja died in 1530, about the time Gowa and Tallo' were forming their alliance. Sanggaria claimed the throne of Luwu' and based himself on the Cenrana River in Wajo'. A rival claimant to the throne fled to Gowa, where Tumapa'risi' Kallona received him and promised to support his claim. Gowa then allied itself with Bone to attack Luwu'. Luwu' was defeated and forced to help Gowa and Bone attack Wajo'. Wajo' was duly defeated, and became a loyal vassal of Gowa. The victories of Gowa and Bone in the Cenrana River basin led to the collapse of Luwu's authority all along the coast of the Gulf of Bone (Pelras 1996: 116). Henceforth, the political history of the Bira Peninsula was to be determined by the rivalry between Gowa and Bone.

Bajeng, Bantaeng, and Gowa

The transfer of power and prestige from Bantaeng to Gowa is acknowledged in the foundation myth of Bajeng, a small kingdom lying to the south of Gowa and one of the first to be absorbed by the growing Empire. Like the other coastal

Makassar foundation myths, the myth of Bajeng traces the ruling family back to Bantaeng. As in the Bangkala myth (M 6.9), power and legitimacy require the union of a foreign prince associated with the sky and an upright tube found growing in the local ground. The myth goes on, however, to account for the decline of Bajeng and the rise of Gowa in terms of an illegitimate transfer of this sacred object.

M 7.3 Karaeng Lowé and the Stolen Blowpipe (Bajeng)

Seven brothers descend in a field along with their house at Tanabangka in Bantaeng. Their leader descends with a wife. They are summoned by the local ruler, but the leader refuses to come because of his poverty. The king comes to him instead and requests him to remain. They insist on wandering through all the lands before they each choose a place to settle. The leader settles in Bajeng and is made king with the title Karaeng Lowé of Bajeng. His followers build him a palace of seven sections. He has a beautiful daughter called I Naima.

Karaeng Lowé's confidant Panai finds a magic bamboo while burning off a field from which he makes a blowpipe and a magic dart that always finds its mark and returns to the pipe. Karaeng Lowé asks for the blowpipe and names it I Bule. He appoints Panai ruler of Galesong as a reward.

King Tumaparisi Kallona of Gowa learns of I Naima's beauty and requests her hand in marriage. Karaeng Lowé refuses him. Tumaparisi Kallona asks Karaeng Lowé to at least invite him to a feast where he might see I Naima. He shows up with his army and challenges Karaeng Lowé to fight. The two sides retire and prepare for war. Karaeng Lowé defeats Gowa's army with the help of I Bule and two champions. Gowa attacks again the next year and is again defeated. The same happens in the third, fourth, and fifth years.

The soothsayer Bonto Lempangang then volunteers to ingratiate himself with Karaeng Lowé and weaken Bajeng from within. He persuades Karaeng Lowé to dig a canal through his kingdom, cutting it in half. But he returns to Gowa without I Bule, and the King of Gowa is afraid to attack.

Panai, now king of Galesong, offers to get I Bule by trickery. He pretends to be at war with the King of Gowa, and while hosting a feast for Karaeng Lowé, stages a mock attack by Gowa on his own house. He persuades Karaeng Lowé to lend him I Bule to fight off Gowa. He rides off with it instead and gives it to the King of Gowa. Panai's descendents suffer from a terrible curse as a result.

When Karaeng Lowé discovers the trick, he tells his human followers that they must remain loyal to the *gaukang* I Bule and follow it to Gowa. He also gives them his belt and his lance as substitutes for himself. Then he disappears along with his wife, his daughter, his brothers, and his champions. Forty people from Bajeng settle in the territory of Gowa and found three new settlements.

Gowa goes on to dominate the entire peninsula, but its power is based on an original act of deceit, so that Bajengers feel no loyalty to the king the Dutch have just deposed in 1905. (Condensed from Tideman 1908b: 488–500)

The foundation myth of Bantaeng begins with seven sisters who are autochthonous. The Bajeng myth begins with seven brothers who descend from the sky in Bantaeng. Their leader comes fully equipped with a house and a wife, but refuses to stay. All seven wander off to the west, like the prince of Bantaeng in the Bangkala myth. The leader is accepted as Karaeng Lowé by the people of Bajeng, who build him a palace.

The rest of the myth is a transformation of the Bangkala myth, designed to explain not the triumph of a new kingdom but the fall of an old one. In the Bangkala myth (M 6.9), the *karaeng* of Kalimporo learns of a beautiful maiden in Ujung Moncong. He tries to obtain her for himself by inviting her to a feast in his kingdom. She visits with an entourage made out of enchanted bamboo and grass but manages to escape back to her place of origin. Her loyal subjects successfully rebuff a subsequent attack by the *karaeng* of Kalimporo.

In the Bajeng myth, the *karaeng* of Gowa learns of a beautiful maiden in Bajeng. He invites himself to a feast so that he can obtain her for himself but is driven off by the power of an enchanted bamboo tube that was given in tribute by a subject to the *karaeng* of Bajeng. Bajeng remains invulnerable until the same disloyal subject gets it back by a ruse, changes sides, and gives it to the *karaeng* of Gowa. The disloyalty of a subject leads to the loss of the chief item of the regalia, which leads to the disappearance of the ruler. The entire realm is absorbed into Gowa, which goes on to dominate the known world.

The Consolidation of the Dual Empire, 1535–1605

The *karaeng* of Tallo', Tunipasu'ru', died in 1546. His partner in expansion, Tumpa'risi' Kallona, died in 1548. At his death, Gowa-Tallo' was firmly in control of the entire Garassi'/Jene'berang watershed and had established its hegemony over the entire west coast of the peninsula. Together, the rulers of Gowa and Tallo' had created a new kind of hybrid state. The chronicle of Gowa says that the next ruler of Gowa, Tunipalangga (born 1512, reigned 1548–1565), was famous only for his skill in war. He is credited with redesigning the spear and shield of the Gowanese army, reducing both in size to make them lighter and more maneuverable. He is also credited with the production of gunpowder and the casting of bullets for muskets (Wolhoff and Abdurrahim [1960]).

Under Tunipalangga, military conquest was followed not just by the taking of booty but by the enslavement of whole populations, who were brought back to the imperial center to work on new irrigation projects. With the surplus rice produced by these projects, he was able to feed his armies and to provide a surplus for trade to Maluku, long dependent on Javanese rice for subsistence. Just as important was the adaptation of hydraulic technology for military purposes. He used the captives to build brick fortifications at Kale Gowa and at Somba Opu. The walls of these fortresses were then lined with cannons.

Although Tunipalangga used captive labor on a large scale, he was careful to maintain good relations with the peasantry of his core constituency in Gowa.

For example, he created a new post of minister of the interior, *Tumailalang*. The Tumailalang served as liaison between the ruler and the Council of Nine, the *Bate Salapang,* and himself. The counselors acted in turn as liaisons between the Tumailalang and the commoners. By codifying the rights and privileges of the core Gowanese from the Jene'berang valley in this way, Tunipalangga created a distinction between the soldiers recruited from the free peasantry of the "interior" and the conscripts brought in from the exterior.

Within the capital itself, skilled labor was organized into what grew to be twenty different guilds, each under a head called a *Jannang*. The guilds included ironsmiths, goldsmiths, house builders, boatbuilders *(panrita biseang)*, and makers of blowpipes, metal armaments *(sappu)*, whetstones, potter's wheels, and spinning wheels. The head of all the *Jannang* was called the *Tumakkajannang* and had a rank just under the Tumailalang. Finally, Tunipalangga was able to attract most of the Malay merchants on the west coast of South Sulawesi to his capital by promising them security in their persons and property. As a further aid to commerce, he set up standardized weights and measures inside the fortresses (Wolhoff and Abdurrahim [1960]: paragraphs 68–73).

Tunipalangga used his army to add the entire south and southeast coasts, the Walannae valley in the center of the peninsula, and the lands north of the Cenrana River to his empire. The limits of Tunipalangga's conquests were reached in 1565, when he and his brother Tunibatta (the Decapitated One) died while waging war on Bone, the last unconquered kingdom on the peninsula.

By the 1560s, a qualitatively new kind of state had been built up, complete with a functionally specialized bureaucracy; sophisticated commercial and financial institutions and codified laws; guilds of full-time urban artisans; large-scale slave labor projects; and a standing army employing a range of gunpowder technologies. Tunipalangga was able to build on the foundations laid by his predecessors to establish a positive feedback circuit in which firearms were used to acquire tribute and slaves from Bugis and Makassar polities all over the peninsula. The slaves were used to build fortifications and to drain swamps to grow large quantities of rice. The rice was used both as a trade item for spices in Maluku and to feed a large standing army. The spices were traded with the Portuguese and others for firearms. The firearms and the army were used in turn to guard the port and to acquire yet more tribute and slaves.

Tunibatta (reigned 1565) ruled for only forty days before he was succeeded by his son, Tunijallo' "The Murdered One" (reigned 1565–1590). Tunijallo' had taken refuge in Bone after quarreling with his father in 1563. When he succeeded to the throne of Gowa two years later, he immediately signed a peace treaty with Bone. New tensions arose in 1582, when Bone's chief minister, Kajao Laliddo, arranged an anti-Gowanese alliance with Wajo' and Soppeng. Tunijallo' began a series of campaigns against the alliance in 1583, which ended only with his murder in 1590 by one of his own men. Five years later, the king of Bone, La Icca (reigned 1584–1595), was also murdered by one of his own subjects.

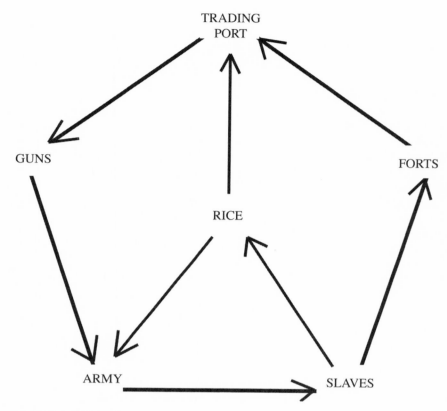

Fig. 7.2 Gowa's Takeoff.

Tunijallo' was succeeded by his fifteen-year-old son, Tunipasulu' (reigned 1590–1593). Tunipasulu' embarked on a thorough centralization of power. He moved the capital of the empire to the fort of Somba Opu at the mouth of the Jeneberang River. He declared himself *karaeng* not only of Gowa, but also of Tallo' and Marusu' (Wolhoff and Abdurrahim [1960]: 193). He turned Marusu' into a virtual slave state by parceling out its rice lands among the Gowanese nobility. He privileged the core Gowanese by further institutionalizing the Council of Nine, giving each a fixed jurisdiction and banner. He created a second office of Tumailalang and increased the rank of both incumbents to *karaeng*. Reid states that it is difficult to understand why a tyrannical ruler would have done this, but I see it as a natural development of a policy of divide and rule, whereby a core of free Gowanese were played off against servile outsiders (Reid 1981: 6).

It was only in the 1590s that the full constitutional structure of the Gowanese Empire was established. At the top was the *karaeng* of Gowa, assisted by his

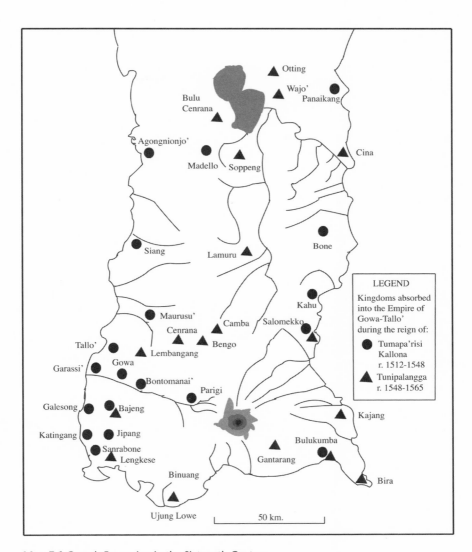

Map 7.1 Gowa's Expansion in the Sixteenth Century

tuma'bicara buttaya, or chief minister, the *karaeng* of Tallo'. Under them were two *tumailalang,* or ministers of the interior, whose rank had been raised from *gallar-rang* to *karaeng* in 1590–1593. They mediated between the throne and the nine *gallarrang*s from the core of Gowa, who composed the *Bate Salapang,* the Nine Banners. Beneath the *tumailalang* was the harbormaster and the guild master.

Tunipasulu's absolutist pretensions got the better of him in 1593. He managed to alienate the community of foreign merchants, an essential element of the imperial economy. The chronicle says, "While Karaeng Tunipasulu' was in

power, even if people were not guilty they were just killed instantly. The Javanese left and all the ana'karaeng (nobles) ran away" (Wolhoff and Abdurrahim
[1960]: 109–191).

The chief minister of Gowa at the time, I Malinkaeng (reigned 1593–
1636), engineered Tunipasulu's exile from Gowa in 1593. He placed Tunipasulu's seven-year-old brother I Mangngarangi (r. 1593–1639) on the throne of
Gowa and forced his own mother, I Sambo, to abdicate the throne of Tallo' in
his favor. For the next forty-three years, I Malinkaeng dominated all of South Sulawesi. He ruled over a consolidated agrarian state in the interior of South Sulawesi and had access to a standing army and large naval and merchant marine
fleets. And it was he who decided that the time was right to convert Gowa-Tallo'
into an Islamic state in 1605. He is best known to history under the titles of
Karaeng Matoaya Sultan Abdullah. But that is another story.

The Incorporation of the Periphery: Bira, 1350–1600

A glimpse of what Gowa's expansion looked like from the periphery is provided
by what I will call "the Bira manuscript."[2] The manuscript contains four parts: a
series of genealogies, a compilation of royal chronicles providing a charter for
Bira's political structure, a collection of political precepts for just rule,[3] and a
Konjo-Makassar version of the *Compendium of Native Laws* prepared for the VOC
Governor of Makassar Roelof Blok in 1759.[4] I will be discussing only the genealogies and chronicles here.

Genealogies

The genealogies begin with the phrase, "This is the story of the ones from
Maluku." The text then launches into a series of fifty-five stem genealogies distributed over twenty-three generations from about 1350 to 1900. All of the genealogies interconnect through frequent cousin marriage, and it is possible to
construct a single integrated genealogy out of them. These interconnections
provide some degree of verification for the accuracy of the count of generations.
Marriages between second, third, or more remote cousins allow one to correct
for a series of descendents born to their parents later or earlier than usual. I
found that, if I calculate an average of twenty-five years per generation, deeds attributed to various ancestors fit in with historical events established by independent sources.

In the end, I was able to compile a single master genealogy containing
the names of about 420 men and 330 women. I assigned each individual on the
integrated chart a generation level based on the twenty-five-year interval during which they were born. Numbering begins at G1 with the generation born
between 1975 and 2000 and goes back to G28, the generation born between
1300 and 1325. All but four of the genealogies begin in the period 1400–1600
(G26–G18), which indicates that they were first written in the sixteenth century, before conversion to Islam. The generations born between 1425 and 1575

(G23–G18) contain more than half the total number of individuals on the genealogy, averaging more than sixty individuals per generation.

By contrast, the average number of individuals shown per generation born after 1575 is less than thirty. After 1600, the genealogies are primarily concerned with an in-marrying lineage of Islamic officials, showing how it was linked to the pre-Islamic royal ancestors of Bira. This in-marrying lineage controlled the post of Kali, the chief Islamic official in Bira, from about 1630 to 1930. During this period, the Kalis are shown in great detail, whereas the ruling line of *karaeng*s disappears.

My working hypothesis is that the genealogies, along with the chronicles, were first written down at the beginning of the sixteenth century by the political rulers, perhaps on the model of the chronicle of Gowa. As we saw above, the chronicle of Gowa attributes the invention of the Makassar script to Daeng Pamatte, the first harbormaster *(shahbandar)* appointed under Karaeng Tuma'parisi Kallona (reigned 1511–1548). Both chronicles show a very similar structure with the earlier portions containing rationalized versions of oral traditions, such as the brief reference to the *tomanurung* in Gowa's chronicle, followed by bare lists of rulers, until a better-remembered period of history, beginning about 1475, is reached.

It is possible to date the period when the genealogies reached their final form a bit more precisely. Genealogies 1–25 trace the ancestry of the Kali known posthumously as Turi Takebere'na—"He Who Recites the Takbir (Confession of Faith)" (G7, born 1800–1825). Genealogies 26–55 trace the ancestry of Dg. Ma'gau (G6, born 1825–1850), a nephew of Turi Takebere'na, and show a single-minded attempt to trace Dg. Ma'Gau's entire bilateral ancestry back to the sixteenth century. These genealogies thus acquired their present form between 1860 and 1900.

According to several informants, including Abdul Hakim, these genealogies and many other heirlooms belonging to the line of Kalis came into the possession of one of Turi Takebere'na's grandsons, Haji Ahmad Rifai (G4, born 1875–1900), and they thought it likely that it was he who copied them out for de Roock in 1936. The genealogies begin with the following preamble:

> *Bismillahi rrahmani rrahim*
> These writings tell the stories of Patturioloang. We do not know them to be truthful, we have not witnessed them. Only an elder, who was a Kali that slept in the mosque, whose soul *(bathin)* was purified by Allah of unbelief and confusion, related them.

Haji Ahmad lived to a ripe old age, dying in 1985. For the last several years of his life, he avoided his relatives and lived as a wandering mendicant and many of the old heirlooms were dispersed.

The earliest recorded ancestor is I Ma'rakki Kalapaya, (born 1300–1325, G28). He is said to have come from Majapahit, which, as we saw in chapter 6, was

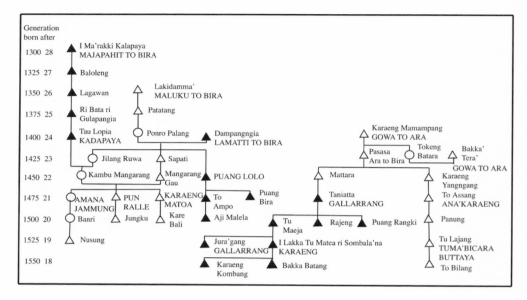

Fig. 7.3 Genealogical Origins of the *Hadat* of Bira.

in contact with the south coast of South Sulawesi in the mid-fourteenth century. The next group to arrive were three siblings from Maluku in eastern Indonesia who settled in Bira Keke in about 1400 (G26, born 1350–1375). Around 1450, a group led by a figure known as the *Dampang* (G24, born 1400–1425) came from the mountains of Sinjai in the north and intermarried with the Malukans in Bira Keke. It is unclear whether they were Bugis speakers or Konjo-Makassar from that area. Around the same time, Karaeng Mamampang (G24), a Makassar prince from an area near Gowa, settled in Ara. His grandchildren, Mattara and Karaeng Yangngang (G22, born 1450–1475), moved to Bira Lohe around 1500.

Bira thus traces its origins from a combination of Javanese, Malukan, Bugis/Konjo, and Makassar noble immigrants. Political power passed on several occasions to the latest in the series of immigrant princes, whereas earlier lines kept control of primarily ritual offices. This process is spelled out more fully in the chronicles that accompany the genealogies. The main characters who appear in both the genealogies and the stories are represented on the above diagram, with the generation into which they were born shown on the left side.

The Chronicles

The individuals in the middle generations of the genealogies are the subjects of the chronicles of Bira. The chronicles are a series of eight narratives concerning the early, pre-Islamic rulers of Bira, Ara, Tanaberu, and Lemo Lemo, focusing mostly on the period between 1450 and 1600. They run to about 7,500 words when translated into English.

The chronicles begin with two stories recounting the process by which an ordered realm came into existence in Bira out of the fusion of four distinct ethnic groups. I will devote most of my discussion to these two stories. A second set of four stories recounts the changing overlords to whom Bira paid tribute. In the third story, Bira is under the control of the Bugis state of Luwu'. According to the genealogies, this story is set between about 1470 and 1510. Then control passed to Luwu's subvassal Tiro, itself under the authority of a prince from Luwu' called Samparaja Daeng Malaja. We have met him before under the name Sapo Hatu, Stone House (M 5.3). Bira soon obtained its independence from Tiro by helping defeat Tanaberu in battle in around 1520. In the fourth story, Bira frees itself from Tiro's control.

In the fifth story, Bira allies with Bulo Bulo in Sinjai to defeat the ruler of Tanuntung, a small realm lying midway between them. Bira then helps the rising power of Gowa defeat Bulo Bulo, probably in the early 1560s. In 1563 a Gowanese force under the Emperor Tunipalangga landed at Cenrana, north of Bone. Tunipalangga was wounded and had to retreat. Two years later, he attacked again, but fell ill and returned to Gowa to die.

The sixth story returns to the mid-fifteenth century, the time when the *Dampang* settled in Bira. It concerns a dispute between Ara and Tiro occasioned by an unintended insult to the people of Ara by a slave woman. In the subsequent war, Bira comes to the aid of Ara and an alliance between them is cemented by their victory. The ruler of Ara at the time is Karaeng Mamampang, a noble from the kingdom of Garassi', which lay just downstream from Gowa and was being incorporated into the new kingdom at just this time.

The last two stories in the chronicle of Bira recount slightly different versions of the events that led the people of Bira to select a great-grandson of Karaeng Mamampang as their paramount ruler in about 1525 and to become voluntary tributaries of Gowa in the 1560s.

The Foundation of Bira

The first story begins with a description of the movements of a Bugis kin group led by a noble identified only by the title of "the *Dampang*." He settled in Bira in about 1450. His descendents served as chiefs of the local community until about 1525, when power was transferred to the descendent of Karaeng Mamampang, the Makassar lord who had settled in Ara in about 1450. The new ruler was given the title of *gallarrang*. In about 1565, Bira was incorporated into the Empire of Gowa, and the office of *gallarrang* was superceded by the offices of *karaeng* and *tuma'bicara buttaya*. This replicated the structure that was established at about the same time in Gowa proper, in which the *karaeng* of Gowa had supreme political authority and the *karaeng* of Tallo' served as his *tuma'bicara buttaya*, "He Who is Speaker of the Land," or chief adviser. At the end of the story, the *karaeng* of Bira is given supreme territorial authority over the whole of Bira, and the *tuma'bicara butta* is given supreme judicial authority.

M 7.4 The *Dampang* Settles in Bira

The *Dampang* and his siblings, Pacindeya and Panyilaya, move from Lamatti on the Tangka River to Bira.[5] Both the *Dampang* and his nephew marry women from Lamatti. Panyilaya's son, La Paranggu, travels north to Tiro where he marries for the first time and then continues on to Lamatti where he marries again. Finally, he moves back to Bone, the land of his mother. In the third generation, a prince, *ana'karaeng,* goes from Bira to Bone and marries La Paranggu's daughter. In the fourth generation, their children returned to Bira, where one of them marries her second cousin. Returning to the original sibling group, the story relates that the *Dampang* himself married a divorced princess from Kanari in Lamatti, that his son by that marriage, Lepa', returned from Bira to Lamatti to marry, and that his son's son, To Paggu, returned to Bira.

Altogether, we are told that three men moved to the Tangka area and one man moved to Bira during the fifteenth century to marry, which indicates a rule of uxorilocal residence. The only exception to this is the woman who left or fled from her husband in Kanari and married the *Dampang* in Bira. On the whole, I think this episode is meant to record the integration of Bugis or Konjo Makassar from the north into the existing society of Bira.

The second episode of the story concerns the displacement of the *Dampang*'s descendents as territorial rulers of Bira by the descendents of Karaeng Mamampang. From the genealogies, we can infer that this episode of the story occurs three generations after the *Dampang*'s arrival, in about 1525. It treats the transfer of power to the Makassar house in this generation (G21) as a purely internal matter.

M 7.5 The Poor One Is Made *Gallarrang* of Bira

The episode begins with a dispute over some millet that had been laid out to dry. To Paggu (G22), son of Lepa (G23) and grandson of the *Dampang* (G24) by his wife from Lamatti, quarrels with a resident of the Malukan settlement of Tampea, at the south end of Bira. The fight escalates, resulting in the death of both To Paggu and some people from Tampea. The leader of the Malukan community, the Amma Tau, or "Father of the People" of Bira Keke, then intervenes. He decides that both sides are at fault and has them both kill chickens in atonement. The people of Tampea give the Amma Tau the disputed millet in payment for his arbitration. Sapati (G23), a son of the *Dampang* by his Malukan wife, goes further and expropriates from Tampea nine parcels of garden land as compensation for the death of To Paggu, son of his half brother Lepa.

This provokes the Polong Tana of Bira Keke to call a meeting challenging Sapati's action. The title *Polong Tana* means "He Who Splits the Earth," referring to the fact that the agricultural cycle began with a ritual plowing of the ruler's land. The Polong Tana states that Sapati has overreached his authority, because none of the locals should assert majesty *[kala'birang]* over the others. Instead, he suggests that one of the sons either of "the *karaeng*" or of Mattara be chosen as *gallarrang* with the power to impose such penalties. *Gallarrang* means simply "the Titled One," but its use tended to spread with the imposition of Gowa's authority over local kingdoms. We know from the genealogies that the individuals referred to by the Polong Tana were Karaeng Yangngang and Mattara, both sons of Passaya (G23) and grandsons of Karaeng Mamampang (G24). Karaeng Yangngang's three sons were called To Assang, Ya'ra, and Yayakanu'. Mattara also had three sons, called Tara', Ngalung, and Muncaranggi. Later in the story, one of these three is called Taniatta.

At first, the people unanimously choose one of Karaeng Yangngang's sons, To Assang, to rule them. To Assang may be a form of *tau-assa'*, "the Noble One." He and his descendents also have the title of *Ana' Karaeng*, "Descendent of the Kings." To Assang refuses the office, noting that he is wealthy enough to take care of himself. He calls instead for the installation of his cousin, Taniatta, the son of Mattara. Taniatta may be a form of *ta-nia'-ta*, "Our Person without Wealth," or "the Impoverished One." It is precisely because of his inability to provide for himself that he is suitable, for he will be unlikely to forget his dependence on his subjects. They must wash him, feed him, and clothe him. The villagers agree to this logic and make Taniatta the *gallarrang,* a Gowanese title. The overall territorial ruler, the *Gallarrang* Taniatta, is thus associated with poverty and dependency. This is reminiscent of the Bugis myth recorded by Acciaioli, in which the noble ruler is completely helpless (M 3.6). He is contrasted with his cousin, the *ana'karaeng* To Assang, who is associated with wealth and independence.

After farming together for three years, Taniatta's appointment is solemnized with an oath that makes explicit the reciprocal character of their relations between ruler and subject and its absolute separation from the relation between master and slave. Two great stones are erected to represent the contract between the ruler and the people. The two stones referred to may still be seen today. They are each about a cubic meter in size and sit behind a house up a hill to the west of the great spring of Bira Lohe.

As in many of the *tomanurung* myths, this story portrays the local population of Bira as divided into several quarreling factions who are unable to resolve their disputes peacefully. They thus turn to an outsider who can be relied upon to arbitrate among them in an impartial way, but who appears so helpless that he will have to rely on his subjects for food and shelter. Although in this case the outsider is only the descendent of a *tomanurung,* the logic of appealing to him to keep the peace is the same as in the other royal foundation myths. The institution of kingship is seen as a contract between a ruler and his subjects, in which the ruler guarantees the fertility of the land by resolving disputes and the subjects provide for the material needs of the ruler.

The last episode of the first story occurs two generations later, in the 1560s

(G20, born 1500–1525). It concerns the formalization of Bira's subordination to Gowa as a "voluntary" tributary and the emperor of Gowa's role in creating a functional difference between the *karaeng* as territorial ruler of Bira and the *ana'karaeng* as *tuma'bicara butaya*, or chancellor in charge of jural deliberations. This correlates with Bira's submission to the emperor of Gowa according to the chronicle of Gowa. That chronicle records that Karaeng Tunipalangga (born 1512; reigned 1548–1565) defeated the lands lying north of Bira in battle, including Kajang and, on the Tangka River, Bulo-Bulo and Lamatti. He also defeated the lands lying to the west and south of Bira: Bulukumba, Ujung Lowé, Pannyakokang, Palioi, Gantarang, Wero, and Selayar. As for Bira, it says only *angngallei sabu kati tu-Biraya*, "he collected war tribute from the people of Bira," not that he engaged in battle with them (Wolhoff and Abdurrahim [1960]: paragraph 60). This episode gives Bira's version of this tribute, as do several of the other stories.

M 7.6 Bira Joins the Empire
The episode begins with a brief recital of the transmission of the Gallarangship from Taniatta to three of his sons, Rajing, Pung Rangki, and To Maeja, and from the latter to his son I Lakka (G19, born 1525–1550). It next turns to the descendents of To Assang, the wealthy noble who turned down the post of *gallarrang*. In this passage, he is identified by the older title *To Bontoyya*, "The One of the Highlands." From the genealogy we know that To Assang's son was called Panung and his grandson To Lajang. They are also referred to in this episode as the *ana'karaeng*, descendents of the *karaeng*.

The group of *ana'karaeng* is then contrasted to the *Polong Tanaya ri Kalumbimbi*, "He Who Cuts the Earth in Kalumbimbi." As we saw in the last episode, the title of *polong tana* refers to the person with precedence over agricultural rites. In this case, the *polong tana* is the *gallarrang*, I Lakka. The dispute in this story arises when the wealthy *ana'karaeng* To Lajang asserts his precedence over the poor *polong tana/gallarrang* in just the manner his grandfather To Assang feared. To Lajang's association with maritime trade is first indicated when the people of Ara obey his orders to prepare a boat to carry tribute to Gowa. The *polong tana/gallarrang* at first resists his orders to load the front part of the boat with agricultural produce. But he soon gives in and prepares several hundred baskets of foodstuffs, while the *ana'karaeng* loads the back with expensive trade goods.

When they arrive in Gowa, the *ana'karaeng* is allowed to sit in the audience chamber of the emperor with the other nobles, while the *gallarrang* is made to sit with the chiefs of the nine villages that made up Gowa's ancient core, the *Bate-Bate*. The *ana'karaeng* offers the emperor a typical tribute of bullion, Indian trade cloth *(cinde)*, and slaves. The emperor is most pleased, however, by the humble agricultural produce presented by the *gallarrang* of Bira, most of which appear to be of New World origin: sweet potato, cassava, and squash.[6]

So that the *gallarrang* may join the other nobles in the audience chamber, the emperor elevates him to the rank of *karaeng*. This selection of the more humble of the two candidates as *karaeng* replicates the earlier selection of the more humble of the two candidates for the office of *gallarrang*. The *ana'karaeng* To Lajang is then appointed as *tuma'bicara buttaya*, the chief judge and minister of the realm.

The model that had come into effect after Gowa and Tallo' signed a peace treaty in 1530 was one in which the inland ruler of Gowa was in charge of agriculture and the army and served as the paramount territorial ruler, while the maritime ruler of Tallo' was in charge of the navy. In 1565, the ruler of Tallo' became, in addition, the *tuma'bicara buttaya* in the kingdom of Gowa. Evidently applying this model to Bira, after elevating the *gallarrang* to *karaeng*, the emperor of Gowa appointed the *ana'karaeng* as chief minister in Bira with authority over judicial deliberations. In Bira, this function was probably transferred to the Islamic Kali in the mid-seventeenth century.

A complementary opposition is at work here between land and sea, agriculture and trade, with the latter term having higher wealth and status but less territorial power. The balance between the two terms was preserved when the emperor granted the *ana' karaeng*'s request that the title of *gallarrang* be preserved alongside that of *karaeng*, despite the elevation of its current incumbent to overall authority as *karaeng*. The episode concludes by noting the posthumous title of Karaeng Lakka', *Tumatea ri Sombala'na*, "He Who Died While Under Sail." The first *tuma'bicara buttaya* To Lajang received the posthumous title *Tumalambusu'na Karaeng Bira*, "He Who was Just to the Karaeng of Bira" because he sailed with him.

The Origin of the Hadat of Bira, circa 1450–1530

The second story in the chronicle concerns the coalescence of a new social whole out of a multiplicity of parts of different origin and the progressive internal differentiation of that whole culminating in the creation of the Hadat (Council) of Bira. Until it was reorganized around the time of the Second Bone War (1859), the hadat consisted of eight members. Concerning the composition of the Hadat of Bira before it was reorganized in 1860, Matthes wrote that there were eight members of the hadat, four of whom were territorial lords and four of whom were the king's advisers (Matthes 1864: 272). Combining his account with some comments of Goedhart ([1920] 1933: 142), we get the following four administrative titles:

1. The *puang lolo*, "young lord." According to Matthes, he served as the *karaeng*'s right hand. Goedhart adds that he also served as commander of the troops in times of war and thus had in his keeping the *salagaya*, the war standard of Bira that originated in Gowa.
2. The *karaeng matowa*, "old karaeng," a retired ruler who continued to provide advice.

3. The *punralle,* "father of the blossom." According to Matthes, this title is derived from the fact that the first person to hold it was born under a *punranga*
tree (*Gemeliana Asiatica* L.), of which *punralle* would be a corruption.
4. The *amanna jambu/jammung,* "mother of the jambu fruit" (according to
Matthes, "father of the jambu fruit"). The title was said to be derived from
the fondness shown by the mother of its first holder for jambu fruit (*jam-
bosa sp.*) during her pregnancy.

And we get the following four territorial titles:

1. The *galla* or *gallarrang* Bira: The ruler of the (upward, northern) settlement
of Bira Lohe, "greater Bira." This would be what the chronicles refer to as
the Tu Kalubimbi. According to Goedhart ([1920] 1933), he was in charge
of carrying out the decisions of the *karaeng* made in consultation with the
hadat of eight or ten advisers.
2. *Lembang keke:* The ruler of the (downward, southern) settlement of Bira
Keke, "lesser Bira," according to Matthes ([1865] 1943).
3. *Lembang lohe:* The ruler of the (seaward, eastern) settlements of Punkarese,
Tuliganra, Dangke, and Langgana, according to Matthes ([1865] 1943). According to Goedhart ([1920] 1933), the only surviving function of the *lembang lohe* in 1920 was to carry the *burangga* or *korontigi,* henna, from the
house of the bride to the groom during weddings. This would associate the
lembang lohe with female gender.
4. *Pundolo/dodo:* The ruler of the (landward, western) settlements of Tunege
and Tapassang, according to Matthes ([1865] 1943). According to Goedhart
([1920] 1933), he was ritually responsible for carrying the henna, from the
house of the groom to the bride during weddings. This would associate the
pundolo with male gender.[7]

Only if one knows these titles and their associated functions can one decode the
second story in the chronicle of Bira.

M 7.7 The Hadat of Bira as a Mandala

The second story begins by stating that it will tell the history of sixteen
groups of people in Bira. Several of the names of these groups survive as place
names in Bira, including Bira Keke, where the *Dampang* intermarried with the
Malukans, Bira [Lohe], where the descendents of Karaeng Mamampang settled, and Tampea, at the southern tip of the peninsula. These sixteen groups
fall into four sets, each with its own leader. The first group is led by To Bara,
who by process of elimination must be a descendent of the Malukan prince
who settled in Tampea in the southeast quarter of the realm. The second
group is led by To Bonto, who is identified in the first story as a descendent
of the Makassar prince Karaeng Mamampang living in Bira Lohe in the northwest quarter. The third group is led by the *Dampang,* a descendent of the

prince from Lamatti who intermarried with the Malukans in Tampea and settled in Kalumpang in the southwest quarter. The fourth group is led by the *kadapa* Tau Lopia, a descendent of the Javanese prince who was first to arrive in the area who settled in Bira Keke in the northeast quarter.

G24: The *Dampang* was recognized by all four groups as their first *karaeng*. When the population increased, he organized it into compact settlements. We later learn that the seat of his power was in Kalumpang Lohe, on the western side of the peninsula. Then the people requested that he marry a local wife. He agreed to do so if they could find a woman of high enough status. They chose for him Ponro Palang, the granddaughter of the original Malukan *karaeng*. We know from the genealogies that her parents were first cousins, children of two of the Malukan brothers who settled in Bira around 1400. "*Karaeng*ship" thus passed from an older lineage to that of an immigrant son-in-law, and not for the last time.

G23: The *Dampang*'s marriage to the Malukan produced two sons, Puang Lolo, "The Young Lord," and Sapati; and twin daughters, Jilang Ruwa, "Jilang the Second," and Sigi Kambara, "Sigi the Twin." Jilang Ruwa married Tau Lopia (G23), a descendent of the Javanese prince who settled in Bira around 1350, who had the title of *kadapaya*. In story 6, Tau Lopia is called the *gallarrang* of Bira. The *Dampang*'s "greatness" *(kalompoang)* or power was inherited by his son Puang Lolo (G22). It will be recalled that this name became the title of one of the advisory members of the Hadat Bira.

G22: Sapati's son Mangarang Gau (G22) married Jilang Ruwa's daughter Kambu Mangarang, thus combining the bloodlines of the Bugis, the Malukan, and the Javanese settlers.

G21: Mangarang Gau's three children were called *karaeng matowaya*, "the old lord"; *pun ralle*, "father of the blossom," and *da jammung* (or *ammana jambu*) "mother of the fruit" (G21). Together with their cousin To Ampa, who inherited the title of *puang lolo* from his father, we have in this generation (G21, born 1475–1500) all four names that will later serve as titles for the advisory officers in the hadat.

G20: To Ampa's son Aji Malela (G20) inherited the title of *puang lolo* in the next generation. Aji Malela assigned the heir of each of Sapati's three children a quarter of the *Dampang*'s legacy, reserving a quarter for himself. The names of Sapati's three children thus became titles in the following generation. Kare Bali became the *karaeng matowa*, Jungku became the *pun ralle*, and Nusung became the *ammana jammung*. The name of Puang Lolo had already become a title in the previous generation.

The story ends by summarizing the structure of the territorial groups that existed at the time the four advisory titles came into existence: the Javanese group of the *kadapa*, the Malukan group of To Bara, the Lamatti group of the *dampang*, and the Makassar group of the *tu bonto*. It comments that power over each of these three groups continued to be inherited internally, and that they

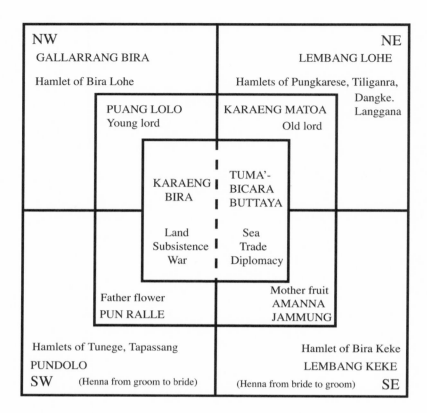

Fig. 7.4 The *Hadat* of Bira as a *Mandala*.

came to share Bira with the *dampang* Aji Malela. There thus came to be four territorial rulers, or *ana'karaeng,* and the whole of Bira came to be divided into four allied parts.

The central functions controlled by the Makassar group then consisted of the territorial office of *karaeng* and the administrative office of *tuma'bicara buttaya.* One of the four subordinate territorial offices was also retained by the Makassar group, that of the *gallarrang* of Bira Lohe. The other three territorial offices were distributed among the descendents of the original Javanese, Malukan, and Lamatti settlers. As the last territorial rulers to be displaced, the Lamatti group was given control of the four all-Bira advisory offices.

We have here an initial bifurcation into an active half of territorial rulers and a passive half of advisers. Turning to the passive half of advisers, we find a bifurcation into those with royal titles, and those with botanical titles. The royal half is then bifurcated into an active half made up of the "young father," whose function it is to lead in war, and a passive half made up of the "old lord," whose function it is to give advice. The *puang lolo* is thus associated with the *gallarrang* and the *karaeng matowa* with the *ana' karaeng*. As for the botanical titles, there is an opposition between male source (*pun ralle,* father of the flower) and female product (mother of the jambu fruit). The *pundolo* carried henna from the house of the groom to that of the bride, while the *lembang lohe* carried it from the house of the bride to that of the groom. This indicates an association of the former with male gender and the latter with female gender. One may thus associate the *pun ralle* with the *lembang keke* as female and the *ammana jammung* with the *lembang lohe* as female. The structure can be represented schematically as shown in figure 7.4.

The generation in which this subdivision of functions and territories culminates is G21, the same generation in which Taniatta was chosen as *gallarrang* of all of Bira in M 7.4 above. Bira had acquired a nested four/five structure by about 1530: one overall ruler in the center surrounded by four advisers and another four territorial rulers (see M 6.4). This structure was further elaborated in the 1560s, when the functions of the ruling Makassar descent group was differentiated into three by the *somba* of Gowa.

In these stories, the younger son of a powerful foreign king goes out into the world and wanders until he marries the sister or daughter of a local ruler in Bira or Ara. Because he outranks the local population, the foreign prince's sons become the highest-ranking candidates for local political office. At the time the chronicles were composed, local royal houses were more concerned to link themselves to foreign imperial centers than to local *tomanurung*. The genealogies record this process as having first occurred when a prince from Majapahit was shipwrecked off the coast of Bira in about 1350.

Conclusion: From Bamboo Maiden to Warlord

Gowa grew from an inland agrarian kingdom to a maritime empire through the use of gunpowder technology and slave-raiding on a massive scale.[8] This was accompanied by a fundamental reorganization of the symbolic system. The complementarity between the sea prince and the bamboo maiden discussed in the last chapter was transformed into a complementarity between the sea king of Tallo', associated with trade, prestige goods and diplomacy, and the land king of Gowa, associated with agriculture, subsistence goods, and warfare. The chronicles of Gowa and Tallo' express this relationship as a division that occurs between two male siblings who later reunite by exchanging sisters. Previously, the relationship had been express as a split between a male and female twin who reunite by finding an identical substitute.

The foundation myth of Kajang (M 6.7) still evokes the old order of coastal chiefdoms. The chronicle of Bira provides evidence that the new conceptualization of the complementary functions of land and sea, agriculture and trade that developed in Gowa-Tallo' was replicated throughout the Makassar world among the vassals of the new empire. Under the Empire of Gowa-Tallo', agricultural productivity was no longer associated exclusively with the feminine role of the goddess who descends from the skies like the rains to unite with the earth. It was now also associated with the shedding of blood in battle. The chronicle of Bira is fully in line with the new order of slavery and conquest stimulated by the appearance of European military technology. Further evidence of the association between violence and fertility will be provided in the next chapter, where I discuss the role of regalia, predominantly made up of battle standards and weapons of various types.

Chapter 8

The Power of the Regalia
Royal Rebellion against the Dutch East India Company

I n this chapter, I will examine the royal rituals that linked the political power of rulers in the present to the mystical power of the founding ancestors in the past. These rituals portrayed the power of the ruler and the power of the ancestors as essential to the natural fertility of all the plants, animals, and humans that occupied a particular territory or realm. These rituals enable us to see how the myths and chronicles discussed in previous chapters functioned not just to organize symbolic knowledge but also to legitimate political power on a daily basis. At the center of the rituals were the *gaukang* regalia. I show how the *gaukang* retained their power from ancient times, through the colonial period, and into the present.

Precolonial Royal Rituals in Bira

Many of the royal houses of South Sulawesi that survived into the twentieth century traced their origins back to the thirteenth or fourteenth century. The continuing identity of these houses was based on the acquisition and intergenerational transmission of an estate that included a variety of symbolic, social, political, and economic assets. Symbolic assets included control of the sacred regalia and their cult, the right to undergo elaborate life cycle rituals and to be addressed by certain titles, and the right to give and receive large marriage payments. Social and political assets included the control of and eligibility for political and religious offices and a network of genealogical and affinal ties that were the residue of previous marriages. Economic assets included land, hereditary slaves, outstanding debts, and long-distance trading partners.

As Lévi-Strauss pointed out, in many "feudal" societies the important point about noble estates like this is that they be preserved intact and passed on through time (Lévi-Strauss [1979] 1982). Just how they were transmitted in South Sulawesi depended on a variety of contingent factors, including descent from the founding ancestor; the marital, military, and economic achievements of subsequent rulers; and the balance of power within the *hadat,* the council that selected successors to the highest political office in a realm.

In South Sulawesi, descent alone defined no more than a pool of potential candidates to high office, according to the purity of the "white blood" each had inherited from all ancestors on both the male and female sides. One of the main uses of the indigenous *lontara* script was to keep track of the myriad kinship connections generated by this bilateral calculation of rank. If a ruler wanted one of his own children to succeed him, he had to take great care to marry a wife of the highest possible rank.

In addition to this genealogical calculus, worldly success could be interpreted as proof of some previously unknown inherent potency. A second use of the *lontara* script was to keep a careful record of precisely these achievements of each ruler. A ruler who succeeded in increasing the military power, economic wealth, or marital alliances of the ruling house while in office would become a focus for future genealogical calculations.

Finally, all Bugis and Makassar foundation myths include the notion that kingship arose when the local chiefs of a certain territory voluntarily placed themselves under the rule of a divine being. These chiefs constituted the original *hadat*, which conveyed the king's commands to the common people, and the people's petitions to the king. Successors to the founding ruler were chosen from the pool of eligible candidates by the successors of the original *hadat*. Members of the *hadat* included both the rulers of lesser territories in their own right and holders of nonterritorial "ministerial" offices like *tuma'bicara butaya*, "adjudicator of the realm" or chancellor. Succession to these subordinate offices followed similar procedures as for the supreme office: a selection was made from a genealogically defined pool of eligible candidates.

Errington entirely overlooks the role of the *hadat* in her discussion of kingship in Luwu', treating the office as passing unproblematically to the candidate with the whitest blood. She also claims that "the ruler was not involved in relations of reciprocity" (Errington 1989: 281). And yet, as we saw in chapters 6 and 7, kingship itself is based on a contract between the king who guarantees social harmony and fertility and the people who feed and protect the king. The relationship between the encompassing office of the king and the encompassed offices of the *hadat* was one of reciprocity. What is more, the representatives of the people who compose the *hadat* were not normally appointed by the king at his own discretion, as implied by the following statement: "A ruler who failed to give a title and arajang appointment (a title and the secondary regalia that located the area) to a high noble with many widely dispersed followers would be courting danger" (Errington 1989: 279). Members of the *hadat* were, like the king, heirs to territorial and ministerial offices each of which was traced back to a founding ancestor. In many cases, these ancestors also left behind physical tokens of their being that served to link the past to the present.

Succession to high office was a deeply "historical" process, dependent on the technology of writing, the balance of power among the subordinate office holders within a realm at the time of selection, the military and mercantile achievements of specific individuals, and, after about 1860, the growing interference of the late colonial state in local government. It is impossible to discuss these public political rituals without discussing the political history of South Sulawesi at the same time. In what follows, I will use the case of Bira to illustrate the way some of the royal rituals operated before the introduction of direct colonial rule.

The Upperworld: Installation on the Palantikan

All over South Sulawesi, the installation of a new king took place on a stone called the *palantikan,* the "place of installation." The *palantikan* was a flat rock usually located just above the main settlement where the original *Tomanurung* had descended. In 1897, Eerdmans published a description of the installation of a king of Gowa, probably based on the installation of Sultan Husain two years earlier.

> The installation takes place in two ways, i.e., *lanti* and *togasa. Lanti* means the installation at Tamalate, a flat area situated within the walls of the old capital of Gowa, where according to some the first Toemanoeroeng made their descent, according to others their palace would have been here.
> The king was installed, standing on a natural stone, clothed in yellow, armed with the *sudang* (the royal weapon), hung with the *Daeng Tanisamaang* (also known in short as *Tanisamaang*) and *Leenjo* (two golden chains, about which more later) and crowned with the *salloko* (golden crown), while the royal parasol was held above his head during the whole installation. . . .
> *Togasa* means the installation of the king in front of his dwelling. The ceremonial customs used for this are less cumbersome than those used for the *lanti,* but the main ones also take place. (Eerdmans 1897: 58–59)

Nine years after this publication, Sultan Husain was killed while resisting the imposition of direct rule over Gowa, earning him the posthumous title of *Tumenanga ri Bundu'na,* He Who Died in Battle.

The Regency of Bira, 1863–1921

After the Second Bone War of 1859, the colonial government decided to carry out a reorganization of local government in the directly administered territories south of Bone. In 1863, the old territory of Boelecomba and Bonthain (Bulukumba and Bantaeng) was divided. Bulukumba was attached to the newly conquered territories to the north in Sinjai and a new division (Afdeeling) was created, called the Eastern Districts. Each divison was administered by a Dutch resident, and each subdivision (Onderafdeeling) by a Dutch controleur.

The next step was to concentrate the numerous native realms into a few manageable units run by salaried native regents answerable to the controleur. By 1871, the seven traditional realms of the Bira peninsula (Batang, Bonto

Tangnga, Tiro, Ara, Bira, Lemo Lemo, and Tanaberu) had all been placed under a native regent of Bira appointed by the controleur. The Dutch chose the existing *karaeng* of Bira to be the first regent. Baso Daeng Raja was the son of the last *karaeng,* Amar Daeng Matoana, who had ruled Bira during the Napoleonic wars (circa 1790–1830). Daeng Raja was selected to succeed him by the *hadat* when he was still a child, in about 1835. He served as ruler of the expanded regency of Bira from 1864 to 1884.

In the interests of uniformity, all the village chiefs were given the title of *gallarrang* and placed under the regent of Bira. This was taken as a grave insult by all those chiefs whose ancestors had carried the higher title of *karaeng.* To add insult to injury, Daeng Raja's immediate successors as regent were not even from the royal house of Bira. They proved singularly unable to command the respect of the outlying villages, and the annual reports of the Dutch controleurs based in Bulukumba are filled with complaints about this fact. The old idea of a contract between a ruler chosen by the *hadat* and the people they represented proved difficult to undermine.[1]

Perhaps in an attempt to increase the legitimacy of the regent, the Dutch appointed Andi Mulia Daeng Raja to the office in 1900. He was a son of the first regent of Bira, Baso Daeng Raja, and thus a legitimate heir to the *karaeng*ship of Bira under the old rules. Although he was not selected by the *hadat* in the traditional way, Andi Mulia was installed according to the customary rites on February 9, 1900. The installation took place on the same two stones described in the extract from the chronicles given in M 7.5. They are each about a cubic meter in size and sit behind a house up a hill to the west of the great spring of Bira Lohe. Andi Mulia described his installation to Collins as follows:

> "It was on this hill that the earliest kampong stood, defended by two little forts. There are two big stones—I expect you've seen them—in an open space among the houses. They are called 'Make Karaeng,' and on one of them I sat. If I had been married, my wife would have sat on the other. At my back were men with all these. . . ."
>
> He waved his hand towards the central pillar of the house, where, lashed by rattan loops, stood seven spears and two old and tattered sunshades on tall poles, emblems of his rank. The longest of the spears was a trident: two had deep horsehair ruffs below their blades; round some were eight-inch bands of gold, embossed in spiral and angular designs, that were begrimed and battered; and one had two blades, like a short-pronged pitchfork, with a sheath or wood carved in the likeness of a lyre-bird's tail.
>
> "The trident and the one with two blades," the Karaeng went on, "may be taken outside only when they follow the Karaeng. And even then, unless there is war or a man runs amok and tries to attack the Karaeng, they are never unsheathed."
>
> . . .
>
> "We had all these spears, Tuan, and the tall sunshades, and gongs and

drums and many cannon. I sat on Make Karaeng, and the chief minister of Bira [*tuma'bicara buttaya*] . . . stood up and shouted:

"'Now we have a Karaeng, raised to power by the stone Make Karaeng! His commands we must obey! What he forbids we must not do. He is our ruler, our leader in battle. We must fight for him. He is our ruler, our Karaeng.'

"Then the cannon roared and all the people shouted, and with booming of gongs and drums began many days of feasting." (Collins 1936: 134–135)

This version of the oath describes the principle duty of the people as military service and stresses the absolute loyalty of the people toward the ruler. But Andi Mulia pays little attention to the reciprocal duties the ruler owes the people.

The Middleworld: Paying Homage to the *Gaukang*

Certain items of sacred regalia, such as the weapons that were carried by Andi Mulia's entourage to his installation and which later served as signs of his office, are known as *kalompoang*, "things of greatness." They are imbued with the power that comes from their former victories in battle, and are carefully preserved however old and decrepit they became. Nooteboom reproduced an inventory of all the *kalompoang* Goedhart found in Selayar (1948–1949: 247–248). The list mostly consists of weapons and battle flags, but items such as walking sticks, betel boxes, and other royal accessories made of precious metals are also common.

The most powerful items of royal regalia are called *gaukang*, "things of potency." Some *gaukang* were linked to the original *Tomanurung*, as in the case of the Tanisanga chain and Sudang sword of Gowa. As we have seen, these objects were carried to the *palantikan* when the kings of Gowa were installed, bringing the new ruler into direct physical contact with objects belonging to the founding ancestors. But the installation of a new king occurred at most a few times each generation. Regular contact with the founding ancestors was maintained at the *palantikan* by means of separate rituals held in honor of the *gaukang* as such. During these rituals, the *gaukang* were carried to the *palantikan,* where the spirits of the founding ancestors were called down into them by special priests, called *bissu* in the great kingdoms and *pinati* in the little kingdoms. Men paid homage to them by performing special military dances with the *kalompoang* weapons of the kingdom, while women performed graceful dances.

The *gaukang* thus provided a symbolic focus for the unity of the kingdom separate from the person of the king. However unstable and violent the political history of a realm might be, the cult of the *gaukang* provided it with a stable identity and source of mystical vitality. This separation of powers became increasingly important as the colonial government usurped the political functions of kingship.

Planting and Harvesting the *Ongko*

The upkeep of the *gaukang* was supported by certain agricultural fields dedicated to them, called *ongko*. These fields were worked by corvée labor, and the produce went to the local ruler acting on behalf of the *gaukang*. The *ongko* of Bira was the barren point of land at Tanetang where the rituals in honor of Sampanena were conducted (see chapter 5). The *ongko* of Ara consisted of two fields. One, at Kaddaro, was the site of a famous battle in which the founding ancestor from Gowa, Karaeng Mamampang, defeated the *karaeng* of Tiro (story 6 in the chronicle of Bira). Recall that Kaddaro means "to kick," and the name of the field is said to derive from the fact that one could not cross it after the battle without kicking the severed heads of the enemy. The field had thus been fertilized by the blood of human victims in battle.

I had to reconstruct agricultural rituals from interviews with several women over the age of seventy, because most rituals have now fallen into disuse. No rice is grown in Ara, because of the poor soil, but long ago the rituals associated elsewhere with the rice spirit were adapted to the cultivation of maize. There are several indications in the chronicle of Bira that the area was one of the first places in Southeast Asia to obtain crops like maize and cassava brought across the Pacific by the Spanish and Portuguese in the sixteenth century.

Until the beginning of the twentieth century, no one could begin work on their own field until the *gallarrang*'s *ongko* field at Kaddaro had been opened by cutting down a shrub or breaking the ground with a digging stick. The clearing and plowing of other fields could then proceed freely. Then the *gallarrang*'s field had to be planted before planting on the other fields could begin. The seed corn was stored in the attic of each house next to the ancestor shrine. Only female members of the household descended from these ancestors were allowed to enter the attic, or even to look into it to see how much maize was left. The reproductive powers contained by the seed corn on which each household depended were thus closely associated with the reproductive powers contained by the ancestor shrine, and both were associated with the link between mothers and daughters. The precedence of the ruler's field over all other fields linked the fertility of the realm as a whole to the fertility of the ruler's field, and the power of all the village ancestors to the power of the royal ancestor.

The selection of the best day to begin work on a new agricultural cycle was made according to a variety of astrological calculations. The day before first planting, the seed corn was brought down from the attic of the house and immersed in a large earthenware pot, which was thought of as "cool." The water activated the life force in the seed. The force was then protected from danger and directed toward its goal by a number of other materials that were immersed alongside it, including the following:

1. Cooking utensils, such as a rice ladle carved from a single piece of *centong* wood, bamboo pincers used to arrange burning logs, and a bamboo tube used to blow on a fire. These utensils were meant to remind the maize of the people's desire for food and of its ultimate destination on the hearth.
2. A variety of leaves, including *taha siri; dingin-dingin,* very cool, a fat leaf that will root if it is planted; and *sinrolo,* another kind of thick leaf. The object of

all these leaves was to make the leaves of the maize thick as well. The same leaves are used in other rituals called *songkobala,* "warding off evil."

3. Tools, including a *parang,* harvest knife, and a *sangko,* sickle for weeding.

The morning following the immersion, the cooking utensils were returned to the hearth, again linking the seed corn to a particular hearth. The leaves were taken out to the field, where they were wedged under the *tangnga koko,* the center or navel of the field, marked by a large boulder or an old tree. This is where the *sumanga'* of the maize resided during the growing season. A special strain of maize was planted each year next to the *tangnga koko,* harvested, stored in the center of the attic, and planted in the same spot the following year. This is a familiar practice throughout Southeast Asia, usually associated with the rice spirit. Planting began at the *tangnga koko,* then moved to the southeast, northeast, northwest, and southwest corners, in that order, proceeding in a counterclockwise direction around the field, gradually dispersing the life force of the maize throughout the field, while keeping it focused on the *tangnga koko.* This ended the ritual and general planting could begin.

When the hairs of the maize first appeared, medicines were placed in the crotch formed where each ear of maize meets the stalk. This is the navel of the maize plant, the point where the life force of each plant is attached. While the medicine was being applied, a *mantera* was recited at the center and corners of the field. After exactly two months, or sixty days, the first young maize would be ready to eat. It was cooked and eaten in the field house while incense was burned and a *mantera* was recited inviting the demons of the wild *setan* to come and share the meal. If they were not fed, they became angry and invited in wild pigs, who could finish off an entire crop in a single night. A portion was also set aside for the maize spirit and placed in the *tangnga koko* along with the ingredients for a betel chew.

All the rituals to this point were small, family affairs. Once sufficient maize had ripened, a feast was held. A huge amount of maize stew, *barobbo,* was cooked and many guests were invited. Special cakes called *lappa lappa* were made from finely pounded maize meal, grated coconut, and palm sugar, all wrapped in a maize husk and boiled. A portion again had to be placed on the *tangnga koko* for the maize spirit.

The day before the full-scale harvest of the field the clumps of sacred maize planted immediately around the *tangnga koko* were bound together. There were usually several stalks growing together, because three to four seeds were planted in each hole. This prevented the life force of the maize from escaping during the disruption caused by the harvest. Three or four people harvested together, starting in the southeast corner and proceeding abreast in a counterclockwise direction, spiraling inward until the center was reached. This inverted the process of planting, with the sacred maize being dealt with last instead of first. The life force of the maize was thus reconcentrated toward the sacred plants in the center of the field, so it could be stored until the next planting season.

As it was harvested, the maize was heaped up in a pile beneath the field house. An ear of maize was taken from the top of the pile, wrapped in a *bungbungan* leaf, and put back on top of the heap under a rock. Next the ears were sorted by size. Seven of the largest ears were placed on the rock along with some salt and leaves from the castor oil plant. The ends of the ears were cut off, causing the dirty outer husks to fall away and leaving just the clean, inner ones. The life force of the maize as a whole was progressively concentrated in the sacred strains, in these seven ears, and finally in the single large ear placed beneath the rock.

The seven plus one ears of maize harvested from the center of the field were tied together, with a maize flower in the center, and placed at the very center of the attic as the *anrong battara*, "mother of the maize." Storing maize in the attic was entirely women's business. The rest of the maize was carefully laid out flat around this, still unhusked, so that air could circulate around every ear and prevent mold from growing. The next year, the "mother of the maize" would be the first to be planted again.

Agricultural rituals like these were both intimate domestic rituals that defined the essence of female power over biological reproduction and public political rituals that placed the ruler and his ancestors at the center of every household. This connection between the biological fertility and political authority was made even more dramatically in the rituals conducted at the navel of the earth.

The Underworld: Sacrifice on the *Possi' Tana*

In South Sulawesi, every village has a stone called the *possi' tana*. Nooteboom served as controleur of Selayar in 1936–1937, just after Collins left Bira. He published the following account of the rituals held in Selayar at the *possi' tana:*

> In various of the older Salayarese villages one finds a great stone, above which the villagers have built a little house and where one brings little individual offerings at irregular intervals. This stone is called the "navel of the earth" *(posi tana)* and stands in close relationship to the origin of the local community. Usually the community includes more than just one village, involving a village complex or even an *adat* community. The village of Salloe in the *adat* community of Batangmata in the north of the island has such a stone. In addition to the individual offerings that occur frequently, every few years a great community ritual must take place. Two or three years after the last one, or else if the maize harvest is bad, the authorities of the village complex, of which Salloe is the center, come together for mutual consultation about whether there is occasion for a new feast by the stone. The Gelarang, or chief of the village complex is paramount, along with his village chiefs and their official helpers. Then comes the Mohammadan leader (imam) along with his religious officials and—last but not least—the *sanro tana*, priest of the sanctuary. They come to an agreement, then they go to the Mohammadan leader of

the *adat* community *(kali)* and to the secular *adat* community head *(opoe)* to ask permission for the feast. This is seldom refused.

In preparation for the performance a little house is installed above the *posi tana* under the leadership of the Kali, imam and sanro, if necessary renovated, and one makes a bamboo enclosure around it. White flags with Arabic expressions rise up from the house. As the great day begins, all the inhabitants arrive to eat and drink with many displays of joy. A small amount of food is placed on the stone for each family, so that all inhabitants of the complex can take part in the sanctity of the *posi tana*. Each takes care for his own part in the expenses, but in addition the *opoe* is responsible for a contribution in the form of a slaughtered buffalo or other offering. This is what they told me in Salloe, when I came across the remains of the latest feast; the newly installed house and the still white flags.

Such stones one finds in many places in the Makassar-Bugis culture area, but alas the data are mostly missing concerning the rituals pertaining to them and concerning their value to the people. (Nooteboom 1948-1949: 246-247)

In Ara and Bira, the *possi' tana* is located just below the main settlement. In Tanaberu it is above the village, right next to the *palantikan*. According to informants, if one lifted the stone one would see a shaft that leads to the Underworld. Periodic offerings are made on this stone to ensure the fertility of the earth. In times of crisis such as droughts and epidemics, it may be determined that the earth itself has been offended by sins like incest or the abuse of royal authority. In this case the most extreme form of sacrifice was performed: the *rumpulangi,* or burnt offering, of a live buffalo on the *possi' tana*. The blood of the animal flowed into the earth, while the smoke from the flame rose to the heavens, invoking the rains. The ashes that remained were carefully collected. A little ash was mixed in with the seed corn each year to ensure the fertility of the crop.

In 1988, the *kapala desa* of Ara, Daeng Pasau, told me that his grandfather Siappe Daeng Masiga (born circa1850) had witnessed the last *rumpulangi* performed in Ara. It took place in the middle of the nineteenth century after a particularly severe drought. Daeng Pasau said that people had stopped performing it because they came to regard it as too cruel. Daeng Elle (born circa 1895) said that he had witnessed a *rumpulangi* in Tanaberu when he was a small child. After another long drought, a buffalo was slaughtered and then burned to ashes at Ere Manerang in Sampung Cina. This is a swampy area next to the Bampang River where groundwater is found just a few inches below the surface of a meadow and is considered to be a point of close contact with the Underworld. Elle considered that, because the buffalo had not been burned alive, it was not as efficacious as it might have been. Elle also claimed that the ritual was specific to Ara and had been copied by Tanaberu. The officiant on that occasion had been the Kali of Ara, Daeng Sijalling.

The *rumpulangi* may have been suppressed, but rituals are still periodically carried out at the *possi' tana* in Ara by a special *sanro,* Daeng Kati Deda. It must be said, however, that the *possi' tana* no longer plays a very important role in the ritual life of the village. It is an unremarkable stone in the front yard of an inconspicuous house just downhill from the main spring at the center of the village. The *possi' tana* of Bira has suffered an even greater eclipse. It took me the better part of an afternoon questioning increasingly older informants to even determine where it was located. Like the *possi' tana* of Ara, it is just down the hill from the main spring of Bira Lohe, about half a kilometer along the road that goes north to Kasuso.

The Regalia in Battle: Sangkilang's Rebellion against the VOC

Because of their importance, generations of VOC and NEI officials left extensive descriptions of certain royal rituals and the role they played in the politics of South Sulawesi. As I have said, the rituals described in the first part of this chapter lost much of their original purpose in the early twentieth century, when the Dutch imposed direct colonial rule throughout South Sulawesi. Many were even actively suppressed as encouraging resistance to colonial rule. We must thus rely on the earlier accounts to understand how they worked traditionally. The meaning and purpose of the *gaukang* became of particular concern to generations of Dutch officials due to a peculiar series of events that took place in the second half of the eighteenth century.

In the latter half of the eighteenth century, a complex trade developed within Southeast Asia between the British East India Company, Chinese merchants, the Tausug of the Sulu archipelago, and specialized slave-raiding groups like the Iranun. The Iranun supplied slaves to the Tausug exchange for firearms, cloth, and opium. The Tausug used the slaves to gather natural produce such as tripang and bird's nests. The Tausug used this natural produce to acquire firearms, cloth, and opium from the British. The British traded the natural produce with the Chinese to acquire tea and silk. The tea and silk was exchanged for more firearms and cloth in Britain. The *To Belo* of of Halmahera served a similar function for the sultan of Ternate that the Iranun served for the sultan of Sulu (Hanna and Des Alwi 1990). The system as a whole rested on the exploitation of slave labor. After the VOC took control of the port of Makassar, it came to serve as one of the most important centers of the slave trade in Southeast Asia between 1670 and 1770.

The Kingdom of Tallo' remained a center of resistance to the VOC long after Gowa's fortifications had been destroyed. The last strong ruler of Gowa and Tallo', Shafi al-Din, died in 1760. The throne of Tallo' was then taken by the former *tuma'bicara* of Gowa, Karaeng Majannang. Shafi al-Din's brother, Karaeng Katangka, became *tuma'bicara butta* of Gowa and guardian of the young king. The throne of Gowa passed to his thirteen-year-old grandson, Amas Madina Batara Gowa.

In 1765 Batara Gowa reached the age of eighteen and was emancipated from the regency of his great-uncle. He chafed under his continued subservience to the VOC governor, however, and in 1766 sailed off to Bencoolen, in Sumatra, where he solicited help from the British who had recently established a base there. Rebuffed, he sailed to Sumbawa, where he took refuge with his mother in the royal palace of Bima. The VOC resident in Bima took Batara Gowa prisoner. The governor-general ordered Batara Gowa to be exiled to the VOC post in Ceylon.

Batara Gowa was succeeded by his brother, Arung Mampu. Arung Mampu grew increasingly distraught over his brother's exile and incessantly demanded his return. In this, he was supported by the royal family of Bone. In 1769, Arung Mampu became so despondent that he, too, abdicated the throne of Gowa and joined his grandmother, Aru Palakka, in her palace at Barombong. In 1770 Shafi al-Din's aging brother, Karaeng Katangka, was installed as Sultan Zain al-Din. With two previous rulers still alive, his legitimacy remained uncertain.

The situation was no better in the twin kingdom of Tallo'. In 1767, the *karaeng* of Tallo', Majannang, had died without heirs. The *hadat* of Tallo' offered the throne to Aru Palakka, the grandmother of the *karaeng* of Gowa at the time. Aru Palakka was one of the most highly born and well-connected nobles in the whole of South Sulawesi. She was the daughter of Sultan Ismail, who had ruled both Gowa and Bone in succession; the granddaughter of a *karaeng* of Tallo', Abd al-Qadir; the widow of a previous *karaeng* of Tallo', Shafi al-Din; and the grandmother of two *karaeng*s of Gowa, Batara Gowa, and Arung Mampu. When Aru Palakka refused to become *karaeng* of Tallo' the *hadat* bestowed the post on another woman, Karaeng Taenga. Over the next few years, Aru Palakka was to play a central role in organizing resistance to the Dutch.

By 1770, the Makassar had thus reached a low point in their political life. The VOC governor may be forgiven for thinking that Dutch rule was now secure. Peace, however, lasted for only six years. In 1776 a prince from Bone bought a slave in Pasir in Borneo and brought him to the VOC territory of Polombangkeng to the south of Gowa. There he escaped and soon built up a following among the inhabitants by claiming to be the exiled Batara Gowa returned to claim his rightful throne. This is how the story came to be handed down orally:

One day in 1776 a prauw appeared at the mouth of the river of Sanrabone. Sitting on a crossbeam at the back of the vessel, the one on which the rudder rests, sat a person, who, when asked his name, appeared to be mute. So they called him Sangkilang, after this beam because that is its name in Makassarese. The prauw went up the river of Sanrabone to Sopu, a forested kampong, where a feast was in progress. Here the boatmen landed and with them Sangkilang, who—having recovered his speech—declared that he was the Batara Gowa banished to Ceylon. According to some reports he was actually a slave of the Bonese prince Aru Patempe, in whose place he had been sent to attend the feast, and who was therefore carrying his *songko* (Makassarese headgear) under a golden cover and who was further decked out with his [master's] clothes and weapons. Arriving at the feast, he immediately occupied the first place and no one there recognized him. When he made himself known as Batara Gowa, a tumult erupted. Some instantly believed in his words, others did not. Finally he was able to make some of them believe him by asking about the different ornaments and family members of Batara Gowa in such a way that the crowd let itself be fooled. By promises and deceptions he was able to create a great following. Some made the story still better, by claiming that Sangkilang, without speaking a word, had come up the river just sitting on the crossbeam of a prauw, then adding to this the assurance that the prauw, which was supposed to have taken him to exile in Ceylon, had overturned, but that he, Batara Gowa, had saved himself by holding fast to a *sangkilang* of the prauw, whereafter he succeeded in sending the prauw out to sea again and sitting on the *sangkilang* to make for land. There are still many who actually think that Sangkilang was the true Batara Gowa. (Tideman 1908a: 360–361)

Among those who accepted Sangkilang as Batara Gowa were his brother, Aru Mampu, his mother, Karaeng Balasari of Bima, and his grandmother, Aru Palakka.

Initial Dutch attempts to capture Sangkilang were rebuffed by armed force. Fighting a mobile guerilla campaign, he took the Dutch post at Maros for a few days in May 1777. The *Punggawa* of the Bone forces was Datu Baringang, son of the former sultan of Bone, Jalil al-Din, and uncle of the current sultan, Ahmad al-Salih. Datu Baringang helped to expel Sangkilang from Maros but then allowed him to escape to Tallo'. The Queen of Tallo' renounced her throne to him. In June 1777, Sangkilang entered Gowa in triumph, and the people proclaimed him sultan. Zain al-Din and his entourage fled with a part of the royal regalia, but Sangkilang took possession of the most important piece, the royal sword Sudang left behind by the royal founder Lakipadada. Zain al-Din died shortly thereafter.

The Bone auxiliaries of the Dutch now refused to take further action against Sangkilang, who had been acclaimed by the people as the ruler of both Gowa and Tallo'. He was forced out of Gowa only when Javanese troops arrived in 1778. For the first time, the walls of Kale Gowa were completely destroyed. Sangkilang escaped to the mountains with his aging "grandmother," Arung Palakka, who died there in January, 1779. Her death was a blow to the rebels, for she commanded the loyalty of both the Gowanese and the Bonese.

In 1780, the *punggawa* of Bone, Datu Baringang, demanded that his wife, Sitti Saleh, be placed on the throne of Tallo'. The Dutch refused and instead coerced the *hadat* of Tallo' into recognizing the VOC as direct ruler of Tallo'. The area south of the river was placed under the senior interpreter of Makassar, and the area to the north under the senior merchant of Maros. In 1781, the Dutch proclaimed Zain al-Din's son, Abd al-Hadi, heir to the throne of Gowa, although they continued to rule Gowa as a conquered province until the British occupied Makassar in 1812. With Sangkilang still at large and without the Sudang regalia, Abd al-Hadi's hold on the throne remained tenuous. Only the lowland Makassar came to recognize him, whereas the mountain Makassar continued to recognize Sangkilang.

When Sangkilang died in 1785, the Sudang passed into the hands of the real Batara Gowa's brother, Arung Mampu, who gave it to the sultan of Bone, Ahmad al-Salih (reigned 1775–1812). The mountain Makassars transferred their allegiance to Ahmad al-Salih, who could also claim descent from the royal house of Gowa. The Sudang was not recovered from Bone by the Dutch until 1816. They then returned it to the ruler of Gowa they recognized, and the regalia were finally reunited after a gap of almost forty years.

Colonial Appropriations of the Regalia

These events left a strong impression on later Dutch colonial officials, who developed something of an obsession with the power of the *gaukang* after the demise of the VOC and the creation of the government of the NEI in the nineteenth century. Following the Second Bone War of 1859, in which he played a prominent role, Bakkers noted that "some days before the start of a battle the royal regalia are brought to an open field in front of both parties, or at any rate out from their normal place of keeping, and smeared there with the blood of a buffalo or other sacrificial animal. Upon this occasion a popular feast is normally held, at which the chiefs and prince *mangaru* [perform a war dance]" (Bakkers 1866: 81). Forty years later, when the Dutch imposed direct rule on the kingdom of Gowa, they took the precaution of destroying royal ancestor shrines kept in the attics of noble houses. Following Bakkers, they believed that armed opposition to them was inspired by blood sacrifices to the *gaukang* they contained (Chabot [1950] 1996).

The first colonial officer to publish extensively on the *gaukang* was P. J. Kooreman.

> When I was temporary Assistant Resident of the Southern Districts in 1876, the regent of Bonthain died, and all the Bonthain ornaments, among which the golden statue called Karaeng Lowé was included, were kept in my house. Apparently one then considered me as the caretaker, for never again so long as I served in South Celebes were my orders so promptly followed, and did one show me so much respect. The same was the case when the ornaments of Montjongkomba (Polombanking) were kept in my office. It struck me much more on that occasion because the people had shown the beginnings of resistance before they were in my possession. (Kooreman 1883: 186–187)

On the basis of these experiences and the history of the Sudang of Gowa, Kooreman convinced himself that whoever had the *gaukang* in his possession would be regarded as the legitimate ruler by the people. Many subsequent authors took Kooreman's assertions at face value.

In part on the basis of Kooreman's theory, when the Dutch finally decided to impose direct rule throughout South Sulawesi in 1905, they seized the Sudang and other *gaukang* and sent them to museums in Batavia and the Netherlands.

The kingdoms of Gowa and Bone were abolished and placed under the direct authority of Dutch controleurs. Installation rituals were suppressed throughout the province between 1905 and 1929. They were deliberately revived between 1929 and 1949 as a way of maintaining the loyalty of the nobility in the face of rising nationalist sentiment. We must thus rely on nineteenth-century accounts of them, or on the rituals stage managed by Dutch colonial officers in the 1930s.

In 1925 a twenty-five-year-old Dutchman, H. J. Friedericy, was placed in charge of what was now the "*adat* community" of Gowa. He had arrived in South Sulawesi in 1922 with a *doctorandus* degree in Indology from Leiden. While in Gowa, he became quite friendly with the pretender to the defunct throne of Gowa, Mappanyuki (Friedericy 1931). Mappanyuki and others apparently persuaded him that only persons of the correct descent were entitled to the *gaukang*, and only they could draw power from it. In 1927, Governor-General Andries de Graeff (1926–1931) visited Makassar. Mappanyuki took the opportunity to request the return of various royal heirlooms that had been seized from his family in 1906. Many heirlooms were returned in 1929, perhaps on the advice of Friedericy. The government, however, retained possession of the *gaukang* themselves. In 1930, Friedericy returned to Leiden to write a doctoral dissertation.

In the late 1920s, the Dutch decided to revive the authority of hereditary local rulers under a sort of simulated indirect rule in the hope that the old noble families would support them against the young modernists agitating for independence. In 1930, a number of reports appeared on ornaments and installation rituals. Van Eerde published an account of Gowa's investiture stones and Le Roux reviewed old archival accounts of coronations of Bone's kings. Commenting on reports that the *gaukang* had also been returned to the royal family of Gowa at this time, Friedericy pointed out that they could not be returned until a legitimate king was once again installed in Gowa (1931). It was not until 1936 that the kingdom of Gowa was restored and, with it, the *gaukang* to their rightful place in Gowa.

Back in Leiden, Friedericy came under the influence of structuralism, specifically, of the argument of Durkheim and Mauss in *Primitive Classification* that all symbolic categories can be traced back to archaic forms of social organization ([1903] 1963). This argument was first picked up by a colonial legal expert, van Ossenbruggen, in an article on Javanese systems of classification published in 1918, and by Rassers, a staff member of the Museum of Ethnology in Leiden, who published an article on the Panji tales in 1922. In the same year, J.P.B. de Josselin de Jong was appointed to the chair in general ethnology in Leiden and trained a generation of anthropologists in this approach.

Friedericy attended the seminars of de Josselin de Jong along with van Baal, Held, Locher, Nooteboom, van Wouden, and Chabot. All, with the exception of Chabot, later produced orthodox structuralist accounts of the societies they studied. Friedericy drew on the theories of Durkheimians such as Rassers and van Ossenbruggen to argue that the division of Makassar society into nobles and freemen was a survival of an earlier moiety system with matrilineal descent and patrilocal residence. In regard to the *gaukang*, he concluded that, contrary to the assertion of Kooreman, "The regalia were inherent to the royal office, the royal office was reserved only for those who were of the purest blood. Thus the regalia belonged in the hands of the highest group" (Friedericy 1933: 501). Academic arguments like these about the importance of the *gaukang* to political legitimacy played a central role in colonial decisions in the 1930s.

In 1931, A. A. Cense was appointed "official for the study of native languages" in the Celebes, replacing the old official for native affairs. One of Cense's first tasks as official linguist in April 1931 was to help organize and observe the ritual installation of the newly reinstated "autonomous ruler" of Bone, who was none other than Friedericy's old friend, Mappanyuki. Because of generations of intermarriage between the royal houses of Gowa and Bone, he was eligible for both thrones. His claim to the title of Arumpone derived from his mother, who was the daughter of Arumpone La Parengi (reigned 1845–1858) and Arumpone Basse Kajuara (reigned 1858–1860).

When Mappanyuki was installed as king of Bone in 1931, no such installation had been performed for over 150 years, perhaps since the installation of Sultan Ahmad al-Salih in 1775. The model Cense used for the ceremony actually seems to have come from the time of VOC Governor van Clootwijk (1751–1756). Cense's unpublished account of how these installation rituals came about is worth quoting in detail.

> When it was decided by the government that the dignity of Self-governor of Bone should be bestowed on Andi Mappanjoeki, it was considered in accord with the gravity of this undertaking that the installation of the new Aroempone should occur in the ceremonial way. Twenty-five years previously the centuries old government, which according to native tradition began with the mythical descent from the heavens of To-manoeroeng ri Matadjang, had been brought to an end; when the circumstances made it again desirable that the old form of administration, albeit on a more modern basis, be established, the announcement of this occurrence had to be made in a manner that was appropriate and unforgettable for the people, and also that the royal ornaments kept in the Museum of the Royal Batavian Society since 1905, without which the royal dignity is unthinkable in this area, should be ceremonially handed over by the Governor of Celebes.
>
> The installation would occur after the swearing in of the Aroempone and the signing of the "Short Declaration" had taken place, on 2 April 1931.
>
> Those who were charged with organizing this ceremony had no easy task. No one in Bone had ever been present at an installation according to the old *adat*-ceremonial, indeed, according to what was contended, it would have been already more than 150 years since such an installation had befallen a Bonese ruler. This contention seems to us credible, since it is in agreement with the information of the deceased Dr. Matthes, that so long as he lived in South Celebes, an authentic installation had never taken place, despite the fact that a new ruler had taken the throne more than once [Matthes: Over de

Bissoe's (1872b: 44)]. Matthes sought to explain this fact in this way: that gradually through the alteration of circumstances it became more difficult to observe the prescribed ceremonial, so that one in the end preferred to abandon it entirely. Thus originally, e.g., it was the tradition that the ruler of Sidenreng went to sit behind the Aroempone; when the first-mentioned grew more powerful, however, he was understandably little inclined to exhibit his subordination in this manner.

It was not only in Bone but also in Loewoe that, according to Matthes, the old tradition had long since been broken. He informs us that the last installation had taken place upon the enthronement of Queen Tanriawaroe, grandmother of the reigning king in his time. Also the present Datoe of Lowoe' was never officially installed.

Now, however, one observes the fact that though one or another of the prescribed *adat* ceremonies perhaps ought to remain in abeyance, there is no reason to think that the whole ceremonial celebration of the installation ought to be relinquished. Although the oral tradition regarding the performance of the usages was no longer wholly reliable, one fortunately found [some relevant] data in a manuscript belonging to Soelewatang Amalai. While the description of an installation in this text is very short, it could still do very good service as a guide. The manuscript was however not followed in its entirety, a few of the ceremonies described had to be omitted; one may compare the report that follows with the translation given as an appendix of the relevant passage from the manuscript. . . .

The Governor made a speech and, following the model of his predecessor Van Clootwijk, who on 28 June, 1753, invested the Bonese ruler Djalalal-Din in his office, and invited the Aroempone to walk with him under the golden umbrella; then both stood, with their right hands embracing the handle of the umbrella—as an explicit sign for the assembled crowd, that a ruler of Bone was again installed by the Netherlands Government—Governor Caron pronounced some words in the Buginese language, which he had committed to memory. (Cense 1931: 2-4)

Thirty-five years later, Cense recalled that many of the details for this ceremony had been drawn from an old Bugis diary, but did not indicate the extent to which the whole thing had been engineered by the colonial government for its own political purposes.

During my stay in South Celebes I witnessed on several occasions how, for the arranging of important ceremonies, old diaries and notebooks were consulted. I can mention here the arranging of the official inauguration of a king of Bone in 1931 when the Government decided to fill once again the office of Arumpone, vacant for nearly 25 years. For the arrangement of the ceremony, use was made of the description of the installation of a king in the 18th century that one had found described in different *surê bilang*. And when in 1935 the old queen of Luwu' was buried, it was once again the old writings which presented pointers for the ceremonial to be complied with, and prescribed the contributions for the occasion. (Cense 1966: 425)

Nooteboom was another classmate of Friedericy's in the early 1930s in Leiden. After graduation, he went to Indonesia, where he served as controleur of Selayar in 1936–1937. During this period, he also felt compelled to comment on the *gaukang* debate.

When a few years ago the realm of Bone was again given a king, the Government decided in wise prudence to return the so-called royal regalia or royal ornaments which had come into its hands in former times. Now that the plans for a the new installation of the Gowa realm has come to pass and the return of the ornaments of the Gowanese realm has taken place, it is of great importance to understand, in connection with these events, what the significance of the objects for the native society is, what the complexes of sentiments that they call forth are, which religious reactions they can evoke. The answers to these questions are necessary for a good understanding of native relations, which may not be absent as a basis for a good and sound governmental administration. (Nooteboom 1937: 167)

As to the debate between Kooreman and Friedericy about whether possession of the *gaukang* can itself give power, Nooteboom adopted a middle position. He also drew on Durkheim in his discussion, but appealed to Durkheim's discussion of Australian aborigines in the *Elementary Forms of the Religious Life* ([1915] 1995). In his account, the *gaukang* turn out to be rather like the *churinga* of the Australian aborigines. He argued that in a "primitive classification" system objects that belong to the same category are closely related yet not identical. Thus, the colonial government did get some power from possession of the *gaukang*, but the legitimate heir to the throne also retained some power. Thus, periods when the heir and the regalia were separated were inevitably periods of division and civil war (Nooteboom 1937: 175).

The last colonial Dutch contribution to the theory of the *gaukang* came from yet another classmate of Friedericy, Hendrik Chabot. He studied customary law in Leiden in 1929, but also attended de Josselin de Jong's seminars without ever falling under the spell of the structuralism being taught. He arrived in Sulawesi in 1936 to study customary law. His notes were lost during the war, but he was able to return to Gowa in 1948 and 1949 to conduct two six-week-long field investigations of "kinship, status and gender." In his dissertation, he jettisoned both the Leiden school of structuralism and van Vollenhoven's school of "*adat* law." which sought to provide colonial administrators with appropriate guidelines for adjudicating disputes. He turned instead to the Oxford structuralism of Evans-Pritchard and to the American school of culture and personality (Rössler and Röttger-Rössler 1996).

Writing after the collapse of Dutch colonialism in 1950, Chabot concluded that the *gaukang* were simply symbols that helped one group of related households to overcome their internal differences so that they could better compete with other groups of households to acquire political power. This is clearly reminiscent of Evans-Pritchard's account of segmentary opposition among the Nuer, applied to a society without unilineal descent. According to Chabot, because the devotees of an "ornament" could include non-kin, and because ornaments could be found even in humble households, they were purely symbols of political factions with no inherent tie to kinship, to royal office, or even to noble descent: "An ornament is supposed to be in the hands of the group member with the purest blood and the best personal qualities. The individual who has the ornament in his possession is therefore believed to have these qualities until it turns out to be otherwise" (Chabot [1950] 1996: 128–129). Thus, the *gaukang* has no inherent power at all: their power derives wholly from the success of the person who owns it.

Chabot's adoption of contemporary British and American models of ethnography meant that his account suffered from a neglect of both the dense network of symbolic meanings in which the *gaukang* is embedded and the larger political and historical forces at play at the time. No one would know from reading his ethnography that he conducted his fieldwork during a bitter guerilla war for Indonesian independence. For the political role of the *gaukang* in the colonial period, more is to be learned from the earlier accounts of Bakkers, Kooreman, Friedericy, and Nooteboom, despite their dated theoretical frameworks. But Chabot's approach proved prescient for their role in the postcolonial world when their tie to political office was severed.

The Modernist Muslim Critique of the *Gaukang*

Although the attitude of the Dutch administration toward the *gaukang* became increasingly positive after 1928, the attitude of local nobles who had come into contact with nationalist and Islamic modernist ideas became increasingly hostile. This may be illustrated by a dispute over the cult of the *gaukang* that broke out in Kajang in 1928 when the old *karaeng* died. He was to be succeeded by his son, Karaeng Yahya Daeng Magassing, but the latter had come under the influence of the modernist Muhammadiyah organization. When it came time for Karaeng Yahya to open the sacred bundle in which regalia of Kajang was wrapped, he reached inside and found the head of a walking stick. This he derisively displayed to a gathering of Kajang's elders, who were deeply shocked at his actions. They reported them to the authorities, and Bapa Daeng Matasa was appointed *karaeng* instead. The well-known modernist writer Hamka, who spent two years in Makassar from 1931 to 1933, remarked on this event:

> This deed of Karaeng Jahja certainly had results: the rulers of other areas also
> got the idea to open their *poesaka,* which had been venerated for a long time

as idols. Among them was Karaeng Sultan Saeng Radja of Gantaran, near Bonthain, and many others: they found the heads of walking sticks, a kris, pieces of deer antlers, bamboo, etc. And most of the rulers became convinced followers of Gods Unity. God be thanked! (Hamka 1965: 9: 248–249)

It was in these circumstances that Andi Mulia had the *gaukang* of Bira sealed up in a cave soon after he returned to office in 1931. He explained this action to Collins as follows:

"The Gaukang, Tuan," he said, "is a little iron figure of a buffalo calf, about three inches long by two high. It has hardly any head and no horns and only one ear. Long ago, whenever the Birans went out to fight it used to be taken with them. And the story goes that it lost an ear in a battle near Gowa.

"There's a small cave at the head of the bathing-pool where the water comes out of the rock. And in this cave, in the middle of a huge plate, stands the little one-eared calf. The plate itself is very old: it came from one of the Dead Men's Caves. But it isn't nearly as old as the calf, which is the oldest thing in Bira. . . .

"Once a year, for hundreds of years, ever since the days when the first kampong was built on the hill, there was a great gathering at the pool. All the men and women of Bira came with gifts of maize and other food and presents for the calf; and all set to and emptied the pool and cleaned the dirt from its bottom. And when the presents had been placed near the cave they worshiped the calf.

"The guardian of the pool took all the food when the Birans went back to their homes. The last keeper died a year or two ago. He was a very old man, and used to heal the sick by herbs and spells.

"The old people of Bira still regard the calf with extreme reverence. They think the earth rests on the buffalo's back, and they fear the Gaukang like a god. But the young men who had been to school used to laugh at them, and wanted to take the little buffalo out of its cave and play with it. To prevent its being taken out and lost, and to forestall any trouble between the old men and young, four years ago I had the entrance to the cave blocked up with concrete when the new bathing-pool was made.". . .

"The buffalo belongs to Bira," the Karaeng went on, "to the whole people. But there are other gaukang that are the Karaeng's and are always kept in his house. For whoever holds them is Karaeng. There are two bronze cannon below, one with its muzzle resting on the pussi [central pillar]. There used to be a drum, but it's fallen to pieces. And a shield and two swords that came from Luwu, which is the oldest state in Celebes. The best sword is in Lemo Lemo now." (Collins 1937: 141–144)

It would appear from his account that in Bira the little iron buffalo represented the power of the local people as opposed to the military objects that represented the power of the king. It was associated with the central spring of the village and had its own caretaker. The annual ritual mentioned by Andi Mulia perhaps refers to an agricultural ceremony in which the buffalo was given the first fruits of the maize harvest. The statue was also carried into battle, again linking the function of agricultural fertility to the function of war.

Contemporary Interpretations of the *Gaukang*

Andaya follows Kooreman in his speculation that among both the Bugis and Makassar *gaukang* were originally objects sacred to small local communities. They were objects that had been discovered by a founding ancestor of the community, who attributed magical powers due to their unusual physical appearance. "The *gaukeng* may have been a mango pit or piece of wood, but most often it was a stone." He goes on to compare the cults surrounding them to the "earth cults of the Chams in Central Viet Nam" (Andaya 1984: 25, 1975). He then argues that the myths of the *Tomanurung* descending from the sky to rule over a cluster of previously autonomous *gaukang* communities must derive from a later period of political evolution. The *Tomanurung* brought a second set of magical objects with them, often made out of precious metals instead of stone. The androgynous *bissu* priests originally ministered to the earth-*gaukang* and later came to serve the sky-*gaukang* as well. When the royal courts later came under Islamic influence, the *bissu* retreated to the local communities and their humbler *gaukang*.

I encountered some evidence of a belief in the magical powers of peculiarly shaped objects found in nature in Tanaberu. In 1988, Abdul Hamid Maming, B.A., was the head of the Department of Education and Culture in Bonto Bahari. One day, he invited me to view his collection of magical objects. He had stacks of beautiful chinaware taken from local graves that contained what looked to me like green Sung and blue and white Ming ware. Some things looked even older, like stone carvings of a pig and little jars. Then he brought out what he claimed was a "fossil man," an eight-inch-long rock dressed in sarong, shirt, and cap. He showed me an even "weirder," *aneh*, figure dressed in "Arab clothes." This time his air of mystery was so great I did not dare photograph it. He pointed out the stone in the ring he was wearing, which he had found himself and which had a magical essence. It had, he said, a stamp of Muhammad on the bottom, put there not by man but by nature. Then he began bringing out a succession of natural objects he had built up in which he saw various forms: objects such as driftwood and rocks in the form of birds, snakes, and men.

Such objects did not, however, seem to form part of the official *gaukang* on the Bira Peninsula. These fell into one of several categories: metal statuettes of animals such as buffalo or birds; androgynous ritual objects representing the union of a bird and a bamboo (snake); androgynous banners uniting a flag and a spear; weapons used in battle by famous warriors, including spears, shields, cannon, and firearms; and relics of royal ancestors such as bits of bone or clothing.

Errington follows Andaya in his adoption of Kooreman's position (Errington 1989: 125–126). Indeed, she goes a good deal further, claiming not only that the regalia (*arajang* in Bugis) is the real ruler of the kingdom, but that the real ruler was just a relatively crude aspect of the regalia.

> The ruler *was* a type of arajang, for his clothing, teeth and so forth could join the store of valuables that formed the arajang. The ruler was the current living aspect of arajang, the arajang quite literally being the leavings of dead rulers. . . .
>
> Hierarchical centrist Indic States, whose ideology was perfect unity, suppressed the intrinsic duality of potency. Or rather, the active aspect of potency was disvalued, seen as a visible crude aspect of unseen potency rather than a nearly equal partner. Viewed in this way, a ruler, being both mortal and mobile, stood a more talle' aspect of the arajang, standing to it as a kind of mouthpiece, in contrast to the arajang's perfectly stable silence. In this sense, the ruler stood to the regalia as the state's spokesman, in Luwu called the Opu Pa'Bicara, stood to the ruler. (Errington 1989: 128–129)

The preponderance of weapons of war among the regalia, the role of the Sudang sword in Sangkilang's rebellion and the blood sacrifices made to the regalia of Bone before battle might lead us to question just how tranquil and immobile Bugis rulers were meant to be. It is not enough to say, as Errington does, that "my work in an era of enforced peace and with high nobles gives me a different perspective (the nobles') from the perspective of villagers on this subject" (Errington 1989: 126). It gives her the perspective of politically marginalized nobles in an era of bureaucratic power.

Conclusion: Warfare, Blood, and Fertility

Taken as a whole, the rituals of installation, veneration of the regalia, and sacrifice on the navel of the earth linked kingship to agricultural fertility by way of blood sacrifice and warfare. Bugis and Makassar kings were not the indolent, cloistered figures depicted in so many accounts of Southeast Asian rulers that rely on descriptions of court ceremonials conducted during colonial rule. They were judges who wielded the power of life, death, and enslavement over their own subjects and war leaders who demonstrated their virility in battle against neighboring kingdoms.

The subjects of a kingdom were always ready to recognize the charisma of a great war leader, however tenuous or fictive their genealogical claim to a throne might be. When a conflict arose between local Muslims and the Dutch, popular support could spread across local political boundaries as shown by the insurrection lead by Sangkilang. Capture of the royal regalia was certainly part of the strategy of these pretenders to the throne. But this was not because possession of the regalia automatically conferred power and legitimacy on an individual. Rather, possession of the regalia allowed a ruler to establish contact with the royal founders and to conduct the rituals that would allow the blessings of the past to flow into the present.

Chapter 9
The Return of the Kings
The Royal Ancestors under
Colonial Rule

I n this chapter, I examine the effects of two centuries of European warfare and conquest on the system of royal houses discussed in chapters 6, 7, and 8. As we have seen, until the nineteenth century, the legitimacy of these royal houses was perpetuated by a whole network of myths and rituals. These royal houses in turn provided a set of reference points according to which a secondary stratum of noble houses jockeyed for power and rank in lesser polities. Only those who could demonstrate bilateral descent from a founding royal ancestor, or from one of their legitimate successors, were eligible for certain political and ritual offices.

The expansion of a centralized bureaucratic state throughout the Netherlands East Indies in the nineteenth and twentieth centuries led to a crisis in the practical and symbolic reproduction of the royal houses of the Bira Peninsula. The very identity and existence of the old noble class was called into question. The rituals dedicated to the royal ancestors acquired new meanings and purposes as they were reproduced in changing political conditions. This process accelerated during the twentieth century, as the rituals came under direct attack, first by the colonial state and then by nationalists and Islamic modernists. That the nobility has been able to survive at all as a distinct stratum in South Sulawesi is due in part to the way the old royal rituals were transformed and preserved in the nineteenth and twentieth centuries.

I have divided the history of royal rituals in South Sulawesi into five periods of approximately forty years each, each punctuated a major armed conflict, some on a global scale. The first period begins with the upheavals caused by the Napoleonic Wars. During this time, the Bugis kingdom of Bone was able to extend its influence over the villages of the Bira Peninsula. Noble houses that traced their descent back to the Sultan of Bone began to compete for office with the older houses that traced themselves back to Gowa. The houses that linked themselves to Bone were associated with To Kambang, the royal ancestor of Tanaberu. The houses that linked themselves to Gowa continued to be associated with *Karaeng* Mamampang, the royal ancestor of Bira, Ara, and Lemo Lemo.

The next three periods concern the gradual expansion of colonial authority during the nineteenth century. In South Sulawesi, this occurred chiefly at
the expense of Bone in the course of three "Bone Wars" that took place in
1824, 1859, and 1905. As the power of Bone was reduced, the royal houses that
linked themselves to Gowa enjoyed a resurgence in the villages of the Bira Peninsula. A local rivalry between two sets of royal houses and two royal cults
came to mirror the regional rivalry between the Bugis kingdom of Bone and the
Makassar kingdom of Gowa.

The fifth period concerns the evolution of the two cults during and after
the First World War. The cult of To Kambang of Bone managed to remain closely
associated with the holders of political office in Tanaberu throughout the twentieth century. While the village was ruled by a series of bureaucrats who were appointed by the central government during this period, many of them married
local noblewomen who had a genealogical tie to the royal ancestor and hence a
claim on the power of the *gaukang*. The cult as thus always enjoyed official tolerance if not outright patronage. In contrast, the cult of *Karaeng* Mamampang of
Gowa has been under attack by the rulers of Ara since 1915. It has survived almost
a century of political repression as an increasingly private cult for noblewomen.

In both cases, royal ancestor cults have been able to survive long periods
when their sponsors were out of power. They have enabled groups of noble families to maintain a sense of internal solidarity and of external exclusivity in reference to both commoners and rival noble factions. When political conditions
changed, a faction was sometimes able to reclaim political power, but the cults
can perform the function of maintaining the coherence of political factions
only because the myths and rituals at their center are embedded in and help organize an entire symbolic world that links the everyday experience of gender
roles, social hierarchy meaning, and economic activity to wider cosmological
schemes. The meaning and purpose of the cults exceed whatever political function they serve at any given time.

The Napoleonic Wars and the Rise of Bone, 1775–1816

The place of Makassar as the center of the regional slave trade was taken by Sulu
in the nineteenth century. Between 1770 and 1835, about 2,500 slaves a year
were sold in the markets of Sulu, peaking at about 3,500 between 1835 and 1848
and falling gradually to 1,000 by 1870 (Warren 1981: 208). This was approximately equal to the volume of slaves exported from Makassar in the eighteenth
century (Sutherland 1983).

Although official British policy opposed the slave trade after 1808, and
abolished it outright in 1833, private British traders based first in Bengal and
then in Singapore made its efflorescence in Sulu possible between 1770 and
1870. Throughout this century, the coasts of South Sulawesi were subject to constant slave raids. Insecurity in the coastal areas of the outer islands of Indonesia
peaked between 1790 and 1820, when the Dutch were distracted by the Napo-

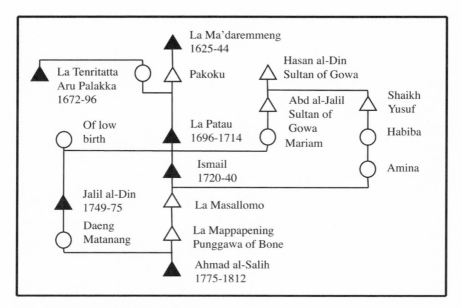

Fig. 9.1 The Sultans of Bone, 1625–1812.

leonic Wars in Europe and unable to send troops, ships, and supplies to defend their possessions in Asia.

The native state that was best positioned to take advantage of Dutch weakness in the late eighteenth century was Bone. In 1772 the Hadat of Bone formally named La Tanrituppu as heir to the throne of Bone. He was chosen in part because he also had a claim to the throne of Gowa through his mother (Tideman 1908a: 359).

In 1775, La Tanrituppu was installed as Sultan Ahmad al-Salih of Bone. Soon afterward, the Netherlands became embroiled in the Fourth Anglo-Dutch War (1780–1784). During this time, the Dutch were able to send only two fleets to the east, in 1783 and 1784. As we saw in chapter 8, after the death of Sangkilang in 1785 part of the royal regalia of Gowa came into the hands of Sultan Ahmad. Because he also had a hereditary claim to the throne of Gowa, many mountain Makassars declared their allegiance to him. Fearing he would attempt to take over the whole of South Sulawesi, an expedition was dispatched from the Netherlands in 1787. It was canceled, however, when the pro-British Orange Party took power. The Orangeists were resolved to take no actions that might antagonize the British in the east, such as fortifying Dutch positions against them.

In 1789 a Dutch party called the Patriots declared their support for the French Revolution and resolved to institute a similar revolution in the Netherlands. News of turmoil in Europe emboldened Bone, which began plundering the Southern Districts of South Sulawesi in 1790. In 1794, Bonese forces took control of the Northern Districts, and Sultan Ahmad established a court there, at Rompegading. In January, 1795, the Patriots marched into Amsterdam and declared the Batavian Republic, forcing the Stadthouder, William of Orange, to flee to England. In his capacity as director of the VOC, William ordered all Dutch colonies to surrender to the British. Governor Nederburgh in Batavia was an Orangeist and so did not prepare to resist the British. Other VOC officials sympathized with the Republic, however, and did try to organize some sort of defense against the British.

In 1795, Sultan Nuku of Tidore in eastern Indonesia also saw an opportunity to expand his power by declaring war on the Dutch. For both the Dutch and the Makassar living along the coast, 1797 was one of the most violent years in history of South Sulawesi. In that year, the British destroyed the remainder of the Dutch fleet in Europe, signed a secret agreement with Bone, destroyed the Dutch post at Bantaeng, and shelled the Dutch post at Bulukumba. In the same year, the fleets of Sultan Nuku were ravaging the coasts of Bantaeng, Bulukumba, and Bira. Among the most fearsome of the forces in the service of Sultan Nuku were Tobello under the command of a man called Tatto. Tatto's son, Robodoi, received his early training in these wars and was later to become one of the most feared pirates in the archipelago (Anonymous 1855: 14).

The governor in Makassar from 1800 to 1808, Petrus Chassé, was one of those who were determined to resist the British. Although he ruled as an agent of the VOC, that organization had officially ceased to exist with the expiration of its charter in 1799. In 1800, the British first blockaded Batavia and destroyed what merchant ships they found there. A few warships arrived in 1803 and 1804 under the command of Dekker and Hartsinck, but by the end of 1806 all had been captured, destroyed, or wrecked. The British blockaded Batavia again and communications with Makassar were cut off completely.

Chassé was thus on his own throughout this period and had to rely on native troops to fend off the attacks from local kingdoms like Bone and Tidore. The most the Dutch could offer the inhabitants of the Bira Peninsula during these years were a few cannons to ward off the raiders. Each village still has the remains of a stone fort built to hold these cannons, and local people can still point out the caves in which their ancestors hid from the dark-skinned Papuan raiders they call *To Seram* or *To Belo*. Chassé later wrote that Bira, Lemo Lemo, and Tanaberu had adhered to the government "without deviation" during this time and had come ready with their weapons to help wherever needed on the island (Chassé [1816] 1917, in van der Kemp 1917: 435).

In 1806, Napoleon declared his brother, Louis, King of Holland. Louis appointed the Patriot Daendels as governor-general of the Indies. He arrived in Batavia in 1808 and prepared to defend Java from the British. He also reinforced the garrison at Makassar, replacing Chassé as governor with van Braam in 1808. In 1809, Makassar was placed under the direct military command of Lieutenant Colonel van Wikkerman. All these efforts were fruitless in the face of British naval superiority and van Wikkerman surrendered to the British in 1811.

The British soon found the chaos they had been fomenting since 1780 in South Sulawesi an inconvenience, especially in the absence of legitimate rulers in Tallo' and Gowa. They pressed their old main ally, Sultan Ahmad of Bone, to surrender the Gowanese regalia still in his possession, but he refused and died soon afterward. His son and successor, Sultan Muhammad Ismail, then tried to place his own candidates on the thrones of both Tallo' and Gowa. In 1814, the British responded by expelling the forces of Bone from their base at Rompegading in the Northern Districts. Muhammad Ismail escaped and fought on against the British until their departure. He did abandon his pretensions to the throne of Gowa, however, and gave the Sudang sword to the *karaeng* of Soppeng. The latter gave it to Arung Mampu, who finally surrendered it to the English in 1816.

In this struggle between the British and the Bonese, the rulers of the Southern Districts sided with Britain, but the *Karaeng*s of the Eastern Districts in Bulukumba, Hero, Lange Lange, and Tiro sided with Bone (Chassé [1816] 1917: 435). The British sent another expedition against these rulers in 1814. Captain Cameron captured the *karaeng* of Bulukumba in Kajang with a force of 500 men. The British tried to persuade him to transfer his allegiance from Bone to England, but the *karaeng* and his uncle were killed while trying to escape (Anonymous 1854: 171).

After Napoleon's defeat in 1814, the British agreed to return the East Indies to the Dutch, but the transfer was delayed by Napoleon's escape from Elba. In April 1816, three commissioners arrived in Batavia to take charge again. Chassé was present to receive Makassar back from Major Dalton.

The Bira Peninsula under Bone's Hegemony

Ara and Tanaberu fell under the influence of Bone during this period. Genealogies in Ara show that the royal house of *Karaeng* Mamampang lost control of the office of *gallarrang* to Salung Daeng Masalo (reigned circa 1800). Salung was a descendent of Puang Rangki, a noble linked to the royal house of Bone who had arrived in the area a hundred years earlier, when Bone was allied with the VOC against Gowa. Salung Daeng Masalo was succeeded by his son, Gau Daeng Mamantang (reigned circa 1820–1840).

The situation in Tanaberu is more complicated. The founding royal ancestor of Tanaberu is called *To Kambang,* but this name occurs in many genealogies in different generations. (In Luwu', the particle *"To"* indicates an honorific title meaning "Father of," while *"Da"* is an honorific for "Mother of"; compare Errington 1989: 198). According to the chronicle of Bira, the ruler of Tanaberu when formal tribute was first sent to Gowa in the 1560s was called To Kambang. According to my calculations, this To Kambang was born about twenty generations before the present (G20). According to other oral traditions and written genealogies, another ruler of Tanaberu called To Kambang was responsible for converting Tanaberu to Islam in about 1610 (G17). A third To Kambang was a contemporary of the famous Makassar saint Shaikh Yusuf, who died in 1699 (G14). Finally, most oral traditions concerning To Kambang identify a fourth in-

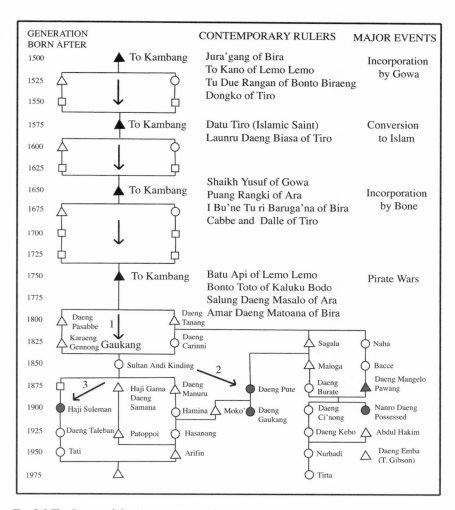

Fig. 9.2 The Return of the *Karaeng*: To Kambang, 1500–2000.

dividual who lived at the time of the Napoleonic Wars (G10). A ruler with the name of To Kambang thus appears about once every four generations. The notion that a powerful ancestor spirit returns to earth in one of his descendents is consistent with many other aspects of kinship and ritual.

The To Kambang who ruled in 1800 is shown on some genealogies as the grandson of a previous king of Bone, possibly Sultan Jalil al-Din (reigned 1749–1775). This To Kambang was succeeded by his son Daeng Pasabbe (reigned circa 1820–1845). In the same generation, a marriage was arranged between another son of To Kambang, Daeng Tanang, and Balole, a daughter of Salung Daeng Masalo. Thus, it would appear that by the end of the Napoleonic period, both

Ara and Tanaberu were ruled by families who claimed descent from the royal house of Bone and that they had cemented an alliance with one another through marriage.

Bira and Lemo Lemo remained in the hands of a royal house that traced its origin back to Gowa throughout the Napoleonic period. From about 1780 until 1830, Bira was ruled by Amar Daeng Matoana, known posthumously as *Tu ri Labbirina*, "the Exalted One." Lemo Lemo was ruled by his brother, known as *Batu Api*, "Fire Stone," because of his exploits in battle. Both were descendents of *Karaeng* Mamampang.

The First Bone War and the Culture System, 1816–1860

One of the first acts of the new colonial government of the Netherlands East Indies in 1816 was to install Abd al-Rauf as *karaeng* of Gowa. The Sudang sword that had been captured by Sangkilang in 1777 was at long last restored to the *karaeng* of Gowa, healing the rift between the mountain and coastal Makassar after forty years of civil war.

Elsewhere on the peninsula, the situation was not so peaceful. Many rulers regarded their treaties of alliance or vassalage to the VOC as abrogated by the British occupation, and they refused to recognize the new colonial government. In 1821 Colonel van Schelle was appointed military commander and governor of Makassar. When the ruler of Tanette refused to renew his treaty with the Dutch, van Schelle occupied the kingdom. He then moved on Supa. This time, the Dutch forces were thrown back, however, and the entire southern peninsula rose in revolt. The governor-general of the Netherlands East Indies, van der Capellen, was forced to intervene in person to calm the situation. In 1824, he managed to convince most of the local rulers to sign a treaty with him.

The Bugis rulers of Wajo, Supa, Tanette, and Bone, however, remained belligerent. Bone was led at the time by a woman, I Maniratu Aru Data (reigned 1823–1835), who had succeeded her brother Muhammad Ismail. As soon as Governor van der Capellen left South Sulawesi in 1824, Bone overran two Dutch garrisons. Much of the population declared its support for Bone, including that of Tanaberu. In October, Bone attacked the Dutch garrison in Bulukumba, which managed to hold out until reinforcements arrived. In February and March 1825, a Dutch force reconquered the interior of Bulukumba and then marched overland to Kajang, planning to attack Bone from the south. Perelaer shows the main route of the Dutch expedition during the First Bone War as crossing the Bampang River into Tanaberu (Perelaer 1872: end map). Local informants say that Tanaberu was burned to the ground at this point. Many members of the local ruling elite, who had been allied with Bone, fled with the retreating troops. Major Le Bron also put Kajang to the torch after the *karaeng* tried to assassinate him.

The Dutch column continued north and defeated a large Bone force at the mouth of the Sinjai River (van Rijneveld 1840: 212; Anonymous 1854: 182).

Le Bron's advance into Bone was interrupted, however, when the Java War broke out on July 20, 1825, and his troops were hastily reassigned to Java. This war lasted for five years and resulted in the final consolidation of Dutch power over all of Java. For the next thirty years, the colonial government was preoccupied with developing the so-called cultivation system in Java. Under this policy, villages were forced to set aside a certain fraction of village land for the cultivation of cash crops that were sold to the government for a fixed price. The system generated unprecedented revenues for the Dutch and allowed them to remit a significant net profit to the Netherlands. Outlying possessions like Sulawesi were neglected during the period of the cultivation system.

Dutch troops had been withdrawn from the campaign against Bone without achieving their original objective of forcing the Aru Data to sign a new treaty. She remained in power until 1835. Bone only made peace with the Dutch in 1838 after her brother, La Mapaseling Aru Panyili (reigned 1835–1845) came to the throne. Bone was left in effective possession of Sinjai, Kajang, and northern Bulukumba.

Dutch interest in Bone only revived when the British adventurer James Brooke visited Bone and Wajo in 1840. His ostensible purpose was to investigate the commercial potential of the region and to sell weapons to the Bugis. His trip caused great anxiety among the Dutch authorities in Makassar, however, who thought the British might make a bid for the allegiance of the more independent native states. In 1847, they laid claim to the entire island of Sulawesi by changing the title of their local representative from governor of Makassar to governor of Celebes and Dependencies. This irritated the ruler of Bone at the time, La Parengi Aru Pugi (reigned 1845–1858), so badly that he imposed a boycott on trade with the Dutch port of Ujung Pandang. Tensions continued to grow until the Dutch launched a second expedition against Bone in 1859.

Lemo Lemo's Rise

While Bone continued to enjoy a significant degree of autonomy after 1824, it lost its hegemony over the Bira Peninsula. The rulers of Bira and Lemo Lemo used their hereditary ties to the royal house of Gowa and their long-standing loyalty to the VOC to their advantage in this period. Lemo Lemo, in particular, enjoyed great prosperity in these years as piracy declined and the Ujung Pandang came to serve as a regional port for eastern Indonesia.

D. F. Liedermoij, who spent five years in Makassar in the 1830s and who held the post of fiscal officer and magistrate, wrote the following account of the "tribe of Limo-Limos" in 1838:

> A not unimportant branch of industry [in Makassar] is native shipbuilding. They manufacture all sorts of prauws here, from the greatest padoeakan of some 75 koyangs [tons] to the least known vessels, or *lepa-lepa*. Those who occupy themselves with this industry form a separate caste, under the name of

"Limo-Limos." Although it is formally under the resident or authority-holder of Boelekomba and Bonthain, this tribe has its own king in Bira or Negrie Limo-Limo, the southernmost cape of Celebes, which king bears the title "Radja Limo-Limo." Many of this sort of carpenter have settled in the capital and other government possessions. Their king collects taxes from them annually of no mean amount. They never complain about them, however. They will also not submit to the usual Kampong chiefs, but choose their own chiefs or *pangawas*. It was an act of weakness to have conceded this to them, unaware of the violent clashes which can often arise between two chiefs belonging to one and the same kampong.

The manners and behavior of the Limo-Limos, especially in respect of their religion, marital affairs and funerals are to some extent different from that of other inhabitants of this coast. Very little ceremonial is in use among them. They are industrious, but disloyal and deceitful, and have the reputation of being great gluttons. It is indeed true that they seem to eat enough on one day for the following day. They only give themselves over to their gluttonous desires, however, when they have been employed to build a vessel and their rice and salt must be supplied in addition to their daily wages. As regards their own food, however, they are very frugal, because they largely neglect agriculture, so that a pikol of rice often costs them F9, or even F12 in silver. . .

A prauw padoeakan of the largest sort costs F2,000 to F2,500 silver, without sail or net. This sum goes mostly for advances and labor charges; if one is in need of wood, one makes a small payment to the King of Tello, who gives a *tjap* or stamp of consent for it, just as for bamboo; then one must go cut one or the other oneself.

A prauw-palarie can cost F400 or F600. A prauuw-padjala F70, F80, F90 or F140. An outrigger canoe F20 to F30 and a sampang, some of which are very big and heavy from F10 to F50; a *lip-lip* from F8 to F30. One can deduce the approximate prices of the other vessels from these remarks. (Liedermoij 1854: 361–362, 366)

Lemo Lemo's prosperity lasted into the twentieth century and only went into decline in the 1940s.

The Decline of To Kambang's House

After the First Bone War, the noble houses of Tanaberu and Ara that linked themselves to Bone went into eclipse. Lompo Daeng Manurungang, "The Great One, The Descendent," became *gallarrang* in about 1840, displacing the descendents of Salung Daeng Masalo from that office. Daeng Manurungang's mother was the daughter of Po Uhang, the last *gallarrang* who claimed descent from *Karaeng* Mamampang. His father was the son of Amar Daeng Matoana, the *karaeng* of Bira from 1780 to 1830.

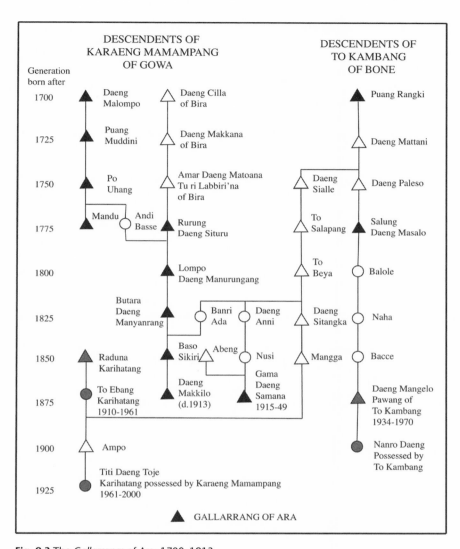

Fig. 9.3 The *Gallarrang*s of Ara, 1700–1913.

In Tanaberu, the royal house linked to Bone managed to hold on to the office of *karaeng* for another generation. Daeng Pasabbe was succeeded by his brother Daeng Malino in about 1845 (the latter was actually listed as the ruler in the *Regeerings Almanak* of 1849), but the village fell into complete destitution in this period. The Dutch missionary Donselaar visited Tanaberu in 1851 and described the effects of the First Bone War on the village as follows: "Tanaberoe has a small population, about 200 souls, under a Regent. The village,

situated on the beach, has extremely shabby houses, without any regular placement, and they are very small and dilapidated. Before the war with Boni in
1824 the population was considerable, but on that occasion many resettled in
Boni. There is no trade and the terrain is unsuitable for rice cultivation" (Donselaar 1855: 174–176).

Thus, after the First Bone War and the restoration of Dutch authority in
Bulukumba, the royal house of To Kambang was faced with a loss of wealth and
power in both Ara and Tanaberu. That it was not completely marginalized like
the allied house of Puang Rangki in Ara was due to the rise of a new ancestor
cult after a young princess, Andi Kinding, received a vision from the royal ancestor To Kambang and his wife Daeng Ma'nasa sometime in the 1840s. Andi
Kinding was a descendent of the union between the son of To Kambang on her
father's side and the daughter of Salung Daeng Masalo on her mother's side.
She was thus a logical choice for an ancestor spirit who wished to unite two
noble houses that traced themselves back to the Kingdom of Bone around one
royal cult.

> **M 9.1 The *Gaukang* of To Kambang Appear (Pawang Bado Unru 2000)**
> The ancestors appeared to her while her grandfather, Daeng Pasabbe, was still
> in power. They told her to expect two golden birds flying east from Gowa. She
> was to wear a skirt made of *cinde* cloth and use it to catch the birds. These
> birds would provide vehicles into which the spirits of To Kambang and his
> wife Daeng Ma'nasa could descend to receive homage from their descendents
> and through which they could distribute their blessings. She carried out these
> instructions and captured the birds just as predicted. No one has ever been al-
> lowed to look directly at these golden birds. If anyone tried, they would be
> blinded by the light that emanates from them.

Thus, even though the royal house of To Kambang had lost much of its
former wealth and power by the 1840s, the royal ancestors returned again in the
fourth generation as they had done before, only this time in the form of sacred
objects rather than as reincarnations. Ever since their arrival, the *gaukang* of To
Kambang and Daeng Ma'nasa have been honored in an annual ritual of homage. During this ritual, the highest-ranking members of To Kambang royal
house reach inside the cloth bundles that covers them and anoints them with
the blood of a sacrificed buffalo. This cult has allowed the royal house of Tanaberu to maintain its cohesion whether in power or not. A new cloth is added to
the old cloths at the end. When I attended this annual ritual in 1988, I counted
more than 143 layers of cloth.

The Second Bone War and Direct Rule, 1860–1905

By the 1850s, the colonial government had sufficiently consolidated its position
in Java that it was able to return its attention to recalcitrant outlying states such

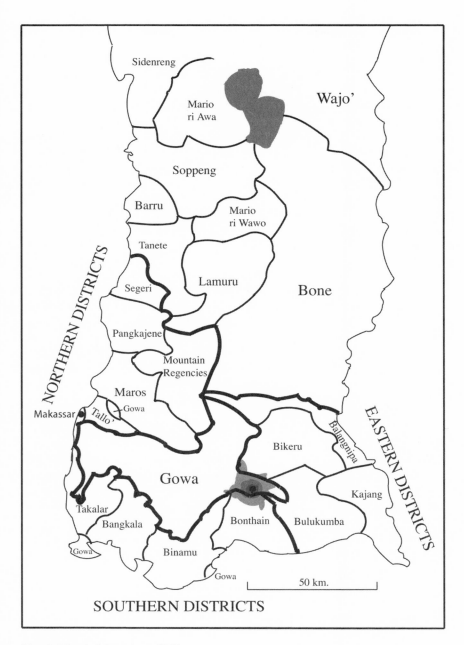

Map 9.1 South Sulawesi, ca. 1865

as Bone. In 1856, the Dutch missionary Matthes attempted to enter Bone to study the Bugis language in its "pure" form, but he was turned back on suspicion of being a spy. When he tried to enter Bone the next year, he was again turned back. This time, the excuse was that the governor's seal on his pass was black, not red. This refusal to admit Matthes was one of the several factors that precipitated the Second Bone War of 1859–1860 (van den Brink 1943).

The Sultan of Bone, La Parengi, died in 1858 and was succeeded by his wife, Basse Kajuara (reigned 1858–1860). She proved just as belligerent toward the Dutch as was her husband. She deliberately provoked them by ordering Bone ships to fly the Dutch flag upside down. The Dutch put together an expedition to place a more compliant ruler on the throne. It landed at Bajoa in February 1859, but then succumbed to malaria and cholera. A second expedition in November succeeded in replacing the queen with Ahmad Singkarru, who was proclaimed "Vassal King" by the Dutch. His legitimacy was only reluctantly acknowledged by a few members of the *hadat* of Bone. He received the regalia on January 20, 1860, and on February 13, 1860, he signed a treaty renouncing all claims to Sinjai, Kajang, and Bulukumba.

In May 1863, authority was granted the governor to "gradually decrease the number of regentships and galarangships" in the area south of Bone (Goedhart [1920] 1933: 140). In 1863, the old Afdeeling of Boelecomba and Bonthain was abolished, and a new unit called the Eastern Districts was created with its seat at Balang Nipa in the territory of Sinjai that had just been wrested from Bone's control. This allowed the assistant resident to keep a closer watch on Bone than was possible from the old seat of Dutch authority in Bantaeng.

In 1865, Bakkers was appointed governor of South Sulawesi. He had now been in the field for ten years and had long been the government's chief adviser on matters of native custom. Bakkers generally adopted a cautious approach to meddling in the internal affairs of the native states. For example, he did nothing about the condition of slaves after he became governor, even though Dutch public opinion was increasingly in favor of abolition. Instead, he focused his efforts on rationalizing the administration of the territories under direct government control.

Matthes was a good friend of Bakkers. He made his second tour through the Bira Peninsula during the week of November 13–20, 1864. His report at the end of his trip may well have influenced the process of government reorganization that began one month later. In 1864, Ara was absorbed by Lemo-Lemo and Bonto Tanga was absorbed by Tiro. Tiro absorbed Tanaberu in 1865 and Batang in 1867. In 1869, Bira incorporated the already combined villages of Lemo-Lemo and Ara. In the same year, Kajang was separated from Bulukumba as a new Onderafdeeling under the authority of its own controleur. The Onderafdeeling of Kajang was composed of the regentships of Kajang proper, Wero, Tiro, and Bira. Finally, Bira incorporated the enlarged Tiro in 1871 upon the death of its regent, Lewai Daeng Matana.

Tanaberu under Direct Rule

The situation in Tanaberu was still bleak when Matthes passed through it in 1864. He wrote, "As there was little good to hold us in this miserable Regentship [of Tanaberu] without trade or rice cultivation, whose people try to provide for their subsistence only from fishing and the planting of djagong, [maize] we stayed there no longer than absolutely necessary" (Matthes [1865] 1943: 269–278).

According to local informants, Tanaberu was subsequently placed under the control of a series of three outsiders between about 1865 and 1896: a man called Kinsang who was of Chinese descent; *Karaeng* Kilong; and Ende Daeng Pasolong, a noble from Lemo Lemo who also served as regent of greater Bira from 1884 to 1896. It was not until Ende Daeng Pasolong was removed from office in 1896 that a local noble, Sajuang Daeng Matasa, was finally appointed *karaeng* of Tanaberu and took control of the cult of the *gaukang* of To Kambang again.

Ara under Direct Rule

Ara remained under the control of the local descendents of *Karaeng* Mamampang until 1915, and the cult dedicated to him continued to play a central role in the official ritual life of the village. The *gallarrang* was the main sponsor of rituals dedicated to this founding royal ancestor. During these rituals, the spirit of the royal ancestor descended into the body of a medium and spoke to his descendents. This phenomenon is referred to as *kadongkokang*, "being ridden" by a spirit. The medium was called the *karihatang*, "mount of the gods," from the Sanskrit *dewata.*

In Ara, the bones of the royal ancestor themselves served as the *gaukang* of the realm. The skulls of *Karaeng* Mamampang and that of his wife Bunga Biraeng were long preserved in an enclosure among the caves of Pilia at the north end of the village. Even now, few dare to enter these caves. One day, Muli, a seventeen-year-old youth with a reputation for recklessness, took me to a clearing among the caves of Pilia where dances used to be performed in honor of the ancestors. Scattered about a clearing in the middle of Pilia were the remnants of old offerings, such as plastic plates and bits of cloth. There were even the remains of a wooden chair in which the *karihatang* used to sit while possessed. In a cave behind the clearing, we found an old skull and jawbone that might have been those of *Karaeng* Mamampang.

The current *karihatang*, Titi Daeng Toje, told me that the *karaeng*'s chair in Pilia is so powerful that no dead leaves ever fall on it. It is guarded by a male spirit in the form of a cock and a female spirit in the form of a hen. She said it was the place where the dancers, the drummers, and the players of gongs used to perform. She recalled that her grandmother, the previous *karihatang*, To Ebang, would first dress in a *baju bodo,* the traditional gauzy blouse of South Sulawesi, dance, and go into trance in her house. Once it was determined who had possessed her, a procession of all the noble descendents of the spirit would set out to the place of that spirit: Pilia in the case of *Karaeng* Mamampang; the graveyard in the case of Ara's village Saint *Bakka' Tera'*, "The Great Belcher"; the boundary rock on the beach between Ara and Tiro in the case of *Sapo Hatu* "Stone House" (see M 5.3), and so on. The procession included musicians playing gongs, drums, rattles and flutes, youths brandishing spears, and maidens in special dancing costumes. Seven people carrying seven umbrellas and flowers walked alongside. These were the *pa'karena* dancers who had already drawn criticism from the hajjis of Selayar in the 1880s (Englehard 1884b). The reigning *gallarrang* would preside and only those of noble birth could attend. When the procession arrived at its destination, a buffalo—or at least a goat—would be slaughtered. More music and dancing would be performed there, and the *karihatang* would dance until entered by the spirit again.

The Third Bone War and the Ethical Policy, 1901–1942

Relations between the Dutch and the kingdom of Bone remained good while their protégé Ahmad Singkarru remained on the throne. When he died in 1871, his daughter, I Banri, succeeded him. In 1880, she married a high noble of Gowa, La Gulaga Daeng Serang. When she died, in 1895, the electors chose her only surviving child, a daughter of twelve, as her successor. The Dutch feared that, with his daughter on the throne of Bone, La Gulaga might try to dominate both Bone and Gowa. They forced the seven electors to change their decision and to appoint La Pawawoi, son of Ahmad Singkarru, as ruler instead. For the next ten years, La Pawawoi ruled Bone in peace (IJzereef 1987).

In 1901, a coalition of right-wing and religious parties came to power in the Netherlands, displacing the Liberal Party, which had ruled for fifty years. This coalition adopted a moralistic stance toward the colonies. In her annual message, the queen spoke of an "ethical obligation and moral responsibility to the peoples of the East Indies" (van Niel [1960] 1984: 32). The justification for maintaining colonies shifted from the making of profits to the moral uplift of the natives. This involved a change in attitudes toward indirect rule and native kings. The Dutch now decided that it was their duty to replace their corrupt and tyrannical rule with that of well-trained colonial bureaucrats. They began looking for pretexts to impose direct rule in all of the native states.

The Dutch excuse for declaring war on Bone came in 1905, when the sultan, La Pawawoi, refused to impose new import and export duties or to pay an indemnity to the Dutch. The government sent three gunboats into the Gulf of Bone with an ultimatum. The king was to pay the indemnity and allow Dutch officials to administer and police the port on his behalf. When the king temporized, the Dutch attacked. By the end of July 1905, the Dutch had occupied Bone's capital. In November, La Pawawoi was captured and exiled to Java. In the months that followed, the subordinate chiefs submitted.

At the same time that they were subduing Bone, the Dutch were also demanding that the ruler of Gowa, Sultan Husain (reigned 1895–1906), submit his actions for Dutch approval. Husain was married to the daughter of the previous ruler of Bone, Basse Kajuara (1858–1860), who had led the fight against the Dutch in the Second Bone War of 1859. Rather than submit, Husain fled to En-rekang in the north of the peninsula to raise a rebellion. There he died in battle in 1906. His brother and son were captured and, like the ruler of Bone, exiled to Java. The Enrekang population held out for four more years, but by 1910 the Dutch had established their control over all of South Sulawesi (Harvey 1974: 53–54). In the aftermath of these wars, the old kingdoms of Gowa and Bone were abolished outright and transformed into Afdeeling under Dutch residents.

Sutherland summarizes Dutch policy in South Sulawesi between 1906 and 1930 as follows:

> Directly after their defeat of the South Sulawesi states (which resulted in the death of the ruler of Gowa and exile of Bone's king) military rule was introduced. The emphasis was on establishing and maintaining control, little attention was paid to the niceties of administration; the general idea was that the states would eventually come under Dutch direct rule, once the various bands and guerilla groups had been crushed. But by 1916 colonial thinking had changed; it was decided to rule through the "native chiefs," but without a central court. The state remained, but the ruler was replaced by the colonial *Controleur*. This was economical, and ran less risk of political upheaval. In 1926, again following general policy which was veering towards a hard conservatism, a further change took place. The old states were to be re-created; their central establishments of king, ministers and council were gradually reborn with the Dutch as midwife, in the hope that they would form an alliance with the colonial regime against trouble-making nationalists, democrats or religious leaders. (Sutherland 1980: 234–235)

In 1920, Goedhart was asked to evaluate the experiment in consolidating the little realms of the Bira Peninsula into one regency. He concluded that the whole project had been doomed to failure because of the way it ran roughshod over local custom.

> Upon the agglomeration of these seven adat communities into the one regentship of Bira, with the karaeng of Bira as Regent over the whole, the existing galarangs of Batang and Ara were retained and galarangs were installed over the realms of Tiro, Bontotanga, Tanaberoe and Lemo Lemo, who serve as the links between the lower chiefs in their jurisdictions and the Regent of Bira up to the present day. The latter has never exercised more than an apparent authority over the adat communities added to his karaengship. The galarangs, who are installed over the territorial subdivisions, are chosen by the population from their old karaeng and galarang families and remain the authority wielding chiefs, whom the successive regents of Bira have constantly tried to

coax so that the orders given them by the European government would be put into effect in the subdivisions of their jurisdiction. . . According to folk tradition, Tiro thus had a karaeng before Bira. In view of this it must be said that the majority of the chiefs and population of the division of Tiro incorporated by Bira are against the incorporation. (Goedhart [1920] 1933: 141–142)

The following year, Daeng Patunru and his son Nape Daeng Mati'no were removed from office and the regency of Bira was broken up again into its constituent villages.

Tanaberu under the Ethical Policy

In Tanaberu, Sajuang Daeng Matasa was kept in office after the abolition of the regency of Bira in 1921. The *gaukang* of To Kambang remained in his possession, and the cult continued to enjoy official favor until he was removed from office in 1934 for embezzlement. Local informants attributed this setback to a sacrilegious act committed by his first cousin, Daeng Manais, who reached into the bundle containing one of the golden birds and broke off its beak. He was struck down with a virulent form of leprosy that soon covered his whole body and killed him. The curse spread to other members of the family, leading to *Karaeng* Sajuang's conviction soon after.

Sajuang was replaced by Abdul Fattah, a man from Bantaeng who married a local noblewoman, Papurampe Opu. She was a niece of Andi Mulia, the regent of Bira from 1900 to 1914 and from 1931 to 1942. This gave him some claim to participate in the local ancestor cults, and the couple took the *gaukang* into their possession.

Ara under the Ethical Policy

When the regent of Bira, Andi Mulia, resigned to go on Hajj in 1914, Uda Daeng Patunru, a noble from Lemo Lemo, was appointed to succeed him. Daeng Patunru and his son Nape Daeng Mati'no took it upon themselves to remove the hereditary rulers of the subordinate districts and to put their own agents in charge. They removed Daeng Pagalla from the office of *gallarrang* in Ara and held a rigged election to put their favorite, Gama Daeng Samana, in his place. Gama had no hereditary claim whatsoever to the office, and his appointment provoked bitter opposition among the noble houses that traced their origins back to *Karaeng* Mamampang.

Gama did have some claim to membership in the local nobility on the side of his mother, Nusi. Her first cousin, Ganna, was the *anrong tau* of the lower settlement of Lembanna. Her mother, Daeng Anni, a descendent of Puang Rangki, a noble from Bone who ruled Ara in the late seventeenth century (see figure 9.3). Another branch of this line had intermarried with the descendents of To Kambang in Tanaberu. Over the years, Gama went on to cultivate his ties to the descendents of Puang Rangki and To Kambang, while trying to suppress the cult of *Karaeng* Mamampang. The relation of the ruler to the royal ancestor cult was thus quite different after Gama came to power in 1915 than the one in Tanaberu under Sajuang Daeng Matasa and Abdul Fattah.

Gama managed to hold onto the office of *gallarrang* of Ara when the regency of Bira was dissolved in 1921. He was reappointed by the controleur, W. Baljet (Batten 1938: Bijlage VIII). Once he was sure of his backing by the colonial government, Gama launched a drive to impose a purified version of Islam on the village. He replaced the small wooden mosque at the Great Spring with a large stone structure. He instituted his own version of *shariah* law, discouraging the consumption of palm wine, keeping track of which men attend Friday prayer services, and banning those who refused to attend from burial in the Islamic cemetery. He even tried to prevent people from praying for the souls of the dead, a practice he regarded as an illegitimate innovation, *bid'ah.*

Gama took an uncompromising approach to local customs he regarded as *shirk,* idolatrous. He personally cut down a huge banyan tree on the beach called Talise to show that the powerful *setan,* demons that were supposed to live in it, could not harm him. He climbed into people's attics to destroy their ancestor shrines and sacred heirlooms. His most determined attack was on the royal rituals that lay at the heart of noble opposition to him. But he was unable to destroy the ancestor shrines of the most powerful noble families.

The shrine of *Karaeng* Mamampang was as large as a regular bed. The *karihatang* from 1910 until 1962 was a woman called To Ebang. To Ebang saved the shrine from Gama by covering it with a mosquito net and pretending it was no longer being used for ritual purposes. Thus, by the 1930s, To Ebang had to be increasingly discreet in her conduct of séances, holding them only in the dead of night on the outskirts of the village. Even so, Gama would disguise himself in old clothes and sneak up on séances, bursting into the room and putting a stop to them.

On the positive side, Gama became an enthusiastic supporter of the cult of the village saint, Bakka' Tera', in which the recitation of the *barasanji* (al-Barzanji's Life of Muhammad) played a central part. Gama's sister married into the family that had controlled the office of *Guru Bakka' Tera'* for more than a century. His son, Patoppoi, described for me the rituals of homage, *a'dalle,* Gama carried out at the tomb of Bakka' Tera' every Thursday night during the 1930s. Only those of good birth were allowed to attend. Four or five men would go and scatter fragrant flowers over the grave and recite prayers. Then a goat would be sacrificed at the grave and taken back to the *gallarrang's* house to be cooked and eaten. On holy days such as the Prophet's birthday *(Maulid)* and in fulfillment of vows *(nazar),* more elaborate offerings would be made. The *barasanji* would be recited in the sponsor's house, accompanied by an elaborate array of food offerings set out on a *kappara bangkeng,* a silver tray with feet. When the *barasanji* was over, the offerings would be carried in procession down to the grave. Seven maidens and seven youths would dance around the tomb to the accompaniment of gongs and drums, while the *gallarrang,* the *kali,* and the *katte* officiated over the recital of prayers. Such rituals involved considerable expense. At that time the grave was surrounded by a high stone wall, and only certain people were allowed to enter it.

The rituals of homage to Bakka' Tera' were remarkably similar to those Gama was suppressing that were performed in honor of *Karaeng* Mamampang. But whereas only direct descendents of *Karaeng* Mamampang could participate in the latter rituals, Gama could approach Bakka' Tera' as a Muslim devotee. By promoting one cult and undercutting the other, Gama tried to reshuffle the local social hierarchy in a fundamental way. In 1938, the government appointed a council of nine electors in Ara, reversing earlier policies in which the electorate had consisted of all the male heads of households in the village. They duly reelected Gama as ruler of the village.

The Second World War and Nationalism, 1942–1989

The Netherlands Indies government capitulated to the Japanese on March 8, 1942. Local officials were mostly left in place by the Japanese between 1942 and 1945. This was true in Ara, where Gama maintained his hold on power. In Bira, however, the Japanese appointed Nape Daeng Mati'no as ruler. He had returned from his exile in Java in 1931, full of modernist and nationalist ideas and was known as a fierce opponent of the Dutch government.

Food was very scarce by the winter of 1944–1945, and the Japanese were collecting as much food and jewelry from people as they could. Most households broke up into nuclear or stem family units and moved to small huts built next to their dispersed fields to be nearer the only remaining source of food, cassava, to escape the attentions of the Japanese, and because they felt ashamed of displaying their poverty in the central settlement. As people began to move back to the central area after the war, they tended to build new houses that would contain only a nuclear or stem family.

After the surrender of the Japanese and the declaration of the Republic of Indonesia in 1945, the Dutch attempted to regain their colonial empire. The Indonesian nationalists declared independence on August 17, 1945. Many Bugis and Makassar fought the Dutch in Java. Among them was Kahar Muzak-kar, a minor noble born in 1921 in a village in Luwu'. In 1934 he completed primary school there and in 1937–1940 attended a Muhammadiyah teacher's school in Surakarta, Java, where he took his new name from a favorite teacher. In 1941–1943 he returned to Luwu to teach in a Muhammadiyah school. In 1943, he was banished from Luwu for denouncing the existing feudal system in South Sulawesi and advocating the overthrow of the aristocracy. He returned to Java and spent 1943–1945 in business in Solo. From 1945 to 1950 he led a group of guerillas against the Dutch in Java. (Harvey 1974: 181–182, 474).

The Dutch were forced to cede Java and Sumatra to the nationalists after heavy fighting in November 1946. They then tried to set up a "United States of

Indonesia" under their control, of which *Negara Indonesia Timor* (NIT) the "State of East Indonesia" was to be a part with its capital in Ujung Pandang. Resistance to the NIT in South Sulawesi was fierce. In December 1946, the Dutch began an all-out "pacification" campaign under General Westerling, during which thousands were killed or imprisoned. A state of war was declared in the divisions of Makassar, Bonthain, Pare Pare, and Mandar. It was lifted in Pare Pare and Mandar in January 1948, but remained in force in Makassar and Bonthain until July 1949.

Estimates of the total number of traditional rulers from *kampong* chiefs to rajas replaced by the Dutch over the next four years range from one quarter to one half. Of those removed, about half were killed, 40 percent were imprisoned, and the rest went into agriculture or commerce (Harvey 1974: 158). In areas such as Ara, which had been subject to Dutch rule since the seventeenth century, they invented entirely new feudal structures. The ruler of Ara was given the title of *karaeng* for the first time since the sixteenth century.

The Republicans claimed that 40,000 were killed by the Dutch during this counterinsurgency campaign, and this figure is still taught to school children as historical truth. The Dutch admitted only to 2,000. In any event, there was great bitterness toward the Dutch all over South Sulawesi (Harvey 1974: 128). "The way in which the pacification campaign was carried out in the countryside also involved Indonesians in the responsibility for the killings. The most usual technique seems to have been to assemble all the villagers in a central area, and to ask them to point out the "extremists" in the group. Those so designated were shot on the spot. If no information was volunteered, several villagers would be chosen at random and shot." (Harvey 1974: 167). It is no surprise that these methods left a number of scores to settle throughout the province.

The Dutch had tried since the 1930s to revive feudal traditions all over the province in hopes that the less-educated nobility would support them in opposing the generation of educated nationalists who favored integration with the new republic. They had little success. In 1945, most nobles declared in favor of the new republic. The *karaeng* of Bonthain was arrested in November 1945 and imprisoned in Makassar, and the *karaeng* of Gantarang was deposed and confined to Makassar. The king of Bone so ceremoniously installed under the observant eye of Cense in 1931, Andi Mappanyuki, was arrested on November 8, 1946, and replaced by Andi Pabbenteng, a grandson of Arumpone La Pawawoi (reigned 1895–1905).

Ever nimble politically, Gama managed to ingratiate himself with the Dutch after their return in 1945. He was ready to play along with their plans to recreate the old feudal order and began to be addressed as Opu Gama. *Opu* is the title of a noble ruler in Selayar, implying that his father Abeng had in fact been of the noble class. But Gama's family still lacked the full social acceptance only marriage into the local nobility could bring. Because of the obscurity of his father's origins, his claims to noble birth rested entirely on his mother. She was a descendent of Puang Rangki, the noble from Bone who had ruled the village in the time of the Dutch conquest of Gowa (see figure 9.3). A collateral line of descendents from Puang Rangki had intermarried with the descendents of To Kambang in Tanaberu. He could thus make some claim to membership in the group of nobles who claimed descent from Bone. In the early 1940s, he succeeded in arranging the marriage of his son Patoppoi (born 1923) to Hasanang, a great-granddaughter of the girl, Andi Kinding, who had caught the *gaukang* To Kambang in her skirt a hundred years before. Although Gama refused as a matter of religious principle to participate in the cult itself until his death in 1954, his own son Patoppoi became a great devotee.

The Dutch made other efforts to win over the "hearts and minds" of the population. Between 1947 and 1949 they sent about 3,000 pilgrims a year to Mecca from the State of East Indonesia.

> The great interest the Indonesian Muslims had always paid the haddj obviously inspired the colonial government after 1945 to follow a liberal haddj policy, hoping to regain the sympathy of the Indonesian *mukims* (long-term residents in Mecca). The Netherlands Indies government had special reason to speculate upon this as the government of the Republik Indonesia in Jogja, despite ambitious plans, was not able to allow pilgrims to leave her territory for Mecca; this was caused by the Dutch navy's blockade of the Indonesian ports and by the fact that the RI had no ships available to transport the hadjis.
>
> On the other hand the colonial government hoped that the arrival of pilgrims from the occupied territories would consolidate the position of the Dutch-created puppet states, both among the Muslims in Indonesia and abroad (in Mecca). (Vredenbregt 1962: 109–110)

Gama's next move to increase his local stature was to take advantage of his close ties to the Dutch administration to perform the Hajj. No one had made the *hajj* from Ara since Haji Daeng Mareha had accompanied Haji Baso Daeng Raja from Bira in 1895. In 1948, Haji Daeng Parani was selected to go from Ara as part of the Dutch attempt to cultivate the loyalty of hereditary rulers. He was the son of the Kali, Baso Daeng Siahing, and had been serving as Gama's *sulewatang* (deputy to the regent). In 1949, Gama was himself selected to go on *hajj*, along with the *karaeng* of Lemo Lemo, Masalolang and the *karaeng* of Kajang, Bapa Daeng Matasa (1928–1949) both of whom had shown their loyalty to the NIT government.

The NIT government granted all the local villages on the Bira Peninsula the rank of *karaeng*ship. When Gama left for the *hajj*, the nine electors designated by the Dutch in 1938 chose his eldest son, Padulungi, to be installed as *karaeng*. Padulungi was the first and last ruler to be formally installed as *karaeng* since the *karaeng* of Gowa demoted the realm to a *gallarrang*ship in the 1560s.

Karaeng Padulungi was favorably enough disposed to the cult of *Karaeng* Mamampang to allow the Karihatang to move his relics down from the caves of Pilia to a shrine next to the road. From 1950 to 1954, the relics were stored together in a small model house that stood under a large boulder just below Pilia.

There the skulls resided in state, each dressed in a sarong appropriate to its own gender. The *karihatang* ("Place of the Gods," the royal medium), To Ebang lived in a large house next to the shrine. To Ebang was in regular communication with the relics. If the skulls were cold or hungry, they would call for more clothing or food in voices that could be heard inside the big house, and someone would be set out to fulfill the request.

Sulawesi was officially incorporated into the new republic on August 17, 1950, five years to the day after Sukarno issued the Indonesian Declaration of Independence. Beginning in late 1949, the Bugis and Makassar guerrillas had begun to return from Java to South Sulawesi and to form themselves into local battalions. In June 1950, Kahar Muzakkar was sent from Java to Makassar to help find a way to either demobilize them or integrate them into the national army. Muzakkar fully expected that he and his men would be inducted into the regular army and that he would be put in command in South Sulawesi. When this did not occur, Muzakkar withdrew into the bush. In August 1953, he declared his support for the Negara Islam Indonesia (Islamic State of Indonesia, or NII). His guerilla movement was known as the Darul Islam/Tentara Islam Indonesia (DI/TII), Abode of Islam/Islamic Army of Indonesia.

After 1953, the guerillas gained control of much of the countryside, including all of Bulukumba except for the city proper. All over South Sulawesi, village officials and schoolteachers fled to the cities for protection. The last rulers of Ara and Bira under the Dutch, Haji Gama and Nape Daeng Mati'no, refused to leave their villages when the Darul Islam guerillas took over the area in 1954. They were executed along with many other local officials. In the face of the growing chaos, To Ebang returned the skull of *Karaeng* Mamampang to the caves of Pilia. Government control was restored only in 1961 when interim officials were appointed in the local villages.

The *Gaukang* of Tanaberu in the Nationalist Era

The *gaukang* of To Kambang remained in the hands of the chief of Tanaberu, Abdul Fattah, from his appointment in 1934 until his death in 1970. Like most other civil servants, he fled the Darul Islam rebellion in 1954 and was only formally replaced as chief in 1961. In 1970, the *gaukang* passed into the care of Abdul Fattah's wife's niece, Basse. In 1985, they passed to a woman named Haji Sulamang, a descendent of To Kambang who lived in Tanaberu. Her daughter married the son of the *Lurah*, "mayor" of Tanaberu, Abdul Azis Lopo. Thus, it continued to be the case that even when the rulers of Tanaberu were outsiders appointed by the central government, they took care to marry a woman from the indigenous line of rulers.

Many devotees of the cult of To Kambang have always lived in Ara. They traced their descent back to Naha, a sister of Andi Kinding's mother. In 1920, one of Naha's grandsons who lived in Ara, Daeng Mangelo, became the *pawang,* or leader, of the cult. He remained in charge until his death, in 1970. Daeng

Mangelo served during this period as the focus of the noble faction in Ara that traced its ancestry back to Bone. After the death of Daeng Mangelo, in 1970, leadership of the cult of To Kambang passed to his cousin, Daeng Gaukang, and to his daughter, Daeng Ci'nong. Thus, from 1920 to 1985, the cult was actually run by people living in Ara.

In 1985, Haji Sulamang and her husband Haji Sanusi took possession of the *gaukang*. Although Haji Sanusi was born in Ara, he had moved to Tanaberu when he married. The two of them began to freeze out the close relatives of Daeng Mangelo who had previously controlled the cult. Meanwhile, Gama's son, Patoppoi, succeeded in marrying his own son, Arifin, to Haji Sulamang's granddaughter. With Arifin's marriage, at least one branch of Gama's descendents finally cemented their status within the traditional social order after four generations of struggle. Arifin's wife will ultimately inherit the house in which the relics are stored and so Arifin was in a position to eventually have full control of the ancestor cult. When I visited in 2000, however, control of the cult had passed back into the hands of another branch of To Kambang's descendents who still lived in Ara.

In 1989 the *pawang* was an old woman named Lolo Inci living in Tanaberu. The main sponsors of the ritual were Haji Sanusi and his wife Haji Salamang, Haji Sanusi's brother Tahir Daeng Kala, and Haji Salamang's brother Bado'mang Rahman. Although many of these people were born in Ara like Haji Sanusi, they all now lived in Tanaberu. Most of the devotees still in Ara seemed to have a hard time getting information about the plans for the annual homage ritual that was held in August 1989. Daeng Mangelo's daughter Nanro complained to me that, whereas once the people of Tanaberu had to come and ask the experts in Ara if they wanted to conduct any rituals for To Kambang, they are now not even informed when they are going to be held.

The ritual in 1989 was postponed several times, because of difficulties in raising sufficient funds to purchase a buffalo and then trouble finding a suitable one to sacrifice. Beginning in 1960, buffalo were replaced by oxen as draft animals in the local area, and when they are needed for ritual purposes they must now often be purchased from as far away as Kajang or Selayar. Only a large unblemished specimen with upright horns is considered suitable. Rituals requiring the sacrifice of a buffalo are thus an expensive business, and the resources of the entire descent group had to be mobilized. When I expressed interest in attending, I was asked for a contribution. I was told that only those descendents who made a cash contribution were going to be allowed a share of the meat.

The Upperworld: Procession to the Palantikan

The first step in holding the ritual of homage to the *gaukang* of To Kambang is to bring the bones of one of his vassals, Bonto Toto, to his shrine. Bonto Toto was the ruler of the settlement of Kaluku Bodo during the Napoleonic Wars. Kaluku Bodo marks the traditional southern boundary between Tanaberu and

Lemo Lemo. Bonto Toto is said to have died at the bottom of a vertical cave while hiding from a pirate raid. His bones are preserved in a cloth bundle.

When the remains of Bonto Toto arrived at Haji Sulamang's house, the *gaukang* of To Kambang and Daeng Ma'nasa were brought down from their resting place in the attic. They were tied inside white cloths and suspended from the necks of two designated male bearers. Other attendants shielded them from the sun with parasols. This is reminiscent of the way the dowry is conveyed to the house of the bride on the wedding day, creating an equivalence between bride and groom as royalty for a day and the ancestors as royal spirits. A procession set off up the hill behind Haji Sanusi's house to *possi'tana*. The *gaukang* were accompanied by a band of men playing drums and gongs; a group of seven youths who were dressed in traditional turbans, trousers, and sarongs rolled above the knee; and a group of seven maidens dressed in *baju bodo* blouses. The youths brandished weapons and performed martial arts movements while the girls danced. A ten-year-old grandson of Daeng Elle later told me that the procession had encountered a black snake on the way up, as big around as a house post. It led the way up the hill, and a second smaller snake came up after it, slithering between the feet of the people.

The procession reached the *possi' tana* while the sun was still rising, about 10 A.M. and circled it three times rotating "to the right," that is, with the right arm pointing outward from the center. The buffalo was sacrificed on the east side of the *possi' tana* while the young men performed martial arts displays. As discussed in chapter 8, in former times a second buffalo would be burnt to ashes in a rite called the *rumpulangi*. Later that evening, a customary meal was served, including the four colors of rice and eggs. Prayers, *doa*, were offered, and people went home.

The *possi' tana* of Tana Beru is a rock no more than a foot high and two feet in diameter. It is surrounded by a circular wall three feet in height and three feet in diameter. Next to it is the *palantikan*, place of installation. Two *tompong* were planted in the earth next to the *possi' tana* and one was planted next to the *palantikan*. At graves, two posts are erected for women, one for men. Thus the *possi'tana* was coded as female and the *palantikan* as male. A *tompong* is a device used in everyday life to pick fruit from the highest branches of a tree. It is made by splitting the end of a bamboo into slats, which are woven together to form a basket. They recall the bamboo vehicles in which the mythical ancestress descends to earth. In this ritual, they were used to transmit offerings to the Upperworld. The *tompong* were filled with bananas and various types of rice. Additional offerings of the same sort were placed directly on the *possi' tana* for transmission to the Underworld.

The Middleworld: Bloodying the *Gaukang*

I arrived in Tanaberu the next day at 9 A.M. and walked up the hill to the *possi' tana* and *palantikan*. All along the path up to the *possi' tana*, fresh green coconut fronds had been hung overhead and on the pavilion in which the *gaukang* were placed. A one-meter-high cloth with one-meter-wide red and orange stripes was hung on the inside wall of the pavilion. I found the *gaukang* of To Kambang, Daeng Ma'nasa, and Bonto Toto sitting in state in the pavilion under red and white umbrellas and more palm fronds. These latter are all perquisites of nobility. Lying in front of and between the *gaukang* of To Kambang and Daeng Ma'nasa was a *ge'no'*, "rattle," a bamboo tube about three inches in diameter and two feet long with a carved bird inserted at one end. This object is similar to "two ceremonial objects used by the *bissu* priests [among the Bugis], the *arumpigi* and the *alosu* (instruments made of long tubes of bamboo filled with little fragments of porcelain or pottery). . . The body of these bamboos figure in effect a serpent, while the head and tail represent those of a cock or calao" (Hamonic 1983: 39).

Seven maidens in *baju bodo* sat next to the *gaukang* inside the pavilion while seven men holding weapons stood guard outside. The weapons included a *barangang*, a spear with a fringe of horsehair at the base of the blade; a *poke pangka*, a spear with an Indonesian flag hanging from the blade end and a forked butt; a *legung*, a long narrow shield with a sunburst pattern in the middle; and a *poke tungala*, a staff with a bulbous shape at the top. These were the *kalompoang*, "things of greatness" of Tanaberu. Between rituals, these *kalompoang* are stored next to the *gaukang* in the royal ancestor shrine.

Then Tahir Daeng Kala, a man in his forties, began to perform martial arts with Bacce Daeng Tiba, a man in his sixties. Tahir is the brother of Haji Sulamang, the woman who has the *gaukang* in her attic. The martial arts movements alternate between long periods when the fighters slowly circle each other in a crouch holding their arms bent in a state of extreme muscular tension and short bursts of speed when they attempt to catch their opponent off balance and throw him to the ground. The older men were much more skilled at this than were the younger men who held the weapons. I saw the old man throw the younger one to the ground several times over the next few days.

I was soon called over to the pavilion where the *pawang*, Lolo Inci, was preparing to start the ceremonial untying of the *gaukang* bundles. First, four older men approached the *gaukang*, including Tahir Daeng Kala. Each threw a few grains of incense on a brazier, filled a woven cup with the smoke, and pushed smoke over the *gaukang*. One of them also sprinkled yellow uncooked rice over them. Then the *gaukang* bundles were tied around the necks of the three young men who had carried them up to the *possi' tana* the previous day. Lolo Inci then covered them in some more smoke while one of the men who had carried the *gaukang* up the hill removed the *ge'no'*. She then began slowly to untie the knots in each layer of cloth around the *gaukang* of To Kambang and Daeng Ma'nasa. It was easy to believe there were more than a hundred layers in each and that the inner layers were over a century old. They were of a coarser, homespun weave than the outer layers. While this was going on, the umbrellas were raised high above them. At the center of the bundle was a basket with a lid. I was again warned that no one could look inside the baskets without being blinded by the

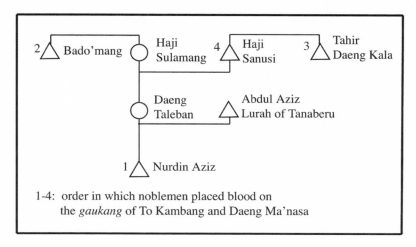

Fig. 9.4 Placing Blood on the *Gaukang* of To Kambang.

light the *gaukang* gave off. The bones of Bonto Toto, on the other hand, were tied up in a single cloth and there was no problem with exposing them.

When the baskets were exposed, Lolo Inci invoked the spirits to descend into the *gaukang,* throwing raw rice into the air over her head. A series of six men approached, dipped their right index finger in a bowl containing the blood of the sacrifice buffalo, reached inside the basket, and anointed the *gaukang.* The men included two I did not identify, then Haji Sulamang's daughter's son, Nurdin Aziz, her brother, Bado'mang Rahman, her brother-in-law, Daeng Kala Tahir, and her husband, Haji Sanusi. When the first *gaukang* had been treated, someone began tying up the cloths again while Lolo Inci supervised the application of blood to the second *gaukang.* When both were complete, they were hung from the necks of the young men again. At this point, some women tore down the palm fronds hanging from the pavilion and knotted them around their wrists "for coolness."

A procession then formed up accompanied by the band of musicians playing gongs, drums, and flutes. The young maidens danced while holding on to a long red and white cloth called a *jinda-birang.* The young men performed martial arts displays with the weapons they had shown me earlier. The *gaukang* were then carried in procession around the *possi' tana,* the graves of To Kambang and his wife, and the grave of Daeng Malino. The procession circled the graves, again passing "to the right."

By 11 A.M. the participants were ready to go back down the hill to Haji Sulamang's house. There the *gaukang* bearers were seated in front of the house with umbrellas over their heads while two pairs of fighters performed another display of martial arts for the spirits. They were taken inside the house, where they were prayed over, censed, and sprinkled with rice again in the main visitor's room before being taken up to the attic and replaced in the *palangka* at exactly noon. The *palangka* was quite elaborate. It was an almost full-size bed with bamboo walls and a canopy. The umbrellas were placed on top of the *gaukang,* and the various banners and weapons were place around the *palangka.* Meanwhile, the bones of *Karaeng* Bonto Toto were carried in procession back to Kaluku Bodo.

The Underworld: Digging for Water in Sampung Cina

On the third day, a group of more than a hundred went to Ere Manerang in Sampung Cina, a water meadow at the northern end of Tanaberu. It is said that this is where the *karaeng* of Gowa used to camp when visiting the area. In the old days, this journey involved a two-mile walk through coconut groves. The power of the *gaukang* was enough to prevent any coconuts from falling on peoples' heads. When I attended, most of the participants rode in rented minibuses. Fifty people traveled from the center of Tanaberu and were joined later by another fifty onlookers. At Sampung Cina, a pavilion had been erected at the west end of the field. The same red and orange cloth used at the *possi' tana* had been stretched vertically between two poles and some other cloths draped over the top of the pavilion. The *pawang*, Lolo Inci, and some other women *sanro* sat in the pavilion and kept up a constant chanting and censing of two cushions placed within it to maintain contact with the spirits of To Kambang and his wife, who were said to be reclining on them. They proceeded to lay out an elaborate offering of some twenty trays. They consisted of cooked and raw rice, various side dishes made of eggs, fish, and vegetables, betel nut ingredients, candles, and incense.

The climax of this phase of the ritual was reached at noon, when Lolo Inci began to dig a shallow hole in the ground. She was soon followed by others who regarded themselves as direct descendents of To Kambang. The little wells are the symbolic counterpart of the *tompong* in the ritual performed at the *possi' tana,* allowing communication with the Underworld, just as the latter allow communication with the Upperworld. It is said that only true descendents are able to reach this subterranean water. They reached water after digging only two feet. (Of course, they were digging right next to a pond and there were puddles in the meadow everywhere there was a small depression.) Some of the water was drunk on the spot, thus establishing physical contact between the powers of the Underworld and the congregation. Some was stored in bottles and taken home for later use. This water is regarded as having powerful curative properties.

While the digging was going on, Arifin and Junedi performed martial arts movements to the accompaniment of three gongs and two drums. When Arifin looked reluctant at the prospect of drinking the murky brown liquid, Bado'mang told him, "Everything from the earth is medicine." An hour later, Bado Rahman entered the pavilion and recited some prayers while the youths performed again. Then the food offerings were distributed and everyone ate. After a final performance, the crowd dispersed and went home. The *gaukang* of To Kambang and Daeng Ma'nasa were returned to the *palangka* in Haji Salamang's house.

Analysis

The symbolic message of the ritual of homage to To Kambang is that the fertility of the land and the people continues to rest on the ability of his noble descendants to connect the present with the past, the Middleworld with the Upperworld and the Underworld, the ascribed rank of the female-centered house with the achieved power of male-centered political office, and the local realm with the cosmos. The cult continues to enjoy official tolerance because the current Lurah of Tanaberu is married to the daughter of the *gaukang*'s custodians. The political message is that large bilateral descent groups continue to form around particular sacred objects and to use the solidarity they derive from collective ritual activity to advance their claims to status and power.

The *Karihatang* of Ara in the Nationalist Era

In contrast to the situation in Tanaberu, the *Karihatang* of Ara, To Ebang, had to endure official hostility to her cult from 1915 until the end of the Darul Islam insurgency in 1961. To Ebang died in 1962. Her granddaughter, Titi Daeng Toje, told me what happened next.

> Soon after To Ebang's death, a spirit came and tried to take possession of Titi's elder sister. She resisted it, sickened, and died. Then, in 1965, an evil spirit from Kajang took possession of Titi.
>
> Seeing this, the Lord God asked the spirit of To Ebang, "Who is that floundering in the sea?"
>
> To Ebang answered, "It is my granddaughter."
>
> So To Ebang flew to the moon and obtained Knowledge, which she put into the body of Titi. Titi was in trance for seven days and seven nights, and remained continuously on the *palangka* of To Ebang. She could only eat a small piece of banana at a time, and would only allow three people into the room with her: her companion Denni, Olong, and one other.
>
> Finally the spirit spoke and demanded that the *palangka* be surrounded by six white mosquito nets and one red one. On the seventh day, Titi emerged from the nets and bathed in the water stored in a clay jug. A drought which had persisted for eight months broke at the same time, and the rains came.

Titi's first patient was her sister-in-law, Lebu. Lebu had a festering sore in her foot and could not walk. Titi commanded her to rise and approach her. Everyone thought she had gone crazy, but Lebu did it. Titi ordered her to make a vow to kill a goat at Ujung Lasoa if the wound healed. She made the vow and soon recovered. This was only the first in a series of miraculous cures that proved that Titi had indeed taken the place of To Ebang.

Titi went on to serve her little group of female relatives as a spirit medium for the next forty years. She has never married, but has always lived with Denni, another woman whom villagers regard as her wife. Denni makes no claim to any ritual expertise. Titi claims not to know anything about *Karaeng* Mamampang or what happens during a séance, because she is supposed to be in a trance. Her "interpreter" on these occasions is her aunt, Olong.

In addition to playing the officially passive role of *karihatang,* Titi has also become a highly knowledgeable *sanro,* or expert, in a variety of other rituals. She prepares offerings for the spirits of the house *(a'pakanre balapati)*; she conducts general protective rituals called *songkabala,* "averting danger"; she can feed the demonic aspect of the human soul called the "black shadow" and has mastered many other ritual procedures. At the same time, she is a highly successful businesswoman who travels all over South Sulawesi and beyond, marketing local textiles.

As I left the field in 1989, Titi and her wife Denni were planning to use their savings from marketing textiles to perform the Hajj in Mecca. They expressed the belief, which was part hope and part fear, that this act would free Titi from possession by the spirits of her ancestors and put a final end to the cult. When I returned in June 2000, I found that the two of them had indeed acquired the title of Haji. This, however, had not put an end to Titi's possession by the royal ancestors. They continued to conduct rituals of homage to *Karaeng* Mamampang whenever they could gather the resources to do so.

The *Lope Lope* Ritual

Because I lived in the house of a well-known Islamic modernist who had once been a Darul Islam guerilla, the women around Titi Daeng Toje were at first reluctant to share much information with me about their royal ancestor. As I gained their confidence, they became eager to have me attend a séance. In August 1989, they told me that, although they had just performed a *lope lope* ritual two months earlier at a cost of 100,000 rupiah ($60), they were planning to hold another one soon, in part just so I could attend it. *Lope lope,* "model boat," refers to the small vessel used at the end of a séance to carry out to sea the spirits that have descended. But they made me promise not to bring along my host Abdul Hakim, or even to tell him about it. I got the clear impression that they felt my presence would help legitimize the ancestor cult. Hakim felt the same way and tried to prevent me from attending by coming up with a whole series of competing events he suggested I go to instead.

The ritual was delayed several times, until Titi was kept awake all one night by spirit familiars who insisted that a ritual was overdue. One of the problems Titi faced in carrying out this ritual is that the model boat had to be made by a man, and there were almost no men willing to participate in the cult. Titi sometimes called on her brother Rasa, but he lived on the island of Buton and visited Ara only rarely. Finally, Titi persuaded her oldest nephew, a boy of twenty called Lari, to make it. The boat itself was an elaborate one, a six-foot-long *pinisi* painted white. Denni sewed seven sails for it. The preparation of all the necessary foods alone took several days of work by Titi, Denni, and their nieces. Altogether, about forty hands of bananas were used, and large quantities of glutinous rice, eggs, and betel chew ingredients. Finally, after several weeks of preparation, they were ready.

I was told that normally the séance would have started out much as it had during the 1930s. According to this procedure, Titi would go to sleep on the *palangka* in the inner room, and the devotees would wait in the outer room for her to become possessed. The first spirit would enter her in the middle of the night. It would be followed by a series of other spirits until dawn. In the 1930s, the medium and her entourage would have then gone up to *Karaeng* Mamampang's throne in Pilia or down to Sapo Hatu's tomb on the beach to complete the offerings. The difference is that these public processions are now prohibited, so the offerings to the spirits are made inside the house. The model boat is carried discreetly down to the sea by a small group in the dead of night.

On this occasion, they accelerated the whole procedure for me so that it only lasted for about three hours. Titi and Denni started setting things up at 4:30 P.M. on the evening of the séance. They laid out an elaborate feast in Titi's back room between the two center posts of the house. These were for the royal spirits and their entourage to consume on the spot during the séance.

1. On a cushion by the west wall, a plate of betel ingredients, cigarettes, and 500 rupiah, and a plate of five unfolded betel leaves.
2. A tray with five mounds of sticky white rice, each with a piece of fried egg on top.
3. Two trays each with four hands of bananas and one coconut.
4. A tray with large mounds of white, black, and red sticky rice, each with a boiled egg on top.
5. A tray with five hands of bananas and a coconut.
6. A plate with seven mounds of white sticky rice with fried eggs on top.
7. A tray with seven hands of bananas and a coconut.
8. A tray with a mound of white sticky rice with a boiled egg on top, half a cooked chicken, and a plate of sweets, including *songkolo* (rice, coconut milk, and sugar cooked into a paste) and three types of fried cakes.
9. A tray with nine hands of bananas and a coconut.
10. A tray with seven glasses of tea.

This was by far the largest and most elaborate display of foods I observed in a ritual and was a mark of the very high status ascribed to *Karaeng* Mamampang and the consequent size of his following.

In addition to this feast, they also prepared a series of offerings appropriate to the Upperworld, the Middleworld, and the Underworld. They would help guide the spirits down from the heavens into the house and then out from the house and down into the sea.

The Upperworld

A tray containing some cooked white rice and betel ingredients was placed on top of a wardrobe. The following offerings were laid out on the *palangka* of To Ebang:

1. Two trays with one hand of yellow and one hand of green bananas and a coconut.
2. A plate of white sticky rice with a boiled egg on top.
3. A plate of betel chew ingredients.

Offerings for heavenly beings consist only of white rice, symbolizing purity, and a single cooked egg, symbolizing unity. This is also true in Islamic rituals when the presence of *malaikat,* "angels," or the *Nabi,* "Prophet" is anticipated. Even if Titi is going to another house to perform a ritual, she is always careful to arrange an offering in this *palangka* first so that her spirit familiars would remember which house she lives in.

The Middleworld

According to Hama, only the royal spirits board the model boat and go out to sea. Their followers are supposed to remain behind on land and share the contents of a basket called the *bala suji,* which contains

1. A coconut inflorescence.
2. One hand of bananas.
3. Seven *ketupat* cakes.
4. A plate of curried chicken.
5. Small mounds of white, black, and red glutinous rice.
6. A special tray containing mixed white, black, and red cooked rice in the center and a boiled egg on top, with five piles of yellow uncooked rice and puffed rice, seven slices of banana, five betel leaves folded "short," and five cigarettes arranged around it.

In contrast to the simple, undifferentiated offerings placed on the wardrobe and the *palangka,* these offerings constitute a fully differentiated, "complete" set. The food offering includes a starch staple, a meat side dish, a ripe fruit, and a sweet snack. The special tray includes the four colors, (red, black, white, and yellow) that represent the four elements (fire, earth, water, and air) out of which all material bodies are made. The rice includes raw, puffed, and steamed forms. The boiled egg represents the way the elements are united into an organic whole. Finally, the offering is completed with two foods that are normally eaten raw (banana and betel) and one that is consumed by smoking (tobacco).

The Underworld

At the end of the séance, the continued presence of the most powerful royal spirits in the Middleworld would be dangerous. They must be sent down in a model boat to the Underworld, whence they will make their own way back to the Upperworld. The model boat was filled with a variety of foods:

1. Three plates with red, black, and white sticky rice and a boiled egg.
2. A bundle of seven rice cakes steamed in a container woven from coconut leaves.
3. A plate of curried chicken.
4. Seven hands of bananas.
5. A green coconut.
6. A plate of sweets containing rice and coconut pudding (*songkolo*) and three types of fried cakes.
7. On either side of the bow of the boat, a tray of uncooked rice, a hand of green bananas, and an unhusked coconut. One of these trays also had five betel leaves folded lengthwise, other chew ingredients, and 500 rupiah.
8. A special tray containing a raw egg in the center surrounded by yellow uncooked rice, puffed rice, and a whole areca nut in an unfolded betel leaf.

The foods placed in the boat also constitute a complete feast that includes a starch staple, a meat side dish, ripe fruit, and a sweet snack. But the special tray includes only raw foods that mark it out as destined for the Underworld.

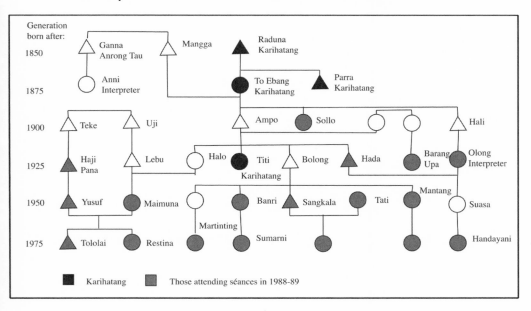

Fig. 9.5 The Ancestor Cult of To Ebang, 1989.

At 5:30, the first group of a dozen women with their small children arrived. By 8 P.M. there were about twenty women in the back room with her, and ten more asleep in front, with a dozen small children. Lari, the model builder, was the only man aside from me. In fact, they were forced to invite Muli, my young companion to the caves of Pilia, to help carry the boat down to the beach, despite their distrust of him. Six teenage boys had been rounded up to help later and had been served tea and cakes. They ate quickly and left, so for a time I was the only man in the house. I later identified all of the women as descendents or collaterals of To Ebang.

The Séance

I was called away by Abdul Hakim at 6 P.M. to observe another ritual being held at the *possi' tana.* By the time I got back to Titi's house at 8 P.M., the séance was already under way. It had begun an hour earlier, when Titi seated herself in front of the large *palangka* of To Ebang and began to chant. An hour later, she was already in trance, taking everyone by surprise. I had been told again and again no spirits would come until midnight. Her assistants, including Olong and some other older women, kept incense burning the whole time and periodically threw yellow raw rice and puffed rice over everyone in the room. Every so often, Titi would break off chanting and talk in a normal tone of voice. Her speech was interspersed with a number of Arabic formulae. She moved restlessly about the room, standing up, going to sit behind the model boat, coming back, and so on. For the most part she kept her eyes closed. Aside from these mannerisms, she seemed normal and was certainly in no way "ecstatic." The women around her listened to her respectfully and punctuated her statements with cries of *ie,* "yes," but did not appear overawed. They appeared to be quite used to this sort of situation.

I learned later from Titi's niece that it was the spirit of To Ebang who first spoke. She had begun by reproaching her followers for having delayed so long in delivering the boat they had promised her. She went on however to praise it. She kept looking at it and touching it, and seemed genuinely pleased. The interpreter, Titi's aunt Olong, did most of the talking, while other older women added incense to the brazier. After two hours, the younger women were invited to each add some incense to the brazier. To Ebang's speech was interspersed with Arabic phrases. While in trance, Titi seemed quite normal, except that her eyes were always at least half closed, and she seemed more animated and talkative than usual.

During this part of the séance, it became clear to me why people sometimes referred to the current *karihatang* as To Ebang rather than Titi: the high point of many of these séances was the chance to chat with the grandmother from whom they were all descended. The following To Ebang had built up before her death in 1962 continued to cluster around her after her death. Titi seemed to be acting quite normally, except that her eyes were half closed and she seemed more animated and talkative than usual. The atmosphere was relaxed and informal, at times even jocular. It was more like a warm family reunion than the supplication of some awesome supernatural power—a matrifocal household extended to the spirit plane.

At some point, To Ebang left Titi and *Karaeng* Mamampang entered her. He spoke in the Gowan dialect of Makassar. He was replaced by a third spirit whose name I did not get. In addition to the three spirits that came and spoke, more than forty of their *joa,* entourage, came to partake of the offerings. This is why so many separate trays of offerings had been prepared: royal spirits never travel without an entourage.

At 9:30 P.M. the tempo of Titi's speech picked up and she started chanting vigorously. She picked up a plate of raw white rice, which she stirred around with her hand and then threw around the room. She called for oil in a special white bowl, which was put on a plate. This she began waving about in the air. I was later told that it did not spill because of the power of the spirit inside her (though it looked like centrifugal force to me). This oil acquired some of the power and later, after the séance, four or five women helped themselves to the oil in the white bowl and rubbed it on their faces, legs, and bellies. Soon afterward she calmed down and came out of trance, as the spirits left her and entered a live chick placed in the model boat. The chick containing the spirits remained in the boat when it was put out to sea. I was told that the sea journey served as a diversion for the ancestor spirits, who enjoyed the change of scenery.

The materials that had been placed in the boat at the beginning of the ritual were now removed and placed in carrying baskets. The six teenage boys were called back into the house, and at 10 P.M. they set off for the beach, a mile away, accompanied by three adolescent girls and two older women. Titi never joins these processions herself, but stays behind to recover from the séance. When they reached the beach, the boys swam out in the surf to launch the boat, while the women immersed a bamboo container called a *bala suji* in the water near the shore. Later, Hama commented that Titi's followers had been wrong in putting the *bala suji* (*bali saji,* according to him) in the water. He said it was meant to be the "opposite" of the boat. Its contents were "for the land," just as those of the boat were "for the sea." It should thus have been placed on a rock for the king's entourage *(joa karaeng),* who remain on the land when he sails off. Only a fraction of the offerings carried down to the beach were put in the water. The rest were eaten on the spot or divided up and taken home by the various participants.

Hama's Commentary

While Titi was insistent on her ignorance of the meaning of any of the rituals she performed while in trance, a male informant called Hama was always ready to supply a commentary. Hama claimed to be full of arcane knowledge he received in dreams and in waking visions. He was of the general opinion that Titi had learned how to perform rituals merely by observing the external actions of other *sanro* but that she did not understand the inner meaning of the actions. As a result, she often made "mistakes" that invalidated her rituals. From Titi's point of view, however, the fact that she did not "understand" her ritual actions and could not provide an interpretation for them was an integral part of their efficacy: as a medium, she was merely a vehicle guided by higher spirits. Only her aunt and interpreter, Olong, was supposed to have the conscious knowledge of these things.

According to Hama, it was not necessary for a *sanro* to be a spirit medium to perform a model boat ritual. One only needed to know the proper incantations to induce the ancestor spirits to descend and bestow their blessings and then to board the boat and depart. Hama was the only *sanro* willing to recite his incantations, or *mantera*, for me. These are the secret essence of ritual knowledge, the part that can be employed without anyone else being able to copy it. He recites the following *mantera* when invoking the ancestors:

> The ancestor spirit says, "I am tired of flying about. I wish to descend but have no vehicle. Make me a ship, because I am tired of going up and down, and have no place to rest."
>
> The *sanro* replies, "Among we seven who emerged together, you are the eldest, you are the highest, you, who have no fixed abode. Please descend to the place you desire, which I have made for you, the boat I Lolo Gading. Please descend to your beautiful vessel, to the body that will be the place of your reclining. Your boat is ready: the boat I Lolo Gading."

Note that *I Lolo Gading*, "The Noble Bamboo," was also the name in a famous Makassar ballad of the boat Datu Museng and Maipa Deapati used to cross from Sumbawa to Ujung Pandang (Gibson, 2004). It signifies a mystical vehicle capable of moving between worlds.

In this *mantera*, Hama also makes a connection between the ancestor spirits and the seven spirits that emerge at the time of a child's birth. The eldest of these seven is the placenta, which was traditionally preserved in a coconut shell and placed in the attic. A person's breath, *nyaha,* goes up into the placenta each night when they sleep and back down into their body each morning when they awake. Because ancestor shrines are also stored in the attic, the relation between ancestors and descendents can thus mapped onto the relationship between the Upperworld and the Middleworld and onto the relationship between elder and younger siblings. The connection between them is maintained through a dynamic process in which the ancestors must periodically descend from the sky like rain and continue to flow out to sea like rivers, only to cycle upward again as mist. If we now refer back to my initial schematic representation of the Austronesian cosmos, we can see that the *lope lope* ritual serves to organize the entire symbolic system into a single coherent process (see figure 3.1).

Conclusion: Royal Ritual and the Bureaucratic State

Between 1930 and 1970, the social hierarchy in South Sulawesi lost its coherence and split into crosscutting social, political, and ideological factions. Hereditary rank, government office, modern education, traditional Islamic learning, and new sources of wealth increasingly marked out distinct groups of people.

Despite colonial and Islamic opposition, the cults of the *karihatang* of *Karaeng* Mamampang in Ara and the *gaukang* of To Kambang in Tanaberu never disappeared. For generations, these cults have allowed noble families in these villages to retain a certain solidarity and exclusivity, despite being shut out of political office. They have also enabled the royal ancestors to continue to guarantee human and natural fertility, despite the loss of judicial and military power by their descendents.

The two cults enjoyed different relationships to political power during the nineteenth and twentieth centuries. Descendents of *Karaeng* Mamampang remained in office in Ara until 1915, and the royal cult remained at the center of official life. Descendents of To Kambang lost power in Tanaberu in 1865, and the cult moved to the margins. The situation was reversed after 1921. Gama consolidated his hold on political power in Ara and began to persecute the descendents of *Karaeng* Mamampang. By contrast, in Tanaberu even officials who were appointed from outside the area sought to marry local noblewomen who could claim descent from To Kambang. By the 1940s, even Gama of Ara adopted this tactic when he arranged the marriage of his son to a woman whose family that controlled the *gaukang* of To Kambang.

In Tanaberu, noblewomen managed to maintain their centrality in the political system. Although the village was ruled by a succession of appointed officials from other parts of South Sulawesi after 1859, in the twentieth century almost all of them married local noblewomen who had some hereditary connection to the founding royal ancestor. They thus played the role assigned in the royal foundation myths to the prince from Majapahit. The cult of To Kambang continued to legitimate the local political order to some extent, while the cult of *Karaeng* Mamampang became a purely private affair of a matrifocal kin group.

In the face of unremitting hostility from the local government, the cult of *Karaeng* Mamampang in Ara has been reduced to a dedicated core of noblewomen. This was part of a more general phenomenon in South Sulawesi, in which indigenous myth and ritual became "the religion of women," while Islam became "the religion of men." Noblewomen were at the symbolic center of the old hereditary system of ritual and political office. Their ascribed ranks defined a fixed hierarchy within which noblemen competed for wealth, status, and power. The new political and religious offices that arose in the eighteenth and nineteenth centuries were largely closed to women and increasingly open to achievement. Men who mastered the sacred scriptures written in the Arabic script could aspire to religious offices even if they were not descended from previous holders of those offices. Noblewomen came to specialize in the indigenous *lontara* script and in the hereditary ritual offices dedicated to the indigenous ancestors. In the twentieth century, men who acquired the ability to read and write the Roman script could aspire to be appointed to the colonial bureaucracy.

Because both these types of office were closed to women, eligibility to participate in the cult of the royal ancestors was one of their most important remaining symbolic assets. The continued vitality of the rituals cannot be explained in this case by their role in legitimating political authority. They continue to be performed at great cost in time and resources because of the way they organize and reproduce the symbolic system as a whole. The women in Titi's persecuted entourage feel obliged to attend the séances of the royal ancestors in spite of the wishes of the current power-holders in Ara. As one woman explained it to me, "If we neglect the ancestors, we will surely die." Neglecting the ancestors would be to neglect everything they "know" about the world of land and sea, Bonto Bahari.

Chapter 10
Knowledge, Power, and Traditional Authority

I n this chapter, I begin by summarizing the argument I have made in this volume regarding the sedimentation of competing ideal models of the regional political order in Makassar myth and ritual. I then provide an overview of what happened to Makassar ideas of the political order after they converted to Islam at the beginning of the seventeenth century. Regional models of the political order were then placed into juxtaposition with global Islamic models. I then discuss the relevance of the life cycle rituals for the reproduction of both the political and the religious systems. I end with some reflections on the relationship between the experiential data collected by the anthropologist in the field and the encompassing historical and geographic structures constructed by the historian in the archive.

Competing Ideal Models in Regional Political Systems

In *Political Systems of Highland Burma,* Leach argued that it was possible for more than one ideal model of the social structure to exist in a single population and that these ideal models were reproduced through what he called the ritual or communicative aspect of social action (Leach 1954). In the case of the Kachin, he argued that competing patterns of marriage alliance provided a framework for competing models of the political order. One pattern, labeled *gumlao,* held that wife takers and wife givers should be of equal status and, in light of asymmetric rules of marriage, that they should be integrated into a closed circle of at least three lines of givers and takers. The other model, labeled *gumsa,* held that wife givers were superior to wife takers and that the central wife giver in a domain should be a tribute-receiving chief. Hierarchical *gumsa* values developed under the influence of the wet-rice growing Buddhist statelets of the Shan people, which were dotted along the trade routes in the Kachin hills.

The breakthrough in this argument was the way Leach treated structural models as modular symbolic systems that could move across local ethnolinguistic boundaries. These models provided a common symbolic language in which relative political statuses within a wider region could be expressed through marriage alliances contracted between local elites despite lower-level differences in culture. Actors were able to organize an ever-changing welter of concrete political situations by reference to these models. The relevance to the situation in South Sulawesi should be clear. I have argued that the myths and rituals surrounding royal weddings set out a number of competing models of how regional political relationships should be organized. I have outlined six such models in this book. These models can be read as both a recapitulation of Makassar state formation and a synchronic structure of competing alternatives.

In the earliest period, outlined in chapter 3, the Austronesian peoples developed an extremely mobile civilization based on the exploitation of the tropical seas and of the coastal littoral. Moving through the sparsely inhabited islands of the Philippines and Indonesia, the members of this civilization were able to maintain a significant degree of cultural coherence on the basis of a shared environment and set of technological adaptations and a shared ancestral language and symbolic system. In the latter respect, there is a clear contrast between Island Southeast Asia and Highland Burma, which is inhabited by ethnic groups deriving from many different language families. At the heart of the Austronesian symbolic system lay the antagonism and complementarity between the male and female principles that animate the cosmos as a whole.

In the second period, outlined in chapters 4 and 5, a network of stable chiefdoms developed along the coasts of the Java Sea. The network was held together by local elites who engaged in intensive trade and intermarriage with one another. Royal marriages were legitimated by a set of myths that portrayed this intermarriage as the reunification of opposite-sex twins. For the most part, these myths and rituals stick to the same Austronesian conceptions of gender and androgynous creation outlined in chapter 3. The distant court of Kediri in Java came to serve as a model of high culture during this period, but the local kingdoms maintained their political autonomy. The model of equal alliance between distinct yet related houses contained in this complex of myths and rituals continues to structure part of the elaborate sequence of rituals surrounding marriage between noble houses to this day (Gibson 1995).

In the third period, outlined in chapter 6, shifting cultivation gave way to fixed field agriculture and reciprocity between polities was supplemented by redistribution within agrarian kingdoms. Local elites now maintained their power partly through their ability to mobilize labor for wet rice agriculture and partly through their continued monopoly on the prestige goods acquired through maritime trade. The female principle was now attached to the noble ruler, who guaranteed the fertility of the soil and domestic harmony in return for the food, shelter, and clothing supplied by the commoners and the male principle to long-distance trade in luxury goods. The royal foundation myths portrayed the polity as based on a complementarity between royal redistribution and feudal service, on the one hand, and long-distance trade, on the other. The origin of the kingdom was traced back to the selection of a heavenly maiden and her earthly consort by a local population as the only ones who could bring an end to internal conflict. The imperial court of Majapahit came to exercise an increasingly hegemonic cultural influence over peripheral courts during this period, as local ancestor cults were drawn into an Indic cult centered on the emperor. As Majapahit's influence declined in the fifteenth century, its place as the symbolic center of the Makassar realms was taken by local successor states like Luwu' and Bantaeng. The complementary opposition between the female products of the land and the male products of the sea, and hierarchical exchange of the fertility provided by the rulers and the tribute provided by their subjects continued to structure agricultural and political rituals well into the twentieth century.

In the fourth period, outlined in chapters 7 and 8, I discussed the astute use of both new forms of practical knowledge and of old forms of symbolic knowledge by the empire builders of Gowa and Tallo'. Gunpowder technology was used to centralize power in the hands of the ruling dynasty in an unprecedented way. War was no longer carried out primarily to seize prestige trade goods like gold and jewels, but to capture slaves who could be put to work on irrigation and fortification projects. The female function of agricultural fertility was taken over by an inland king whose military conquests and ritual shedding of blood on the regalia guaranteed the prosperity of the kingdom. The male functions of long-distance trade and diplomacy were taken over by a coastal king. The complementarity between the two kings was expressed in written chronicles as a bond between brothers-in-law who recognized their equality and interdependence by exchanging their sisters in marriage. The association between warfare, military prowess, and fertility contained in the ritual of the royal regalia continued to legitimate royal warfare until the end of the colonial period.

In the fifth period, outlined in chapter 8, the superior military and bureaucratic methods of the VOC reduced the Bugis and Makassar kingdoms to vassals of a foreign and unintelligible master. The insatiable demands of the Dutch slave markets led to an increasingly exploitative relationship between the local nobility and their own subjects, whom they enslaved for nonpayment of judicial fines, and between the nobility of one kingdom and the subjects of other kingdoms, which they raided for captives. In their desperation, people turned to charismatic figures such as Sangkilang, who claimed to be the true king come back to reclaim his throne, to expel the foreigners and to rule justly. So long as he was accepted as the just king by part of the nobility and by the mountain Makassar, and so long as he had possession of Gowa's heirloom sword, neither the Dutch nor the British could pacify the area. The sword brought by the King of the Sea Nomads from Bantaeng to Gowa in 1300 had once represented the power of the male sea. It now became a symbol of popular resistance. Elements of the charismatic power of the just king continued to structure people's conception of political struggle as recently as the 1950s, when Kahar Muzakkar led a guerilla war against the national government.

In the sixth period, outlined in chapter 9, the place of the VOC as a territorial overlord was taken by a colonial government intent on transforming local social, economic, and political systems in a way that would optimize the generation and appropriation of surplus value through market exchange. During the nineteenth century, the royal cults served sometimes to legitimate the actual rulers of Ara and Tanaberu and sometimes to maintain the cohesion of a noble faction that had been (temporarily) displaced from power. During the twentieth century, the growing demands of the modern bureaucratic state and the market economy pushed the royal cult of Ara into an increasingly marginal position. The current *karihatang* is a successful businesswoman who has used her profits to maintain the royal cult and to acquire a new form of prestige as a Haji.

The myths and rituals associated with each of these six periods provide actors with models for social interaction that privilege, respectively, complementary difference, reciprocity between equals, hierarchical redistribution, military conquest, resistance to predatory outsiders, and the conversion of the profits of market exchange into social prestige. Each of these models has enjoyed a dominant position at a different point in history, but all coexist today.

Now, not only are there multiple models of legitimate political authority within Makassar society, but the Makassar have been engaged with many other societies of greatly divergent scale and complexity for many centuries. Each of these societies has its own array of competing models, so an awareness of social and cultural difference is engrained in every member of the region. These neighboring social formations range from small-scale bands of shifting cultivators and hunter-gatherers, to middle scale societies based on semiintensive cultivation and maritime trade, to large-scale civilizations, both indigenous and colonial in origin, based on the intensive cultivation of irrigated rice and on plantation agriculture. Agrarian kingdoms, maritime chiefdoms, and tribal groups each maintained their own distinctive economic, political, and ideological institutions, all the while interacting with one another at every level. From time to time, regional centers such as Srivijaya, Kediri, and Majapahit have established a certain symbolic hegemony over the region. But they were not in a position to impose their own political or economic systems on the groups they tried to dominate.

The polities of South Sulawesi thus had to operate alongside polities that were both much larger and much smaller than themselves. They occupied the zones intermediate between the forested highland periphery occupied by shifting cultivators maintaining indigenous rituals and cosmologies and the centers of large-scale wet rice cultivation in Java and Bali. They are a useful case to focus on precisely because of their success in this heterogeneous environment. At many points in history, they were able to project their military and mercantile power right across the region, conducting raids throughout the archipelago and even establishing dynasties on the Malay Peninsula. Thus, the periodic emergence of relatively powerful centers in one part of the region did not lead to the extinction of less powerful ones, but rather to a series of mutual readjustments between the heterogeneous social systems of the region.

Competing Ideal Models in Global Religious Systems

The historical narrative traced in this volume reaches a fork at the beginning of the sixteenth century, when the rulers of South Sulawesi became enmeshed with a global symbolic order that had developed throughout the Islamic world over the previous thousand years. On the other hand, the kings of South Sulawesi never completely abandoned the indigenous myths, rituals, and sacred objects that had legitimated the rule of their ancestors. The relevant spatial and temporal horizons of Islamic forms of knowledge are so different from those of Austronesian forms of knowledge that the history of the period after the conversion of the kings must be portrayed from two different angles. I have thus reserved a detailed discussion of the role of Islam in South Sulawesi for another place. I do need to provide a general outline of Islamic models of the state, however, to place the Austronesian models discussed in this volume in perspective.

The best theoretical guide to an analysis of the Islamic era is provided by the work of Tambiah on the role of Buddhism in Mainland Southeast Asia. In my reading of his work, Tambiah developed Leach's basic insight on the role of ideal models in the formation of political systems in his study of the way Buddhist ideas since the time of Ashoka provided the ideological core around which states first developed in many parts of Southeast Asia (Tambiah 1976). In the wake of his contribution, no serious anthropologist of Mainland Southeast Asia could afford to ignore the relevance of Buddhist texts to state formation in the region. This is still not entirely true of anthropologists working on Island Southeast Asia, who often enter the field with little knowledge of Islamic texts.

The kings of Gowa and Tallo' were fully aware of the global Islamic order at least as early as 1511, when numerous Muslim refugees from the Portuguese conquest of Melaka sought asylum on the coast of South Sulawesi. They did not convert to Islam, however, until their control of the peninsula had been secured and they were ready to turn outward to the sea. The kings of Gowa and Tallo' converted at the beginning of the seventeenth century as a way of cementing the new military and economic power they had already achieved. From 1605 on, the kings of South Sulawesi relied increasingly on a range of Islamic scriptures, charismatic saints, and mystical practices, both to legitimate themselves in the eyes of their subjects and to forge new alliances with other Islamic rulers throughout Island Southeast Asia.

One reason the kings of South Sulawesi may have delayed their conversion for a century after the fall of Melaka is that it was not until the end of the sixteenth century that an Islamic model of political authority they found attractive became available. This model was developed by the absolute monarchs of the Safavid dynasty in Iran, the Mughal dynasty in India, and the sultans of Aceh and Mataram in Indonesia, all of whom had also managed to centralize power through the use of gunpowder technology (Hodgson 1974). In this model, the king functions as the embodiment of Ibn al-Arabi's doctrine of the *Insan al-Kamil*, or Perfect Man. According to Ibn al-Arabi and his followers, God created the world so that He might be known by another. In all of creation, it is only a spiritually perfected human who is capable of knowing Him adequately, and thus in a sense the Perfect Man provides the world with its very reason for being. If the ruler claims the status of the Perfect Man, his pretensions are great indeed.

No sooner had the kings of South Sulawesi taken the step of adopting the version of Ibn al-Arabi's theosophy developed in the great gunpowder empires of monsoon Asia, however, than a new circuit of symbolic knowledge was established that linked their subjects directly to the Muslims of the Arabian Sea. Young Bugis and Makassar men set out to perform the pilgrimage to Mecca within a few years of the conversion of the kings. On their way they met Swahili, Yemeni, and Gujarati Muslims who had no place in their religion for sultans claiming to be the Perfect Man. Their rival view of Islamic power and authority soon began to spread in the villages of South Sulawesi.

In this second Islamic model, spiritual excellence resided in cosmopolitan saints, often of humble birth, who kept their distance from corrupt centers of political power. They sought knowledge and power not by climbing the ranks of local social hierarchies, but by circulating through the known world in search of universal knowledge. One of the greatest of these saints was a Makassar of humble origins known as Shaikh Yusuf. After the downfall of the absolutist states of Gowa, Banten, and Aceh in the seventeenth century, charismatic figures like Shaikh Yusuf briefly united diverse ethnic groups in a series of holy wars against the VOC. Yusuf was captured in 1683 by the Dutch, who exiled him first to Sri Lanka and then to South Africa, where he died. His blessings continue to flow to devotees from tombs located throughout the Indian Ocean.

By the end of the eighteenth century, a new model of mystical Islam was gaining ground throughout the Islamic world, partly in response to the growing threat of European expansion. Devotion to local Islamic saints was downplayed in favor of a renewed emphasis on devotion to the universal and final prophet, Muhammad. This model of devotion to the prophet rather than to the king or the saints was expressed through practices such as the recitation of *maulid,* praise poems written in his honor. Many held that the spirit of the prophet became present during the recitation of such poems, allowing devotees to request his intercession with God.

This third Islamic model was adopted in the eighteenth century by the sultans of Bone, who had formed an alliance with the VOC in their struggle with Gowa. In Bone, the Dutch were viewed as instruments of God's wrath, who punished the sultans of Gowa for their arrogance by overthrowing their empire. The sultans of Bone remained central to the religious system, but not by claiming the status of the Perfect Man. Instead they became patrons of Islamic learning and sponsored the translation and dissemination of religious texts within their kingdom. The most popular *maulid* in South Sulawesi was the *barasanji,* a text written around 1760 by Jaffar al-Barzanji, a Kurdish mufti of the Shafii school of law (Kaptein 1992). The *barasanji* was incorporated into almost every life cycle ritual in South Sulawesi, associating the life of every individual with that of the prophet.

A fourth Islamic model developed in the eighteenth century in the areas where VOC officials began to function as territorial overlords. In these areas, local Muslims were faced with foreign rulers who lacked both the traditional authority of descent from the royal ancestors and the charismatic authority of the Islamic saints. Mystical brotherhoods in this period often became sources of resistance to infidel rule. A cult of martyrdom developed in which death in battle became an option for those who suffered unbearable humiliation at the hands of the VOC. The goal of this martyrdom was not the defeat of the enemy in this world, but a quick transition to a state of spiritual grace in the next world. These martyrs are commemorated in a genre of ballads known as *sinrili'*. These ballads helped inspire Islamic guerillas during the Darul Islam movement of 1950 to 1965 (see Gibson, 2004).

A fifth Islamic model developed in the nineteenth century after the predatory rule of the VOC had been moderated and routinized by the new colonial administration of the government of the Netherlands East Indies (NEI). The introduction of steamships and the opening of the Suez Canal made travel to the Middle East much cheaper and quicker than the old methods of navigation. The development of markets for tropical produce also led to pockets of relative prosperity. The result was a great increase in the number of Indonesian pilgrims traveling to Mecca on Dutch ships. Dutch officials actively promoted the separation of politics and religion, tolerating Islamic piety while harshly repressing any criticism of the colonial order in the name of religion. Hajjis returning from the Middle East thus felt free to criticize local ritual traditions they viewed as heterodox, but tended to avoid overt criticisms of the state. As we have seen, it was Haji Gama's affiliation with this movement that led to the marginalization of the royal cult in Ara.

Finally, a sixth Islamic model spread at the beginning of the twentieth century with the introduction of European educational systems in the NEI and the development of Islamic printing presses in the Middle East. These developments gave rise to Islamic modernist movements like the Muhammadiyah that were hostile to the indigenous rituals that perpetuated noble ranking systems, to traditional Sufi brotherhoods, and to European colonial rule. In South Sulawesi, the nationalist movement was closely associated with the critique of all rituals not mandated by the scriptures, according to the doctrine that there should be no innovation, *bid'a,* in matters of religious practice. Followers of the Muhammadiyah will not attend the recitation of the *barasanji,* making every life cycle ritual the occasion for delicate negotiations over who will enter the house at what point.

These six periods of Islamic history in South Sulawesi have left behind six models of the exemplary Islamic figure: the ruler as Perfect Man; the militant Saint; the Prophet as universal intercessor; the otherworldly Martyr; the pious pilgrim; and the religious Nationalist. All six models continue to be invoked in particular ritual contexts.

The outline of Makassar history that I gave in the first part of this chapter

tended to emphasize changes in practical knowledge, such as the new naviga-
tional, agricultural, military, and administrative techniques that allowed for the
construction of ever larger states between 1400 and 1600. But the power of the
rulers was based just as much on their privileged access to foreign sources of
symbolic knowledge as it was on their control of land, labor, and violence. The
possibility that massive social change can also begin at the level of symbolic
knowledge was demonstrated more clearly in the second part of the chapter by
examining the effects of conversion to Islam. In the heterogeneous social space
of Island Southeast Asia, local elites always had access both to techniques and to
ideologies that had developed in more sophisticated social formations. The driv-
ing force of social change in the region has sometimes been the adoption of new
technologies and sometimes religious conversion. Which aspect is playing the
leading role in social transformation at any one time is an open question that
can only be answered empirically.

In summary, it is rather pointless to try to construct a single model of the
state in Southeast Asia. The political systems of South Sulawesi worked rather
differently in the maritime chiefdoms of the twelfth century when revenues
were drawn from long-distance trading and raiding, in the agrarian states of the
fifteenth century when revenues were drawn from the taxation of wet-rice farmers, in the gunpowder empires of the sixteenth century when slaves were used
to produce export crops, in the mercantilist dependencies of the seventeenth
century when local kings exported their own subjects as slaves in exchange for
opium, and in the capitalist states of the twentieth century, when royal rituals
served primarily to reproduce social rank. What is needed, rather, is a model of
interacting models, of the ways in which the longevity of the symbolic knowledge embedded in rituals and myths provides people with a diverse set of metaphors for framing their current experience.[1]

Competing Ideal Models in Local Social Systems

This volume ends where my fieldwork began, with the royal rituals performed
in honor of To Kambang of Tanaberu and Karaeng Mamampang of Ara. A
proper understanding of these rituals required a long detour into the history of
the Java Sea basin. The rivalry between the devotees of Karaeng Mamampang
and To Kambang echoed the long rivalry between Gowa and Bone, a rivalry
that in turn echoed the rivalry between the Makassar kings and the Dutch East
India Company.

The largest portion of my field notes is in fact concerned with the elaborate rituals that occur throughout the life cycle of Makassar nobles, most notably
for pregnancy, childbirth, and circumcision; before, during, and after marriage;
and for dealing with the body, spirit, and soul of the dead. Where the royal rituals
discussed in this book implicated the whole political history of the region, the
life cycle rituals turned out to be even more complex. They implicated not just
the political history of the region but the whole religious history of global Islam

as well. It is through these life cycle rituals that the twelve ideal models outlined above become embedded in the experience of particular individuals.

Such rituals have been a staple of anthropological interest, of course, since the time of van Gennep ([1909] 1960). van Gennep's analysis of their structure as falling into the three phases of separation, liminality, and aggregation was later taken up by many British social anthropologists, who interpreted them largely as mechanisms for moving individuals from one predetermined social role to another. Turner complicated this analysis somewhat by focusing on the potential for freedom and creativity that became possible during the liminal phase, a phase in which normal structural rules were deliberately broken (Turner 1967).

Bloch has shown how social hierarchy and political authority can be reproduced precisely by an emphasis on chaos and disorder in the liminal phase of rites of passage. Order is restored at the end by elders who invoke the traditional authority of the ancestors in formalized speeches. Bloch attributes the political flexibility of Merina symbolic systems to the inherently vague nature of the statements rituals make about the world and to their assault on individual rationality and creativity (Bloch 1986: 191). In a lecture given about the same time his book on Merina circumcision was written, Bloch allowed for another possibility: "metaphysical speculation." He notes that egalitarian peoples like the Batek hunter-gatherers of Malaysia "endlessly indulge in metaphysical speculation without this becoming ideology. This is because this speculation is never *clinched* into an authorized version, however vague such a version might be. Endicott, to the contrary, emphasizes the way in which these people continually disagree with each other about the nature of the supernatural and origin myths and how they seem actually to enjoy the arguments and disagreements" (Bloch [1985] 1989: 122). By contrast, he writes that the Merina are unwilling to discuss their beliefs much at all but insist on orthodoxy when they do, and on obligatory participation in ritual. He then equates ritual with ideological domination in hierarchical societies and draws a clear distinction between ritual and the mythological speculation found in egalitarian societies.

Bloch's argument about the changing political functions of the ritual of circumcision in Merina history inspired much of my analysis of the Makassar (Bloch 1986). Here I want to mention two of the differences in our approach to symbolic knowledge. In the first place, I have argued that ritual and myth are not as different as Bloch would make them appear. The Makassar speculate endlessly using concepts drawn from Western science, Islamic mysticism, and Austronesian myth. Their society is also quite hierarchical and full of obligatory ritual. The only way to deal with this range of attitudes toward speculation and ritual cross-culturally is to admit that between practical knowledge and ideology there is a mediating term: what I have called "symbolic knowledge." Symbolic knowledge contains a great deal more creativity than Bloch's analysis allows. Rather than viewing rituals and myths as generating logically defective propositions about the world, they are better viewed as creating—or, better, revealing—a different kind of meaning that has more in common with art and music than with science and politics.

In the second place, far from resting on vague generalities that negate much of what is known at a practical level about the natural world, myths and rituals presuppose an extremely detailed knowledge of that world. The conservatism of myth and ritual is to be explained by their orientation to unchanging aspects of everyday life, such as the temporal rhythms of the tides, monsoons, and agricultural seasons; the biological cycles of plants, animals, and humans; and the grammatical structures of language. These phenomena of the longue durée are no less real than the events thrown up by the vicissitudes of the political economy. The ideological trick at the root of traditional authority is the linking of transient political structures to enduring symbolic structures.

But as we have just seen, in complex societies like that of the Makassar, there is no one model of the political order, but many competing ones. Just which ideal model of the political and religious order a particular ritual will invoke is often hotly contested. These competing models not only provide political agents with ideological weapons in their struggle for power, but also structure what that struggle is all about. When operating within the symbolic structures that are oriented toward the acquisition and retention of prestige within local systems of kinship and marriage, actors will see themselves as aspects of a larger social agency, that of a corporate house, and they will share a large body of implicit, nonverbal knowledge with their competitors. When operating within the symbolic structures that are oriented toward the acquisition and retention of military power within a regional system that includes not only other Makassar, but also Javanese and Europeans, actors will see themselves as agents with more autonomy from the local social system, and they will also have to function at a more explicit, self-conscious level of knowledge. When operating within the symbolic structures that are oriented toward the acquisition of salvation within the global system of Dar al-Islam, actors will see themselves as ethical individuals whose every conscious choice might affect their fate for all eternity.

It is only when one has understood the way individual agency is defined in each of the relevant symbolic traditions that one can begin to ask interesting questions about the tactics and strategies individuals adopt in the pursuit of a variety of conscious projects such as the accumulation of prestige, wealth, and power. Every individual is at the same time a person in the local social structure, a subject in the regional political system, and a soul in the global religion of Islam.[2] Historical agency, the ability of actors to reflect and make conscious choices, thus depends on an awareness of alternative models of both the past and the future. A more detailed investigation of the nature of historical agency among the Makassar must wait for another time.

From the Field to the Archive and Back

As I argued in chapter 2, the people of Ara have a highly developed historical consciousness. My reconstruction of the Makassar past was based at first on my analysis of interviews, royal and life cycle rituals, symbolic features of the natural and built environments, myths, ballads, and oral traditions, local and Javanese genealogies and chronicles, documents produced for the colonial bureaucracy, accounts published by Dutch missionaries and British adventurers, and many other sources. As I gradually made my way through my field notes and the ever-growing mass of archival material, my understanding of what I had learned in the field changed again and again.

Informants could date the myths, anecdotes, and ballads they told me only in terms of a very rough set of historical periods, such as before the conversion of the ancestors to Islam, during the time of Gowa's dominance, during the time of Bone's dominance, during the time of Dutch rule, and after independence. It was only after I left the field that I learned that Gowa had incorporated Bira in the 1560s, that Bira had converted to Islam around 1630, that Bira had technically become a vassal of the VOC in 1667, but had not paid tribute until 1728, that Bone's dominance over Bira peaked during the Napoleonic wars, that the first attempts at direct rule by the Dutch occurred after the Second Bone War in 1859, and that Dutch colonial officers made their presence felt in the village only between about 1920 and 1950.

While the ability to assign precise dates to key events threw new light on the narratives and texts I had collected, I also came to realize that too much precision could be just as misleading as too little. For example, *zaman Belanda,* "the time of the Dutch," turned out to be an extremely elastic category, accounting for much confusion on my part while I was in the field. In one respect, it lasted for 282 years, from the time of the Treaty of Bungaya, in 1667, until Indonesian independence, in 1949. In another respect, it lasted for just twenty-five years, from the time the Dutch abolished the regency of Bira in 1921 and put the villages of the Bira Peninsula under the direct control of a district officer, until 1941, when the Japanese invaded, and again from 1945, when the colonial administration returned, until 1950, when Sulawesi joined the Republic of Indonesia. Whether or not the Dutch presence in the area was relevant to my analysis depended on the symbolic practice in question. Each of the models I have outlined is the residue of diverse historical processes in which political and economic conditions changed relatively swiftly, whereas the symbolic knowledge accumulated slowly. They thus each have their own, separate histories. The Makassar experience of the past cannot be reduced to a single grand narrative.

Notes

Chapter 4   Incestuous Twins and Magical Boats

1. For a detailed account of traditional South Sulawesi navigation, see Ammarell (1999).

2. A briefer summary of this episode is provided by Koolhof (1995: 28–29).

3. Just before the end of my second visit, Abdul Hakim finally managed to obtain his family's version of the spell for laying a keel from his younger brother. It went as follows:

Lakugiling-giling sai	It will be circled round by me
Pakkaleang alusu'nu	Your body that is subtle
Nu anda bi'bi', nu anda makuliri'	That you not be a shell or *makuliri'*
Arennu "sahang ri langi'."	Your name is "aura of the sky."

Chapter 6   The Sea Prince and the Bamboo Maiden

1. Pelras suggests that the *Nagarakertagama* listing may recall an older tripartite division of Sulawesi found in the La Galigo. There the southern half of the island is divided into a western power on the Strait of Makassar called Wewang Nriwu, to which Bantaeng was heir; a central power that controlled the Gulf of Bone called Luwu'; and a western power in Southwest Sulawesi called Tompo'tikka, to which Uda was heir (Pelras 1996: 66).

2. All Caldwell is prepared to say about the origins of this system of writing is that it is somehow related to other Indic writing systems in Island Southeast Asia, but that it was not directly borrowed from any one of them (Caldwell 1988: 13).

Chapter 7   The Sea King and the Emperor

1. We are told more about this ruler in the chronicle of Gowa, which makes a brief reference to this foundation myth before going on to give a more detailed account of later, "historical" kings. The version published by Matthes (1860) and translated into Indonesian by Wolhoff and Abdurrahim [1960] makes only a brief reference to the origin myth, but other versions of the chronicle as discussed by Noorduyn give more detail (Noorduyn 1991). In most manuscripts, the chronicle of

Gowa begins by referring to a time preceding the coming of the *tomanurung,* when Gowa was a federation of villages called Katangka. Bulbeck places the time of these "lords of Katangka" in the thirteenth century and the coming of the *tomanurung* around 1300 (Bulbeck 1992: 34). The first phrase in these versions is the following:

> Batara Guru, his brother The One Who Was Killed by Tolali, (and) King Whose House was Full of Slaves were (all of them) Lord of Katangka (Noorduyn 1991: 461)

Like Karaeng Lowé, Batara Guru is another name for Shiva. According to Mukhlis, the nine villages near Katangka originally formed a confederation called "Gowa" (from Sanskrit *guha,* cave or hiding place) in order to defend themselves from attack by the neighboring realms of Garassi', Untia, and Lambengi. It was in response to the prayers of this confederation that a female *tomanurung* descended onto a sacred rock on Bonto Biraeng, the Hill of the Fig Tree (Mukhlis 1975).

2. This manuscript was compiled at the request of de Roock, the Dutch colonial controleur of the Onderafdeeling Bulukumba, in 1936. A copy was sent to the Netherlands, where it was lodged with the Royal Institute of Linguistics and Anthropology in Leiden. The late Professor Noorduyn of that institute kindly had a copy of it made for me. The manuscript is written in Arabic script in the local Konjo dialect. In 1989, a group of Konjo informants, including Abdul Hakim, Muhammad Nasir, and Andi Bangun Dg. Ma'gau' transliterated the text into Roman characters and provided a rough translation from the Konjo into Bahasa Indonesia for me. The translations that follow are based on both the transliterated Konjo and the Indonesian versions.

3. This part of the manuscipt includes twenty-eight precepts, proverbs, and other words of ancestral wisdom concerning the responsibilities of both rulers and followers and the cosmic catastrophes that will result if they are not obeyed. These run to about 3,500 words when translated into English. Some of these words come from the mouth of Kajao Laliddo, the chief adviser of the kings of Bone from 1540 to 1582 (La Side' 1967). Influences on conceptions of kingship thus came from both Gowa and Bone in the sixteenth century.

4. A Dutch translation was first published in a legal journal in 1853 (*Het Recht in Nederlandsch Indie* 4 (8): 83–119). Sometime after his arrival in Makassar in 1848, Matthes collected three Makassarese manuscripts for the Netherlands Bible Society (manuscript numbers 25, 26, and 27). In 1855, Matthes completed a version based on these manuscripts for publication in Makassar script, but reorganized into a more "rational" sequence, with notes in Dutch, but no translation (Matthes [1883] 1943: 36; van den Brink 1943: 56). In 1888, a revised Dutch translation was published in the *Indisch Weekblad* (1292, 1293, 1294, 1296) by I. A. Nederburgh (reprinted in 1919 in the *Adatrechtbundels XVII*). In 1889 Niemann published some notes on them in the *Bijdragen van het Koninklijke Instituut* 38: 83–88 (also reprinted in *Adatrechtbundels XVII*).

5. *"Dampang"* is defined by Cense (1979) as an "old title of local rulers in the

Makassarese-speaking lands of Southwest Celebes" (citing Friedericy [1928] 1929: 413–414).

6. Spanish expeditions to Maluku from Latin America were mounted in 1526, 1528, and 1543, and they brought many of the new foodstuffs with them. In light of Bira's long ties to Maluku, it is entirely plausible that these crops first reached Gowa by way of Bira.

7. Matthes ([1865] 1943) listed only eight members of the Hadat, whereas Goedhart ([1920] 1933) lists ten, but Goedhart includes the *ana'karaeng* as a member of the Hadat of Bira, and perhaps also the *karaeng*. The latter two were superordinate positions, however, created by the *somba* of Gowa, as we saw. They were not members of the Hadat itself.

8. As MacNeill (1982) and Hodgson (1974) have shown, a similar centralization of power in the hands of absolute monarchs through the use of gunpowder technology occurred in the sixteenth century in many empires, including those of the Hapsburgs, Romanovs, Ottomans, Safavids, and Mughals.

Chapter 8   The Power of the Regalia

1. For a similar process carried out in Bali at the beginning of the twentieth century, see H. Schulte Nordholt (1996, chap. 8).

Chapter 10   Knowledge, Power, and Traditional Authority

1. At one extreme, Geertz attempted to use fragmentary anthropological data to construct a model of the "theater state" in nineteenth century Bali and to use this model to interpret even more fragmentary data for the rest of "the classical Southeast Asian Indic states of the fifth to fifteenth centuries" (Geertz 1980: 7–10). The notion that the ideal king is the immobile center of a ceremonial court is likely a by-product of the nineteenth century's *pax Neerlandica* (H. Schulte Nordholt 1996: 120). The role of violence and conquest in preserving the vitality of the land and people is also neglected in Errington's work on the Bugis state of Luwu', partly because she relies too heavily on the accounts of her late-twentieth-century noble informants (Errington 1989).

It is the dynamic aspect of traditional Southeast Asian rulers to which Adas refers in his concept of the "contest state" (Adas 1981) and Wolters in the central role he assigns to "men of prowess" (Wolters 1999: 25). In the case of South Sulawesi, we have seen that many of the most dynamic political figures were not those born to the highest rank but the sons of a king's lesser wives. Schulte Nordholt gives several similar examples from Balinese history (H. Schulte Nordholt 1996: 30).

2. There are obvious similarities between my approach to the complexity of knowledge in South Sulawesi and that of Barth in his discussion of Bali. Barth explicitly acknowledges the presence of multiple "traditions of knowledge" in North Bali in a very similar way to the ones I have discussed in South Sulawesi, grouping them under the headings of Islam, Bali-Hinduism, royal courts, modernity, and sorcery.

But he is still driven to identify a level of coherence beneath the surface welter of cultural variation, which he finds in a handful of "concerns" and "orientations" shared by all Balinese actors (Barth 1993: 342). This is very close to Ortner's conclusion regarding the Sherpa: "More specifically one may say that, just as there is one core contradiction in the Sherpa hegemony—between egalitarian and hierarchical discourses —with several variants and transformations, so there is one core 'desire,' with several variants and transformations." (Ortner 1989: 197–198). In both cases, the authors recognize the diversity of subject positions in the complex societies they study, but still wish to identify some ultimate level of unity underlying them all. I see no need to do so.

References

Throughout the reference list, the following abbreviations are used:

BKI—Bijdragen van het Koninklijk Instituut voor Taal-, Land- en Volkenkunde

KITLV—Koninklijk Instituut voor Taal-, Land- en Volkenkunde

TNI—Tijdschrift voor Taal-, Land- en Volkenkunde van Nederlandsche Indie

VBG—Verhandelingen van het Bataviaasch Genootschap voor Taal-, Land- en Volkenkunde

VKIT 91—Verhandelingen van het Koninklijk Instituut voor Taal-, Land-, en Volkenkunde, volume 91.

Abu-Lughod, J. 1989. *Before European Hegemony: The World System, A.D. 1250–1350.* New York: Oxford University Press.

Acciaioli, G. 1989. Searching for Good Fortune. Ph.D. dissertation, Australian National University.

Adas, M. 1981. From Avoidance to Confrontation: Peasant Protest in Precolonial and Colonial Southeast Asia. *Comparative Studies in Society and History* 23: 217–247.

Adelaar, K. 1995. Borneo as a Cross-roads for Comparative Austronesian Linguistics. In P. Bellwood, J. Fox, and D. Tryon, eds., *The Austronesians.* Canberra: Australian National University.

Ammarell, G. 1999. *Bugis Navigation.* New Haven, Conn.:Yale University Southeast Asian Studies.

Andaya, L. 1979. A Village Perception of Arung Palakka and the Makassar War of 1666–1669. In A. Reid and D. Marr, eds., *Perceptions of the Past in Southeast Asia.* Singapore: Heinemann Education Books.

———. 1981. *The Heritage of Arung Palakka.* VKIT 91. The Hague: Martinus Nijhoff.

———. 1984. Kingship-*Adat* Rivalry and the Role of Islam in South Sulawesi. *Journal of Southeast Asian Studies* 15 (1): 22–42.

Anonymous.1855. Berigten omtrent den zeeroof in den Nedelandsch-Indischen Archipel over 1852 en 1853. *Tijdschrift voor Indische Taal-, Land- en Volkenkunde* 3: 1–31.

Anonymous. 1854. Bijdragen tot de geschiedenis van Celebes [by W.R. van Hoevell]. *TNI* 16 (9): 149–186; (10): 213–253.

Asad, T. 1993. *Genealogies of Religion.* Baltimore: Johns Hopkins University Press.

Bakkers, J. A. 1862. De Afdeeling Sandjai (Celebes). *Tijdschrift voor Indische Taal-, Land- en Volkenkunde* 11: 265–374.

———. 1866. Het Leenvorstendom Boni. *Tijdschrift voor Indische Taal-, Land- en Volkenkunde* 15: 1–208.

Barnes, R. 1982. The Majapahit Dependency Galiyao. *BKI* 138 (4): 407–412.

Barthe, F. 1993. *Balinese Worlds*. Chicago: University of Chicago Press.

Batten, R.J.C. 1938. Aanvullende memorie van overgave van de onderafdeeling Boeloekoemba 1938. Amsterdam: Koninklijke Institute voor de Tropen.

Bellwood, P. 1978. *Man's Conquest of the Pacific*. Auckland: Collins.

———. 1995. Austronesian Pre-history in Southeast Asia. In P. Bellwood, J. Fox, and D. Tryon, eds., *The Austronesians*. Canberra: Australian National University.

———. 1997. *Prehistory of the Indo-Malaysian Archipelago,* rev. ed. Honolulu: University of Hawai`i Press.

Bloch, M. 1968. Astrology and Writing in Madagascar. In J. Goody, ed., *Literacy in Traditional Societies*. Cambridge: Cambridge University Press.

———. 1974. Symbols, Song, Dance and Features of Articulation. *European Journal of Sociology* 15: 55–81.

———. [1985] 1989. From Cognition to Ideology. In his *Ritual, History and Power*. London: Athlone.

———. 1986. *From Blessing to Violence*. Cambridge: Cambridge University Press.

———. 1991. Language, Anthropology and Cognitive Science. *Man* 26: 183–198.

———. 1998. Literacy and Enlightenment. In his *How We Think They Think*. Boulder, Col.: Westview Press.

Blust, R. 1991. The Greater Philippines Hypothesis. *Oceanic Linguistics* 30 (2): 73–129.

Boon, J. 1977. *The Anthropological Romance of Bali*. Cambridge: Cambridge University Press.

Bougas, W. 1998. Bantayan: An Early Makassarese Kingdom, 1200–1600 A.D. *Archipel* 55: 83–123.

Bourdieu, P. 1977. *Outline of a Theory of Practice*. Cambridge: Cambridge University Press.

van den Brink, H. 1943. *Dr. Benjamin Frederik Matthes*. Amsterdam: Nederlandsch Bijbelgenootschap.

Brown, D. 1988. *Hierarchy, History and Human Nature*. Tucson: University of Arizona Press.

Bulbeck, F. 1988. Chinese Trade Ceramics in Archeological Contexts from South Sulawesi, Indonesia. Paper presented a conference on Ancient Chinese and Southeast Asian Bronze Age Cultures, Kioloa, New South Wales.

———. 1992. A Tale of Two Kingdoms: The Historical Archeology of Gowa and Tallok, South Sulawesi, Indonesia. Ph.D. dissertation, Australian National University.

Caldwell, I. 1988. South Sulawesi, A.D. 1300–1600: Ten Bugis Texts. Ph.D. dissertation, Australian National University.

———. 1995. Power, State and Society among the Pre-Islamic Bugis. *BKI* 151: 394–421.

Cense, A. 1931. De inhuldinging van den Aroempone te Watampone op 2 April 1931. MS OR 545 (10-A), KITLV.

———. 1951. Enige aantekeningen over Makassaars-Boeginese geschiedschrijving. BKI 107: 42–60.

———. 1966. Old Buginese and Macasarese Diaries. *BKI* 122: 416–428.

———. 1979. *Makassaars-Nederlands Woordenboek.* 's-Granvenhage: Martinus Nijhoff.

Chabot, H. [1950] 1996. *Kinship, Status and Gender in South Celebes.* Leiden: KITLV Press.

Chassé, P. [1816] 1917. Chassé's memorie, gedagteekend Makassar 20 October 1816, gericht aan gouvernuer Kruythoff, over de toestanden aldaar. In van der Kemp, 1917.

Chau Ju-Kua [1225] 1984. Mai. In W. H. Scott, ed., *Pre-Hispanic Source Materials for the Study of Philippine History,* rev. ed. Quezon City: New Day.

Chaudhuri, K. 1985. *Trade and Civilisation in the Indian Ocean.* Cambridge: Cambridge University Press.

Collins, G. 1936. *East Monsoon.* London: Jonathan Cape

———. 1937. *Makassar Sailing.* London: Jonathan Cape.

Connerton, P. 1989. *How Societies Remember.* Cambridge: Cambridge University Press.

Cummings, W. 1999. "Only One Ruler But Two Peoples": Re-making the Past in Seventeenth-Century Makassarese Chronicles. *BKI* 155 (1): 97–120.

———. 2000. Reading the Histories of a Maros Chronicle. *BKI* 156 (1): 1–31.

———. 2001. The Dynamics of Resistance and Emulation in Makassar History. *Journal of Southeast Asian Studies* 32 (2): 423–435.

———. 2002. *Making Blood White: Historical Transformations in Early Modern Makassar.* Honolulu: University of Hawai`i Press.

Dietrich, S. 1984. A Note on Galiyao and the Early History of the Solor Alor Islands. *BKI* 140: (2/3): 318–326.

Donselaar, W. 1855. Beknopte Beschrijving van Bonthain en Boelecomba op Zuid Celebes. *BKI* 3: 163–187.

Dove, M. 1985. The Agroecological mythology of the Javanese. *Indonesia* 39: 1–36.

Durkheim, E. [1915] 1995. *The Elementary Forms of the Religious Life.* Translated by Karen Fields. New York: Free Press.

Durkheim, E., and M. Mauss [1903] 1963. *Primitive Classification.* London: Cohen and West.

van Eerde, J. 1930. Investituur-steenen in Zuid-Celebes. *Tijdschrift van het Koninklijk Nederlandsch Aardrijkskundig Genootschap* 47 (5): 813–826.

Eerdmans, A.J.A.F. 1897. Het landschap Gowa. *VBG* 50: 1–77.

Endicott, K. 1970. *An Analysis of Malay Magic.* Oxford: Oxford University Press.

Englehard, H. 1884a. Mededelingen over het eiland Saleijer. *BKI* 32: 1–510

———. 1884b. De staatkundige en economische toestand van het eiland Saleijer. *De Indische Gids* 6: 519–525, 817–842.

Errington, S. 1983. Embodied *sumange'* in Luwu. *Journal of Asian Studies* 42 (3): 545–570.

———. 1989. *Meaning and Power in a Southeast Asian Realm.* Princeton, N.J.: Princeton University Press.

Foucault, M. 1977. *Discipline and Punish.* Penguin Books.

Friedericy, H. J. [1928] 1929. De Gowa-Federatie. *Adatrechtbundels XXXI* Serie P. No. 62: 364–427.

———. 1931. De Gowasche vorstengraven, de Gowasche huldingssteenen en de Gowasche ornamenten. *Koloniaal Tijdschrift* 20: 630–634.

Geertz, C. 1980. *Negara: The Theater State in Nineteenth-Century Bali*. Princeton, N.J.: Princeton University Press.

van Gennep, A. [1909] 1960. *The Rites of Passage*. Chicago: University of Chicago Press.

Gervaise, N. [1688] 1701. *Historical Description of the Kingdom of Macasar in the East Indies*. London: Thomas Leigh and D. Midwinter.

Gibson, T. 1985. The Sharing of Substance versus the Sharing of Activity among the Buid. *Man* 20: 391–411.

———. 1986. *Sacrifice and Sharing in the Philippine Highlands*. London: Athlone Press.

———. 1990a. Raiding, Trading and Tribal Autonomy in Island Southeast Asia. In J. Haas, ed., *The Anthropology of War*. New York: Cambridge University Press.

———. 1990b. *On Predatory States in Island Southeast Asia*. Comparative Austronesian Project Working Paper no. 2. Canberra: Research School of Pacific Studies, Australian National University.

———. 1994a. Childhood, Colonialism and Fieldwork among the Buid of the Philippines and the Konjo of Indonesia. In J. Koubi and J. Massard, eds., *Enfants et sociétés d'Asie du Sud-Est*. Paris: L'Harmattan.

———. 1994b. Ritual and Revolution: Contesting the State in Central Indonesia. *Social Analysis* 35: 61–83.

———. 1995. Having Your House and Eating It: Houses and Siblings in Ara, South Sulawesi. In J. Carsten and S. Hugh-Jones, eds., *About the House: Buildings, Groups, and Categories in Holistic Perspective*. Cambridge: Cambridge University Press.

———. 2000. Islam and the Spirit Cults in New Order Indonesia. *Indonesia* 69: 41–70.

———. 2004. From Humility to Lordship in Island Southeast Asia. In T. Widlok and W. Tadesse, eds., *Property and Equality* Vol. II. London: Berghahn Books.

Goedhart, O. M. [1920] 1929. De inlandsche rechtsgemeenschappen in de onderafdeeling Takalar. *Adatrechtbundels* 31 Serie P No. 57: 311–352.

———. [1920] 1933. De inlandsche rechtsgemeenschappen in de onderafdeeling Boeloekoemba. *Adatrechtbundels* 36 Serie P No. 64: 133–154.

Goody, J. 1977. *The Domestication of the Savage Mind*. Cambridge: Cambridge University Press.

Goudswaard, A. 1865. Siwa Dienst in Zuid Celebes. *Mededeelingen van wege het Nederlandsche Zendelinggenootschap* 9: 75–103, 289–314.

Hall, K. 1996. Ritual Networks and Royal Power in Majapahit Java. *Archipel* 52: 96–117.

Hamka 1965–. *Tafsir Al Azhar*. Jakarta: Panji Masyarakat.

Hammoudi, A. 1993. *The Victim and Its Masks*. Chicago: University of Chicago Press.

Hamonic, G. 1983. Pour une étude comparée des cosmogonies de Celebes Sud. *Archipel* 25: 35–62.

———. 1987. *Le Langage des Dieux*. Paris: Editions CNRS.

Hanna, W., and Des Alwi. 1990. *Turbulent Times Past in Ternate and Tidore*. Maluku, Indonesia: Yayasan Warisan dan Budaya Banda Naira.

Harvey, B. 1974. Tradition, Islam and Rebellion: South Sulawesi 1950–1965. Ph.D. dissertation, Cornell University.

Hefner, R. 1985. *Hindu Javanese: Tengger Tradition and Islam*. Princeton, N.J.: Princeton University Press.

van Hien, J. A. 1906. *De Javaansche Geestenwereld*. 5 vols. Bandoeng: A. C. Nix.

Hodgson, M. 1974. *The Venture of Islam*. Vol. 3: *The Gunpowder Empires and Modern Times*. Chicago: University of Chicago Press

Horridge, A. 1995. The Austronesian Conquest of the Sea: Upwind. In P. Bellwood, J. Fox, and D. Tryon, eds., *The Austronesians*. Canberra: Australian National University.

Hourani, G. 1951. *Arab Seafaring in the Indian Ocean in Ancient and Early Medieval Times*. Princeton, N.J.: Princeton University Press.

Hugh-Jones, S. 1979. *The Palm and the Pleides*. Cambridge: Cambridge University Press.

IJzereef, W. 1987. *Power and Political Structure in the Kingdom of Bone, 1860–1949*. Royal Institute of Linguistics and Anthropology International Workshop on Indonesian Studies no. 2.

Kaptein, N. 1992. The *Berdiri Maulid* Issue among Indonesian Muslims in the Period from circa 1875 to 1930. *BKI* 148: 124–153.

van der Kemp, P. 1917. P. T. Chassé's werkzaamheid als commissaris voor de overneming van Makassar en onderhoorigheden gedurende September–October 1816, blijkens eenige van hem uitgegane en nog niet uitgegeven rapporten. *BKI* 73: 417–471.

Kern, R. A. 1929. Boegineesche scheppingsverhalen. In *Feestbundel uitgegeven door het Koninklijk Bataviaasch Genootschap van Kunsten en Wetenschappen,* Deel I. Weltevreden: G. Kolff and Co.

———. 1939. *Catologus van de Boegineesche tot den I La Galigo-Cyclus Behoorende Handschriften der Liedsche Universiteitsbibliotheek alsmede van die in andere Europeesche Bibliotheken*. Leiden: Universiteitsbibliotheek.

———. 1950. *Catologus van de Boegineesche tot den I La Galigo-Cyclus Behoorende Handschriften van Jajasan Kebudajaan Sulawesi Selatan dan Tenggara te Makassar*. Makassar.

King, V. 1985. *The Maloh of West Kalimantan*. Dordrecht: Floris.

Koolhof, S. 1995. Pendahuluan. In S. Koolhof and R. Tol, eds., *I La Galigo menurut naskah NBG 188 yang disusun oleh Arung Pancana Toa*. Jakarta: Djambatan.

Kooreman, P. J. 1883. De feitelijke toestand in het gouvernements-gebied van Celebes en Onderhoorigheden. *De Indische Gids* 5 (1): 167–204, 358–384, 482–498, 637–655; (2): 135–169, 346–358.

Lambek, M. 1993. *Knowledge and Practice in Mayotte*. Toronto: University of Toronto Press.

La Side' Daeng Tapala. 1967. Kajao Laliddo. *Bingkisan Jajasan Kebudajaan Sulawesi Selatan dan Tenggara*. 1 (4): 20–24.

Leach, E. 1954. *Political Systems of Highland Burma*. London: Athlone Press.

van Leur, J. C. 1955. *Indonesian Trade and Society*. The Hague: W. van Hoeve.

Lévi-Strauss, C. [1949] 1969. *The Elementary Structures of Kinship.*

———. [1958] 1963. Postscript to Chapters III and IV. In his *Structural Anthropology.* London: Penguin Press

———. [1962] 1966. *The Savage Mind.* London: Weidenfeld and Nicholson.

———. [1964] 1970. *The Raw and the Cooked.* London.

———. [1971] 1981. *The Naked Man.* New York: Harper and Row.

———. [1979] 1982. The Social Organization of the Kwakiutl. In his *The Way of the Masks.* Seattle: University of Washington Press.

Liebner, H. 1998. Four Oral Versions of a Story about the Origin of the Bajo People of Southern Selayar. In K. Robinson and M. Paeni, eds., *Living through Histories.* Canberra: Australian National University.

Liedermoij, D. F. 1854. De nijverheid op Celebes. *TNI* 16: 345–372.

Lineton, J. 1975. Pasompe' Ugi': Bugis migrants and wanderers. *Archipel* 10: 173–204.

Lyotard, J. 1984. *The Postmodern Condition: A Report on Knowledge.* Minneapolis: University of Minnesota Press.

Macknight, C. 1983. The Rise of Agriculture in Southern Sulawesi before 1600. *Review of Indonesian and Malaysian Affairs* 17: 92–116.

Macknight, C., and Mukhlis. n.d. The Chronicle of Bone (draft translation). Unpublished typescript.

MacNeill, W. 1982. *The Pursuit of Power.* Chicago: University of Chicago Press.

Mallinckrodt, J., and L. Mallinckrodt-Djata. 1928. Het *magah liau*, een Dajaksche priesterzang. *Tijdschrift voor Indische Taal-, Land- en Volkenkunde* 58: 292–346.

Manguin, P. 1986. Shipshape Societies: Boat Symbolism and Political Systems in Insular Southeast Asia. In D. G. Marr and A. C. Milner, eds., *Southeast Asia in the 9th to 14th Centuries.* Singapore: Institute of Southeast Asian Studies.

———. 1993. The Vanishing *Jong:* Insular Southeast Asian Fleets in Trade and War (Fifteenth to Seventeenth Centuries). In A. Reid, ed., *Southeast Asia in the Early Modern Era.* Ithaca, N.Y.: Cornell University Press.

Manyambeang, A. K., and Abdul Rahim Mone. 1979. *Lontarak Patturioloanga ri Tu-Talloka.* [Text and translation into Bahasa Indonesia of the Chronicle of Tallo']. Jakarta: Departemen Pendidikan dan Kebudayaan.

Matthes, B. 1860. *Makassaarsch Chrestomathie.* Amsterdam: Nederlandsch Bijbelgenootschap.

———. [1865] 1943. *Verslag van een uitstapje naar de Ooster-Districten van Celebes.* Bijlage 15 in H. van den Brink, *Dr. Benjamin Frederik Matthes.* Amsterdam: Nederlandsch Bijbelgenootschap.

———. 1872a. *Boeginesche Chrestomathie.* 3 vols. Amsterdam.

———. [1872b]. *Over de* bissoe's *of heidensche priesters en priesteressen der Boegineezen.* Bijlage 34 in H. van den Brink, *Dr. Benjamin Frederik Matthes.* Amsterdam: Nederlandsch Bijbelgenootschap.

———. [1883] 1943. *Inleiding op Eenige proeven van Boegineesceh en Makasaarsche poezie.* Bijlage 23 in H. van den Brink, *Dr. Benjamin Frederik Matthes.* Amsterdam: Nederlandsch Bijbelgenootschap.

Mauss, M. [1934] 1973. Techniques of the Body. *Economy and Society* 2 (1): 70–88.

———. [1938] 1985. A Category of the Human Mind: The Notion of Person; the Notion of Self. Reprinted in M. Carrithers, S. Collins, and S. Lukes, eds., *The Category of the Person*. Cambridge: Cambridge University Press.

Mees, C. A. 1935. *De Kroniek van Koetai*. Wageningen: H. Veenman en Zonen.

Metcalf, P. 1982. A Borneo Journey into Death. Philadelphia: University of Pennsylvania Press.

Mills, R. F. 1975. The Reconstruction of Proto–South Sulawesi. *Archipel* 10: 205–224.

Mitchell, T. 1988. *Colonizing Egypt*. Berkeley: University of California Press.

Morris, S. 1980. Slaves, Sago and the Export of Sago in Sarawak. In J. Watson, ed., *Asian and African Systems of Slavery*. Oxford: Basil Blackwell.

Mukhlis. 1975. Struktur Birokrasi Kerajaan Gowa Jaman Pemeritahan Sultan Hasanuddin 1653–1669. Sarjana thesis. Yogyakarta: Fakultas Sastra dan Kebudayaan, Gadjah Mada University.

Nederburgh, I. A. [1888] 1919. Vertaling eener "Verzameling van inlandsche wetten." *Adatrechtbundels XVII* Serie P. No. 11 III: 152–176.

van Niel, R. [1960] 1984. *The Emergence of the Modern Indonesian Elite*. Dordrecht: Foris Publications.

Niemann, G. K. 1889. De Boegineezen en Makassaren. Linguistische en ethnologische studien. *BKI* 38: 74–88.

Nietzsche, F. 1966. *The Genealogy of Morals*. In W. Kaufman, ed., *Basic Writings of Nietzsche*. New York: Modern Library.

Noorduyn, J. 1955. *Kroniek van Wadjo: Een achttiende eeuwse kroniek van Wadjo*. 's-Gravenhage: H. L. Smits.

———. 1961. Some Aspects of Macassar-Buginese historiography. In D.G.E. Hall, ed., *Historians of South East Asia*. Oxford: Oxford University Press.

———. 1965. Origins of South Celebes Historical Writing. In Soedjatmoko, A. Mohammad, G. J. Resink, and , G. McT. Kahin, eds., *An Introduction to Indonesian Historiography*. Ithaca, N.Y.: Cornell University Press.

———. 1991. The Manuscripts of the Makassarese Chronicles of Gowa and Talloq: An Evaluation. *BKI* 147: 454–484.

Nooteboom, C. 1937. Naar aanleiding van de rijkssieraden van Zuid-Celebes. *Koloniaal Tijdschrift* 26: 167–176.

———. 1948–1949. Aantekiningen over de cultuur der Boeginezen en Makassaren. *Indonesia* 2: 244–255.

Nourse, J. 1998. Sawerigading in Strange Places. In K. Robinson and M. Paeni, eds., *Living through Histories: Culture, History and Social Life in South Sulawesi*. Canberra: Australian National University.

———. 1999. *Conceiving Spirits: Birth Rituals and Contested Identities among Laujé of Indonesia*. Washington, D.C: Smithsonian Institution Press.

Ortner, S. 1978. *Sherpas through Their Rituals*. Cambridge: Cambridge University Press.

———. 1989. *High Religion*. Princeton, N.J.: Princeton University Press.

van Ossenbruggen, F. [1918] 1977. Java's Monca-Pat. In P. E. de Josselin de Jong, ed., *Structural Anthropology in the Netherlands*. The Hague: Martinus Nijhoff.

Parry, J. 1989. The Brahmanical Tradition and the Technology of the Intellect. In

K. Schousboe and M. Larsen, eds., *Literacy and Society*. Copenhagen: Akademisk Forlag.

Pelly, U. 1975. Ara dan perahu Bugisnya. Research report, Pusat Latihan Penelitian Ilmu-Ilmu Social, Ujung Pandang, Indonesia.

———. 1977. Symbolic Aspects of the Bugis Ship and Shipbuilding. *Journal of the Steward Anthropological Society* 8 (2): 87–106.

Pelras, C. 1977. Les premières doneés occidentales concernant Célèbes-Sud. *BKI* 133: 227–260.

———. 1979. L'oral et l'ecrit dans la tradition Bugis. *Asie du Sud-Est et Monde Insulindien* 10: 271–297.

———. 1981. Celebes-sud avant L'Islam selon les premiers temoignages etrangers. *Archipel* 21: 153–184.

———. 1985. Religion, Tradition and the Dynamics of Islamization in South Sulawesi. *Archipel* 29: 107–136.

———. 1996. *The Bugis*. Oxford: Blackwell.

———. 1997. La premiere description de Celebes-sud en francais et le destinee remarquable de deux jeunes princes makassar dan la France de Louis XIV. *Archipel* 54: 63–80.

———. 1998. La conspiration des Makassar a Ayuthia en 1686. *Archipel* 56: 163–198.

Perelaer, M.T.H. 1872. *De Bonesche Expeditien*. Leiden: Gualth Kolff.

Pigeaud, T. 1960. *Java in the Fourteenth Century*. Vol. 3: *Translations*. The Hague: Martinus Nijhoff.

Polanyi, K. 1957. The Economy as Instituted Process. In K. Polanyi, C. Arensberg, and H. Pearson, eds., *Trade and Markets in the Early Empires*. Glencoe, Ill.: Free Press.

Ptak, R. 1992. The Northern Trade Route to the Spice Islands. *Archipel* 43: 27–56.

Ras, J. J. 1968. *Hikajat Bandjar*. The Hague: Martinus Nijhoff.

———. 1973. The Pandji Romance and W. H. Rassers' Analysis of Its Theme. *BKI* 129: 412–456.

Rassers, J. 1922. *De Pandji Roman*. Antwerp: O. de vos-van Kleef.

———. 1959. *Panji, the Culture Hero*. The Hague: M. Nijhoff.

Regeerings Almanak voor Nederlandsch Indie. Leiden: KITLV.

Reid, A. 1975. Trade and the Problem of Royal Power in Aceh. In A. Reid and L. Castles, eds., *Precolonial State Systems in Southeast Asia*. Kuala Lumpur: Malaysian Branch of the Royal Asiatic Society.

———. 1980. The Structure of Cities in Southeast Asia: Fifteenth to Seventeenth Centuries. *Journal of Southeast Asian History* 11 (2): 235–250.

———. 1981. A Great Seventeenth Century Indonesia Family. *Masyarakat Indonesia* 8 (1): 1–28.

———. 1983. Introduction. In A. Reid, ed., *Slavery, Bondage, and Dependency in Southeast Asia*. New York: Saint Martin's Press.

———. 1993. *Southeast Asia in the Age of Commerce, 1450–1680*. Vol. 2: *Expansion and Crisis*. New Haven, Conn.: Yale University Press.

van Rijneveld, J. C. 1840. *Celebes, of Veldtogt der Nederlanders op het Eiland Celebes in de Jaren 1824 en 1825*. Breda: Broese.

Robinson, F. 2000. Islam and the Impact of Print in South Asia. In his *Islam and Muslim History in South Asia*. New Delhi: Oxford University Press.

Rodemeier, S. 1995. Local Tradition on Alor and Pantar: An Attempt at Localizing Galiyao. *BKI* 151 (2): 438–442.

Rössler, M. 1987. *Die soziale Realitat des Rituals*. Berlin: Reimer.

———. 1990. Striving for Modesty. *BKI* 146: 289–324.

———. 2000. From Divine Descent to Administration: Sacred Heirlooms and Political Change in Highland Gowa. In R. Tol, K. van Dijk, and G. Acciaioli, eds., *Authority and Enterprise among the Peoples of South Sulawesi*. Leiden: KITLV Press.

Rössler, M., and B. Röttger-Rössler, 1996. From Structure to Practice: Hendrik Th. Chabot and the Origins of Modernist Anthropology in Indonesia. In H. Chabot, *Kinship, Status and Gender in South Celebes*. Leiden: KITLV Press.

Röttger-Rössler, B. 1989. *Rang und Ansehen bei den Makassar von Gowa*. Berlin: Reimer.

———. 2000. Shared Responsibility: Some Aspects of Gender and Authority in Makassar Society. In R. Tol, K. van Dijk, and G. Acciaioli, eds., *Authority and Enterprise among the Peoples of South Sulawesi*. Leiden: KITLV Press.

Rousseau, J. 1979. Kayan Stratification. *Man* 14: 215–236.

Schärer, H. [1946] 1963. *Ngaju Religion*. Translated by R. Needham. The Hague: Martinus Nijhoff.

Schmitt, J. C. 1978. La geste, la cathédrale et le roi. *L'Arc* 72.

Schulte Nordholt, H. 1996. *The Spell of Power: A History of Balinese Politics, 1650 – 1940*. Leiden: KITLV Press.

Schulte Nordholt, H. G. 1980. The Symbolic Classification of the Atoni of Timor. In J. Fox, ed., *The Flow of Life: Essays on Eastern Indonesia*. Cambridge, Mass.: Harvard University Press.

Scott, W. 1982. Boatbuilding and Seamanship in Classic Philippine Society. In his *Cracks in the Parchment Curtain*. Quezon City: New Day.

Scott, W., ed. 1984. *Pre-Hispanic Source Materials for the Study of Philippine History*, rev. ed. Quezon City: New Day.

Soedjatmoko. 1965. Introduction. In Soedjatmoko, A. Mohammad, G. J. Resink, and G. McT. Kahin, eds., *An Introduction to Indonesian Historiography*. Ithaca, N.Y.: Cornell University Press.

Spencer, G. 1983. *The Politics of Expansion: The Chola Conquest of Sri Lanka and Sri Vijaya*. Madras: New Era.

Sperber, D. 1975. *Rethinking Symbolism*. Cambridge: Cambridge University Press.

Sutherland, H. 1980. Political Structure and Colonial Control in South Sulawesi. In R. Schefold, J. Schoorl, and J. Tennekes, eds., *Man, Meaning and History*. VKIT 89.

———. 1983. Slavery and the Slave Trade in South Sulawesi, 1660s–1800s. In A. Reid, ed., *Slavery, Bondage and Dependency in Southeast Asia*. New York: St. Martin's Press.

Tambiah, S. J. 1970. *Buddhism and the Spirit Cults in Northeast Thailand*. Cambridge: Cambridge University Press.

Tideman, J. 1908a. De Batara Gowa op Zuid-Celebes. *BKI* 61: 350–390.

———. 1908b. De Toe Badjeng en de legenden omtrent hun oorsprong. *BKI* 60: 488–500.

toe Water, W. 1840. Vergelijking van den tegenwoordigen toestand der volken van Celebes met dien van Europa in de middeleeuwen. *TNI* 1: 561–594.

Traube, E. 1980. Mambai Rituals of Black and White. In J. Fox, ed., *The Flow of Life: Essays on Eastern Indonesia.* Cambridge, Mass.: Harvard University Press.

———. 1986. *Cosmology and Social Life: Ritual Exchange among the Mambai of East Timor.* Chicago: University of Chicago Press.

Turner, V. 1967. *The Forest of Symbols.* Ithaca, N.Y.: Cornell University Press.

Usop, K.M.A.M. 1985. Pasang ri Kajang: kajian sistem nilai masyarakat Amma Toa. In Mukhlis and K. Robinson, eds., *Agama dan Realitas Social.* Ujung Pandang: Lembaga Penerbitan Universitas Hasanuddin.

van der Veer, P. 2001. *Imperial Encounters.* Princeton, N.J.: Princeton University Press.

Vredenbregt, J. 1962. The Haddj. BKI 118: 91–154.

Warren, J. 1981. *The Sulu Zone.* Singapore: Singapore University Press.

Waterson, R. 1997. The Contested Landscapes of Myth and History in Tana Toraja. In J. Fox, ed., *The Poetic Power of Place.* Canberra: Australian National University.

Weber, M. [1920] 1978. *Economy and Society.* Berkeley: University of California Press.

Wolhoff, G. J., and Abdurrahim. [1960]. *Sedjarah Gowa.* Jajasan Kebudajaan Sulawesi Selatan dan Tenggara.

Wolters, O. 1999. *History, Culture, and Region in Southeast Asian Perspective,* rev. ed. Ithaca, N.Y.: Southeast Asia Program Publications, Cornell University.

Zorc, R. 1994. Austronesian Culture History through Reconstructed Vocabulary: An Overview. In A. Pawley and M. Ross, eds., *Austronesian Terminologies, Continuity and Change.* Pacific Linguistics Series C-127. Canberra: Australian National University.

Index

Abdul Hakim Daeng Paca, ix, 77–79, 94–95, 105, 107, 109, 157, 218, 239n.3, 240n.2

Abu-Lughod, Janet, 45, 47

Acciaioli, Gregory, 56, 161

Aceh, 144, 231–232

Adam and Eve: as transformations of sun and moon, 53–55, 57, 77, 118, 140, 161

adultery, 2, 91, 97–99

advisory offices, 149, 153, 158–159, 163, 165–166, 170

agrarian states, 60, 144

agriculture, ix, 2, 4; and fertility of women, 77, 114, 139; ritual, 173–176

Ajatta-Parreng, 119, 139

Amma' Toa, The Old Father, 8

ancestor cult, 3, 35, 40, 115, 169, 189

Andaya, Leonard, 150, 188

Andi Mulia Daeng Raja, Regent of Bira, 94, 99, 172, 187–188, 206

androgyny, 1, 2, 47, 55, 141; and magical objects, 49, 50, 58–59, 139–141, 188; and supplementary offspring, 54, 59

anthropology, 6, 18, 27, 33, 38, 227, 235

Ara, 3, 26; boatbuilding in, 60, 73, 77–90; and chronicles of Bira, 158, 162, 167; under colonialism, 172, 190–226, 234; informants in, 34; landscape of, 11–17; myths in, 57, 71–73

Arabic language, 33, 225

arajang, Bugis regalia, 170, 189

artisanship, ix, 4, 23, 25, 41, 70, 153, 198

Austronesians, ix, 1, 39–41, 44, 59; symbolic system of, 53, 138, 228, 235

authority: bureaucratic, 3, 22, 33–37; charismatic 35, 37; traditional, 1, 22, 34–35, 37

Babad Tanah Jawi, 92

Bajeng: defeated by Gowa, 147; foundation myth, 150–152; and Karaeng Lowé, 124, 136

Bajo, sea nomads: and Karaeng Bayo of Bantaeng, 132, 144–145, 229; mythical origins of, 72–74, 113, 138

Bakkers, J. A., 181, 185, 202

balapati, spirit of a boat or house, 87–88

Bali, 63, 92, 120, 142, 230, 240n.2

balian, Ngaju shaman, 48

bamboo: containing goddess, 2, 76, 77, 125–128, 131–132, 137–139, 144; magical blowpipe, 151–152, 167. *See also* palanquins; *tompong*

Bangkala foundation myth, 124, 136, 139, 144–146, 151–152

Banjarmasin, 125, 138. See also *Hikayat Banjar*

banners: as androgynous symbols, 50, 168, 188

Bantaeng: under colonialism, 181, 193, 202, 206, 209, 229; foundation

myth, 2, 74, 134–139; and foundation of Gowa 144–146, 150–151,
229; and Majapahit, 121–122, 128
Banten, 144, 232
barasanji, Life of Muhammad by al-
Barzanji: in boat ritual, 85–86; in
life cycle rituals 232–233; as scripture, 33; as substitute for ancestor
cult in Ara, 207
Batara Guru, Javanese term for Shiva,
67, 136
Bate salapang, Nine Banners: Gowa's
advisory council, 153
Bawakaraeng, The King's Mouth: volcanic cone in Bantaeng, 12, 122
Bayo. *See* Bajo
Bima, 73, 179
Bira: under colonialism, 202, 237; and
financing of boats, 80; foundation
myth in chronicle, 3, 118, 156–
167, 162; incest myth, 93; and
Karaeng Lowé, 124; and La Galigo
myths, 90, 95; in Napoleonic wars,
196; origin of *hadat*, 170–173; and
sailing, 73. *See also* chronicles
Bira Peninsula, 6, 60, 64, 67, 70, 190–
191, 193, 202, 205
bissu, transvestite priest, 2, 140, 173,
188; as guardians of regalia, 58; in
La Galigo myth, 68–70, 90; in
Luwu' myth, 129, 131; in Sidenreng myth, 116
Bloch, Maurice, 18, 21, 31, 37, 235–236
Blok, R., VOC Governor, 156
blood: in boat ritual, 82, 84, 86–87; in
exorcism, 109; as fertilizer, 168,
174, 177; and regalia, 215, 229; in
war ritual, 181, 189; white, 55, 170
boats, 39–41, 47; boatyards outside Ara,
79; building of, 4, 10, 19, 66, 77–89,
91, 162; as horizontal mediators,
70, 77; models used in ritual, 78,
99, 103–104, 111, 218–224; mythical origins of, 60, 66–71, 74

bodily fluids: saliva, 75, 86; semen, 55,
59; urine, 74–76
Bone, 8; and Bira peninsula, 210, 234,
237; and colonialism, 179–184,
209; expansion of, 150, 153; foundation myth, 32, 118–121, 133,
134, 136; and local trade, 78; and
Napoleonic Wars, 192, 194; and
origin of Bira, 160; and porcine ancestress, 76; as source of foreign
spirit in Ara, 105–106; and wars
with Dutch, 190–191, 196–203,
237. *See also* chronicles
Bontona, upper settlement of Ara, 11,
14, 111
Boon, James: on twins, 92
Borneo: and long-distance trade, 46,
89, 120, 126; and Majapahit, 128;
slavery in, 42, 179. *See also* Banjarmasin, Kutai, Ngaju
Bourdieu, Pierre, 20
British, 191–197, 237
Buddhism, 44, 60, 120, 143, 231
buffalo, 187–188; value of in 1930s, 78.
See also sacrifice
Bugis, 2, 78; demography, 7; and inland kingdoms, 114–115, 139;
linguistic origins, 40; literature,
34; sailors, 91; spirits, 105; titles,
109; origin myths, 32, 53–57, 64,
67, 90, 125; and origins of Bira,
158
Bulbeck, David, 40, 122, 139, 150; on
origin of agriculture, 115–118
Bulo Bulo: incorporation by Gowa,
159, 162
Bulukumba: in Bone Wars, 196, 200,
202; under colonialism, 171; in
Darul Islam rebellion, 211; feast of
Karaeng Lowé in, 122; incorporated by Gowa, 162; in Napoleonic
Wars, 193–194
burangga, henna, 164
bureaucracy, 190, 230; in Gowa, 153

busung, swelling due to curse, 97
Buton, 72, 121

Cain and Abel, 54, 57, 77, 118, 140, 160
calabai, false women, 105
Caldwell, Ian, 115–119, 129, 239n.2
Cense, A., 183–185, 209
Ceylon, 179, 232
Chabot, Henrik: on *gaukang*, 181–182, 185–186
Chassé, Petrus: on Napoleonic Wars, 193–194
chickens, 50, 68, 80, 99, 100, 223
China, 1; in Kutai myth, 127; and origin of Austronesians, 39; and trade with Indonesia, 43–45, 59, 79–80, 119–120, 142–143
Chola, state of south India, 43, 47, 143
chronicles, 22, 27, 31–32, 35–38, 121, 149; of Bira, 12, 95, 121, 156–167, 172, 174; of Bone, 149; of Gowa, 144–146, 155–157, 239n.1; of Java, 149; of Tallo', 144, 146
Cina: in Bira myth, 91, 93; foundation of, 116, 119, 139; incorporated by Bone, 118, 139; in La Galigo myth, 64–66, 69, 71–74
cockfighting: in myth, 72, 127–128
coconut oil: and boat ritual, 82, 86; in myth of Luwu', 129–130
Collins, G., 176; on exorcism, 99–104, 107, 109–110; on *gaukang*, 187; on human sacrifice, 88; on installation ritual, 172–173; on myth, 93–94
colonialism, 3; and administrators as sources, 6, 38, 237; British, 178–189; and bureaucracy, 229–230, 237; deposition of king of Gowa by, 151, 171; and documentary knowledge, 33–34; and infrastructure, 15; and port of Ujung Pandang, 79; resistance to, 27; and royal ritual, 190–226

color symbolism, 82, 88, 99–100, 106, 220
controleur, Dutch colonial official, 171, 182, 205
coral reefs and islands, 73–75, 91, 112
crocodile, as mediator, 56, 83, 87, 129–131
Cummings, William: on *lontara*, 146, 149–150

dampang, old Makassar title in Bira foundation myth, 160–165, 240n.5
Darul Islam movement, ix, 34, 211, 217, 229
death: funeral ritual, 109; graves, 122; mythical origin of, 58
debt, 42, 75
Demma Daeng Puga, hermaphroditic spirit medium, 104–110
documents, 22, 31, 33–37
Donselaar, W., Dutch missionary: on Karaeng Lowé, 122; on Tanaberu, 199–200
Durkheim, Emile, 19, 22, 28, 35, 62, 182, 185

East India Company, British, 178–179
eggs: in origin myths, 127–128; in ritual offerings, 68, 87, 99, 109, 111, 219–221; as source of Bajo, 74, 138
elephants: as mediating symbols, 50
Englehard, H., 124, 204
epidemics: and infertility, 2, 19, 92, 99, 114, 141, 177
Errington, Shelly, 11, 52, 96, 170, 189, 194, 241n.1
ethnography, 6, 18, 22
Evans-Pritchard, E. E: inspired Chabot, 185–186
exorcism, 92, 99–104, 112

fertility, 2; and agriculture, 12, 41, 174, 177, 188–189, 229; biological, 2, 114–115, 118, 169; of women, 77

fish: in myth, 75–76, 134–135; as a re-
source, 10, 40, 75, 78
flow of life, 2, 52, 95
forest, 1, 41; in myth, 69–71, 114; as
source of trade goods, 61; as source
of wood, 80
Foucault, Michel, 21, 23–24, 26
Friedericy, H.J.: on *gaukang*, 182–183,
185–186, 241n.5

gallarrang, office subordinate to
karaeng: in Ara, 12–13, 15, 198,
203, 206–210; demotion to by
colonial state, 172; in Gowa, 146;
origin of in Bira, 159–165; in Selayar, 176; in Tiro, 8, 98
Garassi', 147, 152, 159
gaukang, sacred regalia, 149, 173–174;
in Bajeng myth, 151; of Bira, 187;
and colonial obsession with, 181–
182; of Tanaberu, 191, 200, 203,
206, 211–218, 225.
Geertz, Clifford: on theater states,
241n.1
genders: antagonism between, 61;
complementarity between, 59, 81,
99; symbolism of, 4, 21, 25, 47, 52,
91
genealogy, ix, 121, 149, 156, 169
Gervaise, Nicolas: on symbolism of sun
and moon, 50–52, 56
Goedhart, O. M.: on Bangkala, 136; on
Bira, 163–164, 205–206, 241n.7;
on Bulukumba, 202; on Selayar,
173
gold and jewels, 40, 49, 60, 64
Goody, Jack: on literacy, 31
Goudswaard, A.: on Karaeng Lowé,
122–124
Gowa: and Bantaeng myths, 138–139;
under colonialism, 204–205; and
conversion to Islam, 232–234; formation of empire of, 3, 142–168,
229, 231; foundation myth, 134,

139, 144; Gervaise's informants
on, 51–52; and gunpowder technology, 32; and Majapahit, 121;
and Napoleonic wars, 192–196;
and noble houses in Ara and Bira,
190–191, 216; regalia of, 178, 181–
182; as source of spirits in Ara, 106,
109; and Toraja and Kajang myths,
131–134; trade with Lemo Lemo,
10. *See also* chronicles
guilds, 153, 155
Gujaratis, 120, 143, 232
Gulf of Bone, 8; under Luwu', 61, 64,
67, 132; and Majapahit's
influence, 128; and regional trade,
72–73, 78, 91; and shipwreck, 94
gunpowder technology, 32; and rise of
Gowa, 142, 148, 153, 167–168;
and sacred objects, 188

hadat, advisory council, 133, 169–170,
172, 179; of Bira, 163–167
hajj, pilgrimage, 206, 210, 232–233
Hamka: on *gaukang* of Kajang, 186–187
Hamonic, Gilbert: on *bissu*, 140; on incest, 61; on sun and moon, 53–54,
56, 58
Harvey, Barbara: on late colonialism,
205, 209
hermaphrodism, 91, 104
hierarchy. *See* ranking
Hikayat Banjar, chronicle of Banjarmasin, 92, 125–126
Hinduism, 44, 60, 101, 124, 128, 136,
138–139, 142–143
history, 4, 18, 38
Hodgson, Marshall: on gunpowder empires, 231, 241n.8
Horridge, Adrian: on boats in Southeast
Asia, 44
house-based societies, 169, 190, 235
Hugh-Jones, Stephen: on myth and
ritual, 30
hunting and gathering, 41, 113, 235

incense, 45, 81, 86-87, 101-102, 104, 129-130, 214
incest, 177; of mothers and sons, 91, 92-97, 141; of twins, 2, 12, 61, 92-97, 141
India, 1, 43-44, 59
Indian Ocean, 33, 43
Indic models of kingship, 115, 229
Indonesian language, 6, 31, 33
installation, 171-173, 182, 189
iron: descended, 48, 68, 70-71, 77; in magic, 76; smiths, 76-77
Islam, 4, 12, 23, 35, 37, 122, 143, 176-177, 188, 231, 234-235; and Chinese expeditions, 142; conversion to, 44, 53, 117, 134, 143, 156; cosmology, 53, 101; as religion of men, 225
Islamic modernism, ix, 109, 186, 190, 208, 233

jangga, Javanese shamans, 121
jannang, guild head, 153, 155
Japan, 45, 208, 237
Java: and Bantaeng myth, 135; and colonialism, 197, 200, 208; courts as models, 126; and Gowa, 145-146; and Hinduism, 142; and incest myth, 92; and Luwu' myth, 73; and Mongols, 119; and origins of Bira, 158, 166; and Panji myth, 62; and trade, 61, 64; and wet rice cultivation, 60, 230
Java Sea, 1, 234; and conversion to Islam, 143; as culture area, 31, 40, 59; and maritime trade, 73, 89, 91, 113; network of royal centers around, 60, 125, 228
Javanese language, 43, 67
Jene'berang River, 148, 152
jin, Arabic spirits, 12, 15
judicial authority. See tuma'bicara butta

Kajang, 8; under colonialism, 194, 196,

202, 210; foundation myth, 132, 134, 139; incorporation by Gowa, 162; and Islamic modernism, 186; as source of buffalo, 212
kali, Islamic official, 157, 163, 177, 208, 210
Kalimantan, 2, 10, 48
kalompoang, objects of power, 149, 172-173, 187, 214
Karaeng Lowé, Makassar name for Shiva, 122, 124, 134, 138, 146, 151, 181
Karaeng Mamampang, royal ancestor of Ara, 12; in Bira chronicles, 158-159, 174; in royal rituals, 190-191, 196, 203-204, 208, 210, 218, 219, 223, 234
karama, sacred power, 13, 106, 108
karihatang, royal medium in Ara, 203, 207, 211, 217, 222, 225, 230
Kediri: and Banjarmasin, 126; and Luwu', 67, 89-90; and Majapahit, 120; as model for region, 2, 228, 230; as successor to Srivijaya, 60, 115; and Vishnuism, 63
keris, dagger, 102, 104, 127, 128
Kern, R. A., on La Galigo, 63, 67-69, 136
kingship, 35; agrarian, 114; as contract with subjects, 161
knowledge: embodied, 18, 22, 24, 37; global, 1, 227; ideological, 18, 21-22, 35, 38; local, 1; objectified, 37-38; practical, 2, 18, 19, 21-22, 37, 38, 234; regional, 1, 227; symbolic, 1, 18-22, 27, 37-38, 169, 234, 235; technical, 20, 38
Konjo Makassar, 7-8, 158; myths, 57, 71-73
Kooperasi Unit Desa (KUD), Village Cooperative Unit, ix, 79
Kooreman, P. J.: on gaukang, 124, 181, 183, 186, 188-189
Kutai, foundation myth, 125-127

La Galigo: Bugis epic, 56, 64–67, 74–77, 90, 114, 131, 239n.1

Lakipadada, royal ancestor of Gowa, 131–134, 145, 180

Lamatti, and origin of Bira, 162, 165–166

language, 18–19

Leach, Edmund: on competing models, 20, 227, 231

legitimation, 169, 226

Leiden school, 61, 182, 185

Lembanna, lower settlement, 10, 111

Lemo Lemo: boatbuilders of, 10, 79; and chronicles of Bira, 158; under colonialism, 172, 196–198, 202, 205; and Gowa, 190; in La Galigo myth, 71, 73; in Napoleonic wars, 193; regalia of, 187

Lévi-Strauss, Claude, 6, 19, 28–31, 35, 169

liden, council of master boatbuilders, 78

Liedermoij, D. F.: on Lemo Lemo, 79, 197–198

life cycle rituals, 4–5; and bamboo palanquins, 140; and birth, 129; and boatbuilding, 77; and Islam, 33; and kingship, 36; and labor migration, 80; reserved for nobles, 169, 234–236

liminality, 81, 86–87

lingga and *yoni,* Shaivite symbols of phallus and pudenda, 63, 100–101, 124

literacy, 6, 25, 31–32; and history, 170

lontar palms, 31; planting of by Sawerigading, 73–74

lontara texts, 6; and genealogical records, 170; and historical writing, 149; and lontar palm, 31; and magical writing, 106; and Majapahit, 120, 149; and origin myths, 52–53; and Philippine scripts, 46; as preserve of noblewomen, 225,

239n.2; and traditional authority, 37

Luwu': in chronicle of Bira, 159; decline of, 150; foundation myth, 114–121, 128–134, 136, 139; and Gulf of Bone, 61, 73; and incest myth, 91–95; and Majapahit, 2, 229; origin myths of, 52–56; regalia of, 187; royal rituals of, 184, 185; rulers of as crocodiles, 83; as source of spirits in Ara, 108. *See also* La Galigo

Macknight, Campbell: on *lontara*, 46; on origins of agriculture, 115–116, 118, 150

Madagascar, 44, 143, 235

Mahabharata, Indian epic, 64, 67

maize, as substitute for rice, 174, 187–188

Majapahit, 2; and Bira, 157, 167, 225; and Gowa-Tallo', 146–147; and Makassar coast, 115, 120–143, 229–230

Makassar: coastal kingdoms, 114–116, 119, 121; colonial port of, 178

Malacca. *See* Melaka

Malagasy language, 44

Malay, 31, 33, 143; language, 43, 109; myth of origin, 115, 125; peninsula, 40, 106, 120, 230

Maluku: annual voyage to, 92, 104; Arabic origin of name, 46; Chinese trade to, 119; Gowa's trade to, 152–153; Malay myth of origin in, 126; Malay trade to, 143; and origins of Bira, 156, 158, 160, 165; raids from, 13, 15; and Spanish expeditions to, 241n.6. *See also* Ternate

mandala: in Java, 101; in Bira, 164–167

Mandar, 7, 79, 209

mantera, spells, 18; in agriculture, 175; in boatbuilding, 77, 80–81, 86, 239n.3; in séance, 222, 224

marriage, 47, 60, 80; of cousins, 66–67, 69, 156; payments, 42, 169; political alliance, 142, 170, 228; ritual, 108, 112, 164, 213; royal weddings, 62; and sister exchange, 147, 167, 229; uxorilocal, 66, 90, 115, 130, 136–137, 146, 160; virilocal, 95, 130, 136

Marusu': allied to Tallo', 147, incorporated by Gowa, 154; Karaeng Lowé in, 124; under VOC, 180

Matano, Lake, 64, 70

Matthes, Benjamin: on Bira, 163–164, 241n.7; on Bone, 202–203; on Cain and Abel, 54, 56; and chronicle of Gowa, 145, 239n.1; on installation, 183; and La Galigo compilation, 63

Melaka: and ancient trade routes, 44; and Bajo, 73; and Bugis dynasties, 230; as successor to Srivijaya, 143, 144, 147; and Yuan dynasty, 119

memory, 25–26

methodology, 4, 18, 27, 38

Middle East, 43, 46, 143

migration, 7, 10, 79

Mindoro, 46, 120

Ming dynasty, 120, 142, 188

ministers, 128. *See also* advisory offices

missionaries, 6, 31, 34, 237

Moluccas. *See* Maluku

moncapat, Javanese five-four symbolism, 101, 167

Mongols, 24–45, 119, 120

moon. *See* sun

mosques, 14, 207

Muhammadiyah, modernist Islamic organization, 208, 233

music, 129–130

myth, 4, 20, 27–38, 47

naga, underground serpent, 82–84, 127

Nagarakertagama, Chronicle of Majapahit, 120

Napoleonic Wars, 190–194, 212

nationalism, ix, 3, 34, 186, 190, 208, 217

navel: of baby, 102; of boat, 82, 85–87; of house, 187. See also *possi' tana*

navigation, 4, 40, 77, 114, 239n.1

Negara Indonesia Timor (NIT), State of East Indonesia, 209–210

Negrito. See *Oro Keling*

Netherlands East Indies (NEI), 3, 178, 190, 196, 233

Ngaju of Borneo: origin myth, 47–48, 63, 70, 126, 136; and slavery, 42

Noorduyn, J.: on Bugis historical sense, 149; on chronicle of Gowa, 145, 239n.1; on languages of Sulawesi, 78

Nooteboom, C.: on Selayar, 173, 176, 182, 185–186

Nourse, Jennifer: on boat ritual, 78, 111; on incest myth, 95; on Malay myth of origin, 126; on Saweriga-ding, 64

ongko, royal fields, 173–176

oral tradition, 32, 34

Oro (keling), Negrito hunter-gatherers: in La Galigo, 65–72, 76, 113

van Ossenbruggen, F., 101, 128, 182

palangka, ancestor shrine, 216–217, 220, 222

palanquins, of bamboo, 69, 70, 99, 140, 223

palantikan, stone of installation, 171–173, 177, 212

Panji, character in myth of separated twins, 2, 61–67, 90–91, 115, 125–126, 129, 182

panrita, ritual specialist, 85, 87

participant observation, 4, 18, 38

pawang, cult leader, 211, 214, 216

Pelly, Usman, 80–82

Pelras, Christian: on Bugis literacy, 31–35; on Bugis origins, 40; on Chinese influences, 46; on Gervaise, 50, 51, 53; on Indic influences, 44; on La Galigo, 63–67, 72, 136, 239n.1; on Lake Tempe, 115; on Luwu', 150

Philippines, 4, 40, 45, 61, 73, 89, 119–120, 228

pigs, 39, 50; as mothers of humans, 74, 76–77; in myth, 74–76

pinati, Makassar priests, 124, 173

pinisi, large sailing boat, 10, 78, 82, 84, 89; and model boat in ritual, 218

Portugal, 143, 147, 153, 174, 231

possession by spirits. See *karihatang*

possi' tana, navel of the earth, 14, 140, 175, 189, 213, 215–216

pregnancy, 81, 88–89, 100; asexual, 54, 55

prestige trade goods, 40, 42–43, 49, 71, 75, 114, 134, 136, 146, 162, 167, 228–229

priests, transvestite, 48. See also *balian; bissu*

punggawa, head of an enterprise, 77, 79–81; as Bugis war leader, 198

Rama, Hindu incarnation of Vishnu, 67, 125–126, 138

ranking, 3, 4, 21, 27, 40, 42–43, 47; achieved, 115, 170; ascribed, 114

Ras, J. J., 50, 60–61, 90, 92–93, 125–128, 138

Rassers, J., 61, 62, 67, 182

reciprocity between king and subjects, 170, 230

redistribution, 115, 118, 230

regalia, 3, 25, 52, 58, 68, 140, 149, 178, 189, 229. See also *arajang, gaukang*

regional political systems, 42, 47

Reid, Anthony, 120, 142, 144, 154

Republic of Indonesia, 208, 237

resi, Javanese priests, 120

rice: cultivation techniques, 1, 7, 19, 39, 41, 60, 121, 148, 152, 228; mythical

origin, 53, 115, 120; in ritual, 68, 82, 175, 214–215, 219–223

ritual, 4, 6, 11; and myth, 28–30; offerings in, 14, 24, 25, 80, 94, 101, 219–223; and practical techniques, 43; and symbolic knowledge, 18–23; and textual knowledge, 33–38

royal centers, 60, 69

rumpulangi, burnt sacrifice of buffalo, 177, 213

sabarana, Shahbandar, harbormaster, 149, 155

sacrifice, 189; of buffalo, 68–70, 84, 176–177, 181; of cattle, 51; of chickens, 68, 70, 86–88, 104, 107; of goats, 51, 87–88, 100–104, 108, 218; of humans, 68–71, 81, 88–89, 103–104, 127; on navel of the earth, 176

sailing, 1, 15, 78–79, 89; in myth, 71

sailor, 2, 113; as mythical figure, 60, 90, 131, 144, 167; payment of sailors in Bira, 79

Sangkilang, rebel against VOC, 3, 146, 178–181, 189, 192, 196, 229

sanro, ritual expert, 14, 100, 111–112, 176–177, 224

Sanskrit language, 44, 61, 67, 120, 138

Sawerigading, Bugis culture hero, 53, 64–75, 91, 96, 101, 129, 138, 141

Schärer, H.: on Ngaju, 48–50

scriptures, 22, 31–37

sea: role in myth, 69–71, 114

Selayar: and Bira, 94; in chronicle of Gowa, 145–146; incorporation by Gowa, 162; in La Galigo myths, 64, 67–68, 70, 72, 74–75, 90; in *Nagarakertagama*, 121; noble titles in, 109; *possi' tana* in, 176; regalia in, 173; as source of buffalo, 212; as source of spirits in Ara, 105

semangat, Malay life force, 11

setan, Arabic for demons, 12, 123, 175, 207

shifting cultivation, 4, 40, 47, 228, 230
shipwreck, 52, 91, 141
Shiva, Hindu god, 44, 67, 101, 115, 119–120, 122, 124, 128, 134, 138, 146–147
siblingship, 47, 67
Sidenreng: defeated by Luwu', 150; foundation myth, 116, 117
Sinjai, 106, 158–159, 171, 196, 202
slaves: capture of, 19, 42, 60, 152–153, 167–168, 229; hereditary, 169; in myth, 75, 159, 161; ritual function of among Ngaju, 48; Sangkilang's origin as, 189; and Sulu sultanate, 178, 191
snakes: as symbols of the Underworld, 50, 76, 127–128, 188
somba, title of Gowa's emperor, 147
songkabala, warding off danger, 86
Soppeng, 105; foundation myth, 116–119; under Luwu', 150; and *sudang* regalia, 194
spears, as male symbols, 50, 188, 214
spells. See *mantera*
spirit mediums, 3, 12, 102. *See also* Demma Daeng Puga; *karihatang*; Titi Daeng Toje
springs, 10, 14, 15
Sri, goddess of rice, 62, 120, 136
Srivijaya, 1, 45, 47, 59, 60, 143, 230
succession to office, 169–170, 190
Sudang, sacred sword of Gowa, 173; in foundation myth, 145–146; in installation, 171; and Sangkilang's rebellion, 180–181, 189, 194, 196, 229
Sufism, 23, 33, 53, 134, 233
Sulawesi: Central, 56; South, 41, 61, 89
Sulu, 120, 191
sumanga', Makassar life force, 88; of maize, 175
sumangé, Bugis life force, 11
Sumatra, 1, 10, 45, 73, 89, 105, 120, 126, 144, 179, 208
Sumbawa, 73, 120, 179

sun and moon, in myth, 44, 49–54, 59, 61, 63, 125
Sung dynasty, 46, 119, 188
Suppa', 118–119
Sutherland, Heather: on late colonialism, 205; on VOC slavery, 191
swiddens. *See* shifting cultivation

Taiwan, 39, 120
Tallo': alliance with Gowa, 3, 152, 167, 229, 231; and Bone, 194; chronicle of, 149; foundation myth, 146; and Karaeng Lowé, 124; and resistance to VOC, 178–179
Tambiah, S. J., 60, 231
Tana Toa, The Ancient Land, 8
Tanaberu, 12, 94; and boatbuilding, 15; and chronicle of Bira, 158; under colonialism, 172; origin of regalia, 200; and royal ancestor, 3, 190–226, 234; and trade, 10
T'ang dynasty, 45
tauhid, Islamic doctrine of God's unicity, 53
Tempe, Lake, 114–115, 150
Ternate, 65, 143, 178
territorial lords, 128, 161, 163, 166
textiles: embroidery, 4, 10; as female symbols, 50, 94, 133; silk, 61, 127, 129; weaving of, 4, 10, 133
texts, 18, 22, 27, 31
textual analysis, 18, 38
Thailand: and Gervaise, 50, 51; and Panji myth, 63; and trade with Sulawesi, 119–120
Tideman, J., 151, 179–180, 192
Tiro, 8; and adultery myth, 97–98; and chronicle of Bira, 158–160, 174; incorporated by Bira, 202; and loyalty to Bone, 194
Titi Daeng Toje, *karihatang* of Ara, ix, 106–107
Tomanurung, heavenly ancestors, 2, 170; of Bone, 183; in Bugis king-

doms, 118; and chronicle of Bira, 161, 167; in coastal foundation myths, 129–138; and earth cults, 188; in Gowa foundation myth, 144–145; and installation stones, 171; in La Galigo, 65; in myth of incest, 93; and regalia, 173; in Soppeng myth, 116

tompong, bamboo basket on a pole, 101, 213, 216

Toraja: demography of, 7; foundation myth, 76–77, 117; and foundation of Gowa, 131, 134, 145; in La Galigo, 68; as source of gold, 40, 64

trade: local subsistence, 78, 162; long-distance, 10, 19, 39–41, 45, 60, 75, 91, 114, 133, 139, 169, 228, 230

tree of life, 50, 54, 63, 70, 135, 136

tribute, 42, 142, 162

tuma'bicara buttaya, speaker of the land, judge, 155, 159, 162–163, 170, 173, 178, 189

tumailalang, Minister of the interior, 153–154

twins: opposite-sex, 54–58, 64–67, 71, 96, 104, 167, 228; same sex, 76

van der Veer, Peter: on Mahabharata, 64

Vereenigde Oost-Indische Compagnie (VOC), 3, 8: decline of, 193, 196; and documentary knowledge, 31–36; Islamic resistance to, 232–234; and Sangkilang's rebellion, 178–181; and slavery, 229

Vietnam, 119, 188

violence, 4, 47; as symbol in myth, 54, 59

Vishnu, Hindu god, 44, 60, 63, 67, 89, 101, 120, 128

van Vollenhoven, C.: on *adat* law, 185

Wajo': chronicle of, 149; and colonialism, 196; foundation myth, 119, 139; and location of Cina, 64; and Luwu', 150; and origin myth, 55–56

wali, Muslim saint, 12, 33, 36

Waniaga, Sanskrit name for Bira, 67–68

warfare, 4; and charismatic authority, 35; as male activity, 114; and regalia, 178–190; and technical knowledge, 47

Weber, Max, 35–36

Welenreng, tree used to build boat in La Galigo, 65, 67–69, 72, 74, 77, 80, 116

Wotu, 70–72

Yuan dynasty, 119

Zheng He, expeditions of, 142–143

About the Author

Thomas Gibson received a Ph.D. in social anthropology from the London School of Economics in 1983. He has done fieldwork in the Philippines (1979–1981, 1985) and Indonesia (1988, 1989, 2000), and archival research in the Netherlands while a Fulbright research fellow at the University of Amsterdam (1994). His previous book, *Sacrifice and Sharing in the Philippine Highlands,* was published in 1986. He is presently associate professor of anthropology at the University of Rochester.

Production Notes for Gibson / *And the Sun Pursued the Moon*

Cover design by Santos Barbasa Jr.

Interior design by University of Hawai'i Press production staff with display type in Stone Sans and text in Stone Serif.

Composition by inari information services.

Printing and binding by The Maple-Vail Book Manufacturing Group

Printed on 60# Sebago Eggshell, 420 ppi